LAKE VILLA DISTR
(847) 356-7711 w
3 1981 0061

D1590268

Brigham Young and the Expansion of the Mormon Faith

Oklahoma Western Biographies
Richard W. Etulain, Series Editor

Brigham Young in Nauvoo.
This is the earliest known photograph of Young.
Lucian R. Foster daguerreotype, PH 497.
Courtesy of the Church History Library, Salt Lake City, Utah.

Brigham Young and the Expansion of the Mormon Faith

Thomas G. Alexander

UNIVERSITY OF OKLAHOMA PRESS : NORMAN

This book is published with the
generous assistance of the
Kerr Foundation, Inc.

Library of Congress Cataloging-in-Publication Data

Names: Alexander, Thomas G., 1935– author.

Title: Brigham Young and the expansion of the Mormon faith / Thomas G. Alexander.

Description: Norman : University of Oklahoma Press, [2019] | Includes bibliographical references and index.

Identifiers: LCCN 2018038895 | ISBN 978-0-8061-6277-5 (hardcover : alk. paper)

Subjects: LCSH: Young, Brigham, 1801-1877. | Mormon pioneers—Biography. | Prophets—Biography. | Church of Jesus Christ of Latter-day Saints—History—19th century. | Mormon Church—History—19th century. | LCGFT: Biographies.

Classification: LCC BX8695.Y7 A64 2019 | DDC 289.3092 [B] —dc23

LC record available at https://lccn.loc.gov/2018038895

Brigham Young and the Expansion of the Mormon Faith is Volume 31 in the Oklahoma Western Biographies series.

The paper in this book meets the guidelines for permanence and durability of the Committee on Production Guidelines for Book Longevity of the Council on Library Resources, Inc. ∞

1 2 3 4 5 6 7 8 9 10

To Marilyn
for her support and eternal devotion

Contents

Illustrations

Figures

Maps

Series Editor's Preface

Stories of heroes and heroines have intrigued many generations of readers and listeners. We are captivated by the lives of religious, political, and military figures and intrepid explorers, pioneers, and rebels. The Oklahoma Western Biographies series endeavors to build on this fascination with biography and link it with two other abiding interests: the frontier and the American West. Although volumes in the series carry no notes, they are prepared by leading scholars, are soundly researched, and include a discussion of sources used. Each volume is a lively synthesis based on thorough examination of pertinent primary and secondary sources.

Above all, the Oklahoma Western Biographies aim at two goals: to provide readable life stories of significant westerners, and to show how their lives illuminate a notable topic, an influential movement, or a series of important events in the history and cultures of the American West.

Thomas G. Alexander, a longtime professor of history at Brigham Young University and a prolific author, more than meets these large goals in this sterling new biography of Brigham Young. Most of all, he gives us just what we have needed: a compact, clearly written, balanced, and revealing story of Young. Rather than portray him as a perfect man or an entire failure, Alexander presents Brigham as a complex western leader and a multifaceted president of the Church of Jesus Christ of Latter-day Saints. We have here a valuable overview of Young's important roles as a major westerner and a leading Mormon, as well as that of a nineteenth-century American.

Young's accomplishments, as Alexander clearly shows, were enormous. As the Mormon Moses, he led his persecuted, driven-out people across a wide West to an isolated area previously unsettled by Euro-Americans. For the next thirty years, he energetically, devotedly, and successfully led his expanding church, helping to found the territory of Utah and advancing a new society in a distant land. As he should, the author touts Young's apt and decisive leadership.

Conversely, Alexander also clarifies Young's shortcomings. His Indian policies and attempts at Mormon Reformation and the United Order did not work well. In addition, some of his unorthodox doctrines never gained his church's acceptance.

In short, Alexander, an active Mormon and a well-trained and experienced historian, has produced an honest, judicious biography of Brigham Young. Latter-day Saints and Gentiles (non-Mormons) alike will find this work extraordinarily illuminating for a larger understanding of one of the most significant westerners of all time.

Richard W. Etulain

Preface

Several years ago, Richard Etulain—a longtime friend, professor of history at the University of New Mexico, and editor of a series titled Oklahoma Western Biographies at the University of Oklahoma Press—approached me about adding a biography of Brigham Young to the series, which consists of short biographies written from published sources. I resisted at first but finally agreed to write the book.

Since this is part of a series, I do not argue that this biography breaks new ground except for the primary research that I have done and incorporated into the book and the primary sources that I have consulted in writing sections of the text. For instance, I had already done research and published an article on the environmental problems that Young and the Mormons faced in the Salt Lake Valley between 1847 and 1858. I have done research in the National Archives and other depositories on federal officials in Utah, especially on the judges, territorial government, and cadastral surveys. Moreover, my own experience as a surveyor helped me to understand the failings of surveys during the 1850s.

In addition, I worked as an editor on a book written by Ronald Walker, Richard Turley, and Glen Leonard on the Mountain Meadows massacre. While reading through the documents that these scholars had collected, I saw the information on Young's efforts to try to bring the perpetrators to justice as early as 1859. This led me to use the information for the Leonard J. Arrington lecture on the massacre that I presented in 2006.

I had also done work on the Utah federal judges for a master's thesis at Utah State University, and I published an article on Judge James B. McKean. I disagree now with many of the generalizations I made about McKean in the article—I treated him too kindly. I believe now that he came to Utah as a judge with a mission and that he broke the law willfully in order to attack the Mormons. I have incorporated this information in this biography.

In addition, I spent forty years teaching Utah history and fifteen years teaching American environmental history. I had studied Utah history at Utah State University under S. George Ellsworth and done research on various topics in Utah history with Leonard J. Arrington. I consider these two scholars generous mentors.

Other scholars have emphasized the importance of Brigham Young and his work. In 1965 economist Jonathan R. T. Hughes published *The Vital Few: The Entrepreneur and American Economic Progress* (Oxford, 1965, 1986). As examples of early entrepreneurs, Hughes selected William Penn and Brigham Young, praising Young's ingenuity in establishing settlements in the West while viewing Young's actions as a model for future entrepreneurs. I found it significant that an economist should select Young and Penn as models of founders of settlements. Furthermore, biographies by Leonard J. Arrington, Newell Bringhurst, and John Turner were of inestimable help in writing this work.

As readers approach my writing, I emphasize that I carry two traditions. My academic education carries a tradition of secular scholarship from Athens through Weber State University, Utah State University, and the University of California at Berkeley. As a scholar, I have taught at several universities, published widely, and served actively in a number of historical and other scholarly organizations, including serving as president and board member in a number of them. My religious culture carries traditions from Jerusalem through New York, Kirtland, Missouri, Nauvoo, and Salt Lake City.

In several previously published articles I have argued that *objectivity*—as scholars generally use the term—is impossible. Every person carries some cultural baggage that no amount of scholarly detachment or persistence can overcome. Historian Charles Beard called the idea of objectivity a Noble Dream. I believe that those who profess to be objective are self-deluded.

I have argued and still believe that *honesty* is the most important virtue historians can seek to achieve. Any written history consists of a text written by weaving together evidence found in clearly fragmentary and often messy documents with prose that links the evidence together in a story or narrative. All too often, historians allow rhetoric and supposition to substitute for evidence. If the available evidence used in the narrative does not support the rhetoric and supposition, I would argue that the resulting story is suspect at best.

In the interest of full disclosure, I acknowledge that I am a believing member of the Church of Jesus Christ of Latter-day Saints. Ancestors on both sides of my family followed Brigham Young and the church leadership west and settled as pioneers in Utah. One great-grandmother came to Utah as a handcart pioneer. Her husband helped to rescue the Willie and Martin handcart companies. I have served as national president of the Sons of Utah Pioneers. These traditions are part of the cultural baggage that I carry.

Recognizing that these two traditions, Athens and Jerusalem, have influenced me, I have tried, as diligently as possible, to write an honest biography. In the text that follows, I have recognized Brigham Young's failings, especially in his Indian policy, the Mormon Reformation, and the United Orders. Some of his doctrinal views are clearly unorthodox. At the same time, I have also tried to treat his successes as a missionary, family man, businessman, church leader, and colonizer. I would like to have known him personally. Unfortunately, the only paths available to explore his life are documents and narratives. The following text is the result of my exploration.

After Brigham Young joined what eventually came to be known as the Church of Jesus Christ of Latter-day Saints in 1832 and moved in 1833 to Kirtland, Ohio, the church headquarters at the time, he became one of Joseph Smith's close associates, with Young's early missions to Canada and the eastern United States and service in Zion's Camp (an effort to redeem the property of the Saints in Missouri) bringing him to Joseph Smith's attention. In 1835 Oliver Cowdery, David Whitmer, and Martin Harris called him as one of the first members of the Quorum of the Twelve Apostles. Thereafter, he would play a central role in the growth of Mormonism, including leading a mission of the Twelve to England, supporting Joseph Smith, leading the Mormon evacuation from Missouri to Illinois, and helming the church after Joseph Smith's murder. In heading up the church, he pressed for the completion of the Nauvoo Temple, the endowment of more than five thousand members, and the sealing of numerous couples for time and eternity.

Leading the Mormons to Utah, Young guided them as they established 350 settlements that he assisted in planning, and helped them weather a decade of shortages and trials. He made a number of controversial and unfortunate decisions, including ordering the extermination of recalcitrant Utes in Utah Valley and ordering the imprisonment of Sanpitch and several other Utes during the Black Hawk War. During the Mormon Reformation of 1855–56, he would try to revitalize the Mormon community through emphasizing plural marriage even with very young women, requiring rebaptism of members, issuing a detailed catechism to which all were required to agree, and violent preaching. As part of the Reformation, he announced a number of controversial doctrines such as blood atonement (the voluntary shedding of blood as atonement for sins) and that Adam was god of this world. However, the church leadership rejected the blood atonement doctrine as part of a comprehensive statement in 1889, and the church never accepted the Adam-god doctrine. At the same time, he served as a comforting religious leader for the Mormon people. While serving both as church president and Utah's territorial governor, Young's career was spotted with controversy.

In retrospect, Young elicits varying opinions. Faithful Mormon people have remembered him fondly. Some scholars praise his accomplishments, while critics continue to vilify him. I find him a successful leader who inspired the communicants who followed him to build a large part of the American West.

On August 16, 2018, President Russell M. Nelson of the Church of Jesus Christ of Latter-day Saints announced that the term "Mormon Church . . . is not an authorized title" for the church. Since then, the church has discouraged use of the term "Mormon" and has abandoned it as a title for its organizations and publications. This notice arrived too late to change all of the references to Mormon and Mormonism in this biography. In addition, such changes might be historically confusing, given that Brigham Young used both terms and in 1871 preached that "Mormon . . . means more good; and Mormonism embraces all the truth that there is in heaven and earth."

Thomas G. Alexander

Acknowledgments

I am indebted to a great number of people who assisted me in preparing this biography. I appreciate the assistance of Richard E. Turley Jr., the late Ronald W. Walker, and Glen M. Leonard, with whom I worked as an editor at the Church History Library of the Church of Jesus Christ of Latter-day Saints. Brian Reeves of the Church History Library helped by supplying copies of documents. Others at the Church History Library who assisted include Mel Bashore, Chad Orton, Chad Foulger, Michael Landon, Steve Sorensen, Brent Reber, Barbara Jones Brown, and Alison Gainer. Thanks also to LaJean P. Carruth and her staff for the transcription of shorthand and Deseret Alphabet entries in various diaries and documents.

My thanks to Brittany Chapman Nash at the Church History Library for her help in securing photographs, and to the Permissions office of the Correlation Intellectual Property office of the Church of Jesus Christ of Latter-day Saints for evaluating their status. Thanks also to Doug Misner, the Library and Collections Coordinator at the Utah State Historical Society, for help with a photograph of the Nauvoo Temple. Thanks also to Elder Steven E. Snow, Historian and Recorder of the Church of Jesus Christ of Latter-day Saints for his help.

I appreciate the kind assistance of the staff of the University of Oklahoma Press, and especially Editors Richard Wayne Etulain and Charles E. Rankin for their insightful critiques of the manuscript. My thanks to Ariane C. Smith for her excellent work as a copy editor, and to Steven B. Baker for coordinating the completion of the project at the Press. Thanks also to Erin Greb for drawing the maps and to Brandon S. Plewe of Brigham Young University for permission to use information on some of the maps in *Mapping Mormonism,* 2nd ed. (Provo, Utah: Brigham Young University Press, 2014), as a basis for those maps. I appreciate beyond measure the critiques of outside reviewers John G. Turner and Richard E. Turley Jr. for their excellent suggestions for improvements in the manuscript. Ordinarily such reviewers remain anonymous, but I requested special permission to thank them here.

My wife, Marilyn Johns Alexander, has been a source of constant encouragement and support during the years I worked on this biography.

Maps

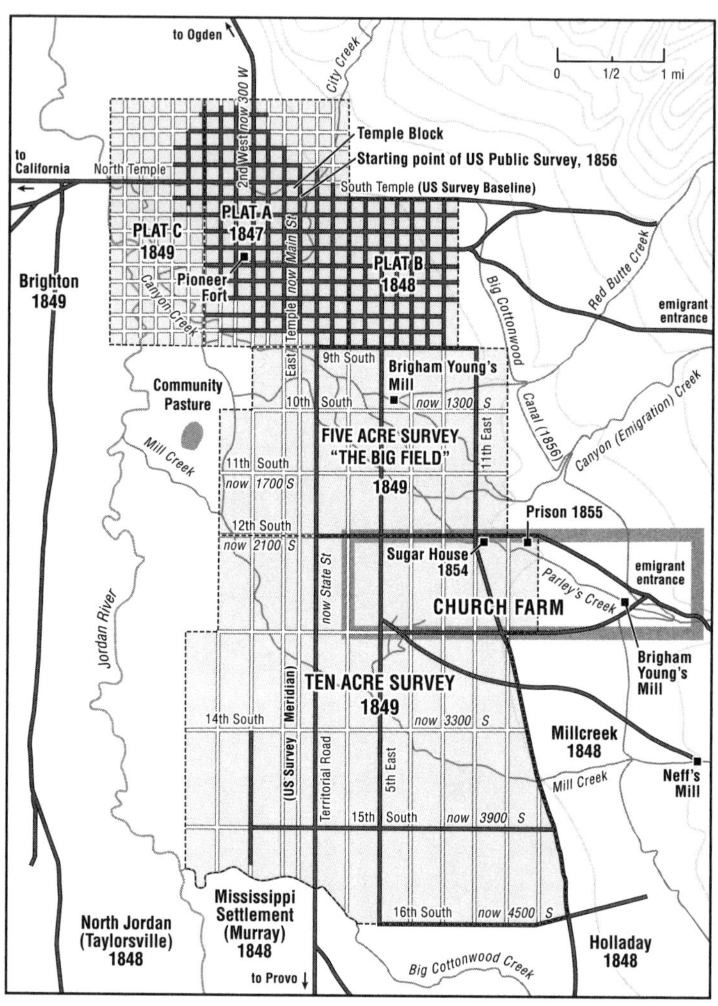

Salt Lake County Surveys and Settlement, 1847–1855

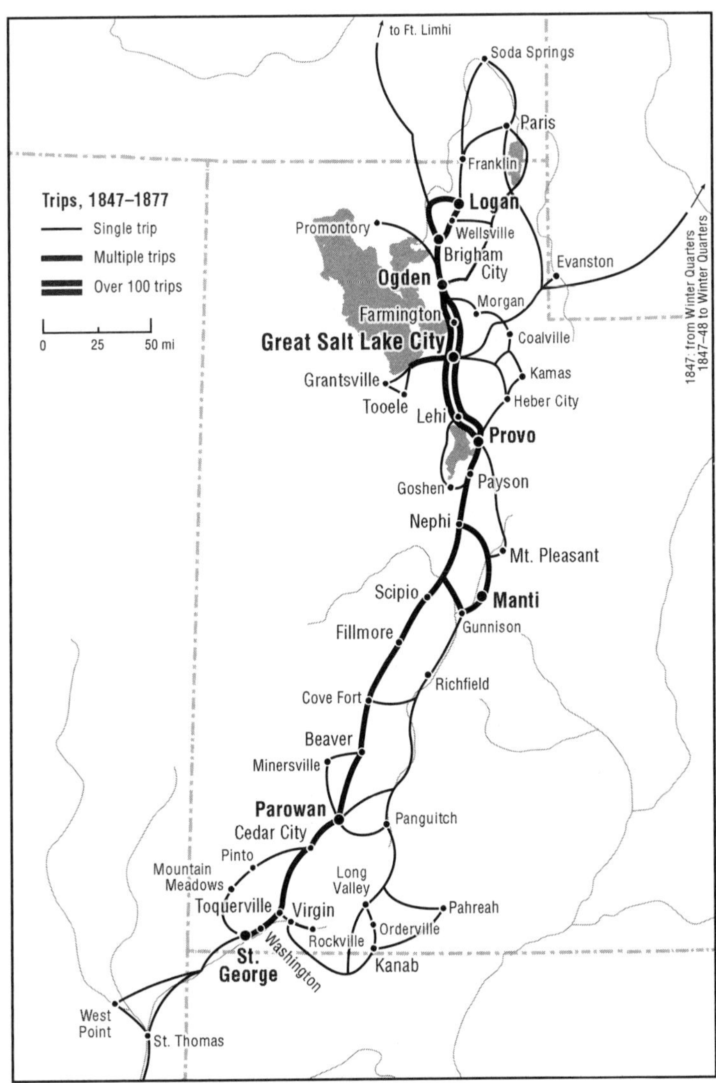

Brigham Young's Travels to the Mormon Colonies

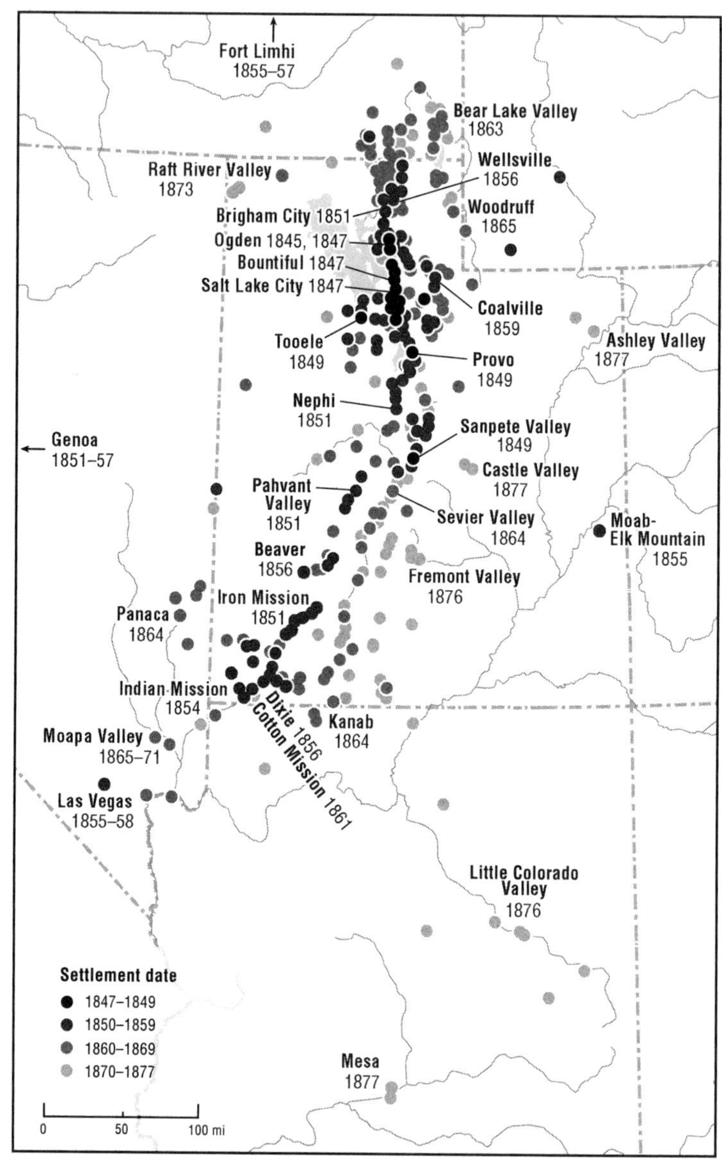

Mormon Settlements in the Intermountain West
in Brigham Young's Lifetime

Brigham Young and the Expansion of the Mormon Faith

1

The Early Years

Between Brigham Young's birth in 1801 and his move to Kirtland, Ohio, in 1833, the future Mormon prophet occupied himself with myriad activities. As a youth, he grew up very fast. Before he reached his teens, he had to help maintain his father's family, and his father made him leave home at age sixteen and support himself. After his marriage to Miriam Angeline Works, Young supported his family financially and cared for their physical welfare, especially after his wife contracted tuberculosis. Concerned about the condition of his soul throughout his early life, he joined the Reformed Methodists before converting to Mormonism. After joining the Latter-day Saints, he became one of their most faithful adherents, finding deep spirituality in Pentecostal experiences. He was also one of the church's most active missionaries, backing Joseph Smith without question.

Brigham Young's ancestors had emigrated from Great Britain to New England in the seventeenth century, with succeeding generations living in New Hampshire and Massachusetts. Brigham's father, John Young, was born in Hopkinton, Massachusetts, in 1763, and he served in the American army during the Revolutionary War. John Young's father, Joseph, was a surgeon, a profession of relatively low social status at the time. He had squandered the family's inheritance in gambling and drinking, leaving virtually nothing for his children, and John had to struggle on his own. Brigham's mother, Abigail "Nabby" Howe, was born in Shrewsbury, Massachusetts, in 1766 to a family of higher social status than John Young's. Despite the objections of her father, she married John in 1785.

In 1797, after failing at farming in Hopkinton, John and Nabby Young moved with their seven children to a farm in Whitingham, Vermont, a town a few miles north of the Massachusetts border. Whitingham had become a popular destination for New Englanders, and a number of other families moved there with the expectation of bettering themselves. The move must have been exceptionally trying for Nabby, who was pregnant with her eighth baby—Brigham Young, who was born in Whitingham on June 1, 1801.

Whitingham and the nearby Green Mountains boasted beautiful summers and exceedingly harsh winters. Land there was cheap, so the Youngs paid an uncle only a dollar an acre for fifty acres. Although inexpensive, Whitingham's earth seemed to curse the farmers who plowed and planted it. Ancient retreating glaciers had deposited rich soil, but they had also left an undulating land surface and, above all, plentiful rocks. Some said the earth grew rocks faster than crops.

Thus, in 1804, ground down by life on a hardscrabble farm in Whitingham, Brigham Young's parents moved the family to Cold Brook in the Smyrna quarter of Sherburne, New York. The family built a log cabin as the first home for the large Young brood. Nabby bore Brigham's youngest sister and brother, Louisa and Lorenzo Dow, there in 1804 and 1807. By 1813, when Brigham Young was twelve, some of his family had married and moved to Aurelius in Cayuga County, a few miles from Cayuga Lake. After struggling at Cold Brook, John and Nabby moved the family to Aurelius as well.

In all these places—Whitingham, Cold Brook, and Aurelius—the John Young family lived in precarious balance between deprivation and starvation. Family members slaved at felling trees, cutting brush, and clearing land. As a teenager, Brigham recalled, he struggled "with insufficient food until my stomach would ache." Like most nineteenth-century rural boys, he wore homemade clothing and walked barefoot most of the time. A strict disciplinarian, his father confronted his sons, Brigham said, with "a word and a blow . . . and the blow came first."

Tuberculosis—a frequent killer in nineteenth-century America—struck down Brigham's mother, Nabby, at Aurelius on June 11, 1815. She had suffered from the disease for many years and had apparently infected her fourth daughter, also named Nabby, who died in 1807. Young's older sister, Fanny, who was previously married to Robert Carr but separated from her unfaithful husband, cared for their mother during the last months of her life.

After Nabby died, John moved with three of his boys—Joseph, Phinehas, and Brigham—to the Sugar Hill neighborhood of Tyrone, a town on the Tioga River in western New York state. The two youngest children, Louisa and Lorenzo, stayed with their sister Rhoda and her husband, John P. Greene, for a time. Although a rough frontier place, Tyrone had advantages, including large acreages and an abundant forest of sugar maples. The family again plunged into the task of clearing the land. They planted corn and tapped the maple trees, boiling the sap to make sugar and syrup. The family worked hard, but they still lacked adequate food and clothing.

In 1815 the family had made sixty pounds of maple sugar, which John took to Painted Post, a village in Steuben County near the Pennsylvania border, to trade for flour, leaving Brigham and Lorenzo home alone for two days. The two brothers, age fourteen and eight at the time, could find nothing in the cabin to eat. Seeing a robin in the yard, Brigham got out his father's Revolutionary War flintlock musket and shot the bird. The two boys prepared and boiled the meat. Hungry for something to eat with the robin, they got out the family's empty flour barrel, held it upside down, and pounded on the bottom, managing to free enough flour from cracks in the barrel to make gravy. The boys subsisted on robin, gravy, and maple syrup—a tasty, if skimpy, diet—until their father returned.

The Young family experienced a number of significant events in the family cycle. After Nabby died, John Young married a widow, Hannah Dennis Brown, and she moved into the Young household. Brigham's oldest sister, Nancy, had married in 1803 to Daniel Kent. His oldest brother, John Jr., married Theodosia Kimball in 1813. His older sisters Rhoda and Susannah married in 1813 and 1814 to John P. Greene and James Little. This left Joseph, Phinehas, Brigham, Louisa, and Lorenzo at home with John and Hannah in 1815. A divorcée, sister Fanny lived in Tyrone, and she apparently remained single until she married in 1832 to Roswell Murray, a brother of Vilate Murray Kimball, who was the wife of Brigham's friend, Heber Chase Kimball. In 1817 John and Hannah sent Joseph and Lorenzo to live with Susannah and James Little, to whom they apprenticed themselves. Phinehas may have remained with John and Hannah for a year or he may have lived with the Littles, but in any case, he married Clarissa Hamilton in 1818. Louisa was only thirteen years old in 1817, and she may have remained in her father's and stepmother's home until her marriage in 1824 to Joel H. Sanford.

Lorenzo Young insisted that his father, John, favored his older brother, Brigham, but when Brigham Young turned sixteen, his father told him to "go and provide for yourself." On his own, Brigham worked first at odd jobs, then apprenticed himself to John C. Jeffries of Auburn as a carpenter, painter, and glazier. Among his tasks, he helped Jeffries paint a home that belonged at that time to Judge Elijah Miller but would later be purchased by William Seward, who would go on to be the governor of New York and still later Abraham Lincoln's secretary of state. Today the building serves as a local museum with a fireplace mantle that locals say Young made. In fact, several Auburn homeowners claim ownership of a Brigham Young mantlepiece, and Karl Butler, a local Mormon leader, donated one such mantle to the Church of Jesus Christ of Latter-day Saints. While in Auburn, Young also helped construct the Auburn Presbyterian Theological Seminary, as well as a number of other buildings, sundry chairs, and other wooden articles.

Young never had an easy life in New York. After struggling with his father, brothers, and sisters to provide a living for his father's family and working as an apprentice, Brigham hit rock bottom in the 1819 financial panic and succeeding depression. The Second Bank of the United States contributed to the severity of the depression by curtailing credit to state banks and by insisting that banks redeem their circulating notes in gold and silver. Unlike the states of Illinois, Kentucky, and Tennessee, New York did not allow banks to suspend specie payments, all of which brought an intensifying hardship to Auburn and to Brigham's own life. Because of a reduced workload, Jeffries dismissed Young before he had completed his certification as a master carpenter. However, unwilling to succumb to the depression, Brigham moved to Port Byron, a town about eight miles northwest of Auburn, where he repaired old chairs, painted boats, and took odd jobs. He also made and painted wooden pails and invented a device for grinding paint.

In Port Byron, Brigham fell in love and married Miriam Angeline Works in 1824. The daughter of Asa and Abigail Jerusha Marks Works, Miriam was born in Aurelius on June 6, 1806, five years after her husband. The couple reportedly made their home in a small unpainted frame house across from the pail factory where Young worked. While in Port Byron, their first child, Elizabeth, was born.

In addition to plying his trade in Port Byron and caring for his wife and daughter, Young joined a debating society and made friends with a tribe of boys who gathered around the pail-factory neighborhood. Local tradition had it that Brigham lined them up and had them wave their hats, shouting "Hurrah for Andrew Jackson." Although he had gone to school only eleven days in his life, Young also spent considerable free time reading. He studied the Bible, ancient history, and a weekly newspaper. Port Byron had no newspaper, so he likely read one or more of four weeklies published in Auburn: the *Castigator,* the *Free Press,* the *Cayuga Republican,* or the *Cayuga Patriot.*

The extent of Brigham's education matched closely that of other members of his family and, with some exceptions, of other early Mormon leaders. Joseph Smith had very little schooling. He wrote that his family was "deprived of the bennifit of an education. Suffice it to say I was mearly instructed in reading writing and the ground rules of Arithmatic which constituted my whole literary acquirements." Historian Richard Bushman opined that Smith "may have attended school briefly in Palmyra," and he may also have improved his education at home. According to Sidney Rigdon's biographer, Mark McKiernan, Rigdon, a member of the church's First Presidency, had only a "rudimentary education." Rigdon, like Young and most other early church leaders, was self-educated. Frederick G. Williams and Willard Richards, both church leaders, had studied Tomsonian medicine, and Richards had sufficient schooling to earn a teacher's certificate. Oliver Cowdery, Smith's scribe and a member of the church's presidency, also taught school, but in the early nineteenth century, school teaching did not require a college education. However, Wilford Woodruff, an apostle and later church president, had studied at the Farmington Academy, and two of the early Mormon apostles and first presidency members, Lorenzo Snow and Albert Carrington, had attended college before their conversion. Brigham's minimal education, though, was more typical.

Brigham, Miriam, and Elizabeth Young moved twice in the late 1820s, first to Oswego on the shore of Lake Ontario for a short period in 1828, and then to Mendon, a town about eighteen miles southeast of Palmyra, the home of Joseph Smith's family, and about seventeen miles northwest of Canandaigua, a market town on Lake Canandaigua. Mendon became a favored Young family enclave. Young's sister, Susannah, with her second husband William B. Stilson, had moved to Mendon before Brigham arrived there. Susannah had remarried to Stilson after her first husband, James Little, died in a wagon accident in 1822. John and Rhoda Young Greene, as well as John Sr. and Hannah Dennis Young, had also preceded Brigham and his family to Mendon. Brigham's brother, Phinehas, and his wife, Clarissa Hamilton Young, and their family joined the others in Mendon in 1829. Lorenzo and his wife, Persis Goodall Young, also lived there for a short time, as did sister Fanny and her husband Roswell Murray, plus John Jr., his wife, Theodosia, and their family.

As Young labored as a carpenter and joiner in Mendon, he built a mill with a waterwheel that powered a lathe and a reciprocating saw, which he used to cut wood and make chairs and other wooden articles. He also worked in construction outside Mendon and took occasional odd jobs such as harvesting grain and hay. Although he worked hard, Young incurred a number of debts while in Port Byron and Mendon, largely in his effort to keep his family afloat. He was unable to repay many of these debts until emigrating to Utah years later, though he did keep track of the notes he had signed. Later in life, he would send his son, John W. Young, and his friend, William W. Riter, at times to repay them with simple interest at 7 percent. Commenting on one such visit from John W. Young, the *Auburn Advertiser Union* noted: "Brigham is honest in some things, but rather slow."

In Mendon, Young experienced great joy but also deep sorrow. Miriam bore the couple's second daughter, Vilate, who was probably named after Vilate Murray Kimball. The Youngs had become close friends with Heber Chase and Vilate Kimball, and they remained close as long as any of them lived. To Brigham's profound grief, Miriam succumbed to the same disease that had killed his mother and sister. During the last weeks of her life, Young cared for her while he worked to support the family. He reportedly got up early, fixed breakfast for the family, carried Miriam to a seat near the fireplace, and left for work. In the evening, he prepared a meal, cleaned up, and carried her to bed. After her death on September 8, 1832, Brigham, Elizabeth, and Vilate Young moved in with Heber and Vilate Kimball.

During these years, religion would play a central role in the lives of the Young and Kimball families and of many others in western New York. Such contemporaries as Presbyterian revivalist Charles Grandison Finney and such twentieth-century historians as Whitney Cross have called the region the "Burned Over District." The area earned the name because of the frequent revivals and intense religious competition. There were Presbyterians, Episcopalians, Baptists (both Calvinist and Free Will), Congregationalists (traditional and New Light), and Methodists (Episcopal, Wesleyan, and Reformed)—all competed for souls throughout the region. Each claimed to represent Christ and His gospel.

Both Brigham and Heber joined Protestant churches. Kimball joined the Baptists. Young said he was revolted by the excesses of revivalism, but in 1824 he joined the Methodists. Like his later decision to join the Mormons, Brigham's conversion to Methodism required a period of intense reflection. Reading the Bible, Young came to believe in its teaching of baptism by immersion, and with that conviction, instead of accepting traditional Methodist baptism by sprinkling, he insisted on baptism by immersion. Methodist ministers resisted, but finally acceded to his wishes. Young's father and stepmother had joined the Methodist Episcopal Church—the orthodox branch of John Wesley's movement. Young and his brothers and sisters joined the Reformed Methodists, however, which was a much more radical denomination. Reformed Methodists renounced showy apparel, alcohol, and circuit riders who traveled around specific geographic territories to organize congregations and minister to the people. Many Reformed Methodists participated in deep spiritual experiences such as faith healing and oral revelation. Instead of functioning under a system of bishops like the Methodist Episcopals, the Reformed Methodists organized congregations like the Congregationalists and Presbyterians. Although they established conferences as central organizations, each congregation chose its own minister. In his recent biography of Brigham Young, John Turner elaborates on Young's experiences as a Reformed Methodist and as a missionary.

Phinehas most likely contributed to Brigham's conversion to Methodism. After struggling for some time, Phinehas joined the Reformed Methodists and later accepted ordination as a minister. He immersed himself in deep spiritual experiences, including faith healing. Through prayer and the laying on of hands, he healed a young woman who suffered from tuberculosis. In another spiritual experience during a prayer meeting, he reported a vision of a "body of light, above the brightness of the sun, that descended upon me," until it filled him with "unutterable joy." The congregation to which Phinehas ministered represented a spiritual haven for him, as its members practiced divine healing, emotional worship, personal revelation, and other manifestations of the spirit.

Others in Young's family accepted calls to the Reformed Methodist ministry. John Jr. and Joseph Young were also ordained ministers, as was Rhoda's husband, John Greene, but Lorenzo declined to join the denomination. Instead, he served as an independent lay minister, but he preached a message much like that of the Reformed Methodists. In a moment of spiritual awakening, Lorenzo had a vision of his dead mother and sister, an event that he said impressed itself deeply on his soul. Eventually, John Young Sr. joined his sons and other family members in Reformed Methodism.

Anxiety over the sinful state of the world weighed heavily on members of the Young family. As they reflected on their own failings, they feared that Satan might carry them down to Hell. Where in the world, they asked one another, could one find a truly Biblical Christian? Many families in the Burned Over District shared the Youngs' feelings—whether from their poverty, their perception of surrounding sinful lives, or both is uncertain. Thoughts and perception of the deplorable state of humanity left them despondent, dejected, and depressed. In this state, Young developed a lifelong friendship with Hiram McKee, a Methodist minister to whom he opened his soul as he did to no one, except his brothers and most likely Heber C. Kimball.

Young remained nominally a Reformed Methodist, but he had become, in truth, a Christian seeker, searching for a religion that he believed actually restored Biblical Christianity. His state of mind and soul had become similar to many contemporaries not only in western New York but throughout the United States during the 1820s and '30s. As the various Protestant denominations called "Lo Here," and "Lo There" (here is Christ, there is Christ), seekers read the Bible, prayed, and sought spiritual experiences. "Convicted," as they said, of their own sinfulness and the sinfulness of others around them, seekers sought some way out of the quagmire into which their spirits and the spirits of others had sunk.

With an understanding of the perceptions of early nineteenth-century seekers, scholars have viewed American culture in a number of ways. Historian William J. Rorabaugh has called it the "Alcoholic Republic." It may have been that for many people, but for seekers it was the Republic of Wonder, abounding in visions, manifestations of the holy spirit, and religious and social experimentation. Scholars have documented and reproduced a large number of reported theophanies in the early nineteenth century in which Jesus Christ appeared to Americans. Many such experiences were undoubtedly not recorded, or the records have not survived. In these experiences, many of those who reported a vision of Jesus witnessed that He had told them that He had borne their guilt and forgiven their sins.

In some cases, individuals experienced personal revelations that convinced them that a restoration of primitive Christianity would take place. A Simsbury, Connecticut, prophet named Robert Mason told Wilford Woodruff he had an extraordinary vision of an orchard with fruit that he could not eat. The vision convinced Mason that he would not find Christ's restored church but that Woodruff would. Similarly, in 1816 Solomon Chamberlain, who was then living in western New York, reported a vision in which he learned that a church that restored the "Apostolic Order"—"a church . . . with the same powers and gifts that were in the days of Christ"—would be organized on the earth.

In 1832 Joseph Smith first recorded a theophany that he had experienced in 1820 or 1821 as a teenager living in Palmyra, New York. Like others who had similar experiences in the Burned Over District, Smith testified that "The Lord" Jesus appeared to him to say: "Thy Sins are forgiven thee, go thy way walk in my Statutes and keep my commandments." Smith also wrote that Jesus told him, "The world lieth in sin and at this time and none doeth good no not one they have turned asside from the gospel and keep not my commandments they draw near to me with their lips while their hearts are far from me and mine anger is kindling against the inhabitants of the earth to visit them according to thir ungodliness." These words would have been especially important to Brigham Young and seekers like him, because they confirmed their belief that humans needed a forgiveness of their sins and that the world needed a restoration of primitive Christianity.

After this experience, Smith would go to revivals and some Methodist services. He also tried to find buried treasure through the use of a seer stone, working for Josiah Stoal in a failed attempt in 1825 to locate treasure buried by pirates. While working for Stoal, Smith attended some Methodist class meetings with the family of his future wife, Emma Hale, reporting additional spiritual experiences between 1823 and 1827 in which an angel named Moroni appeared to him. In 1827 Moroni, a former inhabitant of the American continent, showed Smith the location of a set of golden plates. Smith translated the plates using a seer stone and a set of spiritual interpreters called the Urim and Thummim in Exodus 28:30. He published the translation in 1830 as the Book of Mormon. Responding to revelations he received, Smith and a group of believers organized a church—then called the Church of Christ—that same year. Called "Mormons," Smith and his associates preached that theirs was the restored church of Christ. They announced that His Second Coming was near at hand, and that God had restored the ancient gifts such as visions, revelations, and other spiritual manifestations. Subsequently, Joseph Smith and his colleague Oliver Cowdery experienced visits from John the Baptist and Christ's apostles Peter, James, and John. They testified that these leaders of old ordained them to the ancient priesthood.

In Kirtland, the leadership changed the church's name to the Church of the Latter Day Saints to differentiate themselves from other churches with the name Church of Christ or Christian Church. Mormons called themselves Latter-day Saints or just Saints to confirm their relationship with primitive Christians, not to assert unusual holiness. Significantly, as Mark Lyman Staker has noted, others referred to themselves as "saints" for similar reasons. By 1838 the church had adopted the name the Church of Jesus Christ of Latter Day (by 1851 punctuated Latter-day) Saints.

Confusion could easily have occurred. During the late eighteenth and early nineteenth centuries, other religious groups emerged preaching the restoration of the ancient gospel and the expectation of Christ's imminent return. Some used the name Church of Christ or Christian Church. Some drew on the Bible to preach that they had restored primitive Christianity. Preachers Alexander Campbell and Barton Stone scoured the Bible to find passages from which they expected to restore Christ's ancient gospel. In Mentor, Ohio, Sidney Rigdon, a Baptist associated with the Campbell-Stone movement, preached restorationism as well. Some of the members of Rigdon's congregation, led by Isaac Morley, organized a communitarian society patterned after the collective reported in the Book of Acts.

A number of these religious leaders were Millennialists who took differing positions on Christ's Second Coming. Ann Lee, a British emigrant, organized the United Society of Believers in Christ's Second Appearing, popularly called the Shakers. They believed in the imminence of the return of Christ, and they practiced celibacy. John Humphrey Noyes organized the Oneida community at Oneida, New York. They believed that Christ had already returned, practicing collective ownership of property and complex marriage. Through a study of the Bible, William Miller, who lived at times in Massachusetts, New York, and Vermont, came to believe that Christ would return in 1844. His prediction failed, but some of his followers organized the Adventist movement.

In the meantime, Brigham Young and his family and friends experienced various spiritual manifestations themselves. In a retrospective account, Brigham and Miriam Works Young, Heber C. and Vilate Murray Kimball, John and Rhoda Young Greene, John Young Sr., and Fanny Young all reported that on September 22, 1827, the night that Joseph Smith retrieved the golden plates, they experienced an extraordinary celestial event: a "great light" appeared in the sky, and then traveled from east to west. As the light moved through the heavens, armies of armed men formed in the western sky and then marched toward the southwest. The Youngs and Kimballs knew nothing of Joseph Smith at the time, but a number of them remembered the event and testified to it later in life.

After his 1816 vision, Solomon Chamberlain joined the Reformed Methodists. Later, in 1830, while living in Lyons, New York, he stopped off in Palmyra while Grandin Press was printing the Book of Mormon. He gave the Smith family a copy of a pamphlet he had earlier published that detailed his vision. Convinced of the divinity of the Book of Mormon, he was baptized by Joseph Smith shortly after the organization of the church.

Converted to Smith's message, Chamberlain preached at a number of Episcopal Methodist and Reformed Methodist conferences and services, trying to convince those present of its authenticity and divinity. He also preached to Phinehas and Joseph Young and John Greene. Phinehas became convinced of the divinity of the Book of Mormon, and he tried also—unsuccessfully, as it proved—to incorporate it into Methodist teachings and practice. Through all of this study, preaching, and exhortation, Brigham Young became confident that the Book of Mormon contained some sort of truth, but he was not yet ready to join the church.

After hearing about the Book of Mormon from Solomon Chamberlain, John Greene and Phinehas Young saw it themselves. In June 1830 Joseph Smith called his brother, Samuel Harrison, to preach about the new church and the Book of Mormon. As he traveled, Samuel met Phinehas at an inn in Mendon, and he sold Phinehas a copy. John Greene either obtained a copy of the book or he borrowed Phinehas's. They read it and became convinced of its truthfulness, and Phinehas passed the book on to other family members, including his father, John Sr., his sister Fanny, and his brother Brigham. Instead of converting immediately, however, the Young family members remained for the time being in the Reformed Methodist denomination.

Late in 1831, a group of Mormon missionaries—Eleazer Miller, Elial Strong, Alpheus Gifford, Enos Curtis, and Daniel Bowen—came to Mendon from Columbia, Pennsylvania. Among other things, they explained the miraculous way in which Joseph Smith had received the plates and translated the book. Early in 1832, Phinehas and Clarissa Hamilton Young, together with Heber Kimball, Brigham, and Miriam Works Young, traveled to Columbia, Pennsylvania, to visit a branch of the fledgling church. There they found that the congregation practiced the spiritual gifts they had sought, including oral revelation and the Pentecostal experiences of speaking in tongues and translating such speech.

These experiences excited not only Brigham and Phinehas Young, but other family members as well. After witnessing the spiritual experiences in Pennsylvania, Brigham traveled to Canada to report to and consult with Joseph Young, who had gone there to preach Methodism. They returned to Mendon together. On April 5 and 6, 1832, on a return trip to Pennsylvania, Phinehas, Joseph, and John Young Sr. were baptized into the Church of the Latter Day Saints. Not willing to move quite as rapidly, Brigham accepted baptism and confirmation by Eleazer Miller in Mendon on April 14. Miller also ordained him an elder in the church. Heber Kimball and a number of others from his Baptist congregation had been baptized earlier. In the spring of 1832, the Youngs, Kimballs, and a number of other recent converts organized a branch of the church in Mendon, and the remainder of Brigham Young's siblings and their spouses and families joined the church in 1832 and 1833.

The mass conversion of so many Mendon Methodists and Baptists to Mormonism created a stir in the small community. A Baptist minister commented that Young's "faith and piety were counted for more force than his intellect. Heber C. Kimball, on the other hand, was respected as a man of much more mental power, but not of great devotion in comparison with his associate Young." Whatever the criticisms against him, although slower to convert than other family and friends, Brigham Young gave himself wholeheartedly to his new faith. During the summer of 1832, he preached to congregations, baptized converts, and organized branches. He labored first in Mendon, but afterward his missionary journeys took him as far as Warsaw, southwest of Mendon, and to towns along Lake Canandaigua to the southeast.

While in a religious service at the Kimball home, Young witnessed speaking in tongues by Alpheus Gifford, one of the Columbia, Pennsylvania, branch missionaries. This time, the spirit coursed through his body, and Brigham himself began speaking in an unknown tongue as well. The experience both surprised and elated him because he had seldom seen the phenomenon, but it would recur frequently during the early years after his conversion.

In November 1832 Brigham and Joseph Young and Heber Kimball traveled to Kirtland, Ohio, to visit with Joseph Smith. Located on the Chagrin River east of Cleveland and south of Fairport on Lake Erie, Kirtland became a gathering point for the Mormon community. The young prophet had moved himself and the headquarters of the church there from New York in January 1831, and he encouraged other members to move either there or Independence, Missouri, the other gathering center. Brigham's sister Rhoda and her husband John Greene were among the New Yorkers who had moved to Kirtland, and on their way to visit the town, the Young-Kimball party preached the gospel. They traveled like the apostles of old in the Biblical phrase "without purse or scrip"—that is, with no money. They also experienced additional manifestations of speaking in unknown tongues.

When they arrived in Kirtland, they met with the Greenes before searching out Joseph Smith. They found him chopping wood near the home of his father, Joseph Smith Sr. Later, in a meeting with the young prophet and in yet another event of spiritual engagement, Brigham spoke in an unknown tongue. Excited by the experience, Smith told Young that he had spoken the pure Adamic language, and Joseph Smith spoke in tongues as well. The threesome remained in Kirtland a week before returning to Mendon.

Speaking in unknown tongues became a significant feature of the new church. The practice, which appeared in a number of groups of enthusiastic religionists of the time, had apparently begun in Kirtland as early as December 1830, and apparently migrated from there to the Mormon branch in Columbia, Pennsylvania. Alpheus Gifford introduced it to Mendon, and Brigham, John Greene, and others who had felt the spirit in Mendon carried it with them to Kirtland in late 1832.

Young and Green were not the first to introduce ecstatic experiences to Kirtland. Peter Kerr, generally known as Black Pete, and others—including members of the family of Newel K. Whitney, who would go on to be a prominent leader in the movement—had practiced speaking in tongues in the Mormon community as early as 1831, even before Joseph Smith had moved to Ohio. Kerr had learned such experiences from the African American community in Pennsylvania in which he was raised. Joseph Smith had been skeptical of the earlier introduction, but he welcomed its reintroduction from Young and Greene.

After the reintroduction of these experiences, Joseph Smith, Zebedee Coltrin, and William Smith spoke in tongues at a conference in Kirtland on January 22, 1833. After they had spoken, "the Lord poured out his spirit in a miraculous manner, until all the Elders and several members, both male and female spoke in tongues." At an assembly the next day, many others spoke in tongues as well.

After they returned to Mendon, Brigham and Joseph Young wanted to share the message of the restoration with others, so in December the two brothers left for Kingston, Ontario, where Joseph Young had previously preached Methodism and where Brigham had told him about his experiences in Pennsylvania. In Ontario, they preached principally in and around Kingston but also in other towns along Lake Erie's north shore as well. They remained until February 1833 before returning to Mendon, where they preached again until leaving that spring for a region encompassing northern New York and Ontario.

Commitment to their new faith drew the Young family and their converts to the church center at Kirtland. John Young Sr. joined Rhoda and John Greene in Kirtland. After preaching in Canada in July 1833, Brigham and Joseph Young accompanied the Lake and Wood families from Ontario to Kirtland. Afterward, Brigham returned to Mendon; then he, too, moved with his daughters and Heber and Vilate Kimball's family to Kirtland.

Unlike Methodist circuit riders, who contacted members on America's expanding frontier well into the twentieth century, Mormons sought to gather members in covenant communities they called "towns." The Mormons platted farms on land outside the town while farmers, tradespeople, and businesspeople settled in the towns where they built churches. This practice had both a practical and theological basis. As a practical matter, it enabled those in the Mormon communities to establish such social, cultural, and educational organizations as schools, theaters, and musical groups. It allowed farmers who lived in town but worked the fields surrounding the community to participate in these activities. Town life also encouraged communal support and church activity.

As a theological matter, Smith taught that Christ would soon come for a second time. Following the message of Daniel, chapter 2; Matthew, chapter 24; and John's Book of Revelation, as well as revelations Smith himself received, he taught that violence and tribulation would accompany the Second Coming. The revelations confirmed that righteous Saints who gathered in covenant communities could spare themselves the travail that would accompany Christ's return.

In contrast with William Miller, Joseph Smith predicted no timeline for Christ's return, but he and the church members expected it to occur soon. He preached that the Saints should locate a center place—a new city of Zion—in Independence, Jackson County, Missouri. In Independence and Kirtland, the Mormons were to construct temples and practice the Law of Consecration and Stewardship, a communitarian system similar to that mentioned in the Book of Acts. The revelations said that members were to consecrate their property to the church's bishop, who in turn was to grant property as inheritances to them. Each member was to act as steward to increase the value of the property and to return part of the surplus to the bishop to care for the poor and create new inheritances for others. In practice, the system failed miserably, and Smith eventually abandoned and after an 1838 revelation (Doctrine and Covenants Section 119) replaced it with tithing.

The Mormons who gathered in such covenant communities expected to escape the violence and tribulation that was predicted to occur as Christ, the archangel Michael, and their armies subdued Satan and the wicked. Christ would then reign in righteousness for a thousand years—the Millennium. Although Joseph Smith consecrated Independence, Missouri, for the gathering of the Saints and designated a place for a temple there, he lived for the time being in Kirtland. One of Smith's revelations had promised an "Endowment from on High" to those who gathered in Kirtland, and revelations also instructed the Mormons to construct a temple there.

In Kirtland, Young resumed and expanded his family life. Brigham's brother-in-law John Greene had converted and baptized Mary Ann Angell, formerly a Free Will Baptist. She had moved to Kirtland where she felt drawn to Young after hearing his preaching. An experience in which Mary Ann bore her testimony impressed Brigham as well. The two did not waste time in a long courtship, and their marriage took place on February 18, 1834. Born in 1803, Mary Ann would outlive Brigham by five years. Devoted to her husband and family, she cared for his two daughters by Miriam and bore him six additional children.

Young also resumed the work that he knew best: He began building houses. He also preached and spent time with his daughters and new wife. Within a year of his arrival in Ohio, however, his world would change abruptly as attacks on Joseph Smith intensified, and the Mormons in Missouri endured storms of violence.

Young learned hard work early in his life, and after he left home and married, he was firmly devoted to his family. Moreover, in spite of financial and vocational setbacks, he exerted himself to improve his condition. As a youth, in concert with other family members, he spent long hours clearing land, tapping sugar maples, boiling the sap to make sugar and syrup, and working on the family farm. His father kicked him out of the family home at age sixteen, but he apprenticed himself, and he became an accomplished carpenter, painter, and glazier. During the lingering tuberculosis that eventually killed Miriam, he shouldered a heavy workload while he cared for her and their two daughters. Concurrently, in spite of his woefully inadequate education, he read widely in books and newspapers. Through all of this, first as a Reformed Methodist and later as a Mormon deep faith sustained his life as untoward events led the Mormons to abandon their religious experiment.

In reviewing the early years of Brigham's life, most historians have seen him as a practical leader. His experiences in New York and Kirtland, Ohio, however, reveal a side that historians have often ignored or downplayed. Young took more time than other family and friends to accept Mormonism. Nevertheless, after he joined, he became one of its most stalwart members. Most observers mention the experience of speaking in tongues, At a conference shortly after Smith testified that Young had spoken in the pure Adamic language, the prophet himself and others in the Mormon community had taken up the practice of speaking in tongues. Although Kerr and others practiced speaking in tongues as early as 1830, it does not seem to have occurred in public meetings in Kirtland until Young and Greene reintroduced it. They and others in Mendon learned the practice from Alpheus Gifford and the Saints in Columbia, Pennsylvania. After Young and Greene reintroduced the practice, speaking in tongues persisted in the Mormon community at least into the 1920s when the First Presidency urged the Saints to abandon it.

2

Kirtland and Missouri

From his arrival in Kirtland in September 1833 to his exodus from Missouri in 1839, Brigham Young experienced a number of extraordinary events in his religious and secular life. The vivid experiences of his conversion, missionary travels, and Pentecostal spirituality continued and compounded. Although he recovered briefly from the financial reverses of New York, he fell back into poverty. His financial troubles resulted in part from anti-Mormon violence and the failure of the Kirtland Safety Society, in addition to his continued involvement in uncompensated church work and the financial panic of 1837 and subsequent depression. As he settled in Missouri, his prospects seemed favorable. Living on a farm eight miles from Far West, he remained aloof from the violence of the Mormon Missouri War. Nevertheless, violence soon engulfed him and his family, experiencing the war's excruciating aftermath as he escorted his family and other refugees to Illinois.

When Young moved to Kirtland with his daughters Elizabeth and Vilate and the Kimball family, he had less than nothing. With the deep faith of a convert, he had preached more than he had worked, and he had floated loans that he could not repay to keep his family above water. He had traveled with little money (without purse or scrip, as directed in the Bible), and he had to rely on savings and donations. His missions to New York and Canada and the journeys to Pennsylvania and Kirtland had flattened his pocketbook—he could not work to support his family while away from Mendon. He had so little that he was reduced to wearing borrowed shoes and clothing.

Young experienced a spiritual boost during 1834 as he marched to Missouri with Zion's Camp, an expedition Joseph Smith organized to redeem the Saints in the state. By "redeem," Smith meant that he intended to help the Mormons return to Jackson County and recover the property that Missouri mobs had stolen. By the summer of 1833, around twelve hundred Latter-day Saints had moved to their new City of Zion at Independence in Jackson County, Missouri. They had planned to buy as much property as possible to accommodate themselves and the larger numbers of members who would gather with them.

The non-Mormon settlers in Missouri, most of whom were southern pro-slavery Protestants, reacted with horror to those Mormons who had settled among them and to the prospect of the immigration of free African Americans. The events that followed lit the fuse on a civil war that would continue until Governor Lilburn Boggs ordered the expulsion of the Mormons in 1838. The old settlers feared the political, economic, social, and religious power of the new arrivals, most of whom came from the North. Mormons, who expected to purchase most of the property in the county, held no slaves and seemed friendly to free blacks. After drafting an anti-Mormon manifesto, the opponents organized as vigilantes—the Mormons called them mobs—to expel the Saints from Jackson County. I prefer the term vigilante because the word mob often connotes a lack of organization. The anti-Mormons, by contrast, were generally well organized, often as militia units. Both systematic and uncoordinated attacks included disarming the Mormons, burning their outbuildings and property, destroying homes, wrecking their printing press, and beating them. The vigilantes tarred and feathered Charles Allen and Bishop Edward Partridge.

In response to the anti-Mormon violence, the Mormons hired attorneys to apply to the Missouri courts for protection and petitioned Governor Daniel Dunklin for assistance. Dunklin advised them to go to the courts, where they were rebuffed, and the vigilante attacks intensified. Instead of fighting back, the Mormons fled north across the Missouri River to Clay County.

On the mistaken assumption that Dunklin would assist them and that God would protect them, Joseph Smith organized Zion's Camp. The unit sent to redeem the Missouri Mormons consisted of 204 men, 10 women, and 7 children. Part of Zion's Camp left Kirtland between May 1 and 5, 1834. Brigham joined up, and additional recruits joined them as they marched west.

As spiritual crusaders, they "traveled," Wilford Woodruff wrote, "like the Children of Israel." They prayed together, preached to each other and to people along the way, and heard sermons and revelations from Joseph Smith. According to Woodruff, "Joseph often addressed us in the name of the Lord . . . Clothed upon with much of the spirit of God." In a mound near the Illinois River, fellow Mormon Milton Holmes found the skeleton of a man with an arrow embedded in his back. Joseph said that the man was a Lamanite—a Book of Mormon people—named Zelph, who had died in battle. Woodruff took his thigh bone to Clay County, reburying it as close to the new Zion as possible.

As they marched west, the members passed through towns and farms. The marchers hid their purpose and religious affiliation. Because many of the Mormon sermons resembled those of other churches, the guesses about their identity were often wrong. Brigham Young preached on occasion about baptism, so some of the listeners thought he was a Baptist.

When the recruits reached the Salt River in eastern Missouri, Mormon representatives Parley P. Pratt and Orson Hyde left for Jefferson City to meet with Governor Dunklin. Instead of offering assistance, as they had hoped, Dunklin rebuffed them. Refusing to call out the state militia to aid in recovering their property, he ordered them not march under arms and urged them again to apply to the state courts for damages. But the courts had already failed them, and Dunklin's orders left them at the mercy of well-armed bands of Missouri vigilantes.

On June 19, at Fishing River in Western Missouri, they encountered a force of more than three hundred armed men from Jackson, Clay, and Ray counties. As the vigilantes prepared to attack the Mormons, a raging storm suddenly descended on both parties. The Mormons took refuge in a nearby Baptist church, but wild wind and rain swelled the river and pounded the unprotected attackers. Left in disarray by the storm, the vigilantes retreated from the battlefield.

The traveling Mormons credited their escape to the hand of God, but He had already seemed to add to their troubles. Unused to prolonged marching, the militiamen in Zion's Camp had blistered and bloody feet, and often they could often find only contaminated water to drink. George A. Smith said that he and others had to clench their teeth to strain out "wrigglers" (probably mosquito larvae) as they sucked in water.

On June 21, just two days after the storm protected them from the vigilantes, the waters visited an even more appalling curse on the camp: cholera broke out, most likely from drinking contaminated water. Sixty-eight of Zion's Camp members—about a third of their number—including Joseph Smith and Heber Kimball, contracted the disease, and fourteen of the men died. The uninfected, including Brigham and Joseph Young, nursed the sick. The cholera epidemic continued for several days as the members of Zion's Camp marched on toward Liberty, Missouri. On the advice of Gen. David R. Atchison, one of the Mormons' attorneys, however, they stopped short of Liberty on June 24.

On June 22, the day after cholera first infected the marchers, Joseph Smith announced a new revelation. The disease had struck them as a consequence of their disobedience, and thus the time had not arrived to redeem Zion. Redemption, he said, would not occur until the elders had received an endowment from on high. The Lord would endow them with blessings, he said, at a temple that they were to build in Kirtland. Moreover, the Mormons need not fight those who had gathered against them, he said, but God would fight their battles.

Disbanding the camp on July 3, Joseph Smith told the marchers that they could either remain in Missouri or return to Kirtland. Most who had families in Kirtland, including Young and Kimball, returned to Ohio.

Upon reaching Kirtland, Brigham found Mary Ann pregnant with their son, Joseph Angell. While Young marched to Zion, she had remained "alone with the motherless children consigned to her care"; carrying their unborn child, "she was forced to provide for them and herself the everyday comforts of life." She bore Joseph Young shortly after his father returned.

After he returned to Kirtland, Young continued to work as carpenter, painter, and glazier, and he offered unconditional support to Smith as prophet and church president. He spent much of his time working on the Kirtland Temple, especially after February 22, 1836, when Smith assigned him to oversee the painting and finishing of the building's interior. His brother Lorenzo and their friend Artemus Millet contracted to finish the exterior, a task they had completed in January 1836. The Saints built the temple as sacred space to receive the "endowment with power from on high" that Smith had promised in revelations in 1831, 1833, and again on the Zion's Camp march in 1834.

Unwavering in his support of Smith, Young testified for him in a number of cases. These included charges against the prophet by Denis Lake and allegations by Sylvester Smith (no relation to the prophet). Disillusioned because Zion's Camp had failed to obtain property for him in Missouri, Lake sued Smith for eight hundred dollars. Young considered the charge absurd, and his testimony helped Joseph win the suit. Then, in a trial before the church's common council, Sylvester Smith charged Joseph Smith with misusing Zion's Camp funds. Joseph prevailed, and in fact, the decision led to charges against Sylvester, who reluctantly published an apology.

Young also added to his meager education. He attended adult education classes in common school—we would call it elementary school—and Hebrew school. In 1835 Joseph Smith hired Joshua Seixas of Hudson, Ohio, to teach Hebrew. Son of a prominent New York Jewish family, Seixas had converted to Christianity, and he taught at Oberlin College and Western Reserve College. According to Seixas, a number of the Mormons achieved considerable proficiency in the language.

Smith and other church leaders rewarded Young's spirituality and commitment. In revelations beginning in 1829, Smith announced that the Lord had called the Three Witnesses to the Book of Mormon—Oliver Cowdery, David Whitmer, and Martin Harris—to select members of the Quorum of the Twelve Apostles. At a conference in Kirtland on February 14, 1835, after the three united in prayer, they named the members of the Quorum. They called Brigham Young second in order, and in the end, all but three had marched with Zion's Camp. On May 2, 1835, Smith ruled that the Twelve should rank in seniority by age rather than by date of ordination. This placed thirty-three-year-old Brigham Young third in the Quorum after Thomas B. Marsh and David W. Patten. The Twelve, as they were often called, included a number of men like Young, Kimball, Hyde, Patten, and Parley and Orson Pratt, who would play significant rolls in Mormonism's later history.

In revelations and executive rulings, Smith detailed the authority and responsibilities of the Twelve. A revelation placed them equal in authority to the First Presidency—consisting of the president and his counselors—which was the highest authority in the church, but only outside of the organized stakes. Governed by a president with two counselors and a twelve-man high council, at the time stakes were the local organization in areas with large numbers of members. Outside the stakes, members belonged to local organizations called branches. In practice, however, Smith's rulings ranked the Twelve just behind the First Presidency even within the stakes.

After the three witnesses called the Twelve, Joseph Smith offered them counsel. Two days later, they left Kirtland on proselytizing missions to Ohio, New York, Vermont, Massachusetts, New Hampshire, and Maine. On their missions, they alternated between preaching in various communities, baptizing those who converted to Mormonism, and meeting together for discussion. The apostles met together to assign areas, which they called conferences (probably a designation borrowed from the Methodists), in which they various members were to proselytize. In quorum meetings, they preached to each other, reproved one another for mistakes, and reported on their labors.

After returning to Kirtland, the apostles supported the First Presidency in publishing Smith's revelations and teachings. In September 1834 Joseph had assigned a committee consisting of himself, counselors Sidney Rigdon and Frederick G. Williams, and assistant president Oliver Cowdery to "arrange the items of the doctrine of Jesus Christ for the government of the Church." The result was the Doctrine and Covenants, which consisted of a series of lessons on doctrine taught in Kirtland, called the Lectures on Faith, together with revelations given to Joseph Smith. At a general conference of the church on August 17, 1835, the various quorums met to testify to the divinity of the Doctrine and Covenants. Among the testimonies supporting publication, the Twelve wrote that "the Lord has borne record to our souls, through the Holy Ghost . . . that these Commandments were given by inspiration of God."

Even though the Twelve were supposed to rank equally with the First Presidency outside the stakes, members of the Kirtland Stake leadership sought to subordinate them to the stake high council. The Twelve learned this when they returned to Kirtland from their mission in the eastern states on September 26, 1835. On September 27, at a church trial of Gladden Bishop, who was then away from Kirtland, on charges for "advancing heretical doctrines," the Kirtland High Council questioned the authority of the Twelve to conduct the trial. Joseph Smith supported the Twelve, ruling again that they governed the affairs of the church outside the stakes. He said that the "high Council had nothing to do with the Twelve, or the decisions of the Twelve," who "were accountable only to the" First Presidency for their actions outside the stakes. Joseph reaffirmed this decision in a meeting with his counselors and the Twelve on January 16, 1836.

In subsequent gatherings, however, Smith ranked Young's Quorum above other officers in the Kirtland Stake inside the stake as well. At an evening meeting on March 6, 1836, Joseph ruled that each quorum in turn must vote on a series of resolutions. The voting passed successively in ascending order: deacons, teachers, priests, bishop of Kirtland, bishop of Zion (Independence, Missouri), elders, high priests, presidents of the Seventy (a missionary quorum with seven presidents ranking just below the Twelve), high council of Kirtland, high council of Zion, the Twelve, and finally, the First Presidency. During the dedication of the Kirtland Temple on March 27, the prophet placed the Twelve before the high councils. During a foot-washing ceremony on March 30, the Twelve followed the First Presidency in receiving the ordinance, and after the First Presidency had washed the feet of the presidents of the Seventy, the Twelve and seven presidents of the Seventy washed the feet of the remainder of those in the congregation.

As Young worked to finish the temple's interior, the members gathered in the building for meetings and Hebrew school. A series of extraordinary events unfolded. On January 16, 1836, the First Presidency and Twelve experienced "the gift of toungs, . . . like the rushing of a mighty wind, and my [Joseph Smith's] soul was filled with the glory of God." At a meeting on January 21, Smith saw a vision of Young "standing in a strange land" preaching to "men of colour" who opposed him, with "the angel of God standing above his head with a drawn sword in his hand protecting him." At the same meeting others "saw glorious visions also,—angels ministered unto them, . . . and the power of the highest rested upon us." The next evening, the church leaders enjoyed similar experiences, including the gift of tongues. Smith reported that "angels mingled . . . their voices" with those present.

Similar manifestations occurred in the temple at other times. On January 28, at a meeting with the Twelve and the seven presidents of the Seventy, Roger Orton saw an angel with a flaming sword encircling the house to protect those present, and Zebedee

Coltrin saw the Savior. Visions and manifestations of the spirit occurred on February 6 after the members participated in the Hosanna Shout, in which the congregation repeated three times in unison: "Hosanna, Hosanna, Hosanna to God and the Lamb," followed by "Amen, Amen, and Amen." Some of those present saw visions, which they reported to others. William Smith saw a vision of the Twelve and Seventies presidents preaching in England.

Additional spiritual manifestations and spiritual ordinances occurred at various times. On March 27, 1836, at the temple dedication, several of those present saw angels in the building. After the congregation repeated the Hosanna Shout, Brigham Young and David Patten spoke in tongues. At a meeting on March 29, those present practiced foot washing. At a solemn assembly on March 30, a number of those present prophesied openly about the church and about its treatment in Missouri. In this meeting, the First Presidency retired from the assembly and "left the meeting in [the] charge of the 12," not the Kirtland High Council.

Intense spiritual experiences continued. In a deeply divine experience on Sunday, April 3, Joseph Smith and Oliver Cowdery saw "the Lord standing upon the breast work of the pulpit . . . under his feet was a paved work of pure gold." Prophets Moses, Elias, and Elijah followed Jesus in appearing to the two to dispense blessings and to restore ancient authority, including gathering the Mormons and the Children of Israel and uniting generations of families.

Shortly after the dedication, Joseph Smith called Brigham and Joseph Young, the latter being one of the presidents of the Seventy, to serve a mission to New York and New England. They proselytized in New York, Vermont, Massachusetts, Rhode Island, Connecticut, and Maine. In Hopkinton, Massachusetts, they visited the family of their mother's sister, Rhoda Howe Richards, and Rhoda's husband Joseph. The Richards family and their relatives, the Haven family, joined the church. Joseph Smith later called Brigham Young's cousin Willard Richards, a Tomsonian physician (a herbalist and botanist who followed the teachings of Samuel Tomson), to the Twelve, and Brigham later called him as a counselor in the First Presidency.

Young found it extremely difficult to leave his family in Kirtland, but his commitment to the church made it imperative that he spread the gospel. While living in Kirtland, he and Mary Ann would have three more children: Joseph Angell and twins Brigham Jr. and Mary Ann Jr. While on his mission, he expressed in letters his need to comfort his wife's "hart": "I pray for you and I feele that the Lord will bles you and keep you from danger and bare you upon the arms of faith." He reflected frequently on the children, and he wrote Mary Ann to tell them he remembered them in his prayers. He asked her to tell them to be good, to mind her, and to study their lessons. He became anxious when he did not immediately receive a reply.

As the Mormons in Kirtland enjoyed this season of spiritual feasting during 1836, the city of Kirtland grew. Converts poured into the city, building homes and increasing land values. When Brigham and Joseph Young returned from their mission, they found a bustling community instead of the quiet town they had left.

The community had considerable wealth in land and buildings, but it lacked liquid assets. Recognizing this financial shortcoming, the community leaders decided to organize a bank. The United States had no national banking system at the time, and local banks issued paper currency that circulated at a greater or lesser discount depending on the confidence of the public in their ability to redeem the notes in specie. The church leadership sent Orson Hyde to Columbus to secure a bank charter from the legislature and Oliver Cowdery to Philadelphia to have bank note plates engraved. Cowdery returned with the plates, but after two tries Hyde had failed to secure a charter.

Apparently relying on unsound legal advice, the Kirtland leaders reasoned that if a chartered bank were illegal, an informal association that functioned like a bank was not. They organized the Kirtland Safety Society Antibanking Company, a title they overprinted on some of the bank notes with the word "anti" before "bank" and "ing company" after. Sidney Rigdon served as president and Joseph Smith as cashier. Though popular among most Mormons, the anti-bank engendered animosity among many non-Mormons.

Foremost in opposition was Grandison Newell, a Mentor, Ohio, businessman who hated the Mormons in general and Joseph Smith in particular. Newell lobbied with legislators against the Kirtland bank and refused to hire any Mormons in his businesses. He also sued Smith himself and encouraged others to do so as well. Eventually, Joseph Smith had to answer to seventeen civil suits, ten of which resulted in judgments against him. Smith did not fully satisfy four of the judgments, and he left three only partly satisfied. Smith withdrew from the bank in June 1837.

A financial panic had gripped the United States since May 1837. Banks in New York suspended specie payments on May 10. In September 1833 President Andrew Jackson, who hated banks, had withdrawn all federal funds from Philadelphia's Second Bank of the United States, which had served as a national bank, and the bank failed. Jackson also issued an executive order compelling all who purchased public lands to pay in gold or silver. The Kirtland Safety Society, under the leadership of Warren Parrish and Frederick G. Williams, was already well along to failure before the panic hit, but that and the subsequent depression killed it, and the bank would fail in November.

A number of church leaders who had supported Smith had left Kirtland for various reasons during the year. In March 1837 Brigham Young and his cousin, Willard Richards, had left for a mission to the East. In June, Heber Kimball, Orson Hyde, Willard Richards, and a number of others went on the church's first mission to England. During late July, Young accompanied Smith and Rigdon part of the way on the presidency's mission to Canada. They separated at Buffalo, and Young and his cousin, Albert P. Rockwood, traveled east while Smith and Rigdon went north. At some time, Young purchased a tavern in Troy, New York, apparently with Kirtland Safety Society notes.

Both Smith and Young returned to Kirtland in late August, and on September 3 at a conference there, the church membership voted to sustain the First Presidency and Twelve in their positions. Already, however, dissent had begun to appear in Kirtland. In May 1837, at a high council meeting, several members accused

Warren Parish, Joseph Smith's clerk; Apostles Parley P. Pratt and Lyman Johnson; David Whitmer, one of the Three Witnesses and president of the church in Missouri; and Frederick G. Williams, of the First Presidency, of following a course "injurious to the Church." Because of the prominent positions of the accused, the Kirtland High Council refused to rule on the complaints.

In August 1837, while Smith and Rigdon proselytized in Canada and Young and Rockwood labored in the eastern states, the schism grew rapidly. A group headed by Parrish and aided by Elder John F. Boynton of the Quorum of the Twelve occupied the east pulpits of the temple during a church service. Drawing pistols and bowie knives, they harassed Joseph Smith Sr. while he tried to conduct the meeting. Policemen intervened and arrested the dissidents, but the weapons and violence frightened many in attendance.

Similar discontent reappeared in a conference on September 3. The conference disfellowshipped Apostles Luke S. and Lyman E. Johnson and John F. Boynton. The Johnsons were absent, but Boynton attended and cited the bank failure as justification for his opposition to Joseph Smith. Smith defended himself by arguing that he had insisted that unless those who managed the bank did so "on righteous principles it would not stand."

Smith's financial dealings, the bank's failure, the decline of Kirtland's economic fortunes, and claims of new revelations from several dissident members led a number of local leaders and their followers to again try to take control of the Kirtland Temple and the church leadership. On September 27 Joseph Smith and Sidney Rigdon left for Far West, Missouri, to assist in organizing church units there. During their absence, Parrish, Boynton, Luke Johnson, and some supporters occupied the temple and tried to depose Smith and replace him with David Whitmer. The dissident group called themselves the "old standard," and they proposed to restore the church's original name, "The Church of Christ."

Smith returned from Far West about December 10, and he and his supporters succeeded in excommunicating four dozen of the dissenters. Historian Richard Bushman estimates that over the last half of 1837, more than forty members were excommunicated. By

January 12, 1838, the opposition inside and outside the church, together with lawsuits, mostly over the Kirtland Safety Society, led Smith and Rigdon to flee permanently for Far West, Missouri.

Young vigorously opposed the Parrish group and other dissidents. He believed, as he later told his listeners, that Smith had taken heaven and earth and made them shake hands. This support of Smith caused a group of apostates led by Jacob Bump to turn their wrath on him, and their fury became so great that Young fled from Kirtland three days before Christmas 1838. He traveled to Dublin, Indiana, where Lorenzo had temporarily settled. After leaving Lorenzo's home, Young met with Smith and Rigdon, and the three of them traveled to Far West, where they arrived on March 14, 1838.

Just four days before Young left, Mary Ann had given birth to twins, Brigham Jr. and Mary Ann Jr. Young's flight left her to care for the newborns as well as Elizabeth, Vilate, and Joseph A. Shortly after Young left, his wife wrote to tell him that lawsuits by dissidents had jeopardized all their property and more. The dissenters terrorized Mary Ann and her family, attacking her with "threats and vile language." Mary Ann, with the five children—the youngest two in her arms—left Kirtland later in the spring. The arduous travel by river and overland with five children so sickened and exhausted her that when Young first saw her, she looked "as if you were almost in your grave."

Brigham's short-lived residence in Missouri proved even more grueling than Ohio. When he arrived in western Missouri, Young settled on farmland about eight miles northeast of Far West. He took his family there, and Smith told him by revelation not to leave until he had "provided for" the family. By staying at the farm and visiting Far West infrequently, he managed to avoid most of the conflict that soon engulfed the Mormon community.

Nevertheless, even though he tried to stand aloof from the violence that erupted in northern Missouri, it bore down relentlessly upon him. After civil war had ripped the Mormon community from its moorings, Joseph Smith and a number of other leaders ended up in prison. Young, by then senior member of the Quorum of the Twelve Apostles, had to salvage whatever remained of Mormon possessions and shepherd the refugees eastward to Illinois.

Dissent had quickly spread to northern Missouri. In response, the Missouri High Council excommunicated a number of prominent leaders, including Oliver Cowdery; David and John Whitmer; William W. Phelps; Apostles Lyman Johnson and William McLellin; and Frederick G. Williams, formerly of the First Presidency. Phelps, Williams, and Cowdery would return to the church. The others remained alienated.

Unfortunately, during the summer of 1838, several events had contributed to anti-Mormon violence. On June 17 Sidney Rigdon regaled the Saints with a sermon in which he urged the expulsion of dissenters from the Mormon towns. He built his diatribe on Christ's remark, "if the salt have lost its savour, it is thenceforth good for nothing but to be cast out" (Matthew 5:13). Following Rigdon's address, more than three-score men signed a petition that gave the dissidents three days to depart. Intimidated by the sermon and petition, many dissenters fled on June 19. David Whitmer and some of the others settled in Richmond, Missouri.

More provocative than even Rigdon's sermon and perhaps inflamed by its words, a band of ultra-loyal members organized a notorious paramilitary ring known as the "Danites." In June 1838 Sampson Avard organized a unit in Far West, and in July Lyman Wight organized a unit in Adam-ondi-Ahman (often called Diahman) in Daviess County.

Although scholars do not question that ultra-orthodox members like Avard and Wight belonged to the Danites, Joseph Smith's role is a matter of historical dispute. Historians Stephen LeSueur and Michael Quinn have argued that Joseph was intimately involved in the Danite activities, though Quinn conceded that the Mormons were clearly victims of the Missouri anti-Mormons. Scholar Leland Gentry, on the other hand, has argued that although Joseph supported the dissenters' expulsion from the community and that he approved of the defensive actions against Missouri mobs and militia between June and October, he did not know of the Danites' offensive action during late October. Historian Alexander

Baugh wrote that Joseph knew of some of the Danite activities and participated in some attacks on non-Mormon communities, but that he endeavored "to distance himself from the more militant Danite organization." Historian Richard Bushman believes that the prophet knew much of what the Danites did and that Joseph offered tacit support to some of their activities, but that he declined to participate actively. Bushman also pointed out that both Smith and Rigdon used republican rhetoric to oppose violence but approve resistance. Unfortunately, in Bushman's view, Smith received the blame for much what the Danites did. I believe that Joseph knew of a number of their activities and that he supported some of them.

Young distanced himself from the organization. In a later recollection, Young said that after Lorenzo attended a Danite meeting, he discussed the proceedings with Brigham. Lorenzo heard Avard preach about the oaths of absolute obedience and loyalty and penalties for disobedience, and he declined to join. After listening to Lorenzo's description—apparently unaware of Joseph's personal knowledge—Brigham promised to tell the prophet of Avard's "secret wickedness."

On July 4, 1838, Rigdon gave another speech that inflamed Mormons and outraged non-Mormons. Emphasizing the persecution that the Saints had endured, he said that if a "mob . . . disturb[ed] us; it shall be between us and them a war of extermination." Smith endorsed Rigdon's remarks but insisted that the Mormons would act only defensively. Young later said that Rigdon "was the prime cause of our troubles in Missouri, by his fourth of July oration."

Battles between Mormons and anti-Mormons began in the summer of 1838 and continued through the fall and early winter. The conflicts started with a ruckus in Gallatin, Daviess County, north of Caldwell County, on August 6, when some Mormons who lived in the county went there to vote. The anti-Mormons tried to keep the Mormons from the polls, and their efforts led to a battle in which each side exchanged blows with logs and rocks. These caused bruises and bashed heads, but no deaths.

Throughout August and September, Mormon and non-Mormon units confronted one another. Gen. B. M. Lisle, adjutant general of the Missouri State Guard, ordered Maj. Gen. David R. Atchison and Brig. Gens. Alexander W. Doniphan and Hiram G. Parks to keep the peace and to determine the actual intent of the non-Mormons. In addition, Edgar Flory and Col. Sterling Price, a member of the legislature, conducted an investigation that led to outlandish charges that the Mormons planned to unite with Indians to overwhelm non-Mormons in northern Missouri. Significantly, Atchison and Doniphan served as attorneys for Joseph Smith and other Mormon leaders, so they did not share the anti-Mormon attitudes of most other Missourians. Parks may not have cared about keeping the peace, since he sided with the anti-Mormons. In mid-September 1838, Atchison and Doniphan succeeded in defusing a confrontation in Daviess County between a body of vigilantes from Livingston, Carroll, and Saline counties and Mormons from Diahman under Wight's leadership.

Things did not go as well for the Mormons in Carroll County, southeast of Far West. On August 6, the same day as the battle in Gallatin, anti-Mormons in Carroll County began coordinated movements that led to the expulsion of Mormons from the town of De Witt. The Carroll vigilantes held several meetings, and on October 1 they began burning Mormon buildings. Then, with the help of men from nearby counties, they besieged the town. Brigadier General Parks could not de-escalate the confrontation, and following the attack, the vigilantes forced all Mormons to evacuate De Witt.

Unwilling to remain passive, Mormons from Diahman, augmented by refugees from De Witt, emigrants from Kirtland in Kirtland Camp, and troops from Far West—in part Danites—assumed the offensive. Mormons pled with Missouri governor Lilburn W. Boggs to protect them, but he refused. In an October 14 sermon, Joseph Smith said that Governor Boggs would not intervene, so "they must take care of themselves, as they could get help from no other quarter." On October 18 Mormon units responded in ways Smith had probably not anticipated: they attacked, plundered, and burned the Daviess County towns of Gallatin, Millport, and Grindstone Fork. After these attacks, both Mormons and anti-Mormons ranged through the area burning homes and confiscating property.

Significantly, the civil war within the church had consequences for the Twelve in general and Young in particular. After Smith arrived in Far West, he had increased the authority of the Twelve by calling its three senior members—Thomas Marsh, David Patten, and Brigham Young—as the presidency pro tem in Missouri. The burning of Gallatin, Millport, and Grindstone Fork so outraged Marsh that he resigned from the church on October 24, taking Orson Hyde with him. Marsh's departure left Patten as senior apostle and Young as second in seniority.

Then, further south, on orders from Major General Atchison, Capt. Samuel Bogart and about thirty-five Ray County militiamen patrolled the line between Ray and Caldwell counties. While on patrol, Bogart's unit took three Mormons to their camp on Crooked River as hostages. In an attempt to free the hostages, on October 25 Judge Elias Higbee of Caldwell County authorized a cavalry unit of Capt. David W. Patten and sixty men to move against Bogart's militiamen. In the battle of Crooked River, Patten and two other Mormons died, and no others were wounded. The Caldwell militia killed one man and wounded six others in Bogart's unit.

On October 27, the day after receiving a report of the Crooked River battle and knowing already of the Mormon raids on towns in Daviess County, Governor Boggs issued his infamous extermination order. "The Mormons," he wrote, "must be treated as enemies, and must be exterminated or driven from the state." Boggs also relieved Atchison, an attorney for the Mormons, of his command.

On October 30, with no knowledge of the extermination order, 240 militiamen under the command of Col. William Jennings, sheriff of Livingston County, descended on the small Mormon settlement at Hauns (or Hawns) Mill. They massacred seventeen Mormon men and children and a non-Mormon sympathizer, and they wounded a number of others.

Boggs transmitted his extermination order to Maj. Gen. John B. Clark, instructing him to move on the Mormons at Far West. Clark selected Maj. Gen. Samuel D. Lucas and brigadier generals Doniphan and Parks as field commanders. Declining to wait for Clark's arrival, Lucas moved immediately on Far West. Doniphan stationed his troops near the breastworks the Mormons had erected on the edge of town.

Doniphan considered Boggs's extermination order illegal, but Lucas planned to enforce it. On the morning of October 31, Col. George M. Hinkle, commander of the Mormon troops, met with Doniphan under a flag of truce. Lucas also met with Hinkle, after which he arrested Smith and six others. Hinkle expected Lucas to release the Mormon prisoners, but instead Lucas convened a drumhead court martial in the field. Lucas refused to allow the prisoners to attend their own trial, and the officers voted to convict the Mormons. Lucas ordered Doniphan to execute the seven Mormons in Far West the next day. Doniphan refused, telling Lucas that he would hold the general responsible if anything happened to the prisoners. Instead of killing the Mormon leaders, Lucas took them to Jackson County. Before he left, he forced all the Mormons to deed their real property to the state, allegedly to compensate those who lost property to the Mormons and to reimburse the state for the cost of the war.

After Major General Clark arrived in Far West, he arrested more than fifty more Mormon men. He took them to Richmond, bringing the seven that Lucas had previously taken to Jackson to Richmond as well. Judge Austin King heard the charges and bound twenty-four of the Mormons over for trial. He admitted half of them to bail, but he ordered the other half, including Smith, Rigdon, and Hyrum Smith incarcerated to await trial.

Owing to continued mob assaults, Brigham and Mary Ann had to leave Far West on February 14, 1839. The Young family and other refugees trudged eastward toward Illinois, "their footprints," Mary Ann wrote, "not unfrequently marked with blood upon the snow and ice." She kept "house in eleven different places" before arriving in Illinois.

With the First Presidency in jail, Young, as senior member of the Twelve, and Edward Partridge, as presiding bishop, had to assume responsibility for conducting the refugees to Illinois. Partridge, and William Marks, the Far West Stake president, thought that the members should pay their own way. Young disagreed, and he frequently moved his family eastward from one place to another while he returned to "gather up the poorer and more destitute of the brethren and sisters, the widows and helpless orphans of those who had fallen victims at the hands of the mob." In giving assistance to those in need, Young faced a daunting task. Vigilantes continued to destroy crops and kill the Mormons' animals. The legislature appropriated two thousand dollars to assist the Mormons to move from the state, but mobbers appropriated much of the money through spurious claims, such requiring money for Mormons' animals they slaughtered.

Rigdon managed to secure his release on a writ of habeas corpus on February 5 and traveled to Quincy, Illinois. The last of the Saints who had lived in northern Missouri did not evacuate Far West until April 20, 1839. Joseph and Hyrum Smith and three others remained in custody until April 15, when they escaped with the assistance of the guards who were escorting them to Boone County for trial. Joseph Smith arrived in Quincy on April 22. Charged with treason, he and the others had endured house arrest in Independence, a preliminary hearing in Richmond, and incarceration in Liberty Jail. Judge Austin King charged them with plotting to erect an independent government and planning to wage war against Missouri. King also charged Parley Pratt and four others with murder for the killing of a Missouri militiaman at Crooked River. Pratt and the others secured their release on April 24.

What do we make of the 1838–39 violence in Missouri? It is difficult by any stretch of the imagination to consider the Missouri vigilantes anything but the aggressors. They had expelled the Mormons from Jackson County. In the August 6 election, they tried to stop the Mormons from voting, and later in August vigilantes that had first begun to move on Diahman began what became a siege that led to the expulsion of the Mormons from De Witt on October 11. Mormons retaliated by burnings at Gallatin, Millport, and Grindstone Fork on October 18. The Battle of Crooked River on October 25, in which the Mormons got the worst of the conflict, was an attack on a Missouri militia unit. Even though the Mormons engaged Bogart's unit in an attempt to free three hostages, this battle led to Boggs's extermination order. The massacre at Hauns Mill took place while the Mormons waved a flag of truce. On balance, the Mormons were more sinned against than sinning. In general, though they escalated the violence in some actions such as the Davies County burnings and the attacks on Bogart's unit, they were reacting against vigilante or mob violence directed at them.

Unfortunately, in the civil war that raged in Missouri, that did not matter. In a democratic republic, as Richard Bushman pointed out, citing Alexis de Tocqueville, it is generally impossible to protect the interests of a despised minority when the majority support violence against them. Historically, the principal protection of minority rights in the United States has been an independent judiciary, but that has frequently failed in wartime. In Missouri's civil war, the judiciary provided the Mormons with no protection.

After the war ended, much of the burden of saving the remainder of the Mormon community rested on Brigham Young. With members of the First Presidency in prison and the Far West Stake presidency in disarray, Young and Partridge carried most of the responsibility for helping the refugees to Illinois. As generally happens in the aftermath of war, the number of refugee deaths remains uncounted. Still, as Young helped others flee the state, most of the burden of moving his family rested heavily on Mary Ann, who moved herself and the children to Quincy, Illinois.

3

The Kingdom and the Exodus

The Mormons' experience in Illinois was similar to that in Ohio and Missouri. Members from other states and converts from Great Britain joined Mormon refugees from Missouri, many of whom Brigham Young escorted to Illinois. They settled on a peninsula on the Mississippi River at a place previously called Commerce. They named their city Nauvoo—"beautiful place" in Hebrew—and they constructed homes and built a temple. It seemed at first that the Saints might at last succeed in making a covenant community there. Then everything fell apart. An organized unit of militiamen killed Joseph and Hyrum Smith, and coordinated attacks forced Brigham Young, the Council of Fifty, and the Twelve Apostles to organize and supervise Nauvoo's abandonment.

Respectability and acceptance had seemed within grasp for the Mormons as the city of Nauvoo, its university, and militia (the Nauvoo Legion) obtained charters from the Illinois legislature. This occurred in part because of the influence of John C. Bennett. Bennett had abandoned his wife and family in Ohio to move to Illinois, where he enjoyed close relationships with Illinois governor Thomas Carlin, Judge and later Senator Stephen A. Douglas, and

Joseph Smith. Through Smith's influence, the people of Nauvoo elected Bennett as mayor, and Smith called him as assistant president in the church's First Presidency.

After the chaos of Missouri, Young assumed leadership of the Twelve. On January 16, 1839, Smith confirmed Young's position by calling "the oldest of those" first appointed as "the President of your Quorum." While in Far West, Smith had called the Twelve to a second mission to England by a revelation that instructed them to leave from the temple site in Far West. Braving potential violence and encountering fleeing Mormons as they traveled west, Young, five of the Twelve, and a number of friends gathered at the Far West temple site on April 26, 1839. They replaced two fallen apostles by ordaining Wilford Woodruff and George A. Smith to the Quorum.

The apostles and others asserted their authority by excommunicating dissenters. At a conference in Quincy, Illinois, on March 17, 1839, they excommunicated Marsh, Phelps, Williams, Hinkle, Avard, and a number of others, all in absentia. On April 26, as some of the Twelve gathered at Far West, they excommunicated more than thirty others, also in absentia.

After fulfilling Joseph Smith's command to start their mission from Far West, they returned to Quincy, Illinois, to move their families to Hancock County, Illinois, and Lee County, Iowa. Smith had begun to purchase land in Illinois and Iowa from promoter Isaac Galland. Some of the titles in Iowa proved invalid, but the ones at Commerce were apparently sound.

Instead of settling their families in Nauvoo, Young and several others made their homes in an abandoned military barracks west of the Mississippi River in Montrose, Iowa, but conditions there proved nearly unbearable. After John Taylor left for England, his wife, Leonora, moved in with the Young family, but Young asked her to leave shortly after she arrived—Mary Ann was pregnant at the time, and they had too little space in the cramped barracks for another family.

As Young and the Saints began to gather in and around Nauvoo, by early July 1839 they traded the cholera of Zion's Camp for the malaria of the Mississippi River bottoms. From July 12 through July 19, as malaria spread, Smith, Young, and others of the Twelve walked through the settlements on both sides of the river, healing the sick and providing comfort.

Leaving Mary Ann at Montrose, on September 14, 1839, Brigham Young and Heber Kimball departed for England. They left Nauvoo in the wake of Wilford Woodruff, John Taylor, and Parley and Orson Pratt, who had set off in August in two companies headed for New York to cross the Atlantic. Enfeebled by the alternate chills and fever of malaria, poorly clothed, and virtually penniless, Young and Kimball trudged to Quincy, where Brigham saw his father alive for the last time.

The family now numbered six children, including their baby, Emma Alice—called Alice—who had been born on September 4, only ten days before Young left. Fourteen-year-old Elizabeth and nine-year-old Vilate undoubtedly helped to care for the younger children and assisted in the housework, but the cramped quarters in Montrose and persistent food shortages caused Mary Ann bitter distress. She and other missionary wives remained "at home, lonely and unprotected with the heavy burden of a family on their hands, destitute of means and without suitable habitations, in an ague [malarial] climate, sickness weighing down their spirits." Nevertheless, Mary Ann told her husband to "Go and fill your mission, and the Lord will bless you, and I will do the best I can for myself and the children."

Young had left cash with Mary Ann to settle some debts and to refund Leonora Taylor's rent money. After she had paid his bills, however, she had only a pittance left—$2.72—for herself and their children. The church leadership had promised to provide for the missionaries' families during their absence, but they had very little to offer, so she had to rely on others for help. Because Smith had promised "that the wives of the Twelve should have what they wanted," she apparently received some help from the Nauvoo bishops, who had the duty of caring for those in need. As a result, Mary Ann, feverish from malaria and in abject poverty, frequently crossed the Mississippi to Nauvoo with Alice in her arms to secure a little meat, flour, or potatoes while leaving Joseph (age six), Brigham Jr. (age four), and Mary (age four) in Montrose, in the care of Elizabeth, Vilate, and neighbors. Leonard Arrington believes that Young may have also sent her some money from the donations of the Mormons in England. Later, while Brigham labored in England, Mary Ann would move her family from the army barracks to a log cabin on a swampy lot in Nauvoo.

As Brigham traveled to New York City, the alternating chills and fever of malaria attacked him relentlessly. In Moravia, New York, the disease so overwhelmed him that he stopped for several weeks to recuperate. Fortunately, the families of Caleb and Katurah Horton Haight and William and Julia Ann Haight Van Orden took him in and nursed him.

Wilford Woodruff, John Taylor, and Theodore Turley had arrived in Liverpool on January 16, 1840. Taylor and Joseph Fielding, a Britisher who converted in Canada, proselytized in Liverpool while Woodruff and Turley left for the Staffordshire Potteries. From the Potteries, Woodruff traveled south to Herefordshire, Worcestershire, and Gloucestershire, where he succeeded in converting hundreds of people, including virtually entire congregations of the United Brethren, dissenters from Methodism.

By April 6, 1840, seven of the Twelve—Young, Kimball, the Pratts, Woodruff, Taylor, and George Smith—had arrived in Liverpool to proselytize in the United Kingdom. The apostles found a land of stark contrasts. The missionaries commented on the opulence of the few and oppression of the many, which Friedrich Engels would describe a couple of years later in his *The Condition of the Working Class in England* in 1844. Factories in cities of northwest England, especially Preston and Manchester, manufactured 85 percent of the world's cotton products, but life for poor mill workers ranged from unhealthy to intolerable. Pigs scavenged through the city streets, and although they devoured much of the edible trash, their manure competed for space with human sewage on a constantly accumulating dunghill. Buildings crammed with small apartments bumped up against each other above alleys crowded with the refuse of human degradation.

Many British people wallowed in a sea of quiet desperation, but a number who still held on to hope found an island of comfort in the religion the missionaries preached to them. Shortly after arriving, Young called the Twelve to a conference in Preston at which sixteen hundred British Saints had gathered to hear their message. Those in attendance sustained Young as president of the Twelve, and the apostles ordained Brigham's cousin, Willard Richards, to their Quorum. They also consulted with one another to plan their missionary labors.

Young proposed three projects. He called on the missionaries to print a British edition of the Book of Mormon, prepare a hymnbook, and publish a monthly journal. Although the missionaries incurred debts to print the works, John Benbow and Thomas Kington, who were converts from the mission field Woodruff had opened, helped to pay the costs, so they were able to accomplish all three endeavors. Parley P. Pratt assumed editorship of the journal they called *The Latter-day Saints Millennial Star*, which survived until 1970 as the longest continuously published Mormon journal.

After the Preston conference, Young and Richards accompanied Woodruff back to Herefordshire. The three apostles worked day and night baptizing and confirming the converted and organizing branches and conferences. By April 1841 the British Isles boasted more than sixty-five hundred members, most of them converted by the apostles and the American and British missionaries who labored with them. Although the apostles traveled, once again, without purse or scrip, they lived relatively well on contributions from the British Saints.

The conversion of members of the United Brethren provided the core of the British converts. More radical than the Reformed Methodists to which Young had previously belonged, the United Brethren took readily to Mormonism. Woodruff, Young, and the other missionaries testified of universal salvation; brotherly and sisterly assistance; the restoration of the ancient gospel; and the revival of divine authority, healing, prophecy, and revelation. They also promised the imminence of Christ's Second Coming. Woodruff wrote that Young "addressed the Saints clothed with the power of God." Young, Kimball, and other apostles spoke and sang in tongues, practices that became common in some United Kingdom branches. After one meeting, the apostles joined Young as he healed Mary Pitt, who had walked with crutches for eleven years.

As the Mormon religion generated enthusiasm, it spawned opposition as well, especially from genteel churches. Ministers from the respectable classes railed against them, and mobs sought to disrupt their meetings. The missionaries believed that Satan had rallied the opposition, and they referred to the clergy pejoratively as "priests." Like Grandison Newell in Ohio, the ministers, their supporters, and local politicians encouraged businesses to fire those whom Young and the other missionaries had converted. Many new members found themselves with no jobs, disowned by their families, solitary, and poverty stricken. Nevertheless, the apostles achieved abundant conversions from among the working classes and the despised.

In late November 1840, Young, Kimball, and Woodruff traveled to London, where they experienced little of the success they had had in the northwestern milltowns and the southwestern countryside. The apostles labeled London the seat of "all manner of abominations." Nevertheless, they saw unforgettable sights, including art and curiosity museums and historic places, all the while witnessing the extremes of wealth and poverty in the world's largest city.

The missionaries also urged the converts to gather to Zion. European members traveled to Liverpool, where shiploads sailed from the harbor and the Albert Docks after their construction in 1846. In 1840 and 1841, while the apostles proselytized in the British Isles, at least six companies of British Saints totaling nearly 770 souls left for America.

The conversion and emigration of the British Saints proved a godsend for the Latter-day Saint religion. Those converted in Great Britain gathered with the Mormons in Nauvoo, where they became the strongest supporters of the Twelve in the controversies over the church leadership following Joseph Smith's murder. The

British also followed the leadership of the Twelve to Utah. Scholar Dean May has estimated that more than half of Utah's residents during the early territorial period consisted of converts from the United Kingdom and their children. Utah still has the largest percentage of citizens of British ancestry of any state in the union.

As the Britishers began to gather to Nauvoo, events beyond the control of the Twelve led them to decide to return to America prematurely. Joseph Smith wrote to the apostles in December 1840 urging them to come back to Nauvoo: he trusted their judgment and approved of their labors, but he feared that war might break out between the United States and the United Kingdom. Controversy had arisen because American authorities had arrested a British officer near the Canadian border. On April 21, 1841, Young and six other apostles returned on the ship Rochester. They arrived in New York with a party of 130 British Saints on May 20.

Young returned to Nauvoo on July 1, 1841, and shortly afterward Smith commanded him to spread the gospel and care for his family. As it turned out, his wife would care for him: In November 1842, while Young and his family still lived in the log cabin, Mary Ann saved his life. He lost consciousness in an episode then called "apoplexy," a nineteenth-century diagnosis for a malady that causes a seizure and renders the patient unconscious. Although Smith and Richards blessed him, he lay comatose with a high fever for eighteen days. After his temperature returned to normal, he seemed well enough to sit in a chair. While sitting, his breathing suddenly stopped. Rushing to his aid, Mary Ann threw cold water on his face, clasped his nose, and gave him mouth-to-mouth resuscitation until he started breathing on his own.

When he recovered, Young drained the swamp around Mary Ann's log cabin, and he built a brick home on the lot. The family moved in on May 31, 1843. Kimball and Woodruff also built lovely brick homes in a city where most people lived in log cabins. The three apostles seemed nearly as respectable as the Methodists and Anglicans who ridiculed them in England.

In response to Smith's call, Young served two short missions in 1842 and 1843. The first took him to towns in Illinois from

September 9 to November 4, 1842, to counter anti-Mormon attacks. The second lasted from July through late October 1843. On this mission, Young, Woodruff, and George Smith traveled east to raise money to construct the temple and the Nauvoo House, a boarding house near Joseph Smith's home.

In the meantime, the Young family changed. Mary Ann bore their daughter Luna in 1842 in the log cabin. On July 10, 1842, Elizabeth married Edmund Ellsworth, and she left the Young home. Six children lived at home when they moved into the brick house. In the spring of 1844, Brigham sent fourteen-year-old Vilate to live with the Nathaniel Felt family in Salem, Massachusetts, so she could attend finishing school. Young had baptized Felt in 1843, and he served at the time as president of the church's Salem branch.

Illness and death also plagued the family. While Young was away on his July–October 1843 mission, his wife and all of the children became sick with one or more of such diseases as scarlet fever, canker, and cholera morbus. The latter was a nineteenth-century diagnosis for a gastrointestinal disease characterized by abdominal pain, diarrhea, and vomiting. While on his second mission, Young himself fell ill with a respiratory disease that caused him to stop breathing like the one that had attacked him the year before.

Shortly after learning all his family was sick, Young heard that his daughter Mary, Brigham Jr.'s twin, had died. Mary Ann wrote that she had died from canker and dropsy in her throat. We still recognize canker sores in the mouth and throat, but the term "dropsy" has been replaced by "edema," an expanding accumulation of fluid beneath the skin surface. The combination of canker and edema in the mouth and throat had made it impossible for Mary to eat or drink normally.

In the midst of such trials, Young found some comfort in rituals. Smith received a revelation that those who had died without baptism who would have accepted the gospel had they known about it while living would inherit God's celestial kingdom. A number of churches taught that the unbaptized went to Hell. In spite of this fearful teaching, many believers hoped and prayed for the souls of their deceased relatives and friends. Defiant against the doctrine that good people would spend eternity in Hell, some Christians concluded that baptism was unnecessary.

Smith believed, however, that the Lord required baptism for all except young children, but a passage in First Corinthians suggested a solution. In the scripture, Paul mentioned that early Christians had baptized for the dead. This text apparently led Smith to consider the matter, and as part of the restoration, he instituted baptism for the dead. Young had brooded about the salvation of his mother and other relatives who had died before they had heard the gospel. Gratefully accepting the principle, he was baptized for his relatives, and he baptized others for their kin as well.

Members at first performed vicarious baptisms in the Mississippi River, but Smith halted that practice by ruling that baptisms for the dead must take place in a temple. Early in the construction of the Nauvoo Temple, the Saints installed a temporary baptismal font in the basement. They patterned it, and the permanent font that replaced it, after the molten sea that had rested on the statues of twelve oxen in Solomon's temple in Jerusalem. Young would now supervise and participate in many baptisms in the Nauvoo temple.

In 1842 Smith added the endowment—a ritual consisting of instruction on the way to return to God after this life—to the washing and anointing, that he had introduced in Kirtland, and which he called an endowment from on high. In general, the Nauvoo endowment resulted from Joseph Smith's study and prayer, his reading in the Bible, and his knowledge of Masonic ritual. Smith believed that Masonic rites had originated in ordinances practiced in Solomon's temple, but that parts of the rituals had changed over time. He believed that he had reintroduced the original endowment as part of the restoration.

On October 15, 1841, Illinois Masonic grand master Abraham Jonas had issued a dispensation for a Nauvoo Masonic lodge, which he installed on March 15, 1842. Smith was initiated as an entered apprentice the same day and as a master mason on March 16. The Mormons dedicated a lodge building in Nauvoo in April 1844. Approximately fifteen hundred Mormon men, including Brigham Young, joined the Masons.

Because of Smith's beliefs about the relationship between Masonic and temple ritual, it is not surprising that a number of the signs, symbols, tokens, and stories in the Mormon temple were the same as or similar to those in Masonic rituals. In both, participants learn of creation, life in the Garden of Eden, the expulsion of Adam and Eve, life in this world, and redemption and atonement.

Nevertheless, certain aspects of the two rituals are different. The three degrees of the Masonic ritual in which Joseph participated (entered apprentice, fellow craft, and master mason) are set in Solomon's temple and tell the extra-Biblical story of the murder of temple mason Hiram Abiff and the loss of the "Master's Word." The Mormon temple ritual does not include the Hiram Abiff story or the loss of the "Master's Word," nor does it induct participants into the degrees of Masonry, but participants in the Mormon ritual do visit various geographic realms. Moreover, women were excluded from Masonic ritual in the United States, but they participated in the Latter-day Saint ritual. The Royal Arch Masonic ritual and the Mormon temple ritual have other similarities, but Smith was never a Royal Arch mason.

Perceiving the endowment as a restoration of an ancient ritual, Smith introduced it after he had been initiated into the three degrees of Masonry. To give the endowment, Joseph Smith had rooms above his Red Brick Store fitted out. On May 4, 1842, Smith administered the endowment to nine Nauvoo leaders, including Young, Kimball, and Richards, and called them the Quorum of the Anointed or the Holy Order. On September 28, 1843, Smith inducted the wives of those previously endowed into the Holy Order as well.

In Nauvoo, Young and other Mormons continued to participate in both Masonic and temple rituals and apparently saw no contradiction in doing so. Nevertheless, resentment among some Illinois Masons led the Illinois Grand Lodge to severe its connection with the Nauvoo Lodge. On April 10, 1845, Young advised the Masons in Nauvoo to discontinue lodge activities there.

On September 28, 1843, Smith also introduced a Second Anointing, the highest level of the endowment. Only about thirty-seven men and women received the Second Anointing during Smith's lifetime, and most Mormons do not receive it currently. Given to one couple at a time, it bears no similarity to Masonic ritual. Joseph Smith's journal for September 28, 1843, reported that he "& Companion {d[itt]o.–}" were "anointed & ord[d] to the highest and holiest order of the priesthood." Young commented on the Second Anointing in December 1845 during the intense performance of endowments: "those who have come in here and have received their washing & anointing will be ordained Kings & Priests, and will then have received the fulness of the Priesthood, all that can be given on earth, for Brother Joseph said he had given us all that could be given to man on the earth." On another occasion, Young called it "the fullness of the priesthood."

Mormon women used the same rooms in which Joseph Smith gave the endowment to organize the Relief Society on March 17, 1842, the day after Smith was inducted as a Master Mason. At the organization of the Relief Society in Nauvoo, the women elected Emma Hale Smith, Smith's wife, as president. In Kirtland, only men participated in the temple ordinances. In Nauvoo, however, following the organization of the Relief Society, women joined men in participating and officiating in temple ordinances. Smith said the Relief Society was not the priesthood, but it paralleled the priesthood and, through the Relief Society and temple ordinances, women received "the privileges & blessings & gifts of the priesthood."

In addition to enhancing women's roles in officiating in ceremonies, women participated in other activities through the Relief Society, including charitable service, moral reform, and personal piety. Relief Society women involved themselves in civic and political activity, especially after accusations against Joseph Smith arose both from outsiders and from dissidents. Its role in responding to local divisions generated extraordinary tension in the organization, especially after Smith introduced plural marriage into the church. Emma Smith opposed polygamy quite firmly, but a number of Smith's plural wives were prominent Relief Society members.

As part of the restoration of all things that God had ever revealed, Smith preached plural marriage to select Mormon men. He, himself, contracted one well-documented plural marriage to Louisa Beaman in 1841, and he may have married Fannie Alger polygamously as early as 1833. He published the doctrinal justification for plural marriage in a revelation written in 1843; it appears currently as Section 132 of the church's Doctrine and Covenants. The revelation emphasized the righteousness of polygamous marriages by Old Testament patriarchs, especially Abraham, and by nineteenth-century Mormons.

In that era, the Saints often called plural marriage "celestial" or "patriarchal marriage." Many Mormons believed at the time that plural marriage was necessary for the highest degree of salvation, generally called "exaltation." After the church abandoned plural marriage, James E. Talmage, at the time the church's preeminent theologian, wrote about patriarchal marriages, more properly called "sealings" by Latter-day Saints. On the relationship between men and women in marriage, he reported, it "[i]s not given to woman to exercise the authority of the Priesthood independently; nevertheless, in the sacred endowments associated with the ordinances pertaining to the House of the Lord, woman shares with man the blessings of the Priesthood." That is, in the patriarchal order—also called the eternal marriage—men hold the priesthood, but when endowed and sealed to a priesthood holder, a woman shares in the priesthood with her husband. When so endowed, women may perform some priesthood duties in the temple just as men do.

The Mormons were not alone in introducing forms of marriage unusual in western culture. Various groups experimented with marriage practices that flew in the face of Victorian norms, including the Oneida community's complex marriage, the "spiritual" wives of the Maine Cochranites, and the celibacy of the Rappites and Shakers. Young knew of at least some of the practices by other groups, but when Smith told him of plural marriage, Young said that he would rather die than participate. Nevertheless, he eventually accepted the practice, and he later testified that the Holy Spirit had witnessed to him that plural marriage was a true principle. He became one of the most married of Mormon patriarchs.

When Smith commanded Young that he must "go & get another wife," he sought to obey Smith's bidding by enlisting Kimball and Smith to convince Martha Brotherton to accept his proffer of marriage. Brotherton rejected his advance, and she wrote a report of his proposal that was published by a St. Louis newspaper—to the embarrassment both of Young and the Mormon community. The affidavit had been written and notarized at the urging of John C. Bennett after Bennett's excommunication from the church for adultery. Bennett also published information about plural marriage in a series of letters to the *Sangamo (Illinois) Journal* and in a book. Whether Bennett altered Brotherton's affidavit prior to publication is unknown, but Bennett's description of plural marriage bears little resemblance to its actual practice. Brotherton's affidavit, however, as historian John Turner has pointed out, "is a roughly accurate summary of Smith's doctrine of marriage, which promised those who embraced it eternal glory in the celestial kingdom." Following the affidavit's publication, however, both William Smith and Brigham Young publically attacked Brotherton's character. Clearly, Young's first attempt to follow Smith's direction devolved into a messy, scandalous series of events.

Still determined to fulfill Smith's command, Young next proposed to twenty-year-old Lucy Ann Decker. She had been married previously to William Seeley, but we do not know whether he knew about the marriage to Young. She accepted Young's proposal, and on June 14, 1842, Smith officiated at their marriage. Lucy bore their first child, Brigham Heber, in 1845 before the Mormons left Nauvoo.

Like Brigham, Mary Ann pained when she learned of plural marriage, but her faith in Smith's prophetic calling led her to accept the principle, and she personally witnessed Young's sealing to other women. Young married Harriett Cook in 1843, and their first child, Oscar Brigham, was born on February 10, 1846, just five days before Young and his families left Nauvoo for Iowa and present-day Nebraska. Between 1844 and 1846, Young married

Clarissa Decker, Clarissa Ross, Emily Dow Partridge (previously a wife of Joseph Smith), Louisa Beaman (also one of Joseph Smith's wives), Margaret Maria Alley, Emmeline Free, Margaret Pierce, and Zina Diantha Huntington (also a wife of Joseph Smith), all of whom bore him children after they arrived in Utah. Over the same time period he also married Augusta Adams Cobb, Susannah Snively, Eliza Bowker, Ellen A. Rockwood, and Namah K. J. Carter, none of whom had children by Young.

Young's attitude about sexual relations shocked may staid Victorians. He considered such intimacy natural and enjoyable both for men and women. In a non-contraceptive culture, this led to numerous pregnancies. Over his lifetime, Young fathered at least fifty-seven children who lived beyond birth.

Significantly, Young's participation in the temple ritual and plural marriage seem to have altered his religious experiences. After he accepted these two religious activities, there is little evidence that he continued to speak in tongues. He did, however, continue to engage in priesthood healing and public revelation.

As the Saints settled in Nauvoo, Smith gave more authority to the Twelve Apostles, who were under Young's presidency. On August 10, 1841, shortly after Brigham returned to Nauvoo from England, Joseph delegated the responsibility for the church's temporal affairs to the Twelve. At a special conference on August 16, Smith asked the church membership to sustain the assignment of authority to the Twelve, which they did. With this authority, the Twelve officiated in Nauvoo—an organized stake—as well as in the temporal affairs everywhere. The Twelve began to supervise land sales, the settlement of emigrants, assistance to the needy, and the church's publication program. In September 1841 the citizens elected Young to the Nauvoo city council, a position he held until the Mormons left Nauvoo.

Sometime during the winter of 1844, Smith added to the responsibility of the Twelve. "I roll," Wilford Woodruff remembered him saying, "the burthen and responsibility of leading this Church off from my shoulders on to yours." The apostles considered this delegation of authority their mandate to lead the church in Smith's absence anywhere, including in organized stakes.

Referring specifically to the kingdom envisioned by Daniel (2:44) that would encompass the earth and "stand for ever," Smith encouraged members to gather to Zion and its stakes. The attempts to establish Zion in Independence and Far West, Missouri, had failed. Instead of retreating, Joseph announced in April 1844 that all of North and South America were Zion and that Zion would spread throughout the world. The church organized smaller local congregations, called branches, and in areas with larger gatherings of members, the leaders organized stakes. In Nauvoo, the stake included congregations called "wards," a name borrowed from a city political unit.

In March 1844 Smith also organized a new council, "the Kingdom of God and His Laws, with the Keys and power thereof, and judgment in the hand of his servants, Ahman Christ," or the Council of Fifty. In the short run, it functioned as a group of men assigned to promote the interests of the church. In the long run, however, council members anticipated service as a legislature for the Kingdom of God, when the nations of the earth had destroyed themselves through discord and war and Christ returned to rule the earth. Most important, the Council of Fifty planned and organized the exodus from Nauvoo in 1846.

Smith summed up his views in a letter to the Times and Seasons newspaper, published on April 15, 1844. In it, he declared that the voice of the people is the voice of God. Both "God and the people hold the power," in what he called a "THEODEMOCRACY." "Unitas, libertas, caritas—esto perpetua [unity, liberty, and love be constant]!" he wrote, is the government's watchword. He called for the protection of "life and property," and the exaltation of "mankind."

Earlier that same year, on January 29, 1844, Smith declared his candidacy for the presidency of the United States. He had written in November 1843 to the political leaders whom he expected the Democrats and Whigs might nominate for the American presidency to ask how they would treat the Latter-day Saints. None answered satisfactorily. Significantly, he did not write James K. Polk, who eventually won the Democratic nomination and the presidential election.

Smith's April 15 letter to the *Times and Seasons* elaborated on his declaration of candidacy. With the help of William W. Phelps, Joseph drew up a platform for a political party the Mormons called Jeffersonian Democracy, wherein he called for compensated emancipation of slaves, prison reform, the annexation of Oregon and Texas, the establishment of a national bank, the reduction of the number of congressmen, the reduction of congressional salaries, and the federal protection of minorities.

The Council of Fifty assisted Joseph Smith in organizing his political campaign. In May 1844 more than three hundred political missionaries, including some of the Twelve Apostles, left Nauvoo for the upper South, Midwest, and East to campaign for Smith. They encountered stiff opposition in a number of places, including Boston, where a mob broke up a meeting in which Young was preaching. Others encountered similar resistance.

Meanwhile, the number of Smith's opponents increased. Missouri officials rode into Illinois on a number of occasions, trying to secure Smith's extradition. Their alternative plan was to kidnap and return him to Missouri to face trial either for his escape from his guards or for his alleged implication in an attempt to assassinate former governor Lilburn Boggs. In Illinois, Thomas Sharp, editor of the *Warsaw (Illinois) Signal*, helped organize a plot to murder Smith and rid Illinois of the Mormon people. In fact, Sharp called on the people to exterminate the Mormons. Opposing Smith's introduction of polygamy and theodemocracy, a number of prominent Mormons, including William Law of the First Presidency, resigned from the church and founded a competing organization committed to the principles Smith had taught in New York and Kirtland.

On June 7, 1844, the dissenters published the *Nauvoo Expositor*, a newspaper printed to attack Smith and the church. Its front page carried an editorial asserting, "We are earnestly seeking to explode the vicious principles of Joseph Smith" and to expose the "enormities of crimes practiced by its leaders." The dissidents charged Smith and other Mormons with "abominations," "whoredoms," "crimes," and "blasphemy." Smith considered such charges libelous, and he secured an order from the Nauvoo city council to destroy the press. At Smith's urging, the city marshal carried out the city council's orders, destroying the press and scattering the type. Smith, Young, and other church leaders did not, personally, take part in the destruction.

Destroying the Expositor press proved a fateful turn of events and led to the indictment of Joseph and Hyrum Smith on charges of riot and treason. Under guard, they were taken to Carthage, the Hancock County seat. After a preliminary hearing before a local judge, the sheriff imprisoned the brothers in the upper room of the county jail. John Taylor and Willard Richards accompanied them, and several supporters visited them in the jail. Governor Thomas Ford had promised to protect them, but that proved to be a ruse—Ford anticipated the murder of the two Mormon leaders. On June 27 members of militia units from Warsaw and Green Plains stormed the jail. Joseph and Hyrum Smith tried in vain to defend themselves with a six-shooter and single-shot pistol that friends had smuggled in to them, but they both were killed. Smith succumbed as he fell from a jail window, uttering the Masonic distress call, "O Lord, my God!" The militiamen also wounded Taylor, whose life Richards saved by secreting him away under a straw tick.

A jury, from which Illinois judge Richard M. Young (no relation to Brigham) excluded all Mormons, found the five militia ringleaders not guilty. Orville H. Browning, attorney for the accused, conducted a brilliant defense, in which he had little difficulty convincing the jury that the murderers had acted for the benefit of the community.

On the day of the murder, Young and Woodruff had met in the Boston railroad station. In his diary entry for June 27, Woodruff wrote that Young "was vary sorrowful & pressed in spirit without knowing the cause." Neither man learned of the murders until some time later, and when Young did hear of the killings while in New Hampshire, he hurried to meet with other apostles.

On July 18 a number of the Twelve met in Boston and agreed to return to Nauvoo as soon as possible. They urged the elders in the East to return as well. Shortly after learning of the murders, Young came to believe that the authority to preside over the church now rested in the Twelve. In Schenectady, New York, Orson Hyde, Orson Pratt, and Wilford Woodruff met with Brigham Young, Heber Kimball, and Lyman Wight. Hyde stopped off in Kirtland while the others traveled to Galena, Illinois. In Galena, Kimball had a dream that convinced him and the others traveling with him that "the Prophet Joseph Smith had laid the foundation for a great work and it was now for us to build upon it." The apostles traveling with Young arrived in Nauvoo on August 6.

Other leaders had already begun to gather in Nauvoo, including Amasa Lyman, who had been called to the First Presidency but not sustained. He reached Nauvoo on July 31. Sidney Rigdon, the only remaining member of the First Presidency, got there on August 3. Stake president William Marks had remained in Nauvoo, as had Willard Richards and John Taylor, who was recuperating from his gunshot wounds. The remainder of the Twelve, except Orson Hyde, John Page, and William Smith had gathered in Nauvoo by August 6.

Events on August 8, 1844, confirmed the future leadership of the church. On August 7 and the morning of August 8, the Twelve met at Taylor's home to plan a course of action. On the morning of the 8th, Rigdon addressed the members assembled in the grove where the Saints ordinarily held meetings. He had offered himself in previous addresses as a guardian to "build the church up to Joseph." He reiterated that offer saying that no one had the authority to supersede Smith.

Members of the Twelve agreed with Rigdon. They did not believe they had the authority to take Smith's place as prophet of this dispensation. On the other hand, the apostles believed that Smith had given the Twelve the "keys and power" to serve as the church's presidency in order to "build up the kingdom." Serving as the church's presidency involved exercising significantly more authority than building the church up to Joseph, as the church's guardian with Rigdon in that position, as he proposed. Leaving the discussion with the Twelve on August 8, Young walked to the grove after Rigdon had spoken and announced a meeting for the afternoon at which the people would decide on the church leadership.

Addressing the congregation that afternoon, Young said that Smith's counselors Rigdon and Lyman would need to go beyond the grave to confer with the prophet. He said the Twelve "have the keys of the kingdom of God in all the world. They stand next to Joseph and [in his absence] are the Presidency of the Church." Lyman announced his agreement with Young, but in a series of blunders, Rigdon declined to respond, asking William Phelps to speak in his place. Instead of supporting Rigdon, Phelps said he agreed with Young, which spurred Rigdon to insist that the congregation vote on Young's proposition before they voted on anything else. Instead of voting by quorums, Young called on the entire congregation to vote together, and they voted to sustain the Twelve as the church's presidency. Some in the congregation said that Young, who was considerably shorter than Smith, and looked nothing like him, looked and spoke like the prophet. The congregation also voted to sustain Rigdon and Lyman as counselors to the Twelve in their capacity as the church's presidency. Lyman resumed his position as a one of the Twelve on August 12. Rigdon remained for the time being as a counselor to the Twelve, but as the Twelve consolidated their leadership over the next several weeks, Rigdon, instead of supporting the Quorum, worked secretly to usurp the church's leadership. He gained a number of supporters and announced revelations to support his claim, and on September 8, the Twelve responded by calling Rigdon to a church trial conducted by First Bishop Newel K. Whitney and the Nauvoo High Council. The high council excommunicated Rigdon, who left Nauvoo for Pittsburgh with several supporters, where he organized a competing church.

Because the office of Patriarch to the Church was a hereditary position held by in the Smith family, the Twelve called William Smith, Joseph's only living brother, to that position. William, however, insisted that the Smith family should also succeed to the church's presidency. In the interim, he claimed the church's leadership for himself until his nephew, eleven-year-old Joseph Smith III, Joseph and Emma's eldest living son, reached maturity. By challenging the Twelve, William Smith placed both his role in the leadership and his church membership in jeopardy, and his excommunication followed in October 1845. Joseph III eventually presided over the Reorganized Church of Jesus Christ of Latter Day Saints (now the Community of Christ) from 1860 until his death in 1914.

James J. Strang proved himself the most audacious candidate for the church's presidency. Baptized by Joseph Smith in the temple font in February 1844, Strang produced a letter, apparently forged, naming himself as Smith's successor. Strang offered new revelations and the translation of three brass plates to support his claim. Apostle John Page, Nauvoo Stake president William Marks, some of Wilford Woodruff's relatives, John C. Bennett, and—for a time—William Smith followed Strang to Voree, Wisconsin. (After attempting to organize separate churches, William Smith would eventually join the Reorganized Church of Jesus Christ of Latter Day Saints.) Strang introduced the endowment and plural marriage to his community. Excommunicated in Nauvoo, he was eventually murdered by members of his congregation after he had relocated his community to Beaver Island in Lake Michigan.

Unfortunately, the murders of Joseph and Hyrum Smith did not quell the calls for anti-Mormon violence. Thomas Sharp and other hotheads continued their campaign to drive the Mormons from Illinois. Such sentiment led the legislature in January 1845 to repeal the charters of Nauvoo City, the Nauvoo Legion, and the University of Nauvoo.

Despite opposition within the Mormon community and agitation and violence outside it, the majority of the Saints in Nauvoo and elsewhere remained steadfast in their support of the Twelve with Young as Quorum president. Trying to salvage what they could from an impossible situation, the Twelve gained the support of some friendly non-Mormons, including the county sheriff, Jacob B. Backenstos. In April 1845 Nauvoo's citizens incorporated the central portion of what had been Nauvoo under the Illinois

Townsite Law as "the City of Joseph." Town officials under Mayor Orson Spencer, who was formerly the Nauvoo City mayor, reorganized the police force, led by Hosea Stout, the former Nauvoo police captain. Deacons (older men rather than teenagers as at present) under the supervision of the city's bishops replaced the Nauvoo Legion as an emergency force. Teenagers organized a whistling and whittling brigade—young men formed in groups while whistling and whittling wood with knives—to escort unwanted visitors from town, in a real sense herding people from the town. Recognizing that they would continue to have to protect themselves against militant anti-Mormons, the Latter-day Saints began to rearm themselves by collecting weapons and making a cannon.

The Mormons also completed other projects. They finished building the Seventies Hall and a music hall. They tried, with minimal success, to promote economic development through the Nauvoo Agricultural and Manufacturing Association and its successor, the Mercantile and Mechanical Association. They organized such businesses as weavers, tailors, shoemakers, and tanners. Women and children made hats and baskets. They sent loggers to conifer stands in Wisconsin to cut timber for the temple.

While promoting economic development, the Twelve, under Young's leadership, also tended to their ecclesiastical responsibilities. They sent Wilford Woodruff to England to preside over the church in Great Britain and on the European continent. Young, Kimball, and Richards divided North America into districts. Following a pattern proposed by Smith, Young and the Twelve sent the high priests to preside over districts established in federal congressional districts. Recognizing that not all Mormons could congregate in Nauvoo, the Twelve believed such districts would allow church organizations to expand throughout the United States. Under Young's supervision, the Twelve and the presidents of the First Quorum of the Seventy, then called the First Council of the Seventy, organized nine new Seventies quorums to proselytize. Concurrently, Young and the leaders agreed that they intended to leave Nauvoo for the Great Basin in 1846 as soon as grass on the Iowa prairies had matured enough to feed their livestock.

Young also ruled that during these serious times, members should avoid such frivolities as balls, immodest theatricals, and magic shows. He preached that members should participate in concerts and philosophical and astronomical exhibitions instead. He also encouraged disengagement from non-Mormons, going so far as to encourage Mormons to take their grievances to the priesthood rather than to the courts. The latter suggestion elicited a mild retort from Almon W. Babbitt, an attorney.

Far more important than such directions, Young considered the completion of the Nauvoo Temple as the Mormons' most significant project. William Weeks had designed the temple in the Greek Revival style under Joseph Smith's direction. As planned, the temple was 60 percent larger than the Kirtland Temple. Following the Kirtland Temple pattern, Weeks conceived the temple with assembly halls on both the first and second floors and classrooms and offices in the attic. Unlike the Kirtland Temple, however, the one in Nauvoo had a full basement with a baptismal font.

Perhaps because of the Mormons' general belief that Christ's Second Coming and the Millennium were close at hand, on the exterior of the temple, artisans reproduced in graphic form some features of John's Revelations. The temple's pilasters consisted from top to bottom of starstones, sunstones, and moonstones in an apocalyptic motif. Construction foreman Wandle Mace wrote that the stones were placed in the same order as those surrounding the woman described in Revelation 12:1, which said: "And there appeared a great wonder in heaven: a woman clothed with the sun, and the moon under her feet, and upon her head a crown of twelve stars." She bore, in Revelation 12:5, "a man child, who was to rule all nations with a rod of iron: and her child was caught up unto God and to his throne." Significantly, John wrote in verse 11:19, immediately preceding 12:1, that "the temple of God was opened in heaven, and there was seen in his temple the ark of his testament: and there were lightnings, and voices, and thunderings, and an earthquake, and great hail."

It is no wonder then that Young and the Mormon leadership marshaled their resources to finish building the temple (the House of the Lord) as rapidly as possible. Workers had partially completed the structure by October 5, 1845, when the Twelve announced they would hold general conference there. Young offered a dedicatory prayer for the finished portion. In the conference, the members again sustained the Twelve as the presidency of the church and Young as the Quorum's president. After most members had left Nauvoo, Joseph Young, Orson Hyde, and Wilford Woodruff would hold dedicatory services on April 30 and May 1, 1846.

By December 10, 1845, workers had erected the second story of the temple, although they did not complete its interior construction. After installing the baptismal font in the basement and finishing the endowment rooms on the attic story, the Mormons began to hold endowment sessions day and night. Young himself spent days and nights on end officiating in the endowment ceremonies, and others contributed their time in a haste to endow all worthy members, seal all deserving couples, and perform adoptions of members to leaders before they left Nauvoo. Between December 1845 and February 1846, temple workers endowed an estimated five thousand members.

In addition to completing the temple construction, the leadership planned both the exodus and the means of protecting Mormons in Nauvoo in sessions of the Council of Fifty. The council members elected Young as chairman. To acquaint themselves with the region to which they planned to migrate, council members studied the report of John C. Frémont's 1843–44 expedition to Utah and California, as well as descriptions of the western region by mountain men and others. They also intended to send a scouting expedition to find a suitable place to settle, but that proved to be too little too late.

Until September 1845, Young had seemed unsure just where they should move. Earlier, in discussions with the Council of Fifty, he mentioned a number of possible destinations, and on January 30, 1845, he declared his intention to leave the United States, suggesting a coastal settlement in California, but he also mentioned Vancouver Island, Oregon, Texas, and Soda Springs on the Bear River in Idaho. Historians have assumed that the mention of Texas,

Vancouver Island, or California meant that the Mormons expected to settle outside the United States. In 1845 that would have applied to California, but not to Vancouver Island, Texas, or possibly not Soda Springs because the 42nd parallel had not been surveyed. U.S. president John Tyler had signed a bill to annex Texas on March 1, 1845. Under the Anglo-American convention of 1818, until the signing of the Oregon Treaty of June 15, 1846, the United States and Great Britain jointly occupied all of the territory between the 42nd parallel (the current northern boundary of Utah) and 54°40′. After June 15, 1846, Vancouver Island belonged to Britain and Soda Springs to the United States. Because Young and others had no accurate knowledge of the 42nd parallel, they may have believed in 1846 that Soda Springs lay in Mexican territory.

In a session of the Council of Fifty on September 9, 1845, Young declared the Mormons should settle near the Great Salt Lake, which placed them in Mexican territory, but close to the 42nd parallel, which divided Mexican territory from that which the United States jointly occupied with Britain. After settling, he said, they could explore farther west to San Francisco or Vancouver Island. Whether Young intended to remain at the Great Salt Lake and explore farther west or only settle temporarily at the Great Salt Lake is unclear from the minutes, but Young already thought in expansive terms. After all, Smith had said that all of North and South America were Zion.

Many Mormons seethed with anger in meetings of the Council of Fifty and elsewhere over the failure of the United States and state governments to protect them from anti-Mormon mobs and militias. Some even cursed the United States and, like John Taylor, gloried over the plan to leave his adopted country. Nevertheless, many Mormons still believed that the nation's founders had written a divinely inspired constitution, and some hoped to see a Mormon theodemocratic state enter the union. In 1845 Jesse C. Little, the Mormon agent in the eastern United States, lobbied the Polk administration for federal assistance in the Mormons' move west, perhaps by having the Saints construct block houses on the overland trail. Little's efforts, which led to recruitment of the

Mormon Battalion, succeeded in a way he probably never intended, as the salaries and uniform allowances of battalion enlistees helped to finance the move to the Great Salt Lake Valley.

Not all Mormons were as righteous as the church preferred, and some Mormons engaged in criminal activities, such as stealing cattle and other property from non-Mormons and insisting that they did so with leadership approval. Some Mormons counterfeited U.S. and Mexican coins. Tom Sharp, who continued his verbal attacks and plans to drive the Mormons from Illinois, as well as others, accused the leaders of doing the counterfeiting, and in December 1845 a grand jury in Springfield indicted Brigham Young, Parley P. Pratt, Heber Kimball, John Taylor, George A. Smith, Amasa Lyman, and Theodore Turley on the charge of counterfeiting U.S. coins.

Young avoided arrest on this charge by sending William Miller from the temple in his hat and Kimball's cloak on December 23, 1845. The officers arrested Miller, assuming he was Young. At the time, they reportedly boasted that they would take him to Warsaw and kill him. When arrested, Miller denied that he was Young, but the officers did not believe him. Instead of taking Miller to Warsaw, however, they took him to Carthage, where they found they had the wrong man and had to release him. Young admitted that counterfeiting occurred in Nauvoo and elsewhere, but he condemned it. Extensive research by scholar Todd Kerstetter, in his excellent study of faith and conflict in the American West, concluded that "no reliable evidence implicated Nauvoo's Mormon leaders in the crime."

Pressure on the Saints to leave Illinois arose from multiple sources. Sheriff Backenstos told Young on January 27, 1846, that Illinois's Governor Thomas Ford had assigned Maj. William B. Warren to try to prevent the Mormons from leaving, and Young said the next day that he was "informed" that "the governor's troops . . . are seeking to arrest some of the leading men of the church." To force the Mormons into an early exodus, Governor Ford floated the false rumor that President James K. Polk planned to send troops to prevent the Mormons from leaving, and he left the impression that

Illinois state troops would assist the federal army. The indictment of some leaders for counterfeiting, in addition to the fear that Illinois or federal officials might hinder their leaving—whether accurate or not—led Young and some of the leaders to leave in February 1846, much earlier than they had intended.

Unusually moderate weather in February made the early move accomplishable, although melting snow and spring rains often mired Iowa's dirt roads as the Mormons slogged toward the Missouri River. Contrary to actual conditions, myths later circulated that they left under extreme winter conditions that had led to freezing of the Mississippi River, and that mothers had given birth to nine babies on the Iowa side the first night out from Nauvoo. Research by historian William Hartley and others has shown that the Mississippi froze only between February 25 and 28, and the births occurred much later in the year and not in inclement weather. In fact, the Mormons traversed the river on boats, barges, and ships. Charles Shumway led the first group with fifteen wagons on February 4, and Young, Kimball, and Richards took fifteen wagons across on February 15. All of the early groups camped at Sugar Creek in Iowa, nine miles from the Mississippi.

Many of these early crossings became out-and-back experiences. Some had business in Nauvoo, others returned to try to dispose of property, and many had families who had remained in the city. In fact, so many people came to and from Nauvoo during the early months of 1846 that Young took them to task for their frequent commutes. Even Young and Kimball returned to Nauvoo on February 18, and Brigham preached in the temple on February 22.

In a futile attempt to provide protection until the Mormons could leave, Governor Ford sent two militia units to Hancock County. One unit under majors William B. Warren and Mason Brayman tried without success to stop anti-Mormon violence. They took the murderers of Mormon farmer Edmund Durfee to Carthage for trial, but the judge in Carthage released the murderers without a hearing. A small unit under Maj. James R. Parker sent in late summer also proved ineffective. Mobs continued to burn buildings and physically assault those outside Nauvoo, and anti-Mormon units gathered to storm the city and drive out those who remained.

Under Young's leadership, the Twelve called Brigham's brother Joseph, the senior president of the Seventy, to preside over the Nauvoo Stake until all the Mormons could abandon the city. They assigned Almon Babbitt, Joseph Fullmer, and Joseph Heywood the thankless task of selling the property the Mormons were forced to abandon in Nauvoo. These callings required considerable skill because anti-Mormons organized independent militia forces under Thomas S. Brockman to dislodge the poorest of the poor who could not afford the wagons and supplies to travel, and who remained in Nauvoo until fall 1846. Although Daniel H. Wells led the community in a futile attempt to stop Brockman, the remaining Mormons had to surrender and evacuate. Brockman's forces then ravaged the community. When Young learned of the plight of the poor company, he sent wagons and supplies to assist in their evacuation and travel across Iowa.

Throughout 1846, following the direction of Young and the Council of Fifty, companies of Mormons trekked toward the Missouri or stopped at temporary settlements in Iowa. With the approval of Iowa's territorial governor, James Clark, the Mormons established impermanent farming settlements at various places across the state, including Garden Grove and Mount Pisgah. Eventually, most of those fleeing Nauvoo reached the Missouri River in Iowa at a site they named Kanesville in honor of Thomas L. Kane, who sympathized with the Mormons and wrote and lectured about their persecution and their flight from Nauvoo. Some Mormons settled in Kanesville and in settlements up and down the Missouri in Iowa. Others crossed the Missouri to establish a settlement they named Winter Quarters, near present-day Florence, Nebraska. The refugees remained on the Missouri until they could travel to settle near the Great Salt Lake.

Emma Smith and Brigham Young could not come to terms especially over the division of the church property and Smith family property. She, her children, and her mother-in-law, Lucy

Smith, had remained in Nauvoo. As militia units advanced on the city, Emma left by river for Fulton, Illinois, where she joined with dissenters. Lucy relocated temporarily with relatives in Knoxville, Illinois, but eventually she and Emma both returned to Nauvoo.

The Mormons had expended considerable time and resources to build Nauvoo, but its buildings and homes would end up destroyed or in the hands of others. Although Orson Hyde, Wilford Woodruff, and Joseph Young presided over the temple's dedication on April 30 and May 1, 1846, anti-Mormons would later desecrate it, and the church tried unsuccessfully to sell the building. An incendiary set fire to the building later that year, and a tornado blew a wall down in 1850. Stones from the temple ended up as building material in construction throughout Nauvoo. In the twentieth century, Mormons restored many of Nauvoo's homes and buildings, and the LDS church rededicated a new temple at the original site in 2002.

The Latter-day experience in Illinois evoked a bittersweet memory for Young and the Mormon refugees. By 1844 the Saints had succeeded in building a community of twelve thousand people. An increasingly large number of these were converts that Young, others of the Twelve, and their companions had converted in the British Isles. Mormons founded cultural and educational institutions in the city and farms in the countryside that promised a healthy and flourishing urban and rural life. Unfortunately for their community, however, by congregating together under Smith's leadership, their theodemocracy had bitterly antagonized non-Mormon Illinoisans. In a stunning and revealing letter to William W. Phelps, Governor Ford wrote on July 22, 1844: "Most well-informed persons condemn in the most unqualified manner the mode in which the Smiths were put to death, but nine out of every ten of such accompany the expression of their disapprobation by a manifestation of their pleasure that they are dead." With regard to the surviving Mormon "people," he wrote, "the public feeling is now . . . as thoroughly against them as it has ever been."

Still, those who expected the deaths of Joseph and Hyrum Smith to destroy the Mormon community were disappointed. Young and the Twelve took the reins of leadership, completed portions of the temple, and prepared to abandon the City of Joseph. Their departure, escalated by threats and violence, was inefficient and wasteful, but the evacuation from Illinois would contrast markedly with the relatively effective exodus under Young's leadership from the Missouri River to the Great Basin.

For Brigham Young, Nauvoo had produced mixed results and, eventually, failure. After accommodating his family in a barracks at Montrose, Iowa, he managed to drain a swamp and construct a lovely brick home in the city. The mission to the United Kingdom he led as president of the Twelve produced congregations of more than sixty-five hundred members in England, who generally emigrated to the United States. Young and his people had to flee across Iowa, some under the threat of arrest, and others to escape the guns of anti-Mormon militiamen. In the years following the temporary settlement on the Missouri River, Young led or assigned others to organize a massive movement of Latter-day Saints to the Mountain West to create a new theodemocracy.

4

Trek, Settlement, Starvation, and Persistence

1847–1857

In the eleven years from 1847 through 1857, Brigham Young would experience both success and failure. After leading an advance party to Utah in 1847, he began to direct the relocation of the body of Mormons from the Missouri River to the Intermountain West. In 1850 the federal government organized Utah Territory with Young as governor on land ceded by Mexico in the Treaty of Guadalupe-Hidalgo following the Mexican-American War. The Mormons hoped to govern themselves, but although they controlled the legislature and city and county governments, they obtained only half of the federal appointments. In 1852 Young ordered the abandonment of the temporary settlement in Iowa, and most of those who had remained there moved to Utah. Most migrants who reached the Missouri River outfitting points traveled in wagon trains. Some, however, moved to Utah by handcart, and two of those companies and two accompanying wagon trains suffered terribly from cold and starvation because of faulty planning by others, on top of their own mistakes. After settling in Utah, Young and the Mormon people experienced food shortages and conflicts with the Indian inhabitants that threatened their survival. Through it all, the Mormons nonetheless established permanent settlements in Utah and elsewhere in the Mountain West.

The Twelve had planned to send an advance party to the Great Basin in 1846, but troubles in evacuating Nauvoo and crossing Iowa derailed those plans. Many Mormons had not prepared for the journey, and as the earliest parties moved out along Iowa's designated roads, spring rains and snow turned the dirt byways to mud, frequently miring oxen and wagons in goo. Other Saints who left Nauvoo in late summer and early fall were impoverished by having to vacate hastily under the guns of those who sought to terrorize them. Many did not have enough money or time to assemble supplies for the arduous journey ahead. When he learned of their plight, Brigham Young sent wagon trains back to rescue them.

Young and the church leadership knew that the poor needed assistance, but they also understood that the move west would be extremely expensive for all the Mormons. By late June 1846, Brigham and the Mormon leadership learned that the federal government would assist them. Jesse Little, whom the Twelve had assigned to supervise the eastern branches and negotiate with the Polk administration on behalf of the church, had failed to get the direct help he had sought, but in a stroke of serendipity, his mission in Washington, D.C., ended up succeeding brilliantly. With the assistance of New Hampshire governor John H. Steele and the good offices of Pennsylvania aristocrat Thomas L. Kane, Little convinced President Polk to authorize Gen. Stephen Watts Kearny to recruit a battalion of Mormons for service in the Mexican-American War. Polk and Secretary of War William L. Marcy expected the battalion to aid in the president's plan to expand the American empire from recently annexed Texas to the Pacific.

Kearny sent Capt. James Allen to recruit the battalion, and on June 26, 1846, Allen arrived at Mount Pisgah to begin enlisting five hundred Mormon men. At Council Bluffs, Young, Kimball, and Richards heard of Allen's mission before he arrived, and they heartily assented. They also authorized an additional thirty-three women to accompany the battalion, mainly as laundresses, and fifty-one children also traveled with their mothers. The soldier's pay and uniform allowances, Young realized, would provide a much-needed subsidy for the move west. To seal the deal, Allen agreed to allow the Mormon refugees to establish temporary settlements on both sides of the Missouri River in Iowa and the future territory of Nebraska.

After Allen assembled the Mormon Battalion, he took the recruits to Fort Leavenworth on the first leg of a march into history while Young and the remaining Mormon refugees established temporary settlements along the Missouri River. Young knew he must guarantee the stability of their temporary settlements, so as a shrewd and capable organizer, he negotiated with Peter Sarpy, the American Fur Company's chief at Trader's Point (about ten miles north of the Missouri's confluence with the Platte). Young balanced a contract with Sarpy with agreements with the Pottawattamie Indians and Indian agent R. B. Mitchell. These negotiations resulted in an undertaking to transport furs for Sarpy, permission to construct a ferry across the Missouri, and approval to remain temporarily.

The temporary agreement allowed many of the Mormons to spend the winter of 1846–47 in log houses at Winter Quarters in Nebraska. Unfortunately for the Mormons, the camp at Winter Quarters proved extremely controversial. The local federal Indian agents declined to acknowledge Captain Allen's authority to give the Mormons permission to settle at Winter Quarters, and they pressured the Mormons to move back to Iowa. By 1848 orders from U.S. commissioner of Indian Affairs William Medill forced the Saints to re-cross the Missouri River to Iowa.

As the Mormons returned to Iowa to settle on the eastern shore of the Missouri, many of them reflected on their experience in the upper South and Midwest. Given what had happened to Young and the Mormon people in Missouri and Illinois, one could argue—rightly, I believe—that they were victims of "ethnic cleansing." In a perceptive article comparing genocide and ethnic cleansing, historian Gary Anderson defines the latter as "forced dislocation with the intent to take away lands of a particular ethnic, religious, or cultural group." With the active support of the state government, Missourians had forced Mormons first from Jackson County, and later, under orders from Governor Lilburn Boggs, from the northwest corner of the state. Illinois governor Thomas Ford praised the deaths of the Smith brothers, and he supported the expulsion of the Mormon people from Illinois.

The ejection of Brigham's people from Illinois bred severe consequences. From 1846 to 1848, incalculable numbers died during the exodus. Many suffered disease and death in Iowa and Nebraska; historian Richard Bennett has estimated that more than a thousand died in the settlements on the Missouri. Exposure and dysentery killed many, especially the infants and elderly. Most deaths, however, resulted from scurvy—they called it blackleg—caused by vitamin C deficiency. The hasty departure from Nauvoo and the inability to secure adequate supplies had left the refugees short of vegetables, fruits, and the meat of animals that synthesize vitamin C. Though Governor Ford and Illinoisans who terrorized them must bear most of the blame for these deaths, disease was also an invisible ally. Given the level of scientific knowledge in the mid-nineteenth century, it is difficult to blame the Mormons for failing to understand vitamin C—it wasn't until the early twentieth century that scientists and laypeople would understand the benefits of vitamins. So it was that a half century earlier, when the father in one of the families at Winter Quarters believed he had sacrificed for his family when he peeled potatoes for their meals and ate the peals himself. Members of his family died, but he survived, believing the Lord blessed him for his sacrifice. That may well have been true, but he probably saved his own life by ingesting vitamin C in the potato skins.

Yet scurvy alone does not account for mortality and morbidity among the poverty-stricken Mormon refugees. Travel under pressure without sufficient supplies undoubtedly counted for some deaths. Recent research by Richard Bennett and others shows that even after the excruciating travel over Iowa and the sojourn on the Missouri, the subsequent travel to Utah resulted in a mortality rate among migrating Mormon adults that was higher than the national average. Between 1847 and 1868, when relatively comfortable rail travel became available, the death rate for Mormons in wagon trains averaged 3.41 percent. The death rate in the United States at the time was lower, at an average of 2.5 to 2.9 percent. Significantly, however, the infant death rate of 11.93 percent among the Mormon emigrants was lower than the national average of 12.6 percent. The average death rate of 4.5 percent for those Mormons who traveled by handcart was higher than the rate for wagon companies. Folklore to the contrary, most deaths on the overland trail occurred from disease rather than Indian raids or animal attacks, and half of those resulted from cholera or dysentery. Accidents caused many deaths, but Indians caused only two deaths, and wild animals only killed four.

Even with generally higher rates of mortality among the Mormons, some may argue that with the exception of the forced migration from Illinois, most Mormons emigrated voluntarily. In fact, many of those who converted to Mormonism experienced rejection from their families and communities and lost their jobs. For them, the only viable alternative was apostasy or migration. In fact, as scholar J. Spencer Fluhman has shown, anti-Mormonism was a potent force in nineteenth-century American religion and politics. Even in contemporary religious and political life, sociologists of religion David E. Campbell and Robert D. Putnam have found that only Muslims and Buddhists evoke more hatred than Mormons.

As these events unfolded, Brigham Young, the Twelve Apostles, and the Council of Fifty assumed leadership in organizing the Mormon hegira. On April 5 and 7, 1847, wagons of the vanguard company under Young's leadership left from Winter Quarters for the thousand-mile journey to the Great Salt Lake. The pioneer company consisted of 143 men, 3 women, and 2 children. Among the men were three African-Americans: Hark Lay, Green Flake, and Oscar Crosby. The women were Ellen Sanders Kimball, Harriet Decker Young, and Clarissa Decker Young. The children were Lorenzo S. Young, a son of Lorenzo and Persis Goodall Young, and Perry Decker, a son of Clarissa Decker Young by her first husband.

After leaving Winter Quarters, Young and his company traveled on the north side of the Platte River until June 1, when they reached Fort Laramie in present-day Wyoming. There, a detachment of sick Mormon Battalion members who had left from Santa Fe and wintered at Pueblo, Colorado, and a party of Saints from Mississippi joined the vanguard company. From Fort Laramie, the combined companies followed the Oregon Trail to Fort Bridger, where they turned southwest to travel along the Hastings cutoff. The ill-fated Donner-Reed party of 1846 had blazed the trail they followed on this leg of the journey.

Although Young led the pioneer company, he was not the first to enter the Salt Lake Valley. Erastus Snow and Orson Pratt had entered the valley on July 21, and most of the remainder of the company arrived on July 22. The earliest party camped near current Seventeenth South and Fifth East before moving to a grove of cottonwood trees on City Creek, near present State Street and Third South in Salt Lake City on the 23rd. There they found a plot of land covered with grass, some of it ten feet high, growing in friable loam and small gravel. Orson Pratt dedicated the ground in prayer. At this site, they would cut the grass, plow the soil, and plant buckwheat, corn, potatoes, and other vegetables, and they also would dam City Creek to provide irrigation water.

After most of the others had begun this work, Brigham Young, Heber Kimball, Wilford Woodruff, and several others reached the location of the farm on July 24. Young had contracted what they called "mountain fever"—probably Colorado tick fever—and to recover as they traveled, he had rested in the back of Woodruff's carriage. On a bluff near the mouth of Emigration Canyon, Woodruff turned the wagon around so Young could see the valley. Later, Woodruff remembered that Young had said, "this is the right place, drive on."

After Young joined the group who had begun to work at the garden site, the entire party observed Sunday, July 25, as a day of rest and worship. Young preached to them on land use and theft, saying the Saints could not buy land, but that each "would have land measured out for City & farming," but only "what he could till." All "should be industrious & take care of it," warning of godly judgments against those who took things they did not own. In early August members of the Twelve re-baptized all advance party members for remission of their sins and renewal of their covenants.

After baptism, members began to organize the settlement. Those in the community agreed to herd livestock outside the city, to provide "yards and places appropriate for recreation" for children, and to "have a city clean and in order." On July 28 Young said that when "improved," the owner might "sell the whole Lot or his inheritance in the country and go to some other place." Otherwise, each settler must improve his inheritance.

In addition to instructing the Saints on owning and bettering their property, Young offered a philosophical description of his views on why and how the Mormons could legitimately own property. Young's views seem consistent to a degree with those of philosopher John Locke, who wrote his views in the famous *Second Treatise of Government*—which influenced Thomas Jefferson in writing the American Declaration of Independence—rationalizing how humans could convert common property into private property. Young preached on Mormons converting God's wilderness into private property. Locke, who was a religious man, wrote that God owned all property and had given the property to mankind in common. People could transform the commons into private property if they "mixed [their] . . . labour with, and joined to it something that is . . . [their] own." Young also believed that God owned the land and had assigned stewardship over wilderness to the priesthood to apportion as inheritances. Young said, "the land was given to me by the Indians and I have [given] it to you to use [after paying for] . . . surveying and recording."

County governments issued certificates of ownership that settlers used until they could acquire legal titles from the federal government. To obtain those titles, however, Congress had to extend the land laws to Utah Territory. In spite of his previous claim that the Indians had given him the land, Young, the legislature, and other

Mormons sent repeated petitions to Congress, but it refused to apply the land laws to Utah until 1868, and a land office did not open in Salt Lake City until 1869.

Although Young approved the application of labor to improve the land, he condemned speculation on unimproved land. Land, he said, "is free for you to plow and sow, but not to scope in all creation and then sell." If the Mormons did not improve it, Young said, "then hand it back to me . . . for others to use, . . . [refund the money, or return it to] the public treasury." Notwithstanding Young's admonitions, speculation occurred. Salt Lake City grew very rapidly over the ensuing years, and development drove land values up astronomically. An original owner paid a $1.50 surveying fee for his town lot. By mid-1851 lots in downtown Salt Lake City cost more than $1,000.

After sermonizing on how the Saints could acquire God's land, during the two weeks after arrival, Young and the advance party began exploring the Salt Lake Valley, met some of its Indian inhabitants, and started laying out the city. On Monday, July 26, the leaders climbed Ensign Peak, crossed the Jordan River, reached Great Salt Lake, and made a counterclockwise circuit around Salt Lake Valley. On July 27 and 31 bands of Utes visited the Mormon camp. On July 28 Young designated what eventually became a ten-acre block for the Salt Lake Temple. Under his direction, the Mormons began surveying the city with 10-acre blocks, 8 lots to a block, streets 132 feet wide, and a 20-foot sidewalk. Young is reported to have said that he wanted streets wide enough so an ox team and wagon could turn around without backing up. On Monday, August 2, Orson Pratt and Henry Sherwood established a monument at the southeast corner of Temple Square that served as the starting point for surveys of Salt Lake City and most of Utah.

Beginning with the Pratt-Sherwood monument, historians have generally argued mistakenly that the Mormons laid out their settlements on the Plat of the City of Zion designed by Joseph Smith, Sidney Rigdon, and Frederick G. Williams. In the West, the

Mormons made a number of significant changes in the earlier plan, including wider streets and the absence of twenty-four temples in the middle of the city. Rather, many Mormon towns followed the New England pattern, with farms outside the settlements. Moreover, as author Lowell C. "Ben" Bennion has shown, many Mormon towns did not follow the Plat of the City of Zion pattern at all.

In addition to laying out the city, under Young's leadership, the vanguard began assigning home and garden lots and constructing some temporary buildings. Workers began making adobes, the material used for most homes in the new settlement. Because molding and curing the bricks took several weeks, parties also traveled into the canyons to harvest timber for sheds and fences to protect their supplies, animals, and gardens. On August 7 Young and those of the Twelve who had arrived in Utah chose sites for homes—their inheritances. Young selected the property east of the temple block for himself. Members of the party constructed a fort on the land now known as Pioneer Park between what is now Third and Fourth West and Third and Fourth South in Salt Lake City. A party of mustered-out Mormon Battalion recruits who reached Salt Lake City on July 29 built a bowery on Temple Square, which they used for meetings until they erected the Old Tabernacle in 1852.

As Brigham Young and the vanguard party built temporary homes and shelters, they also designated the Salt Lake Stake as a city government. The apostles selected John Smith, Joseph Smith Sr.'s brother, as stake president, and they called twelve men to a high council. Apostles John Taylor and Parley P. Pratt came to Salt Lake City in early October and November, arriving after the other apostles and some other Mormons had left to return to Kanesville, Iowa. Although they were the highest-ranking church officers in the city during the winter, they left governmental duties to the stake officers.

Several months before Taylor and Pratt arrived, Young and some of the vanguard party had left the Salt Lake Valley. Leaving most of the pioneer company in Salt Lake City, three groups left for

Kanesville, Iowa, to assist in bringing the remainder of the Mormons to their new Zion. Brigham left with the second company on July 26, and his party reached Winter Quarters on October 31. While Young and those with him wintered there, they sent instructions to Mormons still waiting on the Missouri and at large, drafting a "General Epistle" on December 23. The document explained the tragedies and major events the Mormons had experienced over the past two years: the expulsion from Nauvoo, the scattering of the Saints, the founding of temporary settlements, the call and journey of the Mormon Battalion, and the trek of the seventeen hundred people who had reached the Salt Lake Valley in 1847. The epistle encouraged Mormons everywhere except in "Western California" and the Pacific Islands to gather to Council Bluffs and go from there to settle in the Great Basin. The apostles wrote to invite all honest people regardless of religion to assemble with the Latter-day Saints.

Several features of the epistle seem noteworthy. The letter emphasized the trials and starvation the Mormons experienced as terrorists forced them from Nauvoo. It emphasized also how the difficulties were caused by the want of the able-bodied men after so many had volunteered for the Mormon Battalion. The letter also laid the basis for the myth that has plagued Mormon history ever since: that no trees grew in the Salt Lake Valley. Why their collective memories should have erased the grove of cottonwoods near the site of their first plowing is unclear.

In addition to providing counsel to the members, the Twelve took steps to establish a more complete organization for church governance. Since August 1844 the apostles had governed as a collective body, with Brigham Young as Quorum president and Young, his friend Heber C. Kimball, and his cousin Willard Richards as an executive committee. In early December 1847 the Twelve in Council Bluffs began discussing the reorganization of the church's First Presidency. Orson Pratt and several others doubted that they had authority to do this. After all, at the August 8 meeting in Nauvoo, even Brigham Young had said no one could replace Joseph Smith as prophet of this dispensation.

After a long discussion with considerable give-and-take, the Twelve had, by December 5, 1847, reached consensus. Orson Hyde moved that the apostles call Brigham Young as president of the church with the privilege of naming two counselors. Wilford Woodruff seconded the motion, and it carried unanimously. Young nominated Kimball as first counselor, and Richards as second counselor. The Twelve approved the nominations, and then adjourned to Orson Hyde's home in Council Bluffs to enjoy a feast of pie and strawberry wine.

After the Twelve made their decision, Young lost little time in assuming the mantle of church president. Less than a month later, he had provided strong additional guidance for the Saints on marital relations. On December 21 the Twelve excommunicated Milo Andrews, who had abandoned his wife and married another woman. Taking the occasion to preach on marital relations, Young placed a restriction on polygamy by ruling that "There is no Elder in this Church [who has] any right to marry A woman to a man who has A living wife." Rather, anyone who wanted to marry a second wife must obtain permission from the church president. In the nineteenth century the president signed all recommends—certificates of permission—to participate in temple ordinances. William Smith and others had gotten into trouble with the others in the Twelve because they encouraged members to enter into polygamy without permission. Young also admonished the brethren that men who believe "that women should obey their husbands & be passive in their hands . . . act like fools." The "Husband," he said, "should be A righteous man, A man of God" who "ruled his household in righteousness & govern his wife with kindness & love, . . . not with A rod, club, or his fist." He should treat his wife so "that she will love him with all of her heart." He should "pray to God that his wife & children which are jewels given him might be saved & not taken from him." A man, Young said, "ought to . . . treasure" his wife and in "time other jewels might be given him of the Lord."

As Young spoke on the responsibilities of married men, under the church's rule of common consent, the Twelve presented the proposal to reorganize the First Presidency to the church membership. On December 27 members of the Twelve in Iowa gathered with a congregation of Mormons in a newly constructed log tabernacle at Council Bluffs. Orson Pratt urged those assembled to sustain a church president and a patriarch for the "whole Church." The congregation approved motions that "Brigham Young be the President" of the "whole" church with Heber C. Kimball and Willard Richards as his counselors. They sustained John Smith, then serving as Salt Lake Stake president, as "Patriarch over the whole church." Young had recommended him as the member of the Joseph Smith Sr. family who should hold the office.

In the role of church president, Young preached about music and dancing on January 17, 1848. Young said that dancing was "not an ordinance of the gospel"; still, everything "that is calculated to fill the soul with Joy is ordained of God & is proper for the Saints. . . . You will never see any music or dancing in Hell neither Joy or gladness will be there but these things will be in Heaven."

Although the reorganization of the First Presidency took place in Iowa, Young did not intend to remain there—he planned instead to lead those Saints who wanted to go in 1848 to Salt Lake City and to encourage others to gather to Zion. Young left Winter Quarters on May 26, 1848, to escort a party of followers to the Salt Lake Valley. They showed up on September 20, and other companies arrived throughout the fall.

As he accompanied emigrants to Salt Lake Valley, Young contemplated having extensive Mormon settlements throughout the Intermountain West. In his unbounded imagination, Young envisioned the Mormons settling a vast territory. In February 1849, stretching "his arms to the east and to the west," he said, "God would temper the elements so the people could farm." Mormons "will . . . build towns and cities by the hundreds, and thousands of the Saints will gather from the nations of the earth"; the members had to "beautify this earth like the Garden of Eden," he said. "The curse [that God placed on the earth after Adam's transgression] has got to be removed." In 1854 he said that the Mormons "must . . . build up cities, cultivate the Earth and beautify it, and . . . prepare ourselves for the society of God and angels." All told, Young supervised or authorized the settlement of about 350 towns, and during his lifetime more than ninety-nine thousand people gathered to Mormon settlements. He authorized or sustained settlements in Utah, California, Arizona, Idaho, Colorado, Nevada, Wyoming, and Hawaii.

As he encouraged settlement, Young also propounded a salutary environmental theology. In September 1850 he spoke of the duty of God's children to protect His earth. This is "the Zion of our God," he said, "here the air and the water—the grass"— are God's. Settlers, he said, "are not at liberty to foul the water, but let it run free for all. . . . The pasture belongs to our Father in Heaven—then do not destroy it—the timber is free for you—but you have not right to destroy."

He spoke of the earth as a living being designed by God for mankind. Young thought the earth did not currently "dwell in the sphere" in which God created it, but it "was banished from its more glorious state . . . for man's sake." "The spirit constitutes the life of everything we see." This included rocks, mountains, grass, flowers, trees, and even "the different ores of the mineral kingdom." He said, "there is a spirit in the earth; . . . the earth is a living creature and breathes as much as you and I do." Tides acted like the "beating of a man's heart." The earth's breathing causes the tides and "forces the internal waters to . . . the highest mountains which often gush out forming lakes, and springs." He said that the spirits in blades of grass, no two of which are exactly alike, generate the variety we see in nature. In 1855 he said, humans could plant, water, and reap, but a "superior power" springs the seed "into life," and ripens it "for the sustenance of man and beast." If people "are covetous and greedy," their "nerves twich and they have the jerks in their sleep."

Although Young sought to convert wilderness into cities and farms, he also expected Mormons to preserve some wilderness to gladden the eye and heart. In September 1848 he ordered a mill removed from City Creek Canyon because it had polluted the water. He told the "brethren to keep out of City Creek Canyon. . . . He designed to leave . . . every little shrub on the creek. . . . When we came here, the creek was beautifully shaded and cool. . . . This creek should be adorned." Young, however, later constructed a road up the canyon, and he permitted people to log in the upper reaches. In Big Cottonwood Canyon at a Pioneer Day commemoration in 1856, he proclaimed, "Here are the stupendous works of the God of Nature," urging Saints to "calmly meditate . . . upon the wonderful works of God, and his kind providence that has watched over us and provided for us, more especially during the last ten or fifteen years of our history."

As Young preached that the Saints should preserve some land as pristine wilderness, he and the Mormon people also expected to remake the majority of the wilderness they had found into settlements through their labor. Most Mormons would have agreed with historian Richard White, who observed, "What most deeply engaged [settlers in wilderness] . . . was work: backbreaking, enervating, heavy work."

This perceived wilderness was also the home of American Indians. Young and the Mormon people viewed Indian lands in the way that environmental historian William Cronon saw that many people did. Wilderness, Cronon pointed out, is "the creation of very particular human cultures at very particular moments in human history." In a classic example of that observation, the Mormons viewed the Salt Lake Valley and the surrounding Wasatch Front in which American Indians lived as a desert wilderness. They labored to make, in Isaiah's phrase, "the desert . . . rejoice and blossom as the rose" (Isaiah 35:1). We should not be too critical of the Mormons' classification of the Wasatch Front as a desert since even many recent observers have misclassified it as an arid desert as well. By contrast, in Köppen-Geiger's climate classification, the Wasatch Front is a warm-temperate or dry-summer continental climate. Average precipitation in Salt Lake City is 16.5 inches per year—farmers can raise crops if they have as little as 15.0 inches of precipitation during the growing season. Because the Wasatch Front endures a dry summer, farmers must irrigate to grow plants, although some of them would mitigate the need to irrigate through dry farming techniques. Nevertheless, rather than a desert, the first

Mormon settlers occupied rich, irrigable Indian lands that they could transform through work into prosperous Euro-American settlements.

Realistically, although Young sent the Mormons to settle on Indian land, he also said that the federal government must extinguish the Indian title before they could legally own their farms and homes. Like one of many petitions, in March 1852 the territorial legislature pled with Congress to extend the "Land laws" to Utah Territory so the citizens could obtain clear titles.

In what may seem on the surface as incongruous, just as important to Young and the Saints as extinguishing Indian title was the conversion of American Indians to Mormonism. After all, they viewed the Indians as a redeemable remnant of ancient Israel. Moreover, like many Euro-Americans, Young hoped to Christianize Indians and westernize their culture by settling them near the Mormon towns and, integrating them into the Latter-day Saint kingdom.

Unfortunately, Mormon occupation of Indian lands often resulted in bloody conflicts even with Native American converts. Young did not anticipate these conflicts, but he did expect to reshape Utah's landscape, and settlers started on this project while he was away. As Young traveled to the Missouri and back to Utah, church members began to build homes, mills, farms, and businesses in Salt Lake Valley, expanding north into what later became Davis and Weber counties. Mormon Battalion veteran James Brown purchased a farm at Ogden from Miles Goodyear, a mountain man who was Utah's first non-Indian settler. Young invited others to settle with them, but with the expectation that the Mormons would control each of the settlements.

Thus, after Young and his party returned to Salt Lake Valley, he and the other leaders made changes in local government. In January 1849 they formally relieved the stake president and high council of civic responsibilities, and the Council of Fifty assumed control and began meeting weekly, generally at Heber C. Kimball's home. The First Presidency and apostles clearly dominated the meetings.

In addition to governing, Young and the council saw the need to reshape their relationship with United States officials. Although Illinois citizens had expelled the Mormons and they had experienced mistreatment by the state and national governments, they still seem to have considered themselves Americans. After all, Mormons had fought for the United States in the Mexican-American War. In December 1847, well before the United States signed the Treaty of Guadalupe Hidalgo, the church leadership began planning to apply for admission as a United States territory. They proposed a slate of officers for a territory they called "Deseret" (a Book of Mormon word meaning "honeybee") with Young as governor, Richards as secretary, and Kimball as chief justice. The Council of Fifty proposed boundaries for the Territory of Deseret that included present-day Utah and Nevada and parts of Arizona, New Mexico, Colorado, Wyoming, Oregon, and California, including a slice of the Pacific Coast near San Diego. The council approved a memorial asking Congress to organize the territory, and they sent John M. Bernhisel, a physician and council member, to present it to Congress.

Bernhisel left Salt Lake City with the memorial on May 4, 1849, but the arrival in Salt Lake City of Almon W. Babbitt on July 1 triggered a weighty reconsideration of their application for territorial status. As they discussed the matter, Young and the Mormon leaders recognized that they would be much better off as the State of Deseret rather than as a territory. As a state, they could govern themselves rather than subjecting themselves to outside appointees. In a series of informal meetings from July 1 to July 19, the Council of Fifty drafted a constitution based—with several significant changes—on Iowa's 1846 constitution, concocted records of a convention that had never taken place, and chose officers for the proposed state. These included Young as governor, Kimball as lieutenant governor, Richards as secretary, and Babbitt as delegate to escort the constitution to Congress.

As Babbitt traveled toward Washington, the Mormons organized a provisional state of Deseret. Some historians have insisted that the Council of Fifty proposed the State of Deseret to establish the Kingdom of God on earth to prepare for Christ's return. The best evidence, including recent work on the council, shows that rather than preparing for the Second Coming, Mormons wanted admission to the union so they could govern themselves as other states under federalism—America's dual-sovereignty doctrine.

Mormons were not unique in wanting to govern themselves. Residents of other areas drafted constitutions and tried, with varying degrees of success, to obtain admission to the union. These included the provisional states of Franklin in what became eastern Tennessee, Jefferson in what became Colorado, the Champoeg constitution in Oregon, and a constitution drafted in California. Although other efforts failed, California secured admission in the Compromise of 1850. Texas was a separate nation before it entered the union.

Like these other areas, the Mormons knew they had to secure approval from Congress whether they became a territory or a state. After Bernhisel reached New York in October 1849, he learned that the First Presidency had decided to apply for statehood rather than territorial status, so he and Wilford Woodruff visited Thomas L. Kane in Philadelphia in November to ask his advice. Kane urged them to scrap the idea of territorial status and apply for admission as a state. As a territory, he reminded them, they would have to contend with "corrupt political men from Washington strutting around you." Senator Stephen Douglas, chair of the Senate Territorial Committee, did not like the name Deseret, so he introduced both the statehood and territorial propositions to his committee with the name "Utah," borrowed from the Ute Indians. In the prelude to nearly a half century of heartache, the proposal for Utah Territory came before Congress in Douglas's Compromise of 1850 omnibus bill.

Underpinning the omnibus bill was a philosophy of popular or squatter sovereignty. Through the Omnibus Bill, Douglas, Senator Lewis Cass of Michigan, and others tried to sidetrack the issue of expansion of slavery into the territories by allowing the people of each newly organized territory to decide whether to allow slavery or not. President Zachary Taylor opposed the compromise, but that mattered very little because members of Congress killed the bill anyway.

Notwithstanding, events brought about change despite initial opposition by Taylor and Congress. Zachary Taylor died on July 9, after which Douglas shepherded the separate parts of the omnibus bill through Congress. President Millard Fillmore signed the Utah Territorial Act on September 9, 1850, with a popular sovereignty provision that allowed the legislature to decide whether to allow slavery in Utah.

After passage of the act, Bernhisel swung into action to lobby Fillmore on territorial appointments. Using Douglas's and Cass's popular sovereignty arguments, Bernhisel told Fillmore that he considered it the citizens' right to have local residents govern them. He recommended Brigham Young as governor; Willard Richards as secretary; Zerubbabel Snow, Heber Kimball, and Newel Whitney for the territorial district and supreme courts; Seth Blair for U.S. attorney; and Joseph L. Heywood as marshal. Declaring himself a delegate from Utah, however, Babbitt worked against Bernhisel by recommending a combination of Utahns and outsiders for the appointments.

After listening to both arguments, Fillmore's appointments disappointed Bernhisel and Young. Fillmore gave the Mormons half of the appointees that Bernhisel wanted by appointing half the territorial officials from outside Utah, including some from Babbitt's list. He appointed Young, Snow, Blair, and Heywood, but selected Broughton Harris of Vermont as secretary, Joseph Buffington of Pennsylvania as chief justice, and Perry Brocchus of Alabama as associate justice. Buffington declined the appointment, and Fillmore replaced him with Pennsylvanian Lemuel Brandebury. He also appointed Henry Day of Missouri as an Indian sub-agent. Already in Utah, Young took office on February 3, 1851. Brandebury arrived on June 7; Snow, Harris, and Day reached Salt Lake on July 19; and Brocchus got there on August 17.

Relationships between the Mormons and the newly appointed officials seemed pleasant until September 7, when cordiality fell apart. The locals hosted welcome parties for Brandebury and some of the others, and it appeared that things might go well until Brocchus poured cold water on the comity with a speech presenting an invitation he carried for Utahns to contribute a stone for the Washington Monument, which had been under construction since 1848. The judge asked for permission to present the invitation in the LDS general conference that began on September 7. Young agreed, and Brocchus maintained good rapport with the congregation during the first part of his talk, saying that he deplored the persecution of the Saints in Missouri and Illinois. But then he wandered into trouble by telling the Mormons that the federal government had no power to counter the abuses, and he urged the Saints to apply to courts in the two states for redress. He either did not know or did not care that the Mormons had tried this without success, and the speech "stir[r]ed the Blood of the whole congregation." He then waded from water into quicksand by questioning the virtue of Mormon womanhood and impugning the loyalty of the Saints by urging them not to offer a stone for the monument if they could not do so in full fellowship with the remainder of the nation.

Insulted by Brocchus's assertions, the congregation rose in anger. Young intervened to calm the outraged Mormons, commenting nevertheless that Brocchus was "either profoundly Ignorant or willfully wicked." Brocchus's speech and Young's reply bred an appalling response from the officials. Fearing for their lives in a hostile community, Brocchus, Brandebury, Harris, and Day left for the United States on September 28, 1851.

The flight of the officials resulted in grave consequences for both the Utahns and themselves. Harris took with him the money that Congress had appropriated for territorial governmental expenses. Young and the territorial legislature tried to induce him to leave the money, but in a dispute that reached the territorial supreme court, the judges ruled for the secretary. The flight of the two judges left only Snow to preside over the courts in a territory whose settlements in 1851 stretched from Brigham City on the north more than three hundred miles to Cedar City on the south and from Fort Bridger (now in Wyoming) on the east nearly seven hundred miles to Carson Valley (in what is now western Nevada).

To relieve the pressure on Snow, Young and the territorial legislature provided help. The 1852 territorial legislature passed a judicial act that extended the jurisdiction of the county probate courts to include civil and criminal cases. Other territories with scattered populations, including Nevada, Washington, Nebraska, Colorado, Idaho, and Montana, made provisions for expanded probate court jurisdictions as well, but Utah's similar effort elicited much opposition. The federal judges cited the territorial organic act in their opposition, but the same argument would have applied to the other territories. Rather, anti-Mormon prejudice most likely drove the opposition to the Utah provision. In 1874 the United States Supreme Court ruled the expansion of probate court jurisdiction illegal, and in the same year Congress abolished the jurisdiction in a provision of the Poland Act. In the meantime, however, as statistical studies have shown, the probate courts provided equitable justice both for Mormons and non-Mormons in Utah.

The probate court solution to the judicial problem solved only a part of the difficulty Young and Utah Territory faced from the flight of the runaway officials. Even before the passage of the judiciary act, Young apprised Fillmore of the distress the departures caused, emphasizing the steps he had taken under Utah's organic act to get the territorial government up and running and how the officials' departures complicated that. He had begged the runaways not to leave the territory and Harris not to abscond with the funds that Congress had appropriated for Utah. He appointed Richards as territorial secretary pro tem, and recommended that Fillmore appoint James M. Livingston and John H. Kinkead, non-Mormon merchants, to manage the funds Congress had supplied.

As Young tried to obtain relief from the strain caused by the runaway officials, the absent officials argued their case in the court of public opinion. Brandebury, Brocchus, and Harris spoke about and published their charges against the Mormons: they questioned a census that Young authorized and asserted that Young held complete control of the people of Utah. They alleged that Young had engaged in sedition, that the Mormon people were unpatriotic, that elections were fraudulent, that the Mormons claimed ownership of the public lands, that taxes bore more heavily on non-Mormons because most were liquor taxes, and that the Mormons engaged in violence and murder. They also charged that the Mormons practiced polygamy. Young had not helped his cause when, in a speech on July 24, 1851, he had said, among other things: "It was said by Zach Taylor—the poor Mormons ought to be driven from the face of the earth—but as providence would have it—he is in hell and we are here about 1000 miles from hell."

While Young and others argued their case from Utah and the runaways published their views, Bernhisel defended Young and the Mormons in Washington, telling Fillmore that Young's speech "contained a remark which was disrespectful to the government, but the speech contained much more that was favorable to the government than it did against it." He showed a report of the speech to Fillmore to substantiate his claim. He also secured corroboration from the superintendent of the census that the census Young had conducted was accurate in substance and form. He accused Brocchus of insulting Utah's citizens by questioning their patriotism, and pointed out that the local officials had conducted elections in conformity with the organic act.

As he worked to convince Fillmore, Bernhisel found allies in Judge Snow, Thomas Kane, and Salt Lake mayor Jedediah Grant. Snow wrote to Fillmore supporting the Mormon cause, and Kane wrote to the president and collaborated with Grant to publish a letter in the *New York Herald* and a pamphlet of letters supporting Young and lashing out at the runaways. The publications pointed out that Young and local dignitaries sponsored elaborate balls and banquets for judges Brandebury and Snow and secretary Harris. Mormons, the letters said, followed Young because of freely given loyalty, not because of coercion. The letters also criticized Harris for taking the territorial funds with him. Grant and Kane argued that the community was not responsible for the murders to which the runaways referred—they were rather the actions of husbands who had murdered men for seducing their wives. They admitted that the territory levied high taxes on liquor, but pointed out that the taxes bore on Mormons as well as non-Mormons (though they did agree that Mormons imbibed less than non-Mormons). They insisted that the Saints did not claim ownership of the land, but they acknowledged that they had squatted on it—because Congress had not extended the land laws to the territory. They also insisted that tithing was a voluntary contribution, not a tax.

Grant and Kane also employed sarcasm to attack the federal appointees, describing Brandebury's shirt as "about as near to being *the* great unwashed . . . [and] the most Disrespectful Shirt, ever was seen at a celebration." The jab at Brandebury's shirt aroused considerable "amusement" in Washington and became the subject of jokes for several weeks.

After they finished writing, Grant and Kane sought and obtained Bernhisel's approval of the letter and pamphlet, and Bernhisel explained the murder of John M. Vaughn to President Fillmore as the act of a husband killing his wife's seducer. After Grant had published the pamphlet, he sent a copy to Fillmore with a cover letter arguing for religious and political liberty. Grant's and Kane's first letter together with Bernhisel's lobbying led Fillmore to side with the Utahns. When, on March 17, 1852, Bernhisel met with Fillmore at the president's request, their discussion led Bernhisel to conclude that Fillmore appeared eager "to do justice to the people of" Utah, and to assume that he would not remove Young as governor.

Bernhisel's prediction that Fillmore would support Young and the Utahns proved partly accurate. By early May 1852, Fillmore, secretary of state Daniel Webster, and Congress had accepted the Mormon view of the dispute. Kane, Grant, and Bernhisel had played crucial roles in shaping public opinion, and Fillmore seems also to have accepted Young's explanation of his actions. On June 15, 1852, Congress passed a law prescribing forfeiture of pay for territorial appointees who left their posts without permission, and Webster told Brocchus to return to Utah or resign. When Brocchus refused to go back, Fillmore decided to retain the Mormon appointees, keeping Young, Blair, Heywood, and Snow in place. He even nominated Apostle Orson Hyde to replace Brocchus as a territorial justice, but the Senate tabled the nomination because Hyde was not an attorney.

Although Fillmore retained Utah's Mormon appointees, he chose non-Mormons for some positions. After some nominations failed or were withdrawn, the Senate confirmed Lazarus H. Reed as chief justice to replace Brandebury, Leonidas Shaver to replace Brocchus, and Benjamin G. Ferris to replace Harris. Reed and Shaver proved exceptionally popular in Utah, although Reed spent little time there. Ferris remained only six months before leaving the territory and writing an anti-Mormon exposé.

The Utahns had won this skirmish for the short term, but the victory did not last. Claims of Mormon sedition continued to surface in the public press, and the flight of the first round of appointees came back to haunt the Mormons. Conflicts in Utah persisted, and federal officials continued to criticize the Mormons.

In part, these criticisms resulted from the Mormons' attempt to husband resources in the interest of the local community, as well as from Young's economic philosophy. He expected in vain to make the Mormons independent by producing everything they needed themselves. Like other mercantilists, he looked forward to establishing an advantageous balance of trade.

Young expected to draw the commerce of the world to Utah, even though the Mormons had migrated to escape non-Mormon society. Such goals might seem contradictory, but in Utah, unlike the Midwest, the Saints constituted a majority. Trying to grow the goods they consumed, the Mormons imported plants and animals suited to the region. In 1856 they established the Deseret Agricultural and Manufacturing Society to conduct experiments with imported plants and animals and to sponsor a territorial fair to honor the best products grown locally. Moreover, in January 1856 Young spoke of expanding commerce by constructing a transcontinental railroad. "If I was the government of the US," he said, "I would [open traffic] from London to China in 75 days and back again."

By emphasizing commerce and agriculture, Young allied his vision essentially with Thomas Jefferson's conception of the yeoman farmer. Like Jefferson, Young expected the people to work hard and avoid get-rich-quick schemes. He counseled the people to farm rather than prospect. You cannot eat gold, Young declared, but others will "give a barrel of gold for a barrel of flour rather than starve to death." Pessimistically, however, he thought the Mormon "people will stand mobbing, robbing, poverty, and all manner of persecution," but "my greater fear for them is that they cannot stand wealth."

While Jefferson viewed the small farmer from an essentially secular perspective, Young saw the matter from a prophetic standpoint in which he emphasized care for the earth. He said that God created and guided the earth and that its components were all living things. It is no wonder that as he guided the development of towns and farms, he saw the beauty in Big Cottonwood Canyon and sought to preserve lower City Creek Canyon—the reason it remains as a Salt Lake City park today.

Although Young saw many things from a religious standpoint, he also had an extremely practical side. In addition to establishing agricultural settlements, he promoted manufacturing. He said the community was in its "infancy in the art of manufacturing . . . we may stumble and fall sometimes, but we will . . . by degrees gain strength." By 1856 they had tried with both failure and minimal success to refine sugar, smelt iron, and mine lead.

Although they fostered manufacturing, Young and the Mormons also tried to devise rules for the use of natural resources. Instead of privatizing canyon resources such as timber and stone, the Mormons assigned regulation to individuals who would construct roads to access the resources. The builders were supposed to pay for road construction and maintenance by collecting tolls from users, and in 1852 the legislature assigned regulation of canyons to county courts. Many people traveled the roads to harvest timber and stone without paying, however, and violent conflicts often resulted from confrontations between road builders and freeloaders.

Addressing the problem of paying the contractors for their work and controlling access to the resources, in the October 1852 LDS conference, Young said, "We do not own the kanyons . . . , but . . . let them go into the hands of individuals who will make them easy of access." Those at the conference approved, and Young told the county courts to "Put these kanyons into the hands of individuals who will make good roads . . . , and let them take toll from [those] that go there for wood. . . . Note this is my order from the President of the Church," and not from the governor. Young's response to the use of timber resources also militated against the "Tragedy of the Commons." A concept outlined by philosopher Garrett Hardin, this occurs when people can obtain a benefit without paying. Although the toll policy did not prevent profligate use of timber and stone resources, it did prevent "free" use.

As the county courts responded to the problem of timber utilization, they also regulated grazing leases. Under a territorial statute, the county courts issued permits for individuals to graze their livestock on herd grounds. In 1857 and 1858 the legislature also granted herd grounds to individuals. In some cases, the grantees had to allow others to graze and log on the grants, but in other cases, they made no such restrictions. Young, for instance, obtained the exclusive use of some herd grounds in Cache Valley.

The expansion of Mormon settlements and the regulation of access to canyons and herd grounds provoked vigorous opposition from federal officials. Utah surveyor general David H. Burr complained to U.S. attorney general Jeremiah Black that such grants compelled "the settler . . . to pay the Grantees for all the timber and firewood they use." "County Courts," he wrote, "Control all the timber, water privileges and so forth." He deplored that "Minions of the Priesthood" controlled all the "herd grounds" in "neighboring Valleys," and pointed out that the boundaries of Salt Lake City were exceptionally large. The Mormons generally ignored such complaints because they believed regulation served the public interest. Washington, however, added Burr's complaints to the list of other objections to Mormon activities that led to the

Utah War. Despite Burr's opposition, the Mormons expanded their settlements and farms. Soon after settlement began, Mormons occupied virtually all farmland in Salt Lake Valley, and the search for additional land led to the expansion of settlements throughout the West. Young counseled members to live in compact villages and build forts to protect themselves from Indians, all the while encouraging Mormons to beautify towns to build the "New Jerusalem"—settlers should "build their forts, walls, Cities, Houses," in order to "beautify & adorn Zion," he urged—but the Mormons often ignored this directive.

Young's advice to the Mormon people also included his attitude about those alien to the Mormon community. He welcomed friendly non-Mormons to Utah. A stranger, he said, "may live here with us and worship what God he pleases, but he must not blaspheme the God of Israel nor damn old Joe Smith or his religion." He made it clear that although he encouraged others to settle with his people, he did not countenance the attacks of anti-Mormons, whom he angrily declared in 1856 had "driven [us] from the face of man into the wilderness, and now the poor devils follow us to stir up strife."

If Young spoke about the relationship between Mormons and others, he also talked of the Saints' relationship to the environment. Part of the conflict with federal officials had resulted from the Mormons' attempts to regulate access to natural resources in the public interest. The Mormons regulated access to herd grounds, farmland, timber stands, and streams to try to mitigate environmentally induced food and resource shortages that had occurred most years between 1848 and 1858.

Young tried especially over the years to address the problem of food shortages. At first, he proposed some inadequate remedies, such as urging settlers to build fences to keep livestock from their crops. In February1849 a Council of Fifty committee under stake president Daniel Spencer, who had replaced Joseph Smith Sr.'s brother in the calling, divided and fenced farmland. These fences were wooden in large part because barbed wire was not invented until 1867, when Lucien B. Smith received the first patent (in 1874 Joseph F. Glidden patented the type of barbed wire currently in use). In April 1849 Young again urged settlers to keep livestock away from field crops. He also proposed that urban workers assist in solving the problem of starvation by encouraging those city residents who did not farm to give their land to those who did. In 1850 Young said that "hundreds of emigrants [are] now coming here, destitute. . . . Latter-day Saints, let no man go hungry from your doors; divide with them, and trust in God for more."

Young called upon townspeople for assistance in caring for the poor, and he also tried to prevent the loss of crops and livestock to Indians and predators. By late 1848 herders grazed livestock throughout the valley. In order to protect animals from "wolves & Indian[s]," in December 1848 Young assigned a committee led by Amasa M. Lyman to drive the cattle to Salt Lake City. After the drive, herders impounded the livestock until owners could claim them. Young commented that the "natural feelings" of many people were to let their cattle "go to Hell." If others neglected the animals, he said, "we must" care for them because "we are to be saviors of men in these last days."

As Young urged the Mormons to care for their cattle, the settlers also warred against predators that ate crops and farm animals, such as coyotes and wolves. During the winter and spring of 1848–49, the Saints divided into parties under John D. Lee and John Pack, and the two committees competed in the number of predators killed.

If they wanted to protect their crops and animals from predators, the Mormons also had to respond to adverse weather conditions and find ways to feed those who did not have enough to eat. Heavy snow often threatened their food supply. For example, in 1849 snow lay so deep that cattle could not scratch through. Young recognized that some people would be unable to secure enough food, but he opposed price fixing at the time. Rather, he said, "let every man of the Council use his influence to put down extortion." A survey by Bishop Newel K. Whitney showed that food would last only until July 9. Later, abandoning his previous policy, Young directed "if those that have do not sell to those that have not, we will Just take it & distribute amoung the Poors."

Insufficient irrigation water also threatened the food supply. Throughout 1849, for instance, lack of water plagued Young's people. By fall of 1849 lack of precipitation reduced both human and cattle food. Hoping to avoid that problem the next year, Young sent workers to construct canals from the Jordan River, Mill Creek, and Little Cottonwood Creek. Fortunately, snow in the winter of 1849–50 and showers in the spring of 1850 provided abundant moisture, and by March 1850 "good feed" for cattle had grown along the canyons near Salt Lake Valley. To preserve feed for fall, Young urged herders to move livestock to "adjoining valleys in the summer."

Drought that summer of 1850 thwarted the promise of better harvests, however. During late summer and early fall in 1850, rain failed to fall just when it was most needed to mature crops for harvest. Making things worse, wealthier Saints purchased wheat and sold it at a profit to passing emigrants. This practice left poor Mormons short of food, and Young chastised the profiteers. He called those who made such earnings at the expense of poor Mormons unrighteous and rebuked millers who sold "flour to the emigrants."

Deeply concerned about the plight of poor starving Mormons, Young's views on selling grain to passing emigrants ran contrary to the conventional wisdom. Many historians have argued that sales to emigrants who traveled through Utah benefitted the Mormon community, and perhaps in later years it did. But because of food shortages at that time, Young disagreed during the 1850s. He also rebuked those who traded with emigrants or allowed them to pasture on community herd grounds because he knew that if food left the territory in emigrant trains, it would not be available to feed those in the Mormon community.

Lack of food for the poor irked Young considerably, and he tried year after year to induce the wealthy to help the indigent. In addition to speaking against those who traded with emigrants, Young tried, often unsuccessfully, to block profiteers. In 1851 Young was "determined to stop the brethren speculating off the emigrants," and he argued in 1852 that if local merchants sold to emigrants, they would have to pay a higher price for wheat later. Again in 1853, Young chastised those who sold supplies needed by the Mormon community. Young encouraged the wealthy to provide food to the poor, but he also expected them to hire emigrant Mormons and help them find work. Making another proposal, he said the wealthy could distribute their extra oxen to the poor emigrants so they could plow and plant.

In addition to encouraging those who were better fixed to provide food and work for the immigrants, Young spoke at times about the success of the Mormon community, and on some occasions, he noted an adequate grain supply. In March 1853 he said that the community had prospered. In 1852 Young noted that the tithing house contained seven thousand bushels of wheat, and he noted that adequate wheat filled the storehouses in 1853, most of it left from the 1852 harvest.

Nevertheless, despite that bounteous harvest, adverse conditions depleted the food supply by early 1854, and by April, Young said that "the storehouse was empty." The shortages resulted from a combination of drought, replacing crops destroyed during the Walker War of 1853–54, and supplying Lt. Col. Edward J. Steptoe's troops and camp followers. Steptoe had about 350 people with him, including troops and the camp followers who regularly relieved the soldiers of their pay.

Young recognized those two causes, but he could not have understood how long-term climate change might also diminish the food supply. Tree-ring data indicate that the West experienced a drought from the mid-1850s through the mid-1860s. Under these conditions, by 1855 starvation of the poor accelerated as food shortages persisted. Oblivious to this condition, some profiteers continued to sell food to emigrants. Trying to thwart speculation, Young purchased as much grain as he could for the tithing house. Some profiteers found themselves in short supply, and even though they appealed to Young, he refused to sell "tithing wheat" to replenish their supplies.

Profiteers and long-term weather patterns did not present the only problems—excessively harsh winter conditions exacerbated food shortages. Northern Utah experienced a harsh winter during 1855–56. Wilford Woodruff reported that the winter "killed four out of every five head of cattle in the northern counties." In Weber and Cache Counties, "hundreds of persons lived [first] on dead cattle . . . and [later] . . . on weeds, roots, and greens."

Still, despite the lack of beef and the necessity of gathering native plants to provide food, Young had high hopes for the year 1856. He expected spring wheat and garden vegetables to mitigate the starvation, but his hopes were shattered. Instead, food shortages reached critical proportions by June, and Young did not have enough grain for his own family, his employees, and the tithing house. He did not "turn away any that are in need," and he tried to "induce the next brother to do the same." Instead of sharing, some profiteered and caused "a few to suffer."

Besides Young, others in the community understood the dire needs and some of their causes. By July 1856 the previous harsh winter and persistent drought, as well as insect invasions, had taken their toll. *Deseret News* editor Albert Carrington, later one of the Twelve Apostles, said grasshoppers had destroyed "the entire . . . crops . . . in Cache, Box Elder, and Utah counties." "Tobacco and other worms" had "ravaged . . . potatoes and corn." Carrington hoped that "strong faith . . . great skill, strict obedience to . . . commandments of the Lord and . . . counsels of his servants, . . . economy, and . . . well-directed industry" might preserve the community "until a harvest in 1857."

Wilford Woodruff and others did not comment on insect invasions, but they were acutely aware of the damage to crops caused by lack of precipitation. By August 30, 1856, Woodruff lamented that wheat "stocks were so small that in many instances the farmers have had to pull their grain [by the roots] instead of cutting it." "Potatoes are generally a failure; on the lower and farming lands there are moderate crops, having mostly grown to tops." The one bright spot was that "corn crops in many places looked well." In October, Isaac Bullock, a prominent territorial legislator, wrote that farmers had harvested about half a wheat crop. Young explained in October that "potatoes and late corn" had suffered from lack of water.

The shortages in 1856 led Young in July and August again to exhort the Mormons to save wheat for the poor. He said that more than three thousand people depended upon the tithing house for food. Chastising profiteers, he declared that this "is the Almighty's grain and [by denying food to the poor] you may just as well steal" ancient Israel's "shew bread."

Recognizing the distress caused by food shortages, Young and the First Presidency tried to rally the community to take measures to mitigate suffering. In June 1856 the First Presidency sent out a circular letter urging farmers to "freely" permit "gleaners" to accompany the harvesters into their fields to offer a way for "the poor . . . [to] contribute to their own support." They asked bishops to "deal with [those who refused to allow the gleaners into the fields] according to the law of Zion."

Albert Carrington wrote about current food shortages, but he also tried to summarize changing conditions during the entire decade. Carrington editorialized about agricultural conditions between 1847 and 1856, urging the Saints to engage in raising stock. Forgetting the shortages of 1854, he argued that between 1852 and 1854, wheat had become plentiful. By late 1856, however, "it became too scarce." Contrary to Carrington's expectation, in mid-January 1857 heavy snow caused cattle deaths "in the ranges all over the valley."

Disastrous weather conditions continued to beat on the Saints in early 1857. Lack of rainfall coupled with frost on May 9 devastated some vegetable and fruit crops, and the frost left some pools "covered with ice in some places nearly half an inch thick." It also killed "the potato and bean vines" and damaged fruit trees. Reports noted some relief on May 13, when a heavy rainfall accompanied by snow offered the promise of irrigation water, though observers thought that "it will take much water to wet it down to any considerable depth."

Fortunately, early predictions of disaster in Salt Lake Valley in 1857 proved premature, and grain from central and southern Utah helped those in the territorial capital as well. The supply of wheat in Salt Lake increased because of a warm summer and irrigation water from the newly constructed Big Cottonwood Canal. Then, coming to the rescue, in February 1857 Sanpete Valley shipped a large quantity of grain and flour to the Salt Lake tithing office. In March Iron County sent wheat to the tithing office as well.

Such developments encouraged Young. By early June 1857, he noted that "our bins" were "full of flour." He attributed increased crop yields to "renewing our covenants, keeping the commandments of God, and walking humbly before Him" in the Mormon Reformation, then in its later stages. In early September, Young reported that nearly "all the men are engaged in harvesting and securing our grain."

The Reformation may have helped, but the canals provided the essential irrigation water. Mormons in Salt Lake Valley, Davis County, and Box Elder County noted the deliverance from canals. Young delivered sermons on the critical need to provide food for the poor, but he also encouraged able-bodied men to assist in constructing canals. In November 1855 Young had admonished the bishops to send men "to work" on the Big Cottonwood canal. From 1855 through 1857, under Young's orders, workers had toiled on it. As construction proceeded, Young asked the people not to waste water and instructed water masters to control access. In addition to the Big Cottonwood Canal, Mormons would divert the Jordan River to western Salt Lake Valley, the Weber River to Davis County, the Provo River in Utah County, and the Bear River throughout Cache and Box Elder Counties.

Even before its completion, water from the Big Cottonwood Canal assisted while construction workers continued to dig the canal. By June 1856 workers had dug the canal to Parley's Canyon east of central Salt Lake City. This allowed farmers to irrigate lots in the Big Field, the area between current 9th South and 21st South. In 1857 workers built the canal into southern Davis County, and on

January 3, 1858, wards in Salt Lake and southern Davis counties reached agreements on the division of water. Still, because the Mormons built no reservoirs until 1870, with the exception of the water they could retain in the canals, streams had to supply enough water for the entire growing season.

As construction on the Big Cottonwood Canal proceeded, Young promoted additional irrigation projects. On July 16, 1856, Farmington citizens met with the First Presidency to plan the diversion of Weber River as far south as Warm Springs in northern Salt Lake City. Territorial surveyor Jesse W. Fox ran levels to confirm a practical route for such a Weber River canal. By fall of 1857, as Mormons prepared for possible battle with the Utah Expedition, Young thought they had enough food "to supply the people from two to three years." They had begun to prepare to abandon settlements so their "enemies shall find nothing but heaps of ashes and ruins." By early October, however, the mustering in of the Utah militia had reduced the numbers of farmers who could plow for the 1858 growing season.

Additional factors continued to reduce food supplies. Notwithstanding the oft-told tale of the seagulls eating crickets and saving crops in early 1848, the settlers continued to encounter cricket and grasshopper invasions into the 1870s. In addition, the move south, which Young had ordered to avoid troops of the Utah Expedition, hindered agricultural production. Because most people had abandoned Utah's northern settlements, few farmers remained to oversee irrigation, and "orchards have suffered much with the drought." By 1858, also, a new enemy—smut (*Tilletia caries* or *T. foetida*) —had appeared and was attacking wheat crops. Brigham Young met with Elder Amasa Lyman, presiding bishop Edward Hunter, Salt Lake Stake president Daniel Spencer, and Joseph and Lorenzo Young to try to figure out how to eradicate the "smut" and to determine whether they had enough "bread stuff . . . to last another year." They seem to have been able to do very little at the time, as smut continued to attack the grain until 1950. By 1950 scientists had produced both fungicides to control smut and fungus-resistant strains of wheat.

Clearly the experiences of 1847 to 1858 show that some historians have overestimated the power Brigham Young held over the Mormon people. It is certainly true that the Mormon community was a theodemocracy with Young as the leading theocrat. Nevertheless, because the LDS church was a voluntary organization, he had to rely on the democratic element of the political system to implement his demands. He consulted with leading officials, the Twelve, and the Council of Fifty in formulating policy and practice. Still, at times his attempts to regulate the actions of church members proved futile or only partly successful. He could not control profiteering, and his failures resulted in a shortage of food for poor Mormons. As we shall see, especially during wartime and Indian conflicts, Young often had difficulty inducing Mormons to follow his orders. In practice, Young's authority extended only as far as those in the community willingly followed his advice.

5

Conflict in the Kingdom

Brigham Young and the Mormons faced numerous challenges during the 1850s. The Mormon Reformation of 1856–57 led to violence that disrupted the Mormon community. Considerable distress occurred from conflicts with non-Mormon federal officials that Washington sent to supervise various functions. The most serious of these occurred between the Mormons under Brigham Young on the one side and the federal judges, land surveyors, and Indian agents on the other. When these federal officials and others sent their perceptions of the events to various departments in Washington, their missives led President James Buchanan to conclude that the Mormons had engaged in "substantial rebellion" against the authority of the federal government. That perception resulted in the removal of Young as territorial governor and the dispatch of an army to escort a set of both friendly non-Mormon and assertive anti-Mormon officials to Utah.

In the meantime, under the direction of Young as governor and prophet, the Mormons were establishing settlements throughout Utah Territory and in California. Conflicts often ensued because Young and the Latter-day Saints had moved into a territory where an estimated forty thousand folks already lived. The Indians who resided in Utah Territory had changed the landscape by, in historian Richard White's words, "farming, hunting, fishing, and grazing their animals." In Utah Valley, the Timpanogos Utes engaged in a thriving fishing business that attracted others to Utah Lake and its tributaries. Chief Walkara, an entrepreneurial Ute, operated an extensive trading empire throughout the Hispanic southwest and northern Mexico. Goshutes harvested plants and animals. Navajos hunted and gathered, and they herded Churro sheep obtained from the Spanish. Paiutes hunted and gathered, but they also raised corn, squash, melons, and sunflowers along the Virgin, Santa Clara, and Muddy rivers in southern Utah.

Although the Indians had made extensive changes to the land, with the possible exception of the Paiutes' farming and the Navajo's sheepherding, the Mormon settlers did not recognize the changes as improvements. The Saints did not acknowledge the brush enclosures the Paiutes and Goshutes lived in or even the tents occupied by Utes and Shoshones as proper dwellings. They viewed the land through the eyes of Euro-Americans, who saw the Intermountain West as a wilderness that they expected to transform into familiar houses, outbuildings, farms, and towns.

As they proceeded to change the Indians' land, like most people, the Mormons saw no inconsistency in holding contradictory views. From a religious perspective, Young and the Latter-day Saints viewed the Indians as remnants of the House of Israel, a blessed people who would play a key role in establishing Zion in preparation for Christ's Second Coming. As Euro-Americans, they often reacted violently when Indians resisted the Mormon efforts to acculturate them, when they rustled the Saints' livestock, and when they opposed their new settlements. Militia units or posses trailed the Indians and responded with gunfire rather than with forgiveness and brotherly kindness.

The militia pursued various parties of Indians under several leaders. (Like other Euro-Americans, the Mormons used the term "chief" to designate the men they perceived as leaders of various tribes or bands, but this term does not rightly apply to such leaders.

Various tribes could change leaders rapidly, and many operated under systems of radical individualism in which each Indian might choose to obey a "chief" or not. Nevertheless because Mormons, other Euro-Americans, and federal officials used the designation, I will also call their leaders "chiefs" as well.)

Whether the Mormons dealt with chiefs or other Indians, Brigham Young had previously told the settlers not to kill Indians for stealing. Still, between 1849 and 1852, he often violated his own policy. In March 1849, after Indians had stolen some livestock, Young ordered Capt. John Scott to muster a unit of the territorial militia and pursue them. Unknown to Scott or Young, the militia unit found itself in the middle of an intra-tribal conflict. A Ute that the Mormons called Little Chief convinced the militia that the culprits, who were his enemies, had camped in Battle Creek canyon east of present-day Pleasant Grove in Utah Valley. Scott's unit attacked the camp, killing all the men except a sixteen-year-old boy. The surviving women and children trailed the soldiers back to Salt Lake City.

Shortly after the battle, Young and the Council of Fifty authorized John S. Higbee to lead a company of settlers south from Salt Lake to Utah Valley. Extending south of Salt Lake Valley and east to west between the Wasatch Front and Utah Lake and embracing Provo, Orem, Springville, and other towns and cities today, Utah Valley was home to the largest concentration of Utes in Utah Territory. The Timpanogos Utes who lived there understandably resisted the incursion of the Mormons into their homeland. Dimick B. Huntington, the settlers' interpreter, told the Utes that even though the Mormons planned to make a permanent settlement, they would not take their land, although Huntington must have known that any such town would occupy Ute ground. Nevertheless, the Utes under Chief Big Elk reluctantly agreed, and the Mormons established Fort Utah near a Ute village on the Provo River several miles east of Utah Lake.

In February 1850 a vicious and tragic set of events unfolded in Utah Valley. According to one account, three of the Mormon settlers came upon a Ute, called Old Bishop because he resembled presiding bishop Newel K. Whitney. Richard A. Ivie, one of the three, claimed that Old Bishop was wearing a shirt stolen from him. Old Bishop denied the charge, but Ivie's companion John R. Stoddard shot the Ute anyway. The three men then gutted the body, dragged the corpse to the Provo River, filled the body cavity with rocks, and deposited it in the river.

When Old Bishop's friends found the body, they responded with outrage, but instead of attacking the Mormon settlement, they angrily killed and rustled cattle. Ignoring the murder of Old Bishop, Alexander Williams, a settler, wrote to Brigham Young about the renewed spate of stealing. Young replied to the letter warning the settlers not to kill Indians for stealing, but Isaac Higbee, John Higbee's brother and the settlement's leader, was unwilling to accept Young's ruling and scurried to Salt Lake City to petition Young for permission to exterminate the Indians. When Young learned that the three settlers had killed and mutilated Old Bishop is a matter of dispute, but apparently believing that the Utes had precipitated the conflict, he consulted with his advisors, all of whom recommended extermination. On Young's decree, the militia's commander, Gen. Daniel H. Wells, ordered Capt. George D. Grant to lead a unit to Utah County, and in concert with local militia, to engage in "exterminating such as do not separate themselves from their hostile clans, and sue for peace."

Grant's militiamen, reinforced by a few U.S. soldiers visiting from Oregon Territory, chased a band of Chief Big Elk's Utes into Rock Canyon east of Provo. In the ensuing battle, the militiamen killed eight Utes, wounded one woman, and suffered one militiaman killed. A force of fifteen to twenty Utes escaped from the battle site and traveled south to Table Mountain (also called West Mountain) near Payson, where the militiamen, now commanded by General Wells, attacked them. They killed eleven more Ute men and captured some fifteen to twenty women and children. U.S. Army surgeon Dr. James Blake and two militiamen decapitated the dead Indians, allegedly for scientific research. When one of the militia units saw a band of Utes in the area several days later, they killed three of them, and members of another unit killed three more Utes the next day.

Shortly after that conflict, a force of twenty-four militiamen came upon an equal number of Utes. In view of the parity, they invited the Indians to the settlers' fort, where they negotiated a truce. Wells and the main force returned to Salt Lake City with the wounded militiamen, accompanied by a number of Indian women and children.

Despite this truce, several more battles occurred during 1850 and 1851, but a policy change was in the offing. After the Utes rustled sixty head of cattle in June 1851, Wells, with Young's approval, ordered captains Grant, Peter W. Conover, and William McBride to raise forces to "chastise them." In a short time, however, again by Young's command, Wells rescinded the order, and by June 14, 1851, Young and the Mormon leadership had reached a turning point in their Indian policy. Instead of sending out more troops, Wells ordered Conover to take "proper care and watchfulness."

His orders to Conover were apparently Wells's first tentative steps toward inaugurating Young's policy of defense and conciliation. In orders to Captain Grant, Wells weighed the cost of sending out troops against the cost of the losses incurred by theft, and calculated that military action was much more expensive. In July 1851, in response to a report by Weber County's Lorin Farr of action against the Shoshones for stealing horses, Brigham Young was quoted as saying, "do not the people all know that it is cheaper by far yes hundreds and thousands of dollars cheaper to pay such losses, than to raise an expedition . . . to fight Indians."

Although the Mormons initiated some punitive actions in 1852, by the time of the Walker War of 1853–54, Young had settled on the more peaceful policy. In a message to the territorial legislature in December 1854, he had apparently forgotten the earlier extermination orders and insisted that he had "uniformly pursued a friendly course toward" the Indians. "Independent . . . of exercising humanity towards so degraded and ignorant a race of people, it was manifestly more economical and less expensive," he said, "to feed and clothe, than fight them."

Young's message followed the conclusion of the Walker War, which had been spurred by at least three sources of contention.

First among them were Mormon efforts to halt the Ute slave trade in Paiute captives. Second, the Mormons had settled on desirable lands on the Wasatch and Plateau fronts, which kindled Native resentment, and third, Euro-Americans hoped the federal government would extinguish the Indian title to lands on which they had settled. Unfortunately for the Mormons, the federal government never extinguished the Indian title, and such settlements became sources of conflict.

During the Walker War, many of the settlers again refused to follow Young's policy of defense and conciliation. In Utah Valley, Peter Conover, now a militia colonel, initiated aggressive action against the Utes. When Young learned what Colonel Conover had done, he ordered Wells to remove Conover from command. In his place, Wells assigned Col. George A. Smith, a member of the Quorum of the Twelve Apostles, who followed Young's policy by issuing orders to defend and conciliate. Smith ordered residents of small towns to move to larger ones and communities to fort up rather than to take combative actions. In the face of belligerent resistance on the part of Mormon settlers, especially those in Cedar City, Smith also ordered cattle from the settlements driven to Salt Lake City to protect them from Indian raids.

Smith's orders did not satisfy many of the settlers, some of whom initiated violence contrary to orders. Settlers in Nephi massacred eight Indians who came to their camp seeking "protection and bread." Such inhumane tactics led to the deaths not only of Indians but also of Mormon settlers: the Utes retaliated. Uncontrolled action caused Young considerable distress, and in December 1853 he offered amnesty to the Utes, although he could not meet with Walkara to negotiate a peace treaty until May 1854. The Mormons called the conflict the "Walker War," but Walkara was in the south, outside the area of conflict, much of the time. After he returned to central Utah, however, Young met with him and his associates on May 11 at Chicken Creek, near present-day Levan in central Utah's Juab County.

After Young arrived there, Walkara refused at first to meet with the governor, but as a gesture of conciliation, Young and

George A. Smith walked to Walkara's tent. As they entered, they found Walkara's daughter lying ill inside. Walkara had been baptized and ordained as an elder in the LDS church, and, touched by the young girl's illness, Young and Smith gave her a blessing. Young also gave him cattle and other gifts. As Howard Christy, a historian who has written extensively on Young's Indian policy during the early 1850s, has pointed out, the policy of defense and conciliation succeeded in ending the Walker War not because the Mormon settlers agreed to follow Young's policy, but because Young persisted in spite of their resistance. Young may not have been the successful autocrat that some historians have portrayed him as, even if he wanted to be.

Conflicts such as the Walker War would seem a logical result of Mormons occupying some of the most desirable lands in Utah, but at the same time, it is important to understand that Young's policy spawned disagreements with both the federal government and Mormon settlers. Due to the resentment that Young and other Mormons felt toward the non-Mormons who had expelled them from Missouri and Illinois and their belief that federal officials had condoned that violence, in addition to the generally antagonistic policy most Americans exhibited toward Indians, Mormons encouraged the Indians to settle near the towns the Mormons were establishing. Young and the Mormons expected to convert them into Mormon farmers by doing so. They also actively sought to induce the Indians to differentiate them from other American citizens. With Mormon encouragement, Numic speakers (Utes, Shoshones, Bannocks, Paiutes, and Goshutes) transformed the designations Mormon—"Mormonee"—and American—"Mericats"—into their language as different words.

In an attempt to promote better relations and to convert the Indians to Mormonism, Young established many settlements as Indian missions. Some of these, such as Jacob Hamblin's Southern Indian Mission with headquarters at Santa Clara and later at Kanab, succeeded to a degree. Others, like the Elk Mountain Mission near present-day Moab and the Fort Limhi settlement in present-day Idaho, ended in abject failure. Indians—the Utes in the case of Moab and the Bannocks and Shoshones in the case of Fort Limhi—drove the settlers off with some loss of life on both sides.

In contrast with these failed missions, some of Young's efforts succeeded. When he saw the success of some farming by the Pahvants in Millard County, he established the Corn Creek Indian farm in cooperation with Indian agent Garland Hurt. Young also helped Hurt set up similar farms near Benjamin in Utah Valley and near Gunnison in Sanpete Valley. He expected the federal government to appropriate money to help sustain the farms, but Congress refused to do so. Nevertheless, Young and Hurt went ahead without federal approval, and during 1856 Young overspent Utah's federal appropriation for Indian affairs by $31,000. That seems little enough, but that would amount to $839,000 in 2017.

Moreover, unlike the punitive expeditions against the Indians, the burden of feeding them under Young's policy fell on individual settlers rather than on the community at large. Indians visited the homes of settlers to beg for—and in some cases to demand—food and clothing. From a humanitarian perspective, Young considered the donations of meat and bread a small enough price to cement peaceful relations, but as we have seen, Young promoted this peaceful policy in the face of starvation or near-starvation in his own community. Food shortages among the Mormons occurred every year between 1847 and 1858 except 1852, part of 1853, and 1857. This was the result principally of the harsh climate and lack of irrigation water, but also of supplying food to Indians, hostilities such as the Walker War of 1853–54, and provisioning the Steptoe expedition of 1854–55.

In 1854 Bvt. Lt. Col. Edward J. Steptoe brought 350 soldiers and civilians and more than 800 horses and mules to Utah. Steptoe had come from Fort Leavenworth for three reasons. His superiors ordered him to provide troops and livestock for Pacific coastal garrisons, and they wanted him to find a better route from Utah to California. He was also to investigate the massacre of Lt. John W. Gunnison and his exploration party in October 1853. Steptoe's command stayed into 1855, and the Utah community had to supply food and shelter for it the entire time. Although the government paid well for the supplies the Utahns sold them, provisions for the expedition reduced the food available for poor Mormons.

The massacre that Steptoe had come to investigate proved extremely controversial in Utah and the nation. Gunnison, who had had served in Utah in 1849–50 with Maj. Howard Stansbury's exploration of the Great Salt Lake, had returned in 1853 as part of the federal government's survey for a projected transcontinental railroad. Young, who approved both explorations, had assigned Albert Carrington, the *Deseret News* editor and a well-educated Mormon, to work with Stansbury and Gunnison. Carrington and Gunnison became good friends. After his service with Stansbury, Gunnison had published a book titled *The Mormons.* He did not approve of the Mormons' theodemocracy, but his literary treatment was fair and evenhanded.

In 1853 Secretary of War Jefferson Davis assigned Gunnison to survey a strip of land between the 37th and 39th parallels. The lieutenant and his party had proceeded west until October 26, 1853, when they camped on the Sevier River west of the current city of Delta, Utah. During the night, a party of Pahvant Utes attacked and massacred Gunnison and seven of his men in retaliation for the murder of a respected Ute by members of a passing wagon train some time before. In Pahvant culture, indeed in many cultures, the murder of one of their folk demanded retribution against either the person responsible or members of his cultural group.

A number of people blamed the Mormons for the massacre, but careful investigations exonerated the Latter-day Saints. Gunnison's second in command, Lt. Edward G. Beckwith, investigated and reported that the Pahvants had perpetrated the massacre, and that Mormons were not involved. Indeed, one of those massacred was a Mormon who worked as the party's guide. Concurring with Beckwith, Steptoe reported that Pahvants committed the massacre and that the Mormons were blameless.

Gunnison's wife, Martha, and a number of anti-Mormons, including Utah territorial justice William W. Drummond, insisted, however, that the Mormons had either committed or arranged the massacre. They falsely asserted that the Mormons had opposed the surveys because they opposed the construction of a transcontinental railroad. In fact, the Mormons had petitioned Congress for the railroad's construction, and Young had publicly urged its building to improve trade and facilitate the gathering of the Saints to Utah. Moreover, when the railroad finally came, Young took contracts to assist in grading the roadbed.

Although Steptoe exonerated the Mormons of blame in the Gunnison massacre, his unit created unprecedented tension with Utah's citizens. A violent confrontation between drunken enlisted men from Steptoe's command and Salt Lake City citizens broke out on Christmas Day in 1854. It required the concerted effort of both Steptoe's officers and those of the Nauvoo Legion to quell the melee. In addition, serious disputes resulted from the amorous adventures of several of Steptoe's officers, especially Lt. Sylvester Mowry and Capt. Rufus Ingalls. Unlike Mowry and Ingalls, Steptoe himself and his second in command, Bvt. Maj. John F. Reynolds, did not consort with Utah women. Nevertheless, at the urging of Mowry and Ingalls, as many as seven Mormon women accompanied Steptoe's command as they left for California in May 1855.

The women's departure outraged Young, their fathers, and their husbands. Clearly, Young and other Utahns considered Mowry and other seducers as thieves absconding with their property. He said that the Mormons ought to have killed some of the officers because their only motivation was to treat the Mormon women as prostitutes rather than to enter into legitimate marriages with them. Mowry's own correspondence shows that the lieutenant did view them as convenient sex partners rather than as potential wives.

To understand Young's anger with Mowry, we should recognize that in Utah and most of the United States, women had few rights. Until the passage of Married Women's Property Rights Laws in various states in the late nineteenth century and in Utah in 1872, under the common law, married women were the chattel property of their husbands. Married women had a dower right of a third of her deceased husband's property, but very little else. Unlike many states in which only men could sue for divorce, until 1878 women or men could easily obtain divorces in Utah. All that married couples had to do was to agree to divorce, though women had to apply for the divorces; they could not legally escape a marriage by running off with a lover or seducer.

Although Steptoe declined to consort with the Utah women, he did become involved in an abortive threat to Utah's theodemocracy. When President Franklin Pierce decided to remove Young as territorial governor, Pierce nominated Steptoe to the position in Young's place, and the Senate confirmed him. Steptoe, however, refused to accept the governorship. He believed that no matter whom Pierce appointed as governor, Brigham Young would remain the people's de facto governor. Steptoe averted what could well have become another source of conflict between Young and the non-Mormons.

If conflicts with the Steptoe's military unit soured Mormon relations with federal troops, tension between Young and the Indian agents created another source of conflict. Differences between Young, as superintendent of Indian Affairs, and some of the non-Mormon Indian agents, especially Joseph Holeman, Henry Day, and Garland Hurt, damaged dealings with the federal government and with the Indians. After their arrival in Utah, the non-Mormon agents enjoyed a short honeymoon with Young, but that relationship degenerated rapidly into antagonism and hostility. In correspondence with Washington, Hurt condemned the expansion of Mormon settlements and the settlers' economic activities. He rightly pointed out that settlements depleted the food supply on the land and streams on which the Indians had traditionally hunted, gathered, and fished.

In addition to his concern about the Indians' food supply, Hurt also complained about the missions the Mormons sent to convert the Indians to Mormonism, and he resented the distinction the Mormons cultivated between themselves and other Americans. These activities were not illegal because two acts passed in 1834 gave Young, as superintendent of Indian Affairs, and, with his approval, the Indian agents and subagents, authority to consult with Indians in Utah. With his authority, Young could send missionaries to visit the various tribes in his jurisdiction, but his authority did not extend to New Mexico and Oregon territories, where Mormons tried to convert Indians as well.

Hurt understood that Young's policy of expanding settlements caused additional Indian conflicts. In large part, the Tintic War of 1856, like the Walker War of 1853–54, resulted from the pressure the Mormon settlements in Utah Valley put on the Indians' economic base. Young advocated contradictory policies, urging the settlers to respect Indian land rights even as he sent settlers to establish towns and farms on Indian lands. He expected to mitigate the impact because he believed the federal government would extinguish Indian title to the lands on which the Mormons settled.

When that failed to happen, in an effort to temper the conflicts caused by his policy, Young tried to reduce the tension by direct negotiation, yet another authority he had as superintendent of Indian Affairs. He instructed Indian subagent George W. Armstrong to arbitrate disputes between whites and Indians. In Utah Valley, the Mormons had enclosed four hundred acres of the Timpanogos Utes' grazing land for herd grounds and farms. Settlers also reportedly killed several horses that belonged to Chief Tintic, a son of Chief Big Elk who had been the principal chief in the Ute's Provo River settlement. By 1855 the disputes between the settlers and Utes had become so serious that Young sent militia Col. George A. Smith and Indian interpreter Dimick B. Huntington to try to negotiate an agreement. The negotiations with Tintic led the Ute reluctantly to accept an agreement to divide the herd and crop grounds.

Even this agreement did not patch up the relationship, however. Shortages of food during 1855 and 1856 caused starvation among both Indians and Mormons, and as the agreement unraveled, Tintic demanded ten kegs of powder and ten head of cattle as reparations. In view of the shortages and the danger from the powder, Young declined to meet his demands, and the war continued.

Young continued his policy of defense and conciliation, but he had virtually no success in mending the Mormons' deteriorating relationship with Tintic and other Indians. Federal officials, including Judges John Fitch Kinney and William W. Drummond and

Indian Agent Garland Hurt, opposed Young's policy and urged him to take punitive action against Tintic's Utes. Drummond sarcastically chided what he called Young's "breadbutter" policy, and after Tintic's band stole some livestock, he ordered Deputy U.S. Marshal Thomas S. Johnson to arrest Tintic and members of his band. As territorial governor and superintendent of Indian Affairs, Young tried to intervene because Johnson was an executive officer, but his actions led to a dispute with Drummond, who insisted that Johnson go after the Indians. Throughout early 1856, Drummond dispatched posses headed by marshals Johnson, Peter Conover, and others. Although the posses scoured the country, their efforts to arrest Ute raiders were futile.

Throughout the Tintic War, as Young became aware of the deputy marshals' efforts to capture Tintic and his raiders, he tried unsuccessfully on the one hand to convince the Mormons to live in peace with the Indians by adhering to his policy of defense and conciliation. On the other hand, he ignored the advice of federal officials to go after the Indians and instead urged the federal government to extinguish Indian title to lands occupied by Mormon settlements. Despite Young's efforts, the war brought pitched battles that cost the lives of at least six Mormons and three to five Utes, as well as the rustling of scores of Mormon cattle by Tintic's raiders in a time of famine. Opposed to Young's policy, Kinney, Drummond, Hurt, and Surveyor General David H. Burr wrote confidential letters to Washington blaming the conflicts on Young's policies of settlement expansion and defense and conciliation. Young also stirred opposition among many Mormon settlers whose views corresponded more with those of the federal officials than with their church president.

Although Young failed with Tintic, he succeeded in maintaining relatively good relations with at least four of Utah's Indian chiefs and a mixed relationship with another. He had good relations with Kanosh (Man of White Hair), a Pahvant leader in Millard County; Peteetneet, a Timpanogos Ute leader in southern Utah Valley; Sowiette, also a Timpanogos chief, in central Utah Valley; and Tutsegavits, a Shivwitz Paiute chief in Southern Utah. By contrast, Arapeen, a brother of recently deceased Walkara, a leader in Sanpete and Utah Valleys, tried to appease both the Saints and the federal officials by professing friendship with Mormon leaders while complaining about them to Garland Hurt.

As the Mormons struggled to maintain satisfactory relations with the Indians, they endeavored to replace the temporary land titles issued by the county courts with clear titles from the federal government. Some historians have alleged that Mormon settlers did not want Utah lands surveyed or the federal government to open a land office so they could obtain clear titles to the property they occupied. In fact, Brigham Young, the legislature, and other Utah citizens petitioned Congress and the president to extend the land laws to Utah. They also wanted a government land office so they could obtain titles to their farms under the Preemption Law and urban lots under the Townsite Act. Young and the Utahns suffered continued disappointment because they could not purchase the land on which they were legally only squatters. Until 1869, when the federal government finally opened a land office in Utah, Utahns had to content themselves with a temporary system administered by county surveyors and the county courts. The temporary titles identified lands occupied by settlers, and although they helped to prevent claim jumpers from stealing the land the residents occupied for farms or businesses, the interim titles also led to conflicts and the murder of at least one non-Mormon.

Expectations for clear titles rose slightly when Surveyor General Burr began surveys in 1855, but they proved a major disappointment in part because Burr's deputy surveyors made land acquisition even more difficult by running fraudulent surveys. Utahns complained about this and, following the Utah War, President Buchanan and later presidents ordered investigations by surveyors general Samuel C. Stambaugh and Courtland C. Clements. These investigations showed that the surveys Burr's deputies allegedly made had resulted in massive frauds on both the Utahns and the federal government. One of the surveyors, Charles Mogo, was the worst offender, but Burr's son Frederick H. Burr and Joseph Troskolawski also contributed to the frauds. The federal government had previously forbid Troskolawski from contracts to survey after the California surveyor general discovered frauds in his surveys there, but Burr hired him anyway.

When confronted, Burr and his deputies blamed the Mormons, charging that Mormons had destroyed the survey stakes and monuments. Brigham Young replied that the deputies themselves had planted such flimsy survey stakes that the "wind could almost blow [them] over." Young underscored his charges by countering that Burr and his employees had erected corner monuments without the pits and subsurface charcoal that were necessary to install relatively permanent markers. Other Utahns complained to the General Land Office in Washington about the fraudulent surveys as well.

Anyone who understands the rudiments of surveying knows, on the one hand, that it is quite easy to destroy stakes and other evidence of surveys on the ground. On the other hand, it is very difficult to alter survey notes and plats drawn by office staff, and by law the surveyor general had to send copies of those documents to Washington, D.C. Comparative evidence from the survey plats and notes from Burr's office revealed that the surveyor general's deputies had run fraudulent surveys. Sent to Utah by Buchanan, Stambaugh detailed these, especially those by Charles Mogo.

One such fraudulent survey was similar to others Mogo submitted. In 1872 Surveyor General Clements dispatched deputy surveyor Augustus D. Ferron to survey a portion of Township 13 South, Range 5 East in central Utah. Mogo had submitted a survey of the township in 1856, and Burr had approved the survey on February 25, 1857. Clements's examination showed that "the topography of the country on the two plats of survey [Mogo's and Ferron's] are so entirely different as to throw discredit upon one of the surveys." To investigate the discrepancy, Clements sent surveyors J. H. Cox and John F. Sanders with Ferron to examine the land he and Mogo had reported as surveyed and Burr had approved. The investigation showed that Mogo had neither seen nor surveyed the ground.

Frustrated at the fraudulent surveys and their inability to secure clear titles to the land they occupied, some Utah settlers attacked

David Burr's employees and deputies. William A. (Bill) Hickman and a number of his band raided Burr's office and severely beat some of his employees, including Troskolawski. Several, including Mogo and Burr, escaped unscathed. Referring to Young or some other church leader, Burr said the attacks were approved by higher authority, but in August 1857 Brigham Young chastised Hickman and his gang for the attacks, rightly admonishing them that they would hurt the Mormon cause.

It is difficult to believe that Burr did not know of the frauds. Part of his responsibility as surveyor general was to check the work of his deputies. To have been unaware, he would have had to have been ignorant of the flimsy corner monuments and the poorly driven survey stakes. He would also have not compared the ground where surveys allegedly took place with the notes that the surveyors submitted and the plats drawn in his office. Nevertheless, Burr sent letters to Washington, D.C., complaining of the Mormons. He attacked the system the Mormons established to regulate grazing land, timber stands, and water resources, and he criticized the "very extensive" areas covered by cities. Amplifying his complaints, he attacked the exemption of churches from taxes, school tax elections, liquor regulation, liens for debt, probate court jurisdiction, inheritance laws, numbering of ballots, ferry grants, and court rulings. Most seriously, he charged that Brigham Young had ordered a number of murders.

Burr also made the astounding charge that Young controlled all the land in Utah. In 1854 Young tried to restore the United Order that Joseph Smith had taught in the 1830s. With his knowledge of deeds that church members had signed, which transferred property to Brigham Young as a "trustee in trust" under the United Order, Burr asserted that Young controlled the land. The surveyor general wrote that "he did not know how many had obeyed, but nearly all of them will." Two recent authors, Will Bagley and David Bigler, were mistaken when they wrote that Young actually took the property. In fact, many members, including Young, signed deeds pledging to turn their property over to the church for redistribution to themselves and to poor Mormons to promote equality. Contrary to Burr's assertion and that of the two authors, however, research by Leonard Arrington, Dean May, Feramorz Fox, and Polly Aird demonstrates that resistance to turning the land over became so strong that Young could never actually take control of the property either for himself or for the church.

Such charges, fraudulent surveys, and Mormon relations with the Indians were not the only sources of conflict between the Mormons and non-Mormon federal appointees. By the mid-1850s Brigham Young was convinced that the faith of church members had weakened. Since 1848 Utah had suffered from drought and food shortages, and Young believed that if the Saints rekindled their faith, God would bless them with plentiful harvests and prosperity. Believing a Reformation would renew the Mormons' faith, Young knew just the man to stoke the fire of renewal. In fall 1856 Jedediah M. Grant, the late Willard Richards's successor as Young's second counselor, had recently returned from a mission. Young called him to travel north from Salt Lake City to call the Mormons to repentance. Grant spoke first in Bountiful and then sermonized in other northern Utah communities, calling on the residents to repent and be rebaptized.

Grant's preaching inaugurated the Mormon Reformation, but Young had paved the way for his counselor six months earlier. In a sermon of March 16, 1856, Young preached that Christ's death and resurrection did not cleanse sinners of some serious transgressions, such as first-degree murder and adultery, if those who committed those offenses had taken an endowment oath. For such offenses, Young said, "The blood of Christ will never wipe that out, your own blood must atone for it." Young believed that only a sinner's voluntary offering of his own life would expunge the sin. Sermonizing on September 21, 1856, Young again preached "blood atonement," saying, "There are sins that men commit for which they cannot receive forgiveness, . . . and if they had their eyes open . . . they would be perfectly willing to have their blood spilt upon the ground, that the smoke thereof might ascend to heaven as an offering for their sins; . . . whereas, if such is not the case, they [their sins] will stick to them and remain upon them in the spirit world." On February 8, 1857, Young chastised sinners who apostatized rather than repent. Such recreants would have had a "chance" in the final resurrection "if their lives had been taken and their blood spilt on the ground as a smoking incense to the Almighty, but who are now angels to the Devil." In a violent interpretation of brotherly love, Young said that helping unrepentant sinners to take their own lives "is loving our neighbour as ourselves; . . . if he wants salvation and it is necessary to spill his blood on the earth in order that he may be saved, spill it."

Significantly, however, Young seems to have backed down somewhat in his sermon. He had prefaced his teaching of blood atonement by promising that Christ would eventually save those who were "now angels to the devil." He said that eventually "our elder brother Jesus Christ raises them up—conquers death, hell and the grave." Even with the mitigation, it is difficult to understand how Young could believe in blood atonement because the Book of Mormon teaches that Christ's sacrifice "must needs be an infinite atonement" (2 Nephi 9:7). Recognizing Young's mistake, the First Presidency and Quorum of the Twelve Apostles repudiated blood atonement in a public declaration, but not until 1889.

Historians have argued whether Young preached blood atonement in 1856 and 1857 as doctrine or hyperbole. Whatever the case, some church members and officers took it literally and applied it in ways he never intended.—Young had called it a voluntary act by endowed members who wanted their sins forgiven at once, and by February 1857 he had limited it to those who did not want to await the effect of the Savior's atonement.

Nevertheless, perverting Brigham's teaching by applying it to those who had not applied to have their blood spilled, Springville bishop Aaron Johnson ordered the murder of William Parrish and his sons Beeson and Orrin, who had lost faith in Mormonism and made arrangements to leave for California. Johnson rationalized the murders by noting that they had some debts they had not paid. He knew of their plans because a "friend" of the Parrish family,

Gardner "Duff" Potter, reported on them. When William Parrish learned of his possible fate, he said he would take the matter to Brigham Young. One of Johnson's subordinates, A. F. McDonald, told Parrish that if he tried to tell Young, he would never reach Salt Lake alive.

As Johnson explained his plan to a council of Springville leaders, he lied to them. He exhibited a letter from Brigham Young that instructed local officers to be on the lookout for and possibly execute two ex-convicts, John Ambrose and Thomas Betts. Young thought Ambrose and Betts might try to steal livestock as they rode to California. Johnson apparently exhibited the letter, but he did not apprise his council of its content. Rather, he told them it applied to the Parrish family. In this way, he left the local leaders with the false belief that Young had authorized the murders.

Johnson put his murderous plans into action on March 15, 1857. As the Parrishes stole away from Springville in the night, Orrin lagged behind Potter, who was leading them to their doom. In the darkness, Johnson's assassins killed William and Beeson Parrish, as well as Gardner Potter, caught in the crossfire, but Orrin escaped. In 1859 a first grand jury refused to consider the case, but a second one indicted Johnson for the murders. Johnson hid out in the mountains, and U.S. marshals, with warrants for his arrest, were never able to capture him.

The deaths of her husband and son distressed William Parrish's wife, Alvira, deeply, and she decided to tell Brigham Young about the atrocity, meeting with the Mormon leader in July 1857. Some historians have insisted that Young already knew of the murders and had, in fact, ordered them. If Young already knew of Johnson's plans, one wonders why McDonald would have threatened William Parrish if he went to tell Young about what might happen. It seems more likely that Brigham Young was truthful when he told Alvira Parrish "he would have stopped it had he known anything about it." She asked him about the horses "stolen to satisfy the debts." Young, Alvira Parrish said, replied, "He would do everything he could do to have the horses restored to me—he would write to me after seeing . . . [Provo mayor B. Kimball] Bullock and others. I told him," she said, "that [Lysander] Gee [of Tooele] had the horses, and that he said that nothing but an order from Brigham could get them. . . . Brigham never wrote to me." Brigham Young wrote to Bullock, who had already returned the two horses to William Parrish, but we do not know whether the family recovered the horses in Gee's possession or not.

We can understand but not excuse why Young did not spend more time addressing the Parrish-Potter murders. As William MacKinnon has pointed out, a number of serious problems occupied Young's time and energy in early 1857. These included the "loss of emigrant life among the Willie and Martin handcart companies", Jedediah Grant's death in December 1856, the Tintic War and the accompanying extensive livestock thefts, "the viability of . . . Mormon colonies in San Bernardino and Carson Valley," and the tenuous launching of the "ambitious, expensive Y.X. Carrying Company."

Turning his thoughts to Washington, Young worried about rapidly deteriorating relations with the federal government. Federal officials in the West maintained an almost unrelenting correspondence with Washington departments making charges against the Mormons in general and Young in particular. Responding to these charges, congressmen attacked polygamy and introduced bills in Congress to reduce Utah's borders, "repeal [Utah's] organic act," and split the offices of Utah's governor and superintendent of Indian Affairs. It also seemed probable that Utah's proposal for statehood would fail and that Buchanan would remove Young as governor.

Carrying these burdens, Young also suffered from what one historian called "a mysterious, debilitating illness that kept [him] . . . absent from church services for weeks." Because he carried so many concerns, the disease may well have been psychosomatic: he may simply have worried himself sick.

To add to the already hefty pile of charges, the territorial legislature, unconcerned about the consequences, did nearly irreparable damage to Utah's relationship with Washington. On January 6, 1857, the legislature sent a memorial to Buchanan asserting the right of Utah's people to choose their own executive and judicial officers. Members of the legislature undoubtedly considered their demands justified under the popular sovereignty doctrine espoused by Illinois senator Stephen Douglas, who chaired the Senate Committee on Territories, and Senator Lewis Cass, whom Buchanan appointed as secretary of state in March 1857. Despite the fact that the State Department supervised territorial affairs, Buchanan bypassed Cass—with whom he had strained relations—and gave the memorial to Interior Secretary Jacob Thompson, who oversaw the Bureau of Indian Affairs and the General Land Office. Unlike Cass, Thompson and his wife Kate were close confidants of the president, and they visited the White House frequently. Thompson called the legislature's memorial a Mormon declaration of war with the United States.

Thompson's reaction must be seen in the context of all the letters sent to Washington by federal officials, including Indian agents, surveyors, and federal judges. The most bombastic charges came from Judge Drummond. As William MacKinnon has shown, Drummond's famous resignation letter of March 30, 1857, post-dated the Buchanan administration's decision to remove Young and send an army to escort a new governor, judges, and other officials to Utah. An earlier letter written by Drummond in California, however, reached Washington on March 19, the same time that Buchanan learned of the Utah legislature's memorial, and before the decision to send troops.

However great the role Drummond's charges played in the decision to dispatch an army to Utah is unknown, but whatever its effect, the letter was a colossal fraud. Not only had Drummond conducted himself extremely injudiciously in Utah, his charges contained damaging lies. He had abandoned his wife and family in Illinois and brought a prostitute, who went by the name of Ada Carroll, with him to Utah. Drummond introduced her as his wife and invited her to sit with him on the bench during some trials. In Fillmore, where he held court, he became angry at a Jewish resident, Levi Abrams, and ordered his African-American slave to attack Abrams. A probate court charged the judge with the assault, but Drummond escaped punishment because federal judges overruled the probate court's jurisdiction and refused to try him. Nevertheless, Judge John Fitch Kinney wrote Attorney General Jeremiah Black that Drummond was unfit for judicial appointment because of his personal immoral conduct.

If the impact of Drummond's charges is unknown, so is the full extent of his charges, because his first letter has disappeared. But newspapers published parts of the letter, and in those reports, Drummond reiterated the frequent assertion that Young held complete power in Utah. It is true that Young was the lead theocrat in Utah's theodemocracy, but he clearly did not hold complete power. A careful examination of Young's relationship with church members shows that sometimes they obeyed Young and sometimes they did not, even defying his orders on occasion. Ignoring mitigating examples, Drummond insisted that Brigham Young and the Mormons were so treacherous that the federal government would require "an efficient military force . . . to carry out the laws to the fullest extent."

Drummond also made specific charges that Buchanan could easily have refuted had he investigated before sending an army. He complained that Mormons had destroyed territorial and district court records and that they had killed Lieutenant Gunnison. After the Utah War, the clerk of the federal district court produced the records for inspection. Two investigations by federal officials showed that Pahvants, not Mormons, killed Gunnison. Drummond said that Mormons, not Cheyenne Indians, had murdered Utah territorial secretary Almon W. Babbitt and members of his party as they traveled toward Utah. Capt. H. W. Wharton, commander at Fort Kearny, investigated the murders and verified that Cheyennes had committed the murders. Probably ignorant of their value, as Wharton pointed out, the murderers had actually scattered United States Treasury drafts at the massacre site rather than taking them for their own use, something Mormon perpetrators would most likely not have done. Drummond also alleged that

Mormons had murdered retired federal judge Leonidas Shaver. An examination by two physicians, Dr. William France and his personal physician, non-Mormon Dr. Garland Hurt, reported at an inquest that included non-Mormons that Shaver had died of natural causes. Drummond also accused the probate courts of jailing people without cause. Recent statistical studies have shown that the probate courts dispensed equitable justice to all.

As damning as Drummond's assertions were, William MacKinnon has argued that Buchanan, who had access to reports showing Drummond had lied, probably paid more attention to the charges of Utah chief justice Kinney. Before he came to Utah, Kinney had a sterling reputation, having served as chief justice of the Iowa Supreme Court. In Utah, however, the probate court indicted him for gambling, and he owned a disreputable hotel. Kinney associated himself with Burr's charges by carrying a letter from the surveyor general to Attorney General Black speculating that the Mormons might assassinate a new governor.

Whatever Buchanan thought of Drummond's case, Kinney's own charges were just as serious. He wrote that "the Mormons are inimical to the Government of the U.S. and to all its officers who are not of their peculiar faith." As evidence, he claimed that in fall 1856 the Mormons had tried to incite the Indians to murder David Burr and Garland Hurt. He cited Hickman's attack on Troskolawski in August 1856, and he quoted Salt Lake bishop Edwin G. Woolley as saying that "they would cut the throats of all the Gentiles, throw their heads into Salt Lake and use their bodies for manure."

Significantly, claims that Young and the Mormons cooperated with the Indians may have influenced Buchanan most in his decision to send troops. Nearly 30 percent of the letters Buchanan sent to Congress, in response to a request for the evidence on which the president based his decision to order the Utah Expedition, charged collusion with the Indians. Letters from Judge Kinney, Surveyor General Burr, Indian agent Hurt, and other Indian agency officials carried unsubstantiated charges of Mormon connivance with Indians in attacks on federal officials and on emigrant trains. These stoked the antagonism of the Buchanan administration.

Although some Mormons undoubtedly cooperated with Indians in such raids, they did so without the approval of church leaders, and the leaders tried to stop those who did. Nevertheless, some claims about Mormon relations with Indians were accurate. The Mormons did try to convert Indians to their religion, they did encourage Indians to live near their towns, and they did encourage Indians to favor them over other Americans.

Without a thorough investigation, however, Buchanan had no way to evaluate the charges Kinney, Burr, Hurt, Drummond, and others made. Delegate John Bernhisel, Thomas Kane, and Jedediah Grant had effectively refuted the charges of the runaway officials in 1851 and 1852. Kane wrote to Buchanan during early 1857, but he did not meet with the president in person on the proposal to send an army until November, when the army had already reached eastern Utah. The two were not close friends; the Kanes belonged to a different faction of the Pennsylvania Democratic Party than Buchanan. And in contrast to the affair of the runaway officials, Bernhisel was not in Washington to counteract the claims of Mormon critics. Tired of the give-and-take of Washington politics and anxious to see his family, the delegate visited relatives in Pennsylvania while Buchanan ordered a third of the United States Army to descend on his home territory.

Washington's response to Utah Territory contrasted markedly with the treatment of Kansas Territory. In 1854 Congress had passed the Kansas-Nebraska Act, which divided the unorganized territory in two and established governments under popular or squatter sovereignty. Violence broke out in Kansas Territory as pro- and anti-slavery forces, citizens, and governments fought with one another in what Horace Greeley called "Bleeding Kansas." Violence overwhelmed the people as partisans contended for the pro-slavery Lecompton and anti-slavery Topeka constitutions. In 1856 Congress sent to Kansas Territory a special investigating committee, whose report concluded that if an election that had taken place on March 30, 1855, and had been limited to "actual settlers," it would have elected a free-state legislature. By contrast, Buchanan sent an army to Utah, and Senator Stephen Douglas repudiated the doctrine of popular sovereignty as it applied to Utah and the Mormons, saying the Utahns misused popular sovereignty and sought statehood only to "protect them in their treason and crime, debauchery and infamy."

Although it is counterfactual history, we can ask ourselves if an investigation might have prevented the dispatch of an army. A thorough investigation would have undermined many of the specific charges, although some of Garland Hurt's charges were undoubtedly true. The establishment of Mormon settlements did in fact undermine the Indians' economic base. Nevertheless, similar conditions resulted from settler colonialism throughout the American West. Young's policy of defense and conciliation fell most heavily on the Mormon settlers, but the proposal of Hurt, Kinney, and Drummond to fight Tintic and his raiders would have been extremely expensive. Mormons did try to induce the Indians to prefer them to other Americans, but this did not always work, especially in the case of the Utes. Kinney's charge that Mormons were antagonistic to many federal officials was accurate. On the other hand, Young's intemperate rhetoric would undoubtedly have concerned the Buchanan administration, as would his unauthorized travel to Fort Limhi. While there, Young distributed gifts to the Indians without the approval of the Oregon superintendent of Indian Affairs. He apparently did this with his own or church funds, however, because a subsequent investigation by Utah superintendent of Indian Affairs Benjamin Davies cleared Young of the misuse of public funds and approved his accounts.

It is unclear how Indian relations would have balanced out in an investigation, but neither Congress nor the president solved the problem after the war. Instead, beginning in the 1860s, the federal government started removing the Utes and Shoshones to reservations distant from the principal Mormon settlements. The government negotiated treaties with the Shoshones but removed the Utes to the Uintah Reservation without adopting a treaty or extinguishing Indian title.

Much of what David Burr charged was true. Mormons did try to control the use of grazing, timber, and water, and they did incorporate large areas into their cities. However, an earlier investigation would have revealed the massive surveying frauds over which he presided. Significantly, Buchanan did not reappoint Burr as surveyor general.

The Buchanan administration and Congress might have paid more attention to the general charges of the central direction of Mormon violence. Nevertheless, given the decidedly negative reputation of Mormons in the mid-nineteenth century, the administration most likely discounted Young's insistence that he had not ordered attacks on federal officials or the murders that Bill Hickman and Aaron Johnson committed. An investigation would have shown the Mormons had not destroyed court records. The Mormon Reformation, Young's preaching of blood atonement, and the practice of polygamy all counted against the Mormons and helped to bolster the reputation of Utah as a violent theocracy.

Choosing not to investigate, Buchanan concluded that Utah was in "substantial rebellion" against the authority of the United States, and he ordered Bvt. Brig. Gen. William S. Harney to assemble twenty-five hundred troops at Fort Leavenworth. Buchanan ordered them to serve as an escort or posse comitatus to conduct Governor Alfred Cumming of Georgia and other federal officials to Utah. Although Congress confirmed Cumming's appointment, Buchanan did not notify Young he was being replaced as governor, most likely because he did not believe he had to do so. Preparations for the Utah War had begun.

6

War and Peace

Events between mid-1857 and spring 1858 must have been the most challenging in Brigham Young's life. His preaching of blood atonement and his letter encouraging all to watch for the ex-convicts may have justified in Aaron Johnson's mind the murders of William Parrish and his son. In spring 1857 the Tintic War engulfed central Utah. Fraudulent surveys plastered the territory with sham stakes and monuments, all recorded on useless office plats. Utahns could not obtain titles to property anyway because Congress had refused to extend the land laws to Utah. Bill Hickman and his band had severely damaged the relationship with federal officials by attacking the surveyor general's employees. Young had no supporters among federal officials except two Indian agents, and by mid-April all the other federal officers had fled the territory. In turn, the runaway officials barraged Washington with charges against Young and his people, while some vented their grievances in person. In late May 1857 Young learned that President James Buchanan planned to send an army to Utah. He later heard that the Utah Expedition harbored officers and men, including the commander's adjutant, who intended to kill the Mormons. In September 1857 a burden crashed down on Young when he learned that Mormon militiamen in southern Utah had murdered 120 innocent emigrants in cold blood. In view of these challenges, it is remarkable how much Brigham Young showed himself to be a stalwart, creative, and flexible leader who responded effectively and successfully to the challenges.

As events unfolded in early 1857, James Buchanan decided by late March—shortly after his inauguration—to remove Young as governor, and by sometime in May had concluded to send an army to escort a new governor and new set of executive and judicial officers to Utah. At its peak in January 1858, 5,606 troops had orders to march to Utah—about 30 percent of the soldiers enrolled in the army. To carry out these orders, Buchanan instructed Secretary of War John Floyd to have Com. Gen. Winfield Scott issue orders to Bvt. Brig. Gen. William S. Harney as the expedition's commander. Dated June 29, 1857, Scott's orders asserted that "The community and, in part, the civil government of Utah Territory are in a state of substantial rebellion against the laws and authority of the United States." The orders authorized Harney to use military force should the new governor, judges, or marshals require it. The instructions also left to Harney's discretion whether the troops might forage forcibly for supplies among Utah's citizens.

Following Buchanan's instructions, Secretary of State Lewis Cass sent a letter to Governor Alfred Cumming on June 30 outlining his duties. Cass told Cumming that the army was ordered to perform "the ordinary military duties of security and protection upon our frontiers, and also, if necessary, to aid in the enforcement of the laws." He also wrote that the governor and other civil officers might call upon the army as a posse comitatus if "forcibly opposed or have just reason to expect opposition." Somewhat tamer than Scott's assertion of "substantial rebellion," Cass's letter added: "The President trusts that occasion for resorting to the employment of military force will not arise; but should actual resistance take place, while you meet it with prudence and discretion, it must be met with firmness."

Why had the relations between Brigham Young and the Mormon people and the United States government become so muddied that James Buchanan believed he must appoint a new cadre of officials—none of whom were Mormons—and muster a military

CVS/pharmacy®

$1.00 off

$1.00 off Tylenol, Motrin or all Bengay

(Up to $1.00 value)

Expires 6/29/2019

7139 5589 0200 1003 MFR

ExtraCare Card #: ********3426

ExtraCare card required. Offer redeemable and savings applied to qualifying [illegible]chase only. No cash back. Tax charged on pre-coupo[illegible]equired. Not valid in specialty centers wi[illegible]ludes trial / travel sizes +CRV on be[illegible]ges where applicable.

CPN#: 44070 [illegible]4039558902

force to escort them? One reason was Buchanan's low opinion of Utahns. In his December 1857 State of the Union address, Buchanan cited popular sovereignty as a reason to allow Kansas citizens to choose between slavery and free soil, but he did not grant Utahns the same privilege. The clash between Governor Young and President Buchanan amounted to, in the words of historian William MacKinnon, "conflicting philosophies of governance." Young called Utah either a theodemocracy or a theocracy, seeing it as a divinely inspired state preparing for Christ's Second Coming. In either case, he considered it the purist form of republican government. Buchanan, by contrast, viewed Young as a theocratic despot in "substantial rebellion," in a federal territory that should have functioned under the pupilage of Congress and the administration.

To arrive at his conclusions, Buchanan had become convinced of the accuracy of the complaints lodged against Young and the Mormons. Most of the charges, detailed in the previous chapter, had been lodged in Washington by former territorial officials who had fled Utah while Franklin Pierce was still president or shortly after Buchanan took office. Whatever the accuracy of the complaints, in his December 1857 message to Congress, Buchanan cited them in arguing that Young and the Mormons had made life unbearable for non-Mormons, especially federal appointees. Perhaps the crux of the matter was his belief that Young held absolute power over church and state, with which, Buchanan asserted, Young had marshaled the Mormon people to oppose the United States. Young, he also said, had succeeded in "tampering" with some Indian tribes. Excusing himself from charges of religious discrimination by insisting that with "religious opinions . . . I had no right to interfere," Buchanan—convinced by runaway federal judge Drummond, or someone with similar views—believed a non-Mormon governor required the support of a substantial military force.

As a lawyer, Buchanan may have used his message to build the case that conditions in Utah met the requirements of the 1807 Insurrection Act. If he did not do so then, he clearly did in the pardon he sent to Utah in 1858. In his address, Buchanan used the term "rebellion" as a synonym for "insurrection." Similarly, the federal government called the Civil War the "War of the Rebellion." A few years later, the Insurrection Act would serve as the basis for federal action in the Civil War. It said that insurrection—or in these two cases, rebellion—occurred when the insurrectionist "(A) so hinders the execution of the laws of a State or possession, as applicable, and of the United States within that State or possession, that any part or class of its people is deprived of a right, privilege, immunity, or protection named in the Constitution and secured by law, and the constituted authorities of that State or possession are unable, fail, or refuse to protect that right, privilege, or immunity, or to give that protection; or [the insurrectionist] (B) opposes or obstructs the execution of the laws of the United States or impedes the course of justice under those laws."

Whether Buchanan was right about the need to dispatch an army or not, he was right about one thing. One can argue with Buchanan's assertion that Young was a despot, but the Mormon prophet was without question a theocrat. Buchanan seems to have discounted, if he even knew about it, that Young had insisted that he would welcome others to Utah no matter what their religious persuasion as long as they did not attack the Mormons. In fact, Young generally had excellent relations with non-Mormons—in businesses or other private occupations—if they left his religion alone. These included businessmen like James M. Livingston, John H. Kinkead, and William Bell. The list also included some sojourners like Solomon Nunes Carvalho, a painter and photographer.

Traveling as the company artist, Carvalho arrived in Utah during winter 1853–54 with John C. Frémont and his explorers. Frémont's party became snowbound in the plateau east of Parowan in southern Utah, and when his party reached the town on February 7, 1854, local Mormons nursed them to health. After Frémont and most of his men left for California, Carvalho remained in Utah until May 1854. Traveling to Salt Lake City, he "called on Governor Young, and was received by him with marked attention."

Said Carvalho: "He tendered me the use of all his philosophical instruments and access to a large and valuable library." Visiting with Brigham Young and other Mormons, Carvalho was impressed with a people who "preach morality . . . [and] practice it."

Although Young got along well with people who did not oppose him and his people, he made no secret of favoring theocratic republicanism. Unfortunately for the Mormons, Young's persuasion countered the historical trend in America's democratic republic. Historically, many republics had functioned either as theocracies, as governments by religious leaders, or as quasi-theocracies with established churches that citizens had to support. But Young lived in the nineteenth-century United States, not in Savonarola's Florence, Calvin's Geneva, Cromwell's England, or even England's American colonies.

From an eschatological perspective, Young argued that a theocracy and a republic were essentially the same. He expected Christ to rule in such a government after His Second Coming. In the United States, however, in the nineteenth century, Protestant churches controlled the religious life of the United States, and some states established them as state churches. The Bill of Rights prohibited the federal government from establishing a state church or prohibiting the free exercise of religion, but until the approval of the Fourteenth Amendment in 1868, the national Bill of Rights did not apply to the states.

Young's views seem to have blinded him to the realization that since the late eighteenth century, disestablishment and the elimination of theocracy had become the clear trend in America. In the seventeenth and eighteenth centuries, most Americans lived in colonies with established churches, generally either Anglican or Congregational. Many states retained established churches in the early republic. Election sermons, in which state-supported ministers counseled their parishioners about how to vote, were regular features of each balloting cycle.

Such conditions changed slowly. Many states had test acts that required office holders to be Protestants, Christians, or members of a specific church. Until 1877, the year Young died, New

Hampshire's constitution required all legislators to be Protestants. Nevertheless, disestablishment took hold in the states during the 1780s and gained momentum in the early nineteenth century. Connecticut in 1818 and Massachusetts in 1833 were the last states with established churches. Clearly, Young defended as authentic republicanism a form of government that the people of the United States had come to believe was increasingly outmoded.

Whatever his views on republicanism and theocracy, Young did not know until long after Buchanan's inauguration on March 4, 1857, that the president would confront the Utah Mormons with an army. After Steptoe's troops left in 1855, Young feared that the federal government might dispatch another army to Utah. That did not happen in 1855, but Young discovered his people faced that prospect at least by May 29, 1857, when George A. Smith called on him to report his disappointment that Congress would not consider their 1856 constitution. Smith also reported "that a new Governor would be sent to the Territory accompanied by two or three thousand soldiers." Traveling with John Bernhisel, Smith had stopped briefly on May 2 at Leavenworth, Kansas, where he may have seen preparations for mustering the army, after which Smith's party continued to Salt Lake City. Young knew more on June 23, when Ephraim Hanks and Feramorz Little brought the mail along with further intelligence on the marshaling of an army. They also brought the sad news of Parley P. Pratt's murder. Bill Hickman may have provided additional information after he arrived two days later on June 25.

Young may have kept the information confidential until July 24, 1857, when Abraham Smoot, Judson Stoddard, Porter Rockwell, William Garr, and Elias Smith rode into the Saints' Pioneer Day celebration in upper Big Cottonwood Canyon. Brigham Young and some Salt Lake businessmen had established the Brigham Young Express and Carrying Company (called the Y.X. Company) to transport goods to and from the Missouri River and Utah. The federal government had awarded a contract to the Y.X. Company to carry the mail between Independence, Missouri, and Salt Lake City. When Smoot and Stoddard arrived at Leavenworth, the postmaster refused to give them the mail, saying the government had cancelled the contract. The messengers confirmed that Buchanan had dispatched a new governor and an "entire set of officers" to be escorted to Utah by an army of twenty-five hundred troops commanded by General Harney. Harney's reputation as an Indian killer preceded him, and Young said, "if General Harney came here, I Should then know the intention of [the] gover[n]ment." Those present voted "unanimously that if Harney crossed the South Pass the buz[z]ards Should pick his bones." The Mormons claimed that "The feeling of Mobocracy is rife in the 'States' the constant cry is kill the Mormons." Young's reply: "Let them try it."

Some historians have asserted this was the nation's first rebellion, its first civil war. It was not. At least two rebellions took place before the Utah War, both of them over taxation. Daniel Shays's rebellion of farmers in 1786–87 over high taxes in Massachusetts occurred first; it was crushed by Massachusetts troops under Gen. Benjamin Lincoln. A second rebellion in western Pennsylvania against the 1791 federal Whiskey Tax was similar to Shays's Rebellion in that it was initiated by local farmers. Five hundred armed men attacked the fortified home of tax inspector general John Neville to prevent collection of the monies. President George Washington himself rode at the head of an army of thirteen thousand state militiamen to suppress the rebellion, and his army arrested twenty Pennsylvanians who were later released or pardoned.

Three other incidents of rebellion or potential rebellion occurred prior to the Utah War. After the passage of the federal Alien and Sedition Acts of 1798, the legislatures of Virginia and Kentucky passed resolutions condemning the acts, and in contradiction to the U.S. constitution's supremacy clause (Article 6, Clause 2), the Kentucky resolution said states could nullify unconstitutional laws. During the War of 1812, Massachusetts and Connecticut refused to permit the federal government to enlist their militias to fight in the war as required in the U.S. constitution, Article 1, Section 8. Delegates from a number of New England states held a convention at Hartford that proposed nullification of federal laws.

Perhaps more famously, the South Carolina legislature enacted nullification in 1832, declaring the tariff acts of 1828 and 1832 void in the state. When Andrew Jackson's administration refused to back down, South Carolina and the federal government prepared for war. At Jackson's request, Congress passed the Force Act in 1833, authorizing military action to collect the tariffs. Jackson avoided war by inducing Congress to pass a tariff act in 1833 that substantially reduced the taxes. In a defiant gesture, the South Carolina legislature passed an act nullifying the Force Act. In a revelation of December 25, 1832, Joseph Smith said at the time: "the rebellion of South Carolina . . . will eventually terminate in the death and misery of many souls." The Palmetto State did not actually rebel against federal authority until its forces attacked Fort Sumter in April 1861, but those events did lead to four years of unimaginable death and destruction.

As Joseph Smith announced this revelation, he and his people had already suffered from violence, and they would experience a great deal more. They endured attacks by militias, mobs, and vigilantes in Missouri and Illinois, and during Steptoe's stay in Utah, they experienced the soldiers' amorous adventures, drunkenness, and violence. It is not too much to say that Brigham Young, the Mormon leadership, and the Mormon community feared for their lives as the army descended on Utah. William MacKinnon has rightly argued that these perceptions contributed to Mormon opposition to the Utah Expedition. At best, the army would cause insufferable disruption in Utah, and at worst, soldiers might kill Mormons as militia groups had in Missouri and Illinois.

Young considered the dispatch of an army unwarranted anyway because he regarded the Mormons as law-abiding Americans who were abused by anti-Mormon federal officials. Some historians have argued that the Mormons intended to create an independent nation. If they did, they certainly went about it in an odd way. It is true that in the Midwest and to some degree after they arrived in northern Mexico, many Mormons had condemned the United States and hoped to separate from it. Brigham Young had told the Council of Fifty in Nauvoo that he expected to leave the United

States. Nevertheless, after the American victory in the Mexican-American War and the Treaty of Guadalupe-Hidalgo, instead of trying to create an independent nation, the church leadership petitioned for admission to the union as a state. Utahns applied for statehood under a constitution drafted in 1849. Then, with Young's approval, memorials from the territorial legislature in 1852, 1853, and 1854 petitioned Congress for an enabling act to draft a new constitution to enter the union. After Congress refused to pass one, Elders George A. Smith and John Taylor of the Quorum of the Twelve Apostles traveled to Washington in summer 1856 to present a newly drafted constitution for admission, despite both Stephen Douglas and John Bernhisel urging them not to submit it. Then the two apostles tried to see Thomas Kane in Philadelphia to ask him about applying for statehood, but he had left town. Disappointed, they returned to Utah with Bernhisel shortly thereafter. These were surely not the efforts of a community that did not want to be part of the United States.

As the army assembled at Fort Leavenworth, conditions in Kansas prompted Buchanan to order Harney to remain at Leavenworth. Kansas Territory had started to bleed from a seemingly interminable conflict between pro- and anti-slavery forces. Instead of Harney, Buchanan ordered that Col. Albert Sidney Johnston replace Harney as commander of the Utah Expedition. Johnston did not take command until November 3, 1857, after the troops ground to a halt in what was then eastern Utah under the burden of the indecision of their interim commander, Col. Edmund B. Alexander; the harassing tactics of the Nauvoo Legion; and the assault of high-country winter weather.

As the Mormons mobilized for war, Young and others criticized some local non-Mormons while attempting to maintain good relations with many of them. On August 19 Young "took measures" to stop "Some men" who were causing trouble with non-Mormon businesspeople. Commenting on his policies, Young said he intended "to give my enemies fair warning." "I wish," he wrote, "to meet *all men* at the judgment Bar of God without any to fear me or accuse me of a wrong action." He leveled a blistering public attack in particular on Charles Mogo, the deputy U.S. surveyor who came under serious criticism from the Latter-day Saint community for his work. Yet Young later wrote a letter of apology in response to a letter from Mogo that explained his views of Young's criticism.

Young believed he still held the governorship since Buchanan had never notified him of his removal "as required by law." The president had never told Young of the appointment of a new governor or a military escort, and Young chose to consider the massive force as an invading army. In fact, no president had appointed Young since 1850, and Young had already served four years, as specified under Section 2 of the Utah Territorial Organic Act. In 1857 he served at the chief executive's pleasure.

Throughout that late spring and summer, Young and his advisors prepared to defend themselves and to wage aggressive war if they needed to protect themselves. Under Young's orders, the Mormons had burned Forts Bridger and Supply, both of which they owned. Acting on Young's instructions in August, Gen Daniel H. Wells, commander of the Nauvoo Legion, Utah's territorial militia, ordered his adjutant, Brig. Gen. James Ferguson, to muster the militia. Acting as executive of a threatened territory, Young declared martial law on September 15.

Young's actions rested on wobbly legal grounds, although the precedents for a territory declaring martial law are mixed. In 1849–50 it appeared that the State of Texas might invade New Mexico Territory in a dispute over the boundary between the two jurisdictions, so Secretary of War Winfield Scott urged the acting governor of New Mexico Territory, Bvt. Col. John Monroe, to issue a proclamation—countering one expected from Texas—and to summon troops to parry the anticipated invasion. In 1856 Washington territorial governor Isaac I. Stevens declared martial law in parts of the territory during an Indian war. President Pierce's secretary of state, William Marcy, wrote that in the case of "rebellion, or a formidable insurrection . . . Martial law has been occasionally resorted to as the only means left for its re-establishment. [It might be] resorted to in aid of the government when in imminent danger of being overpowered by internal or external foes." Disagreeing with Marcy, Attorney General Caleb Cushing wrote that "the power to suspend the laws and to substitute the military in the place of the civil authority, is not a power within the legal attributes of a governor of one of the Territories of the United States."

Young probably cared little or not at all for such opinions. He may have learned about the Stevens incident from Wilford Woodruff, but it is unclear whether he knew of Marcy's advice, Cushing's ruling, or Monroe's potential confrontation with Texas. Whatever the case, Young was acting in the defense of his people, and he moved aggressively to order the U.S. Army to stand down. He sent a letter to the commander at Fort Bridger, where the army had wintered at a camp named after Gen. Winfield Scott. In the letter, Young ordered the federal army to "retire forthwith from the Territory." Should they find that "impracticable," he offered, the force could remain in "peace" if they deposited their arms and ammunition with Utah territorial quartermaster general Lewis Robison. Col. E. B. Alexander offered to refer Young's letter to his superior when Johnston arrived at Camp Scott.

Under Young's leadership, the Utahns prepared to repel the invasion. To obstruct and paralyze the army until the people could organize a satisfactory response, Young and General Wells mounted a series of delaying tactics. Under Young's orders, Wells ordered Maj. Lot Smith, Col. Robert T. Burton, Maj. John D. T. McAllister, Maj. Warren Snow, and Capt. Porter Rockwell to harass the army. Remembering Napoleon's dictum that an army marches on its stomach, these units cut supply lines by rustling stock, burning grass, and torching seventy-six wagons in three trains. On one such foray, Smith and his unit reportedly appeared at a freighter's camp. "For God's sake," the wagon master implored, "don't burn the wagons!" "It's for His sake," Lot Smith replied, "we are burning them!"

If we consider the Utah War a Mormon rebellion, we have a number of choices about the date of its beginning. Young broke the law when he traveled to Oregon Territory in April because he had not obtained permission to leave the territory. Though illegal, we would be hard pressed to consider Young's journey an act of rebellion. We might date the rebellion from August, when Brig. Gen. James Ferguson began mustering the militia and assigning them to posts for Utah's defense. We might also consider Brigham Young's declaration of martial law on September 15 as the date the rebellion began. However, we do not usually date the beginning of the Civil War from enactment of the Southern states' ordinances of secession. Rather, we generally believe the rebellion began with the Confederate attack on Fort Sumter. Therefore, my vote goes for the overt act of burning wagon trains in October as the beginning of the Mormon rebellion.

As the Mormons prepared to engage in offensive war, they undertook a defensive response to prevent or delay the army from murdering them, as anti-Mormon militiamen had in Missouri and Illinois. Although Johnston did not propose to murder Mormons, a number of his officers, including his adjutant, Maj. Fitz John Porter, did. Had he acted on Secretary Floyd's orders to Harney, Johnston had the authority to wage war on the Mormons if attacked, but not otherwise.

Young, Wells, and Ferguson had ordered the militia to engage in offensive war if the army moved to the Wasatch Front, either through the passes that led from Fort Bridger or by following the Bear River through Oregon Territory. Under Young's orders, Wells sent Nauvoo Legion units to fortify Echo Canyon, a narrow defile and the most direct route to Salt Lake City. He also ordered small contingents to Soda Springs and the Blackfoot River. Much to the relief of Utah's people, however, the weather pinned the soldiers down at Camp Scott, and Wells recalled most of his men.

Meanwhile, Young and Wells mobilized the people at home. To prepare for wartime conditions, they sent George A. Smith to settlements south of Salt Lake City on August 4 to call out the militia units and meet with the leaders. Warning the people in each town of the approach of a hostile army, Smith reminded them of how people in the United States hated the Mormons. He cautioned the Saints to keep their weapons ready, and told them not to sell supplies to non-Mormons. He also warned them that troops might attack from California through southern Utah. After hearing Smith's instructions and recognizing the importance of keeping the Indians either neutral or on the Mormons' side, Jacob Hamblin, leader of the Southern Indian Mission, assembled twelve chiefs from the Paiutes and Pahvant Utes and took them to Salt Lake City for a meeting with Brigham Young on September 1.

These events preceded the most tragic and abominable event of the Utah War—the Mountain Meadows massacre. A number of authors, including William Wise, Sally Denton, and Will Bagley have argued that Brigham Young ordered the massacre. A number of other authors, including Juanita Brooks, Ronald Walker, Richard Turley, and Glen Leonard, and Young's four scholarly biographers—Stanley Hirshson, Newell Bringhurst, Leonard Arrington, and John Turner—argue that Young did not.

William MacKinnon, the most knowledgeable authority on the Utah War, has argued for a Scotch verdict on Young and the massacre—that is, he believes it has not been proved that Brigham Young ordered the massacre. Such a verdict is legal in Scottish courts, but it is not accepted in U.S. or English courts; a jury must either convict or acquit the accused in our system. Nevertheless, MacKinnon, like Michael Quinn, argues for a number of reasons that Young bears some responsibility, including his rhetoric, preparations for war, tolerance of violence and thefts, unleader-like language, and the dispatch of George Smith to warn settlers in the south to prepare for possible war. By contrast, Ronald Walker argued in his Arrington Lecture at Utah State University that Young was a pacifist. Leonard Arrington has argued that we should understand Young's violent speech as rhetoric rather than as counsel.

Available evidence suggests that Young was an extremely complex person and that his response depended on his perception of a particular situation at the moment. At times, he was very harsh; other times he could be compassionate. He was brutal when he lectured on blood atonement. Young's letter authorizing the possible killing of two fleeing ex-convicts reveals a much harsher disposition than we would expect from a governor. By contrast, some non-Mormons who met with Young found him very friendly, and at times urbane. These include not only Carvalho and such non-Mormon business leaders as William Bell, but also Episcopal bishop Daniel S. Tuttle, although he met Young some ten years later. Young apologized to Mogo, someone who, as it turned out, hardly deserved an apology. He supported Alvira Parrish's efforts to recover her deceased husband's horses; and he reprimanded Bill Hickman for his raid on the surveyor general's office.

In the narrative on the Mountain Meadows massacre that follows, I have tried to follow the rule to which all historians should strictly adhere. That is: give evidence. Evidence consists of facts verifiable from existing documents. It is not supposition or rhetoric. Nor is it conclusions drawn from circumstances. It is rather what the always incomplete and often controversial, but nevertheless, verifiable record can show. But, after examining the evidence, historians must weave the verifiable facts into a narrative.

We know much about the Mountain Meadows massacre and Brigham Young's involvement in it. But there is much we do not know and, most likely, never will know. On their way north to Salt Lake City, Jacob Hamblin, George Smith, and the Indians camped at Corn Creek, south of Fillmore, near a company of Arkansas migrants led by John Twitty "Jack" Baker and Alexander Fancher. These emigrants and their families were moving to California with valuable possessions, a cattle herd, and money. Some of their party had visited California previously, discovering a central California area where they believed they could establish ranches. To stock them, they drove with them six hundred or more cattle. The Arkansans had decided to take the southern route. They reportedly did so—and evidence lines up on both sides of this question—because, as Brigham Young remembered twenty years later, Charles C. Rich had advised them *not* to go south, emblematic of the theme of distrusting the Mormons. Also two decades later, Malinda Scott, who decided to take the northern route, said that the Mormons had convinced her father, William Cameron, who went with the Baker-Fancher company, to take the southern route. Jacob Hamblin said a member of the party told him that, as southerners, they preferred to go south. Whatever motivated them, this decision led them through the settlements along approximately the present I-15 corridor to Cedar City, then southwest on the main wagon route to Mountain Meadows. The Baker-Fancher party consisted of the first outsiders to reach southern Utah after Smith had warned people in the settlements south of Salt Lake City to prepare for an impending invasion.

Will Bagley has argued that Young gave orders to attack members of the Baker-Fancher party to the Indians whom Hamblin took to Salt Lake City. We have no evidence of such an order, and there is no evidence that the Indians who met with Brigham Young were present at the Mountain Meadows massacre, which occurred on Friday, September 11, after an initial attack on Monday, September 7. Research by Walker, Turley, and Leonard shows that the Paiutes and Pahvants who accompanied Hamblin had remained in Salt Lake City after their meeting with Young on September 1, spending time with Wilford Woodruff and others and visiting workshops and gardens. Kanosh and other Pahvants had remained in Salt Lake City at least until September 4. Whether they remained longer, existing records do not show. At any rate, there is no evidence that Pahvants participated in the massacre. We know that at least some of the Paiutes remained in Salt Lake City until after the massacre. Tutsegavits, a Shivwitz Paiute leader, was ordained an elder in the LDS church in Salt Lake City on September 13, two days after the massacre.

Instead of encouraging the Indians to attack the Baker-Fancher Party, Young tried to recruit them to steal cattle on the overland trails. Young believed that the Mormons could hold the army at bay, but that, as a consequence, their tactics would lead to an extended siege. To prepare to feed the community during such a siege, Young reversed his previous policy of discouraging the Indians from raiding emigrant trains. He spoke with some Indians himself, and he sent Dimick Huntington and other emissaries to those Indians with whom he did not meet, to encourage them to steal cattle on the northern and southern overland routes. According to Walker, Turley, and Leonard, Young told the Indians through Huntington that he expected to store stolen livestock and local grain in the mountains to feed the people during the siege. With the exception of a few Paiutes, Young's policy did not bear fruit.

Armies have frequently lived off the bounty of their enemies. Alexander the Great fueled his march to Babylon and India from local populations, and William T. Sherman would use similar tactics in his campaign from Atlanta to Savannah in November and December 1864. A dearth of food and water often forced besieged peoples to capitulate to the enemy. To avert this possibility, Young intended to feed his people in part with cattle taken from overland emigrants.

In addition to the Indian policy, Bagley also argues that the murders of Parley P. Pratt and Joseph Smith contributed to the decision for the Mountain Meadows massacre. He asserts that it was meant, in part, to avenge the blood of martyred prophets. Pratt, a popular member of the Council of the Twelve, had married Eleanor McComb McLean in 1855 as a polygamous wife. Eleanor had recently left Hector McLean, a Unitarian minister and, at the time, an Arkansas resident, who had abused her. Against Brigham Young's counsel, Pratt had gone to Arkansas to meet Eleanor, who had left Utah to retrieve her two sons by McLean. Pratt suffered an excruciating death on May 13, 1857, as the outraged minister, aided by a small group of vigilantes, shot and stabbed the apostle to death on a road about twelve miles west of Van Buren, Arkansas. Word of the murder reached Utah in early June, and Eleanor Pratt, who had watched in horror as her husband died, reported the details and called for vengeance in Salt Lake City after arriving with the Judson Stoddard mail party. Hailed as a hero in Arkansas, McLean never stood trial for the murder, and the Latter-day Saints viewed Pratt's death as the latest episode in a never-ending saga of violence and abuse at the hands of the American people in general and Protestants in particular.

Although one can find an extensive discussion in Bagley's narrative, he presents no evidence that Young and church leaders linked Pratt's or Smith's deaths or the Indian policy with the massacre.

In fact, Bagley pointed out that although Eleanor Pratt expected retribution, after she had reported the murder in Salt Lake City in August, "Mormon leaders in Salt Lake barely mentioned Pratt's death over the next month." In a sermon, Brigham Young linked Pratt's death and those of Joseph and Hyrum Smith with aims of the governments of the United States and of European countries, not with the people of Arkansas. Moreover, on October 4, 1857, Young preached, "God will fight our battles." Nor is there evidence of an oath—reportedly taken in the Endowment House to pray to the Lord to avenge the blood of Joseph Smith—having anything to do with the massacre. Contrary to Bagley's later assertion, although some anti-Mormons avowed otherwise, the oath did not commit those who took the pledge to take action themselves to avenge the death of the prophets. Rather, it was a prayer that God would avenge the prophets' deaths.

In Utah, however, as Young learned, the Arkansan emigrants had trouble enough over local issues. After they arrived in Salt Lake Valley, the local settlers urged them to move on as quickly as possible. Hamilton Park, a Salt Lake City businessman, later reported a near brawl in Salt Lake City between the Arkansans and local Mormons. Farther south, the Mormon settlers had staked out herd grounds for winter feed, which they considered extremely critical in time of war and food shortages. The Arkansans disputed Mormon control of these herd grounds, and they drove their cattle onto Provo's winter feed grounds. Under Young's policy of preparing for war, Lyman Woods, a Provo policeman, asked them to move to a different site. The Arkansans' captain reportedly told him that they had herded their cattle onto Uncle Sam's grass and that they had a "better claim to it than a bunch of rebel Mormons." Woods told the emigrants they had to move in an hour and called out the local militia. When the militia reportedly set up a firing line, the emigrants moved on, and stake president James C. Snow congratulated the militiamen on their preparation.

As the Arkansans pushed south from Provo, and as the residents tried to implement Young's policy, threats arose in other communities. Leaders in Springville and Payson chastised Saints who sold supplies to the Arkansans, and conflicts over winter feed reportedly took place in those communities as well. Non-Mormons reported disputes over the refusal of the settlers to sell supplies to the emigrants in Holden—then called Buttermilk Fort—or in nearby Fillmore.

Some evidence points to trouble boiling up between the settlers and one of the emigrants called the "Dutchman." Both the Arkansans and the Mormons labeled him a troublemaker. In the nineteenth century, the term Dutchman referred to both Netherlanders and Germans (*Deutsch*). In addition to verbal attacks on the women, the Dutchman reportedly heaped verbal abuse on the "g.d . . . ed" Mormon people in general and Brigham Young in particular. Walker, Turley, and Leonard suggest that the Dutchman may have been John Gresly, a German-American originally from Pennsylvania.

Nevertheless, in an attempt to justify the massacre at Mountain Meadows, unlike the controversies over refusing to sell to the emigrants or to permit them to use herd grounds, many of the reports of verbal abuse were undoubtedly blown out of proportion or fabricated. Indeed, many of them were clearly post-massacre rationalizations. Virtually every overland emigrant train relied on trade with settlements for supplies, and all expected to graze their livestock on the open range. The refusal of many Mormons to trade with them may have left them short of supplies, and the embargo on herd grounds may have aroused the Baker-Fancher party's concern for the survival of their large herds.

A number of false stories of abuse and death at the hands of the Arkansans originated in Corn Creek, the Pahvant settlement at which George Smith and Jacob Hamblin had seen the Arkansans. Some clearly took place, while others were attempts at shifting the blame. A conflict ensued when Peter Boyce, a federal Indian farmer, tried to prevent the Pahvants from trading food for ammunition. Critics after the massacre charged the Arkansans with Indian deaths from poisoning water or beef and the death of settler Proctor Robinson. These incidents had nothing to do with the assault. These deaths occurred after the Baker-Fancher party had left, and evidence assembled by Walker, Turley, and Leonard suggests they actually resulted from anthrax, and, at least in Robinson's case, putrefaction from skinning a dead animal.

The Mormons applied Young's policy against trading with the Arkansans quite inconsistently. Jesse N. Smith at Paragonah traded flour and salt to the emigrants. At Parowan, the stake president, William Dame, sent "a crowd of dogs" led by Barney Carter, his son-in-law, to bash William Leany's head with a fence post, leaving him marred for life because he gave some vegetables to William Aden, the son of a man who had befriended him while he served on a mission in the East.

Conflict peaked in Cedar City, which by 1857 had devolved into a failed industrial experiment. Brigham Young had sent the settlers there to exploit an iron mountain. After fabricating a few iron implements, failed financing, inadequate technological knowledge, and poor leadership had left the people with little prospect for prosperity.

The Arkansans encountered a folk in Cedar City who considered them alien enemies. When stake president Isaac Haight learned that the government had dispatched an army to invade Utah, he reminded his community in a sermon of the abuses borne by the Mormons in Missouri and Illinois. He charged that the United States had sent an army "to exterminate us," and said that he was "prepared to feed to the Gentiles the same bread they fed to us." Because he learned details of the army's expedition from George A. Smith, Smith's admonition to prepare for possible war may have reinforced his animosity.

After the Baker-Fancher party reached Cedar City, confrontation soon erupted in two and possibly three incidents. The first involved Samuel Jackson Sr., who farmed outside the city, selling the emigrants fifty bushels of wheat. When they took the grain to a flourmill owned by Haight and operated by Bishop Philip Klingensmith, Haight told Klingensmith to demand a cow for grinding the wheat. This exorbitant price led some in the Arkansas party who had, according to reports, imbibed too freely of locally distilled whiskey, to threaten to come back with the army and exterminate the Mormons. Alexander Fancher rebuked the drunken loudmouths, but further confrontations flared. In a second incident, members of the company had a run-in with company store manager Christopher Arthur, Haight's son-in-law, when they discovered the store did not stock supplies the Arkansans badly needed. Disappointed, the would-be customers directed abuse and profanity at Arthur. A third incident, which may or may not have occurred—the evidence is sketchy—holds that one of the Arkansans, angry that he could not purchase the supplies he needed, killed two of Barbara Morris's chickens and threw them in his wagon. Barbara was the mother of Elias Morris, Haight's second counselor, and the wife of John Morris, Klingensmith's second counselor.

After these incidents, a party of drunks threatened abuse at Haight's front door. Haight escaped through the back door, but not before he heard the unruly crowd threaten to send an army from California to kill Young, the local leaders, and every other "g.d . . . ed Mormon." Haight ordered the town marshal, John M. Higbee, who was also his first counselor, to arrest the troublemakers, but the Baker-Fancher party evaded him and left town.

A major in the Iron County militia, Haight had no authority to act against the emigrants without approval of his militia commander, Col. William Dame, the stake president in Parowan. Haight immediately sought Dame's permission, but Dame refused to grant it, replying that "words are but wind" to the report of the threats, bravado, and claims of complicity in Smith's death. Dame's refusal did not satisfy Major Haight.

Bent on vengeance, Haight worked around Dame's refusal. He thought of an Indian raid as way to punish the emigrants. Haight expected his militiamen to recruit Indians to attack in the Santa Clara Canyon just beyond its confluence with Magotsu Creek. John D. Lee, Haight, Higbee, Klingensmith, and Lee's son-in-law, Carl Shirts, recruited Paiutes from Southern Utah. Then, bent on punishing the Arkansans, in a meeting that lasted from late Friday evening, September 4, into Saturday morning on September 5, Haight assigned Lee to supervise the Indian raid. Haight and Lee were both majors in the Iron County militia, but Haight reportedly convinced Lee that Colonel Dame had approved the attack.

Although Lee held no ecclesiastical position at the time, he had previously served as presiding elder in Harmony, and he was a ceremonially adopted son of Brigham Young. Never a bishop, as later reports alleged, Lee's only authority was his personal prestige and his military rank. Nevertheless, on Sunday, September 6, 1857, Major Lee substituted a war council for the regular church service. He called on the congregation to support what he called the decision of Haight and Dame, and few opposed him. Then he rallied two score or more Paiutes and marched around in Harmony with them. From the town, Lee and the Indians headed for Mountain Meadows by way of Leach's Springs. Carl Shirts also brought Indians and militiamen from Washington and Santa Clara for the attack.

On the same Sunday at 4 P.M., Haight presided at a council meeting in Cedar City. The council included his counselors, Klingensmith and his counselors, members of the high council, and other leading citizens. Laban Morrill, a high councilman and blacksmith from Fort Johnson (now Enoch) north of Cedar City, arrived late, and when he learned of Haight's plans, he reminded those present that their "principles of right teach us to return good for evil and do good to those who despitefully use us."

Taken aback by Morrill's opposition, Haight had to admit that Dame had told him not to attack the emigrants. But he did not tell those assembled that he had already sent Lee to exterminate the Arkansans. Morrill persisted until the council agreed unanimously to send a "dispatch to Governor Young to know what would be the best course." Haight agreed to send a rider the next day. Some evidence indicates that Haight may have sent two men in a failed attempt to assassinate Morrill as he returned to Fort Johnson.

In the meantime, Haight had sent William Stewart and Joel White to contact Lee. We do not know what he told them, but when Stewart and White learned that two of the emigrants had returned toward Quichipa Lake southwest of Cedar City to look for lost cattle, they decided to kill the two. They met William Aden and the foul-mouthed Dutchman at Little Pinto Creek. Stewart shot and killed Aden and wounded the Dutchman as he galloped away for the emigrants' camp.

Unaware of Stewart's and White's actions, James Haslam rode the 250 miles from Cedar City to Salt Lake beginning Monday, September 7, carrying a note from Isaac Haight to Brigham Young. Some difficulties in securing fresh horses along the way delayed him. Nevertheless, Haslam arrived exhausted on Thursday, September 10, at about noon. He interrupted a meeting Young held with Capt. Stewart Van Vliet, assistant U.S. quartermaster, who was there to negotiate for supplies for the army at Fort Scott. In the letter he sent back with Haslam, Young ordered the Iron County militia to stand down. He penned: "In regard to the emigration trains passing through our settlements, we must not interfere with them until they are first notified to keep away. You must not meddle with them. The Indians we expect will do as they please but you should try and preserve good feelings with them [the Indians]." A still-weary Haslam obtained a fresh horse and galloped immediately to Cedar City, arriving on Sunday, September 13, two days after the massacre.

Haight did send Joseph Clewes to advise Lee to use his best effort to prevent the Indians from continuing the attack "until further orders." Clewes turned the dispatch over to Amos Thornton, who delivered it to Lee. But Clewes considered conditions hopeless because the attack had already begun, and it continued while he remained at the meadows. Meanwhile, Stewart and White returned to Cedar City to report the Monday attack by Lee, a number of Mormons, and some Indians. They also told of Stewart's murder of Aden and wounding of the Dutchman.

Given the alternative of persisting or desisting, Haight persisted. On Tuesday, September 8, he sent Klingensmith with additional militiamen to the meadows. To try to understand conditions at the meadows, Dame sent Jesse N. Smith and Edward Dalton to investigate. They reported that, contrary to Lee's later effort to deflect guilt from himself, he, the Mormon militiamen, and the Indians were aggressively attacking the Arkansans. They also reported Haight's aggressive attitude as well.

On Wednesday, September 9, Haight met with Dame and the stake high council in Parowan. The high council voted to call off the massacre, but, undeterred, Haight held a rump session with Dame on a pile of tanbark near Parowan's east gate. He convinced Dame that Lee, the Indians, and other militiamen had commenced the conflict, and the Mormons would have to massacre the emigrants to protect themselves both from public opinion and from James Buchanan.

According to plan, on Thursday, September 10, militiamen who were mostly from Cedar City gathered at Jacob Hamblin's ranch at the northern end of Mountain Meadows. On Friday, September 11, Lee approached the embattled emigrants under a flag of truce and convinced them that if they agreed to disarm, the militiamen would escort them to safety. After sending the women and children ahead, each soldier walked northward from the camp by the side of one of the disarmed men. At a signal from John Higbee—"Halt"—each militiaman either murdered the immigrant by his side or ducked out so someone else could do it. The militiamen and perhaps some Paiutes also murdered the women and older children.

According to Nephi Johnson, militiamen did most of the killing. Somewhere between 90 and 115 immigrants died at Mountain Meadows on September 11, 1857—we do not know the exact number. The Mormons and their Indian allies had killed others previously for a total of about 120. The Mormons saved seventeen of the children age six and younger, and Philip Klingensmith distributed most of them among Latter-day Saint settlers. Eventually, Jacob Hamblin would gather them up and Indian superintendent Jacob Forney would return the children to their relatives. Young proposed to send them home in wagons, but Forney secured ambulances from the army and a dragoon escort.

How do we interpret all of these facts as we know them? It seems almost beyond comprehension that God-fearing and Christian militiamen could commit such an atrocity. Nevertheless, we begin to understand such crimes when we compare them with the massacres of Christian Armenians by Muslim Turks, of Jews by Christian Germans, of Muslim Bosnians by Christian Serbs, of Shia and Sunni Muslims by each other, and of black Christian Republicans by white Christian Democrats at Colfax, Louisiana. The Democrats massacred more Republicans at Colfax than the militiamen did Arkansans at Mountain Meadows, but those who killed Republicans at Colfax had not disarmed their victims or promised them safety. High on the list of reasons for such massacres appear fear and hatred of domestic minorities, of other religions, and of people the aggressors consider alien—the other. As an ethnic or religious minority like the Armenians, Bosnians, Jews, and African Americans, the Mormons, who were not Protestants, suffered murder, rape, and expulsion at the hands of a Euro-American Protestant majority who hated and feared them.

Brigham Young and the Mormons lived in a constitutional republic that was supposed to guarantee the free exercise of religion and prohibit religious establishment. No constitution is self-enforcing, however, and most national and state leaders opposed the protection of a despised minority. Catholics, Jews, Masons, and Mormons suffered the wrath of America's Protestant majority. As southern Utah militiamen massacred Arkansas emigrants at Mountain Meadows, the U.S. Army marched on Utah with officers and men who trumpeted their hatred for the Mormons and who openly boasted of their intention to punish or kill them. In response, Brigham Young declared martial law and confronted the army with guerrilla tactics. Given the wartime conditions, the massacre seems at least in part a fearful and angry response by Mormons to the anticipated violence against themselves.

Authors Sally Denton and William Wise have argued that something as heinous as the Mountain Meadows massacre could never have occurred without Young's approval. We have seen, however, that in the Walker and Tintic wars and the Reformation, commanders in the field and Utah townspeople committed murders and massacres without Young's approval and, in some cases, against his express orders.

Will Bagley is undoubtedly right in believing that part of the motivation for the Mountain Meadows massacre included both a desire for retribution for the blood of the prophets and the use of Indian allies to conduct military campaigns. The known facts provide ample evidence of the culpability of Isaac Haight for the assault, but they do not provide such evidence for Brigham Young.

In addition, we have the contradictory assertions of John D. Lee or his attorney and editor, W. W. Bishop. Throughout the years following the massacre and, indeed, until late in the effort to convict him in the 1870s, Lee insisted—often in vigorous confrontations with others—that Young had not ordered the massacre. After Lee's capture and indictment, federal prosecutors offered him leniency if he implicated Young and other senior church officials, but he refused to do so, even though Young had engineered Lee's excommunication in 1870. In Lee's later confession to U.S. Attorney Sumner Howard, he testified that he had "considered" that Young had ordered the massacre. We do not know if it was Lee or Bishop who wrote in *Mormonism Unveiled: The Life and Confession of John D. Lee, Including the Life of Brigham Young*, "I now believe that he [George A. Smith] was sent for that purpose [murdering the Baker-Fancher party] by the direct command of Brigham Young." Lee had written a manuscript while in prison and gave it to Bishop in partial payment for his legal services. Lee's original manuscript has not survived. Nevertheless Bagley, Wise, and Denton believe that Lee's public statements mutated from absolute belief that Young was not guilty to an absolute belief he commanded the massacre. Yet as I read the evidence, a juror would have more than a reasonable doubt about whether Young ordered the massacre or whether Lee even believed he actually did.

Moreover, historian Chad Orton has made an extensive textual analysis of *Mormonism Unveiled* and of supposed newspaper reports of Lee's last words at Mountain Meadows. His work has demonstrated beyond a reasonable doubt that W. W. Bishop and various associates and editors altered Lee's words, inserting additional material into statements and texts allegedly written or quoted from Lee. Also, he shows that many of the passages in *Mormonism Unveiled* contradict each other, and some passages are favorable to Young and other LDS leaders.

On the other hand, we have more than enough evidence from available sources to convict Isaac C. Haight, the commander who sent Lee and the militia to kill the Arkansans. If Brigham Young had ordered the massacre and exercised the sort of theocratic authority that his critics believe he had, why did not Haight and Dame simply tell the church members and militiamen in southern Utah that Young had ordered the massacre? Instead, Haight sent out Lee, then backtracked because of counter pressure in the Cedar City High Council. He sent out Clewes to tell Lee to stand down, and he sent Haslam to find out what Young wanted them to do. The high councils in Cedar City and Parowan vetoed the massacre, but Haight pressured Dame into to authorizing him to move ahead with plans he had already put in motion to murder the emigrants.

Haight and Dame visited the massacre site on Saturday, September 12. The number of dead appalled Dame, and he argued with Haight about how to report the massacre to Brigham Young. Haight insisted that Dame shared responsibility. As far as we know, neither of them spoke of Brigham Young's culpability. After some discussion and a lengthy wait, Haight sent Lee north to report the horrible deed to Brigham Young as an Indian massacre. Ultimately, Brigham Young punished two men for the crime. In 1870, at Young's instigation, the church excommunicated Haight and Lee. For some unknown reason, Young reinstated Haight within four years. Perhaps to comfort Lee family descendants, church leaders reinstated him posthumously in 1961. Even though the Cedar City militia had committed the massacre, in a gesture of genuine reconciliation, the church leadership participated in the dedication of a monument to the massacre victims at Mountain Meadows in 1999.

A federal grand jury indicted nine men for the massacre: William Dame, Isaac Haight, John Higbee, Philip Klingensmith, John D. Lee, William Stewart, George Adair, Samuel Jewkes, and Ellot Willden. Klingensmith turned state's evidence, and the federal prosecutors could not gather enough evidence to try Adair, Dame, Jewkes, or Willden, whom they captured. Haight, who was most responsible for the massacre, Higbee who gave the order to massacre the emigrants, and Stewart, who killed William A. Aden, escaped capture and trial.

In the end, the law punished only one person for all the murders. Abandoning an oath to remain silent, some of the militiamen tried to clear their consciences by revealing the names of local participants. Superintendent of Indian Affairs Jacob Forney, Maj. James H. Carleton, and Judge John Cradlebaugh all investigated the massacre, and federal officials searched without success for the other murderers. Captured in Panguitch in November 1874, John D. Lee sat through two trials, the first of which ended in a hung jury. The only person convicted of a crime for which more than fifty Euro-Americans and a small number of Paiutes also bore guilt, Lee died before a firing squad at Mountain Meadows on March 23, 1877. In dying, Lee suffered for his own sins and the sins of others: Iron County militiamen, Paiutes, and Isaac Haight, who bears the greatest responsibility for the massacre.

In the immediate aftermath of the massacre, Young searched for a place of refuge to protect his people from the advancing army. He had visited Mormon settlers at Fort Limhi, Oregon Territory (present-day Idaho). That site proved untenable when the Bannocks and Shoshones, with the connivance of some mountain men and possibly of army civilian scout Benjamin Ficklin, killed two Mormons, wounded five, and drove the remainder away. Young did not like the site anyway because he considered it too distant. He considered the Bitterroot Valley in today's Montana, but the large number of Indian tribes and mountain men there made it unattractive. He negotiated in a desultory way with promoters who wanted the Mormons to move to the Mosquito Coast of Nicaragua, expecting that the United States would annex the region if the Mormons moved there. He sent a party under William Dame to investigate the White Mountains of western Utah (present-day Nevada), but ultimately, he rejected all of these options and instead ordered an expensive and Move South from Salt Lake to Provo.

Meanwhile, Utahns remained on a wartime footing, dreading the spring thaws that would clear the road into their communities. In September 1857, as the entrenched Fanchers awaited their fate at Mountain Meadows, Capt. Stewart Van Vliet, quartermaster of the approaching army, arrived in Salt Lake City to buy supplies.

Seeing the preparations for war firsthand and learning of the determination of the Mormon people and leaders to resist the army, Van Vliet found also that he could expect little succor from the Utahns. Young did offer to send the army some lumber, but that was clearly not what they needed most. Young later sent a supply of salt to Camp Scott, but Colonel Johnston refused to accept it.

As both the army and the Utah militia sought refuge from the winter storms of 1857–58, events on the East Coast lay the groundwork for a resolution. During early 1857 Thomas L. Kane, who had previously interceded for the Mormons, had been devastated by the death of his brother, Elisha Kent Kane, a noted Arctic explorer. Plunging into depression after Elisha's funeral on March 12, Thomas Kane could do little more than try to influence Buchanan and Attorney General Jeremiah Black through correspondence that they should wait to appoint a replacement for Young. He was not successful. Although Kane's father knew the president, Kane himself was not close to Buchanan, and the two of them belonged to different factions of the Pennsylvania Democratic Party.

Still, in view of the seriousness of the conflict, Kane approached Buchanan in November 1857. He had received correspondence from Samuel Richards, a Mormon whom Young had sent to meet with Kane, and from Brigham Young himself, warning that Buchanan intended to "hang, shoot, burn, debauch, lay waste, drive and destroy us as in times past." Through the good offices of James C. Van Dyke of Philadelphia, one of Buchanan's closest advisors, Kane met with a skeptical Buchanan. After a lengthy discussion, as historian Matthew Grow has noted in his studies of Thomas Kane, Buchanan offered Kane an official appointment, which he declined. In correspondence of December 31, 1857, Buchanan praised Kane's "philanthropy," but made clear that if he traveled to Utah, he went without official sanction.

Kane traveled pseudonymously as botanist Dr. Anthony Osborne, a name he adopted from an African American servant. His travels took him to central America, across the Isthmus of Panama, then to California and by the southern route to Salt Lake City. For part of the overland journey, he traveled as William MacKinnon has shown with the assistance of several Mormon women, and, as Leo Lyman has shown, the help of Elder Amasa Lyman of the Twelve.

Reaching Salt Lake City on February 25, 1858, Kane met with the church presidency and the Twelve, then with Young alone. After some argument, Young agreed that Kane should "go to the" army under the influence of "the spirit" and "all would be right." On March 8, 1858, Kane left for Camp Scott in the company of Mormon scouts. To try to influence the government officials and the military, Kane devised the fiction that the Mormon leadership consisted of a peace party led by Brigham Young and a war party, with a vague unspecified leadership. As Kane left Salt Lake, Brigham Young learned of the attack on Fort Limhi, which destroyed any possibility of using the fort as a way station for a Mormon escape. He hurriedly sent a dispatch to Kane offering cattle and flour to the army, which Johnston rejected, as he had the salt Young had sent in November. Young now clearly hoped for peace rather than war.

After arriving at Camp Scott, Kane met with Johnston and then with the newly appointed territorial governor, Alfred Cumming. One of Johnston's soldiers arrested Kane, and Kane challenged Johnston to a duel. The two abandoned the duel, but from then on they carried a razor-sharp dislike for one another. Kane had better luck with Cumming. After a number of discussions, Kane convinced the new governor to accompany him to Salt Lake City without the army. Shunning and verbally condemning the opposition of Johnston, his officers, and most of the federal officials, the two left Camp Scott on April 5, 1858, under the protection of Mormon militiamen. Arriving in Salt Lake City a week later, Kane and Cumming occupied rooms at William Staines's mansion on South Temple on April 12.

Cumming was greeted as Utah's governor by the militia escort, Brigham Young, and the Mormon leadership, but he encountered skepticism among the people. Nevertheless, Kane's ploy of fabricating a peace party headed by Young and an anonymous war party worked exceedingly well. Kane told Young that "he had caught the fish, now you can cook it as you have a mind to." Contrary to Judge William W. Drummond's lie, Cumming found the territorial law library, the papers of the district court, and the court seal intact and well preserved. In letters to Secretary of State Lewis Cass and House Speaker James L. Orr, drafted by Kane and signed by Cumming, the new governor confirmed as lies some of the most prominent charges that federal officials had lodged against Young and the Mormons. Cumming also tried to dissuade Young and the Mormons from abandoning Salt Lake City and moving south.

In a speech in the tabernacle, Cumming emphasized his wish to help those who wanted to leave Utah. In response, Young said that he had told them "that we would help you away. If there are any such here who want protection at the hands of Governor Cumming, men or women, will you have the kindness to be manly enough, to manifest it here. Four people raised their hands." During 1858 and 1859, more than 230 dissatisfied Utahns left the territory. Contrary to the assertions of a bevy of federal office holders, Cumming found no one abused or detained by the Mormons.

In a study of the reasons that people left and the barriers to their leaving Utah, Polly Aird found a number of both. Although Brigham Young encouraged those to go who wanted to leave, some local leaders made it difficult for them to leave. Poverty and debt prevented some dissenters from leaving, many of whom owed money to the Perpetual Emigrating Fund. According to James Linforth, one of those who left, however, "the chief fault expressed . . . was 'no work and no provisions [in Utah].'" In a study of seven defectors, Aird found each had more than one reason for leaving, including a desire to seek a better life, disillusionment with Utah conditions, lack of freedom of thought, loss of confidence in church leaders, the Mormon Reformation, the Mountain Meadows massacre, and fear.

Kane and Cumming remained on the Wasatch Front until May 13, when they departed with a Mormon militia escort for Camp Scott. On May 5 Young had broken the news to Kane of the death in February of his father, Judge John K. Kane. Young had known of the death since April 24. The news devastated Thomas Kane, and hastened his decision to return to Philadelphia, escorted by Maj. Howard Egan.

In the meantime, Buchanan had sent official commissioners Lazarus W. Powell, senator elect and former governor of Kentucky, and Maj. Ben McCulloch, a former Texas Ranger and U.S. marshal to whom Buchanan had previously offered Utah's governorship. They met with Cumming at Camp Scott before departing for Salt Lake City, where they arrived on June 7.

Buchanan had sent the commissioners with a two-part peace proclamation. Part one reiterated the charges lodged by federal officials, largely by repeating Drummond's lies. Buchanan's proclamation provided no specific examples for most of them, except those that "the records of the courts have been seized and either destroyed or concealed," and "They have organized an armed force" and "a train of baggage wagons, . . . was attacked and destroyed by a portion of the Mormon forces." The first charge was false because the records remained in the possession of the clerk of the U.S. courts. The last charge was undoubtedly true, although George A. Smith opined that the document contained forty-two lies overall.

Part two of the document offered an unconditional pardon for treason and other offenses. Buchanan instructed the commissioners that the Mormons must either accept or reject the whole document as it stood, a provision that the commissioners insisted upon. Young and the Mormons tried to negotiate, but Powell and McCulloch rebuffed them at every point. They had no authority, they insisted, to negotiate the terms, only to offer "a free and full pardon to all who will submit themselves to the authority of the federal government." Young feared political slavery, but salved his conscience by accepting with the comment: "If a man comes from the moon and says he will pardon me for kicking him in the moon yesterday, I don't care about it; I'll accept of his pardon."

With that, the army marched through a nearly deserted city on June 26. The soldiers camped west of the Jordan River and proceeded to Cedar Valley, where they established Camp Floyd, named after Secretary of War John Floyd. The camp was the largest military installation in the United States at the time.

The Utah War was not a bloodless conflict, as it sometimes has been represented. The worst atrocity during the war occurred at Mountain Meadows. Other murders included the death of Richard E. Yates, a mountain man–trader who sold munitions to the army and whom the Mormons considered a spy. The Nauvoo Legion captured him close to Fort Bridger in mid-October 1857, and the notorious murderer and thief William A. Hickman admitted killing Yates after capturing him. Hickman insisted that Brigham Young had ordered the murder through his son, Joseph A. Young, but in a newspaper interview, Joseph Young denied telling Hickman to commit the murder. Daniel Wells and Daniel Jones supported Joseph Young's version of the events, and Brigham Young insisted that he had ordered Hickman to release Yates. By the time Hickman published his confession and gave a newspaper interview implicating Young, the church had excommunicated him, and he had begun working for Patrick Edward Connor, who hated the Mormons. An illegal grand jury empaneled by Judge James B. McKean indicted Daniel H. Wells, Hosea Stout, Brigham Young, and Hickman for the murder, but the U.S. Supreme Court ordered the indictments dismissed.

Part of the problem in assessing Young's complicity is Hickman's previous association with Young. Young had recommended Hickman for an appointment as U.S. attorney, and Hickman had worked for the Y.X. company. Young had also secured Hickman's help in impugning Judge Drummond's character, and the Mormon leader had offered to pay some of Hickman's personal debts. Hickman insisted that he had not benefited from the murder, but a witness saw him wearing Yates's overcoat and riding Yates's horse through Springville.

Other disputed murders include those of the six members of a party headed by John and William Aiken. Part of the party died on the Sevier River about twenty-five miles south of Nephi. Porter Rockwell and Sylvanus Collett may have murdered the Aiken party. David Bigler believes that Brigham Young ordered the murders but offers no evidence, only his own supposition. Rockwell died before he could be tried, and Collett may have been acquitted through perjured testimony.

Other murders took place as well. Army deserter Pvt. George W. Clark was hanged either by mountaineers or Mormons near the Smith Fork of the Green River. Henry Forbes died on the road between Springville and Provo at the hands of unknown assailants. As Ardis Parshall has shown, an attack on John Tobin, John Peltro, and two companions took place on the Santa Clara River on the mistaken belief that they were accused thieves John Ambrose and Thomas Betts. Mormons carried out a number of these affairs, including the murder of the Aiken party, the killing of Forbes, and the attack on the Tobin-Peltro party. It is unclear, however, whether Brigham Young bears responsibility for any of them except the mistaken attack on the Tobin-Peltro party, because in the letter he ordered the pursuit of Ambrose and Betts.

The army itself may bear some responsibility for the mayhem. Johnston had sent Benjamin F. Ficklin to secure horses in Oregon Territory, and there is some evidence that he encouraged Bannocks and Northern Shoshones to attack the Mormon fort. The attack killed two of the Mormon settlers. Just as the Mormons recruited Paiute allies in their attack at Mountain Meadows, Johnston authorized Indian agent Garland Hurt to recruit Uintah Utes to fight against the Mormons. Hurt may have failed, though Brigham Young believed he succeeded.

Could the United States and the Mormons have avoided the war and its consequences? The Utah war proved to be a tragedy of unimaginable magnitude, but only in counterfactual history could it have been avoided. William MacKinnon believes that a conference between Buchanan and Young or Young and Cass might have prevented the war. Historian and Brigham Young biographer John Turner suggests that instead of sending an army without an investigation, Buchanan might have dispatched representatives to discuss the charges with Young and the Mormon leadership. In such a discussion, Young might have admitted that republican theodemocracy was no longer compatible with American democratic republicanism. In counterfactual history, Thomas Kane and John Bernhisel might have met with Buchanan to clarify the issues. Rooting through the charges might have refuted most of Drummond's allegations and shown that Young could not control the Indians. An early probe might have revealed the massive fraud perpetrated by the surveyors under David Burr's supervision and raised questions about the motivation behind his charges. On the other hand, an investigation might have corroborated Judge John F. Kinney's complaints that the jury in Nephi refused to follow his instructions in the trial of Pahvants accused of murdering Gunnison, but it might also have revealed why the jury rendered such a verdict.

Unfortunately, counterfactual history is not actual history. I would argue that in spite of Buchanan's protestations, anti-Mormonism factored into the decision to delay an investigation until the new federal officials with their military escort had reached Utah. After all, Congress conducted an investigation in Kansas more than a year before preparation for the Utah Expedition. In spite of Buchanan's insistence that the government paid no attention to religion, it is telling that the president applied "popular sovereignty" to Kansas but not to Utah. Religion undoubtedly played a role in other ways. The roster of new federal officials Buchanan appointed included no Mormons. Moreover, Hosea Stout was the only Mormon appointed to a prominent federal position between 1857 and 1890—by Abraham Lincoln. Religion played a role with the army and some of the new officials, since some members of the expeditionary force threatened to kill the Mormons, and various federal officials expected to exact retribution against the Mormons and their leaders as well. Judge Delana R. Eckels proposed to indict Mormon leaders for practicing polygamy, but the grand jury he empaneled at Fort Scott refused to return such indictments.

In actual history, the Buchanan administration relied entirely on the reports from federal officials and interested private parties who harbored deep antagonism to Young and the Mormons. Buchanan and his advisors discounted the explanation of conditions in Utah by Mormons and their supporters. Kane's letters to officials in Washington sent early in 1857 were either ignored or not received. Personal concerns, especially his brother Elisha's death in Cuba in mid-February and his delayed funeral in Philadelphia, left him at least in despair and probably in clinical depression. For whatever reason, he could not offer a timely response as events unfolded as he had with the runaways. Kane did not speak directly with Buchanan until the army had already reached Utah Territory. Bernhisel, who had played a critical role in the affair of the runaway officials, had left Washington and could not represent an alternative viewpoint until he returned—after the administration had already dispatched the army.

Although treasonous, the Mormon response to Buchanan's army was understandable. Brigham Young had witnessed the expulsion of Mormons from their homes, the rape of Mormon women, and the deaths of hundreds twice in Missouri and again in Illinois. As a responsible leader, Young could not stand idly by while another army marched against his people, especially when he believed the soldiers planned to kill him and other Mormons. Tragically, scores of people died in the war, most of them at the hands of Mormons. Thousands of dollars' worth of goods perished, also at the hands of Mormons. Moreover, Mormons died at Fort Limhi.

To end the conflict, at Buchanan's initiative, but largely because of the efforts of Kane and Cumming and the response of Young and the Latter-day Saints to their work, the Mormons received a full pardon for their activities in opposing the army. Unfortunately, as we will see in the next chapter, although many of the federal officials acknowledged Buchanan's pardon as official policy, others refused to do so and instead strived to work against the interests of justice and the Mormon people.

The Kirtland Temple. *PH 725.*
Courtesy of the Church History Library, Salt Lake City, Utah.

Mary Ann Angell Young (1803–1882). *(Opposite, top)*
Savage and Ottinger, photographer, PH 1716.
Courtesy of the Church History Library, Salt Lake City, Utah.

Heber Chase Kimball (1801–1868). *(Opposite, middle)*
Savage and Ottinger studio portrait, PH 200.
Courtesy of the Church History Library, Salt Lake City, Utah.

Willard Richards (1804–1854). *(Opposite, botom)*
PH 327. Courtesy of the Church History Library, Salt Lake City, Utah.

Jedediah M. Grant (1816–1856). *(Top)*
PH 327. Courtesy of the Church History Library, Salt Lake City, Utah.

George A. Smith (1817–1875). *(Bottom)*
Daguerreotype, PH 100. Courtesy of the Church History Library, Salt Lake City, Utah.

Nauvoo Temple.
Louis Rice Chaffin daguerreotype.
Used by permission, Utah State Archives.

Eliza Roxcy Snow (1804–1887). *(Top, left)*
Savage and Ottinger portrait, PH 200.
Courtesy of the Church History Library, Salt Lake City, Utah.

Zina Diantha Huntington Young (1821–1901). *(Top, right)*
PH 327. Courtesy of the Church History Library, Salt Lake City, Utah.

John Taylor (1808–1887). *(Bottom)*
PH 6248, Box 1, Folder 40. Courtesy of the Church History Library, Salt Lake City, Utah

Wilford Woodruff (1807–1898). *(Top)*
PH 6821. Courtesy of the Church History Library, Salt Lake City, Utah.

Daniel H. Wells (1814–1891). *(Bottom, left)*
Savage and Ottinger, photographer, PH 1716.
Courtesy of the Church History Library, Salt Lake City, Utah.

Lorenzo Snow (1814–1901). *PH 6248. (Bottom, right)*
Courtesy of the Church History Library, Salt Lake City, Utah.

Orson Pratt (1811–1881).
Savage and Ottinger, photographer, PH 1716.
Courtesy of the Church History Library, Salt Lake City, Utah.

Amasa Mason Lyman (1813–1877). *(Top)*
PH200, Savage and Ottinger studio portrait.
Courtesy of the Church History Library, Salt Lake City, Utah.

John M. Bernhisel (1799–1881). *(Bottom)*
PH 327. Courtesy of the Church History Library, Salt Lake City, Utah.

The Sons of John and Abigail (Nabby) Howe Young. (*left to right*) Lorenzo Dow (1807–1895), Brigham (1801–1877), Phinehas Howe (1799–1879), Joseph (1797–1881), John Jr. (1791–1870).
PH 200. Courtesy of the Church History Library, Salt Lake City, Utah.

Brigham Young's Properties, South Temple, Salt Lake City. (*left to right*) Lion House, Office, Beehive House.
PH 499. Courtesy of the Church History Library, Salt Lake City, Utah.

Brigham Young.
Savage and Ottinger, photographer, PH 1716.
Courtesy of the Church History Library, Salt Lake City, Utah.

Chiefs Walkara and Arapeen,
from a portrait by Solomon Nunes Carvalho.
PH 1700. Courtesy of the Church History Library, Salt Lake City, Utah.

Party of Pahvant Utes. Kanosh is the
second from the right in the front row.
PH 200. Courtesy of the Church History Library, Salt Lake City, Utah.

John D. Lee (1812–1877).
James Fennemore, photographer, PH 1700.
Courtesy of the Church History Library, Salt Lake City, Utah.

Thomas L. Kane (1822–1883). *(Opposite, top)*
PH 327. Courtesy of the Church History Library, Salt Lake City, Utah.

Alfred Cumming (1802–1873). *(Opposite, middle)*
PH 327. Courtesy of the Church History Library, Salt Lake City, Utah.

Patrick Edward Connor (1820–1891). *(Opposite, bottom)*
James M. Hardie photograph, PH 200.
Courtesy of the Church History Library, Salt Lake City, Utah.

The St. George Temple.
PH 500. Courtesy of the Church History Library, Salt Lake City, Utah.

The Salt Lake Theater.

Charles R. Savage photograph, PH 499.
Courtesy of the Church History Library, Salt Lake City, Utah.

7

Investigation

Shortly after the Mountain Meadows massacre occurred, Brigham Young began to hear of massive bloody killings in southern Utah. The earliest reports blamed the slaughter on the Paiutes. On September 20, 1857, Ute chief Arapeen told Young "that the Piedes had killd the whole of a Emigrant company & took all of their stock & it was right[.]" On September 28 Leo Hawkins in the Church Historian's Office recorded that "reports reached town that the companies of Cala Emigrants" consisting of "100 men & 1000" cattle "were all used up by the Indians" at Mountain Meadows. Young received a letter dated September 30 from George W. Armstrong, Indian agent at the Spanish Fork Indian Farm, also blaming the Indians.

On September 29, 1857, John D. Lee told a similar story to Young and Wilford Woodruff. Young arrived at his office at 7 A.M., and Lee came in later in the morning. Because Haight and Lee had waited so long before informing Young of the massacre, they agreed to date the massacre two weeks after the event. Lee's report, which Woodruff recorded in his diary, blamed the Paiutes, and it included the half truths and downright falsehoods that became part of the massacre's folklore. These included verbal attacks on church leaders by Baker-Fancher party members that may well have taken place, and a number of fabrications, including Indians eating poisoned beef, the Arkansans poisoning the water at Corn Creek, and the party's women being cursed with venereal disease. When he told Young the Indians had slit the throats of women and children, Lee remembered Brigham saying, "it was heart rending," and replying that emigration must stop. Lee tried to justify the massacre by insisting that the Indians had shed not a drop of innocent blood. The story so sickened Young that, Lee wrote, the church president "wept like a child. . . . He said this transaction will bring sorrow and trouble upon us in Utah. I would to God it had never happened." After hearing Lee's story, at eleven o'clock that morning Young had his driver take him to his upper mill at the mouth of Parley's canyon, most likely to recuperate, "his health being feeble."

It seems clear that after reflecting on the horrors of September 11 and learning of Young's disapproval from the message Haslam gave to Haight, Haight and Lee misread Young's reaction to the report. Haight and Dame had argued about how to report the massacre, finally agreeing to tell Young it was an Indian massacre. Taking all of this into consideration, Haight and Lee tried to cover themselves by lying to the prophet.

In December 1857 and January 1858, relying on the reports he had received, Young repeated the story of an Indian massacre as told by Arapeen, Lee, and Armstrong in letters to church members in Southern California, to the commissioner of Indian Affairs, James Denver, and to others. Perhaps trying to cover himself, Lee insisted in 1870 that he had told Young the truth except for "one thing": that he had assumed responsibility for the massacre himself. In his journal written at the time of Lee's report and in an 1882 affidavit, however, Wilford Woodruff recorded that Lee had laid the entire blame on the Indians and had taken credit for leading a party to bury the dead.

Word soon reached Young that non-Mormons blamed him and the Mormons. Various Californians said "the Mormons" had killed the emigrants. Judge John Cradlebaugh, appointed U.S. associate justice for the district of Utah in June 1858, and Maj. James

Carleton, who made one of the first investigations of the site and whose command buried some of the dead in May 1859, also blamed Young. Carleton even urged the extermination of all the Mormons, not just the ones guilty of the massacre. Young most likely dismissed the charges by anti-Mormons, Cradlebaugh, and Carleton.

Soon, however, reliable reports began to filter in. On December 4, 1857, Indian agent Garland Hurt wrote on the basis of messages from Utes that the Paiutes and Mormons had perpetrated the massacre. Hurt heard that Lee had urged the Paiutes to participate. Hurt's incomplete version received further clarification from Utah's superintendent of Indian Affairs, Jacob Forney. Forney, who was often friendly with the Latter-day Saints, wrote reports in May and August 1859 based on his visit to southern Utah and on having spoken with John D. Lee and others. Like Hurt, Forney blamed a group of southern Utah militiamen and Paiutes rather than Brigham Young.

By late June 1858 Young knew that Mormons had helped commit the murders, although he probably did not know the full extent of their involvement. Jacob Hamblin related on June 20 to Brigham Young and George Smith regarding a conversation with Lee about the massacre, but that report would have left Young with incomplete information on the extent of the involvement of Mormons in the massacre. Hamblin's report corroborated part of Hurt's and Forney's stories. Much later, on November 13, 1871, Hamblin wrote a report to Young, and he filed an affidavit on November 28, 1871.

In the report and the two documents, Hamblin said that he had met Lee near Fillmore on September 24, 1857, as Lee came north to report to Young. He later learned further information that incensed him. Hamblin said Lee told him that he and "the Indians had commenced" the attack. Lee said that some "brethren" participated and the "immigrants were all wiped out excepting a few children." When Hamblin asked why, Lee said, "They were enemies to us, and that this was the beginning of great and important events." The massacre, Lee said, was necessary to protect "the lives of the Brethren." In Lee's second trial in 1877, Hamblin testified that Lee had told him that he had killed a woman. In a conversation with Hamblin, William Dame also justified the massacre just as Lee had. Such justifications outraged Hamblin, and he told his wife, Rachel, that the massacre was one of the worst disasters in church history and that neither Young nor the church leadership had approved of them.

After hearing Hamblin's report, Young told him to keep the information confidential for the present. He said they would soon get a "court of justice" to investigate the massacre and reveal the truth. Subsequently, Hamblin often described the murders as an Indian massacre, probably to obey Young's request.

After hearing Hamblin's report, and anticipating the need to follow up and obtain further information, Young sent apostles George A. Smith and Amasa M. Lyman to investigate. Leaving on July 15, 1858, Smith and Lyman reached the massacre site on July 29. Massacre participants led them through the area, carefully obscuring their involvement. The sight of scattered bones and decomposing corpses filled the two apostles with revulsion, as it had others. After visiting towns in southern Utah, they returned to Cedar City on August 6.

On August 6 in Cedar City, Smith and *Deseret News* reporter James McKnight wrote a report to the Church Historian's Office that repeated the story told by the massacre participants who had duped the apostles as they guided them through the area. This report blamed the massacre on Paiutes and dated the massacre September 21 through 25, 1857, the dates that Haight and Lee had concocted to explain Lee's belated report to Brigham Young. After returning to Salt Lake, Smith endorsed the document with the comment: "This statement is doubtless incorrect as to the dates, as the massacre must have occurred earlier in the month, say about fifteen days." Young, who probably never saw the document, did not endorse it.

Continuing under Young's direction, Smith and Lyman traveled to Parowan, where they stayed from August 8 through 12. They summoned Isaac Haight, John Higbee, Nephi Johnson, and Samuel White from Cedar City to testify. On August 9 Smith and Lyman heard charges against Dame for ordering the assault on William

Leany. Dame managed to deflect guilt from himself by diverting the discussion to his efforts to save the Turner-Dukes party from a Pahvant attack at Beaver even as the massacre occurred. The Turner-Dukes were the first emigrants that traveled through southern Utah after the Baker-Fanchers. The Pahvants had attacked the party because of deaths from what was probably anthrax, and they tried to avenge themselves by attacking the Turner-Dukes train. The Indians clearly did not understand that cattle rather than the emigrants had carried anthrax.

In Parowan, Smith and Lyman heard evidence that Lee and other Mormon militiamen had probably been at Mountain Meadows during the massacre. Lyman returned to Cedar City, but Smith remained in Parowan until August 17, when he wrote to Brigham Young with some findings from the second investigation. Smith and Lyman had learned that the massacre took place from September 6 through 11 rather than the 21st through the 25th.

The August 6 message described the massacre as "The Emigrant and Indian War," but Smith's August 17 report called it "the horrible massacre at the Mountain Meadows." On August 6, when Smith believed the Haight-Lee version, he thought the Indians had sought revenge for "the death of several" of their tribe. The August 17 report detailed the stories participants had told to justify the violence at Mountain Meadows. The report mentioned conflicts at Fillmore and the threats from the Arkansans to return to Utah from California to attack the Mormons, both of which were true. It also contained descriptions of the death of Proctor Robinson, which occurred after the Arkansans had left, as well as fabricated reports of events that did not take place, such as poisoned springs at Corn Creek south of Fillmore, where Smith and Hamblin had seen the Baker-Fancher party.

As much as they had learned, Smith and Lyman were still in the dark on many details. Haight seems to have deflected blame from himself by placing Lee and unnamed others at the scene of the massacre, as Lee had told Hamblin, rather than afterward, as Lee had told Young and Woodruff. Reflecting Haight's explanation, Smith's August 17 report said, "John D. Lee and a few other white men were" at the meadows "during a portion of the combat." Smith conceded his information was still incomplete, and he backed away from his previous statement, saying he had not determined why they were there, "or how they conducted, or whether indeed they were there at all" for what he still thought was a Paiute massacre. Why Smith doubted that militiamen were at Mountain Meadows is unclear because Hamblin had already placed Lee and other "brethren" at the massacre site. Perhaps he just could not believe it, or he may have wanted further corroboration.

Whatever the case, the lack of information, Smith's reluctance to place the blame where it belonged, and the inconsistencies in the Lee, Arapeen, Armstrong, Hurt, Haight, and Hamblin versions necessitated further investigation. Traveling north from Parowan, Lyman and Smith met in Beaver with apostles Charles C. Rich and Erastus Snow on August 18. Rich and Snow had come to southern Utah to collect Deseret scrip, a paper currency the church had issued, but they agreed to assist Lyman in continuing the investigation. Smith continued northward the next day, and Lyman, Rich, and Snow traveled from Beaver to Cedar City and Harmony.

On August 23 the three apostles took Lee from Harmony to Cedar City to further their examination of the conditions surrounding the massacre and problems in the city. On the 23rd and 24th, they "held [what Lee called] a council of inquiry in relation to many complaints made against" Haight and Klingensmith. In a misdated journal entry, Lee wrote that he "was also accusd of having used an influence against Pres. Haight but was exhoneratd from the charge." Lee also wrote that the three apostles reproved the stake president and bishop and "told the People that they were at liberty to remove to any settlement where they thought that they could better their condition." Although Lee wrote in his diary that he felt exonerated, his employee, Marion Jackson Shelton, wrote that the "inquisition" at Cedar City upset Lee. The entries in Lee's diary from August 6 through September 15 are garbled with many dates missing.

By late summer 1858, the apostles had reported to Young, and the information they gathered led him to believe that an official investigation could result in court trials of the participants. But Young now held no governmental post, so he could only ask the federal appointees to cooperate with him. He could conduct his own investigation, but he could not require federal officials to assist him.

In view of the intense anti-Mormonism of some federal appointees, it is unclear just how serious President Buchanan was about his assertion that religion had nothing to do with his Utah policy, but Jacob Forney, along with a party of moderates that included Governor Alfred Cumming and U.S. Attorney Alexander Wilson, tried to ignore religion in their effort to bring the perpetrators to justice. Anti-Mormon federal officials that Forney labeled as "Ultras" included the federal judges Delana Eckels, John Cradlebaugh, and Charles E. Sinclair; U.S. Marshal Peter Dotson; Bvt. Brig. Gen. Albert Johnston; and other army officers.

The Ultras showed their colors when Judge Cradlebaugh, who had arrived in Utah in November 1858, took a detachment of the Tenth Infantry from Camp Floyd with him to Provo in March and April 1859. Summoning Provo mayor B. K. Bullock and the community's civil and religious leaders to court, he summarily imprisoned them in the guard tent. Like Young and most of the Mormons, Provo citizens feared the army and protested Cradlebaugh's action. Instead of relenting, Cradlebaugh issued subpoenas for the arrest of numerous citizens from Springville, Spanish Fork, Nephi, and Pleasant Grove, including Bishop Aaron Johnson of Springville, who had ordered the Parrish-Potter murders and deserved to stand trial. A grand jury in 1859 issued indictments charging him with the murders.

Another Ultra, Marshal Dotson, with a force of two hundred soldiers, tried without success to find Johnson, who had secreted himself in the mountains. Searching for him, Dotson's soldiers invaded Johnson's house where they found the bishop's nine wives in bed—they had to retreat under a barrage of pillows and blankets the women threw at them. Johnson avoided capture and died in 1877, still a fugitive from justice. Undeterred by Johnson's escape, Cradlebaugh sent troops to Manti, American Fork, Sanpete, and Goshen to search for additional suspects.

In response to Cradlebaugh's actions, Nauvoo Legion commander Gen. Daniel H. Wells called out the militia to guard the roads from Camp Floyd, and Brigham Young drafted a petition to Governor Cumming that emphasized his fear of the army. Young said that such violence as that in Utah, Sanpete, and Juab Counties seemed to presage another massacre like the attack in Carthage that killed Joseph and Hyrum Smith, and he urged Cumming to act to preserve the peace. After all, the Mormons had capitulated and accepted Buchanan's amnesty proclamation with the expectation they would be treated like other American citizens. Instead, Cradlebaugh and the army had subjected them to military tyranny.

After his crusade in Provo, Cradlebaugh and a military contingent went south to Cedar City and the Mountain Meadows massacre site. The judge succeeded in interviewing some people with knowledge of the massacre before returning to Camp Floyd. He could not, however, bring any of the perpetrators to justice.

These and other conflicts between townspeople and the soldiers led Cumming to appeal to Washington to place the military under civilian control, and U.S. Attorney General Jeremiah Black issued orders to that effect, which the local papers published on June 29, 1859. But Cradlebaugh did not seem finished. He had returned to Camp Floyd with the soldiers on April 2, 1859, but he apparently still planned to use army support, a prospect that disturbed Young. Young still wanted an investigation, but he wanted it done without the army's involvement. On May 25 Young had told George A. Smith that "so soon as the present excitement subsided, and the army could be kept from interfering with the Judiciary, he intended to have all the [Mountain Meadow massacre] charges investigated." Young said he "would try to get the Governor & Dist. Atty. to go to Washington County, and manage the investigation of the Mountain Meadow Massacre, themselves."

Young also took steps to clear himself of any charges in connection with the massacre. In May 1859 Salt Lake County probate judge Elias Smith issued a warrant for Young's arrest, accusing him on the basis of Cradlebaugh's allegations with sending written and verbal messages that led to the massacre. When Young appeared voluntarily before Smith on May 12, he denied the charges and demanded a "fair and impartial" investigation and trial. Smith ordered county sheriff Robert T. Burton to arrest Young, which he did, but as Will Bagley noted, the charges may have been dismissed for lack of evidence. In any event, nothing came of them, and Young was released.

On June 18, 1859, Young met with George A. Smith and Jacob Hamblin to explain his expectations for the eventual prosecution of the perpetrators. He said he had urged those accused to come forward to stand trial, and if the federal judges conducted the trials impartially without military interference, Young said they should do so. In a March 8, 1863, sermon, Young said he had "told . . . Governor [Cumming] . . . that if he would take an unprejudiced judge into the district where that horrid affair occurred, I would pledge myself that every man . . . should be forthcoming . . . to be condemned or acquitted as an impartial . . . judge and jury should decide." Young promised to protect the court from "any violence or hindrance," and the guilty should "suffer the penalty of the law." In a hearsay statement published after Cumming's death, an unnamed informant said that the governor had accused Young of lying to him. Why Cumming would have said this is unclear. Young had tried to do as he said he would, but the Ultra officials thwarted him.

On July 5, 1859, after the public knew that Cumming would control the army, U.S. Attorney Wilson met with Young. Young told him "that if the judges would open a court at Parowan or some other convenient location in the south, . . . unprejudiced and uninfluenced by . . . the army, so that man could have a fair and impartial trial He would go there himself, and he presumed that Gov. Cumming would also go." Young "would use all his influence to have the parties arrested and have the whole . . . matter investigated thoroughly and impartially and justice meted out to every man." However, presumably referring to Cradlebaugh and the army in Provo, he said he would not exert himself "to arrest men to be treated like dogs and dragged about by the army, and confined and abused by them." Young said that if the judges and army treated people that way, the federal officials "must hunt them [the perpetrators] up themselves." Wilson agreed that it was unfair "to drag men and their witnesses 200 or 300 miles to trial." Young said, "the people wanted a fair and impartial court of justice, like they have in other states and territories, and if he had anything to do with it, the army must keep its place." Wilson said he believed "the proposition was reasonable and he would propose it to the judges." After talking with Wilson, Young met with George Smith, Albert Carrington, and James Ferguson to discuss the "reaction to the Mountain Meadow Massacre." Young reported that Wilson had called "to consult with him about making some arrests of" the accused.

In sermons, Young, Lyman, and Smith elaborated on doctrine emphasizing peace and brotherly love, and decried the shedding of blood. In a speech in the Tabernacle on May 22, 1859, Young said that although he was "accused of having great influence" with his people, "he would to God that he had influence sufficient to make every man that calls himself a Saint do right." Praising the American government, Young also spent time "admonishing the Saints to be faithful and patient and not to take judgment into their own hands, and by the help of the Lord, he would lead them to the fountain of light."

On June 15, 1859, Young repeated to George Smith and Jacob Hamblin the promise he had made to Alexander Wilson. He again sent Smith and Lyman south, this time to urge the accused to prepare for trial and to try to suppress Mormon-authored crime. The two apostles spoke in various cities, denouncing murder, blood atonement, and the stealing of gentile property. They preached against blood atonement, and, based on the fact that George Smith was very close to Young, they may have reflected Young's changing views on blood atonement, even though the church leadership did not officially repudiate the doctrine until 1889. When Smith and Lyman visited Parowan, even William Dame "called on all to keep the laws of the land as well as those of the church." Civil authorities, he said, should "suppress all fighting and other disturbances."

Acting on Young's instructions, Smith and Lyman shook up the leadership of the church in Cedar City on Sunday, July 31, 1859.

Smith "disorganized the Stake," releasing Philip Klingensmith, Samuel McMurdy, and John Morris from the bishopric and Isaac Haight, John Higbee, and Elias Morris from the stake presidency. In their place they called Henry Lunt, Richard Morris, and Thomas Jones, none of whom had participated in the massacre, as a combined bishopric-stake presidency.

Cedar City's plummeting population, according to Morris and Kathryn Shirts, "undoubtedly [contributed to] the decision to combine normally separate offices into one," but the massacre also contributed. Haight said he asked for a release because he expected to be hiding out—"In consequence of the persecution of our enemies." Klingensmith had not asked for a release, however, and all of the church officers except perhaps John Morris had planned or participated in the massacre. Still, the apostles told the massacre leaders to prepare for trial, and the perpetrators took the prospect of facing a judge and jury seriously. Sending a deed to his property in Cedar City as a retainer, Klingensmith wrote to Smith, asking that Smith and Hosea Stout defend him in the forthcoming "proceedings . . . against me in a case of alleged murder at the Mountain Meadows." A few days later, Lyman met with Lee on "special business." Again proclaiming his innocence, Lee nevertheless wrote to ask Smith and Stout to defend him if he were arrested "upon the charge of aiding in the Massacre at the Meadows." On September 11, 1859, Lee confided to his journal that the perpetrators could expect "neither Sucor, Simpany, or Pity" from the church leadership. Haight sent Smith a letter on October 17 asking Smith to serve as his attorney and transferring half ownership of his woolen factory to Smith as a retainer.

On August 6, 1859, U.S. Attorney Wilson asked Marshal Dotson to deputize territorial marshal John Kay to arrest massacre suspects in southern Utah. Wilson said Kay "was a Mormon, had a knowledge of the country and of the people, and expressed a determination, if legally deputized, to make arrests if possible." Wilson also told Dotson that Brigham Young had promised to cooperate. Wilson also knew that William H. Hooper, Utah's delegate to Congress and a prominent businessman, had offered to donate $1,500—more than $40,000 in 2017 dollars—to help finance the investigation and trials. Dotson refused "to appoint Kay his deputy," however, because Kay "was a Morm[o]n." Wilson asked Utah's Chief Justice Eckels to intercede with Dotson, but Eckels refused, asserting that Kay was "a notorious Mormon." Eckels said that accepting the church's help was acknowledging its power, writing, "I never will acknowledge a power . . . above the law." Clearly because of his anti-Mormonism, Eckels failed to acknowledge that Kay was territorial marshal, and that his rant about the church's power was irrelevant. Citizens had an obligation to cooperate with authorities to bring criminals to justice, and Kay was a territorial official who could assist the federal officers if Dotson gave him the authority. As a citizen, Young had offered help as well, which Eckels and Dotson shunned.

In what seems an exceedingly fruitless decision, instead of holding court in Parowan or Cedar City where Dotson and Wilson might have brought participants and witnesses to the court, Eckels held trials on August 22 in Nephi, 175 miles north of Cedar City over extremely rugged frontier roads. Eckels assembled most of his grand jurors from among camp followers from Camp Floyd, claiming that citizens of Utah County had fled before him. Although some had indeed departed, his district included Provo, the territory's second largest city, from which he could easily have empaneled jurors. Unable to attend court himself, Wilson sent Stephen DeWolfe to Nephi as prosecuting attorney. DeWolfe would later reveal himself to be a bitter anti-Mormon when he became editor of the *Valley Tan* in January 1860.

Even with a stacked jury and an anti-Mormon prosecutor, Eckels could obtain neither indictments against nor convictions of massacre participants. He complained of inadequate funding, neglecting to mention Hooper's offer to help defer court expenses or Brigham Young's and John Kay's endeavor to help the U.S. marshal because Kay was territorial marshal—a proposal made as a public service. DeWolfe, however, cited the main barrier to prosecution when he noted the distance between Nephi and the settlements south of Parowan "and the difficulty, if not impossibility, of bringing . . .

[witnesses] before the court [in faraway Nephi] in any reasonable time." Wilson agreed, and Cumming scolded the judges for their obsession with hounding "the leading men of the Mormon Church." Citing a list of those he believed most guilty—all from southern Utah—Forney complained of the judges' inaction, of the stupidity of publicly naming the suspects before trying to "catch them," and of refusing the help of Young, Kay, or Hooper.

Significantly, Eckels's prejudices did not signal the end of Brigham Young's willingness to bring the killers to justice. On September 2 Young met with Hooper as the latter was about to depart for Washington. He told Hooper that if someone asked him "why he had not brought the guilty parties to justice," he should answer that "if law and justice could take place no one could be more willing than he would be." Echoing Young's statements, the Mormon-controlled *Deseret News* attacked the federal judges for talking tough but refusing to act.

Still, Eckels reiterated his scorn for Mormon help. Writing to Secretary of State Lewis Cass, he defended his decision to hold court in Nephi instead of southern Utah, attacked the moderate federal officials, and asked again for army support. As for Young's attempt to help, he wrote that he believed a competent attorney "could show that Brigham Young directed the Mountain Meadow Massacre." He may have believed in Young's culpability, but he lacked verifiable evidence to support his supposition.

Cass sent a copy of Eckels's letter to Cumming to inquire about Eckels's complaints. The governor replied that contrary to anti-Mormon propaganda, he believed "Person's unbiased by prejudice" would agree that they had "seldom seen" a community "more marked by quiet and peaceable diligence, than that of the Mormons." Instead, he blamed the "hundreds of adventurers" who accompanied the army for the violence and theft then occurring in Utah.

By 1860 the church leadership knew that Lee had lied to Young and Woodruff, but the church president apparently still did not know everything. Young probably did not yet know of the large number of militiamen who participated in the massacre, and he may still have believed that Indians under Lee's command and a few other Mormons had murdered the emigrants. In addition, he may not have known that the militiamen who participated did so under church and military duress. Summarizing his understanding of murders committed in the territory, Young wrote his Methodist pastor friend, Hiram McKee, in May 1860 that the massacre was "far more repugnant to my feelings than I suppose it can be to yours." He added, "Indians and wicked [white] men" had committed the murders, although he may have been referring to violence in Utah generally rather than specifically to the massacre. But Young may also have been less than forthright even with a close friend like McKee. After he failed in his effort to secure cooperation from the Ultra federal officials to bring the perpetrators to justice, Young seems to have given up the efforts to induce the judges to convene trials. He may have done this in part because of the loud and long public denunciations calling him the author of the massacre.

It tests belief, however, that as late as 1861, Young still thought Baker-Fancher crimes had led to the massacre. Woodruff recorded that when he visited the massacre site with Young in May 1861, they noted the message—"Vengeance is mine; I will repay, saith the Lord"—on the cairn and cross Carleton had erected on the mass grave he had created the year before. Woodruff recorded that Young said the message should read, "Vengence is mine and I have taken a little." Later that same month, Young told John D. Lee that the emigrants "Meritd their fate, & the only thing that ever troubled him was the lives of the Women & children, but that under the circumstances [this] could not be avoided." Dudley Leavitt reported that Young ordered those with him to pull down Carleton's cross simply by raising his hand, but Edwin Purple, a non-Mormon businessman, recorded seeing the monument that spring, and John Turner argues that a massive flood may have destroyed the monument the following winter. Whatever the case, it may have been destroyed and rebuilt numerous times.

Young's comments in 1861 at the massacre site were clearly insensitive. His conclusion that the murdered men merited their fate and that the murder of women and children could not be avoided was unwarranted. Although he may not have known everything about the massacre by 1861, he did know enough from Jacob Hamblin's report to place Lee and some other "brethren" at the massacre site. He knew that Haight, Lee, Klingensmith, and Higbee bore some responsibility for the massacre, and he had tried two years before to make arrangements with federal authorities to bring them to court. As unlikely as it seems, Young must still have believed the stories of the murderous acts members of the Baker-Fancher party committed at Corn Creek.

By 1863 Apostle Erastus Snow, the principal leader in the southern Utah colonies, had found that the massacre had outraged the settlers in the Cotton Mission, virtually all of whom had settled in Washington County since 1861. "After colonies of our people began to locate in Washington County," he reported, we "began to learn that . . . Lee had taken a direct hand with the Indians in that affair; and I felt it my duty to acquaint the Presidency of the Church with the facts so far as I had been able to gather them." Most of the new settlers were horrified to learn that Mormons had murdered 120 emigrants a few miles from their homes. As the community leader, Snow believed he had the responsibility to find out who had perpetrated the massacre. He had some background because he had undoubtedly learned various facts during the 1858 hearings in Cedar City. Now, Snow enlisted Bishop Lorenzo W. Roundy of Kanaraville to help him and later testified that he and Roundy "communicated to President Young the facts as we had learned them, and the sources of our information."

Between 1861 and 1863, Young had learned more about the massacre, and his perception of the fault had changed radically. Young again urged the government to bring the perpetrators to justice, saying that his offer to Cumming "still held." Probably because his understanding remained incomplete, Young still believed that John D. Lee was the principal culprit. In April 1863 Young, Heber C. Kimball, George A. Smith, and Orson Hyde headed south with a large party. On May 6, 1863, they visited Lee in Washington, Utah, and Young condemned Lee before those present. Observing and recording the event in his journal that day, David John wrote:

"Young spoke to . . . [Lee] about the 'Mountain Meadow'. . . , [Lee] tried to blame the Indians for the massacre, but Pres Young . . . said, 'John D. Lee, do all the good you can, while you live, and you shall be credited, with every good deed you perform, but, where God and the Lamb dwell, you shall never be.' Lee wept bitterly." Although the General Authorities did not officially excommunicate Lee until 1870 at Young's direction, Lee reportedly said he considered himself cut off from the church in 1863. In spite of their disaffection from Lee, both Erastus Snow and Brigham Young interacted with him on business and church matters until 1870 and on business until 1874, when deputy marshal William Stokes finally captured him.

Even by the mid-1860s, federal officials continued to refuse Young's assistance in apprehending and prosecuting the perpetrators. Consequently, Young expected them to bring the guilty to court without his help. On May 8, 1866, in a conversation with several military officers, Young said that he had "urged, from the days of Governor Cumming . . . for Judges from the First Judicial District to go south and investigate" the massacre and "pledged . . . to protect them with my life in so doing but they would not do it." He told them he believed that the officials really did not want to investigate because by leaving "the matter in an unsettled condition," they could "reflect evil on me." He said that "if there were Mormons guilty in that act . . . let them be brought to justice." Addressing a congregation in the Salt Lake Tabernacle on December 23, 1866, Young urged the authorities not to "cease their efforts until you find the murderers." In 1869 he again reminded George Hicks of his offer to Governor Cumming, adding that he had made it "again and again" and concluding that "God will judge this matter and on that assurance I rest perfectly satisfied."

Despite Brigham Young's open statements that white men had been involved in the massacre, George A. Smith misrepresented the massacre. In the fall of 1869 Smith, responding to reporter's questions, still attributed the massacre to Indians. He admitted whites were there, "but arrived too late" to prevent the tragedy. However, Smith explained truthfully that Young and his associates were always "ready to give every aid in their power to discover and bring to Justice the participants in this massacre."

By 1870 the major participants had continued to hide out in various locations. With Young's encouragement, Lee settled, with extreme reluctance, for a time at Skutumpah northeast of Kanab, then at Lee's Ferry on the Colorado River, upstream from the Grand Canyon and at Moenave in northern Arizona. Haight, Higbee, William Stewart, and George Adair lived and worked at various places in Arizona and southern Utah. Klingensmith moved to Nevada and eventually turned state's evidence against Lee.

Young met with Lorenzo Roundy on a date over which there is some controversy, although it was probably in September 1870. Roundy said the president "did not know the truth" and told him he had "been misled and deceived." "If you want to know the truth," Roundy said, "ask Nephi Johnson." After his meeting with Johnson, Young "expressed great astonishment, and said if such were the facts, Lee had added to his crime lying and deceit."

Young's party traveled north from Virgin City to Cedar City, and the following morning he spoke at the local meetinghouse. Afterward, according to a 1927 reminiscence by Young's nephew, John R. Young, the president asked him to walk with him. They met Lee who, according to John R., "reached out his hand, to shake hands." Brigham refused to take it and said, "'John what made you lie to me about the Mountain Meadow Massacre?'" Lee refused to answer. Brigham bristled and told Lee never to "come again into my presence" or seek to be "Refellowshiped into the Church." Nephi Johnson's memory of his meeting with Young differed from both John Young's and Lorenzo Roundy's versions. Johnson dated the conversation in Salt Lake City "fifteen or twenty years" after the massacre rather than in Virgin City, and John Young placed the event in 1865. Johnson said that as he spoke, Young "walked the floor, . . . and several times said why did Lee lie to me." Johnson said he told Young that most of the men were young, went under orders, and believed "when they left Cedar City, that the emigrants had been killed by the Indians . . . [and they] were going to bury the dead, . . . they took their shovels along, and their arms to protect themselves" from possible Indian attack. These were reminiscent accounts, and all of the men were clearly confused about the date of the meeting.

What could Brigham Young have learned from Nephi Johnson if the interview took place in 1870 that he did not know before, and what effect did the new knowledge have on his attitude about prosecution? The evidence suggests that he learned that some of the militiamen who took part in the massacre did so under false assumptions. Some thought they were going to save the emigrants from the Indians. Others believed they were going to help bury the dead from an Indian massacre. Still others, like Johnson, went under church and military orders. Young told Johnson he would not hold responsible the men who were forced to go, "but . . . he would hold . . . [the leaders] respon[s]ible." Both Judge Jacob Boreman, who presided at Lee's trial, and the anti-Mormon *Salt Lake Tribune* agreed on the need to hold the leaders responsible rather than men they ordered to go to Mountain Meadows.

Brigham Young's company returned to Salt Lake on September 24, 1870, and on October 8 between general conference sessions, Young called a "council" of the Twelve Apostles. After laying "the facts before them," Young "proposed, and all present unanimously voted to expel John D. Lee and Isaac C. Haight, who was his superior officer in the Church, for failing to restrain him, and to take prompt action against him." Snow said Young instructed that "Lee should, under no circumstances, ever be again admitted as a member of the Church." Wilford Woodruff said that the same applied to Haight.

When Lee learned that the Twelve had excommunicated him and Haight, he accepted it stoically, though he professed not to know the reason. He became disturbed, however, as the excommunication disrupted his family and turned others against him. He blamed Erastus Snow and Lorenzo Roundy for his fate, and he reported a dream in which he tried to clean a dirty, half-naked Erastus Snow. In another dream, he concluded that Young would punish him for a short time to deflect persecution of the church by apostates.

Confronting Roundy directly at a party in Kanarraville on January 3, 1871, Lee responded with anger to Roundy's friendly greeting. Accusing Roundy of trying to poison "the Mind of" Brigham Young "in an Evil hour," he told the bishop: "Every Dog will have his day, . . . Now is your day. By & by it will be my day."

The disruption of his family led Lee to try to patch things up between himself and Young. Driving a wagon to St. George on December 22, 1870, Lee asked Young why the leaders should have cut him off thirteen years after the massacre. Young told him that he had not learned the "particuelars until lately." Instead of blaming the Paiutes as he had in 1857, Lee insisted that he had told the president "the whole Truth . . . with the Exception of one thing." That "one thing" was that he "suffered the blame to rest on" himself. Instead, he told Young, he should have told of the others who were present, noting that "what we done was by the mutual consent" of church leaders after prayer. "Righteousness alone prompted the act," he insisted.

After Lee begged him, Young agreed to give him a rehearing, sending him to Erastus Snow to arrange it. Snow, however, who knew many facts in the case, refused to hold the rehearing, arguing "it would result in no benefit." Although upset at the refusal, within a few days, Lee thought that there would be "Justice in the rulers of Iseral yet," probably thinking Young would forgive him.

Haight, who lived in Toquerville at the time, responded much differently. Haight told Lee that "he feared he would never get a hearing until" the church got a new president. Significantly, despite Lee's optimism and Haight's pessimism, Haight, rather than Lee, managed to get his excommunication reversed in his lifetime. In February 1874, when a new Toquerville bishop, William A. Bringhurst, spoke with Young about Haight's membership, Young replied, "Isaac Haight will be damned in this world and will be damned throughout eternity." In spite of this, Haight's defenders—particularly a son-in-law—persuaded Young that he had "misunderstood" Haight's role in the massacre. Apparently, Haight's defenders succeeded in convincing Young that, because he was not actually on the killing ground, his only sin was in his inability to restrain Lee. Whatever the argument, Haight was re-baptized into the church on March 3, 1874, and his blessings were restored.

In 1872 Young again reiterated and renewed the offer he made to Cumming in 1858 to help with investigating the massacre. Still fearful of army violence, he argued at the same time against the establishment of Fort Cameron, a military post opened east of Beaver, Utah, later that year. Young argued that Cradlebaugh and Eckels had "accomplished absolutely nothing." Now, he wrote, after fourteen years, instead of trying "to prosecute the accused . . . some of the Judges, like Judge [Cyrus] Hawley, have used every opportunity to charge the crime upon prominent men in Utah, and inflame public opinion against our community."

Events in early 1874 were also moving steadily toward a prosecution of John D. Lee. On April 5, 1874, Lee met with Brigham Young for the last time. Lee said he found Young outwardly cordial, but Young, by contrast, said he berated Lee, urging him if had killed the emigrants to "hang yourself." Lee's account was written at the time, so it may have been the more accurate. Whatever the case, federal marshals subsequently arrested Lee, Dame, Ellott Willden, Klingensmith, and Adair, but the U.S. attorneys could not assemble enough evidence to prosecute Dame, Willden, or Adair. Klingensmith had turned state's evidence in Lee's first trial, but did not testify in the second. Haight, Stewart, and Higbee avoided capture by U.S. marshals, but as Lee, now in custody, wrote in 1859, "Catching is before hanging."

Young and Smith both said they were too sick to travel to Beaver to testify at Lee's trial, but offered sworn depositions instead. The prosecution introduced them, and Lee insisted that the judge admit them. The depositions, in which both declared themselves innocent of the massacre, were generally accurate, except that Brigham Young through George A. Smith had counseled the settlers in 1857 not to sell grain or to trade with the emigrants. The depositions said they only told settlers not to sell grain for animal fodder.

The record is vague on just when Young learned various details about the massacre. Available evidence currently does not reveal the actual date he knew most things, except that he knew them before 1870, when he was clearly aware of nearly everything except probably that Lee was behaving under Haight's orders. Most likely, Young picked up bits and pieces over time. From Jacob Hamblin's and George A. Smith's 1858 reports, for example, Young knew that John D. Lee and other "brethren" participated in some way. With this information, Young and his associates, William H. Hooper and territorial marshal John Kay, told the federal attorney, marshal, and judges they would help bring the perpetrators to justice, assistance the judges and marshal rejected.

Contrary to the usual story, which interprets Young's role as the author of the massacre or faults Young either for refusing to investigate it or for erecting a stonewall against the investigation, it is clear that he consistently asked for an investigation and trials. Nevertheless, he wanted to protect his people, and he did a number of things to try to accomplish that end. At times, as his story to his friend McKee shows, he could be less than forthright, and until 1870 he encouraged Lee to avoid public exposure and the federal marshals by living in secluded places in such as Skutumpah and Lee's Ferry. Nevertheless, Young, Smith, Lyman, Snow, Rich, and Roundy investigated the massacre, and in 1859 Smith and Lyman advised the participants to prepare for trial. They also meted out some punishment in 1859 by releasing leading participants from their church positions. Significantly, these leaders took the apostles seriously enough to retain attorneys for an anticipated trial. Young and the church leaders did not officially excommunicate any of the participants until 1870, but Lee considered himself cut off in 1863.

Whatever culpability Brigham Young might have had in delaying the prosecution of the perpetrators and in helping Lee to secret himself, the Ultra federal officials erected the major barrier to speedy prosecution. Had the marshal and judges cooperated with Young and the moderate federal appointees, they might well have succeeded in bringing the leading criminals to justice as early as 1859 or 1860. The lack of cooperation by federal officials resulted from their anti-Mormon convictions and their inability to muster enough evidence to indict Young. After Lee's capture in 1874, it seems evident that leading anti-Mormons intended to pin the murders on Young rather than Lee. This is clearly shown from the way in which Robert N. Baskin prosecuted Lee in his first trial. He refused to focus his prosecution on Lee, but tried unsuccessfully to elicit evidence of the culpability of Young and other general authorities. His prosecution was either incompetent or cleverly aimed at swaying public opinion against Young and the Mormon leadership.

Could Young have done more to bring the perpetrators to justice? Certainly. Utah's probate courts had jurisdiction in civil and criminal cases under territorial law until 1874 when passage of the Poland Act and the U.S. Supreme Court decision in *Ferris v. Higley* took it away. Federal judges disputed such jurisdiction, and in a number of cases, the federal district courts forced transfer of cases from probate courts to their courts, but the county or territorial attorney could have initiated prosecution in the county probate court. The territorial marshal could have organized a posse to search for the accused, and Young could have urged territorial officials to act against the accused. In addition, instead of urging Lee to hide out, he could have asked him to turn himself in.

If anyone deserves credit for investigating the massacre, it was Erastus Snow, although it seems unfortunate that he apparently pinned the principal guilt on Lee rather than Haight. Historian Juanita Brooks was right that Snow persevered because he found the work of building the kingdom in southwestern Utah hampered by the rumors circulating about the massacre and the role that church members—especially Lee and Haight—had played in it. Lee, himself, understood the central role Snow and Roundy played in clarifying the matter for Young, as evidenced by his dream of a filthy naked Snow and his confrontation with Roundy.

I fail to understand why Brigham Young punished Lee more severely than Isaac Haight. Juanita Brooks may well be right that Brigham Young decided to excommunicate Lee because his name continued to surface as responsible for the massacre and "sentiment from within the church became so strong that by 1870 the leaders were forced" to act. Will Bagley thought the church leaders picked Lee as a scapegoat because they believed he accept the decision and take what was coming to him because his excommunication would deflect attention from church leaders. My view is that Lee was a fall guy rather than a scapegoat because he played so major a role in the massacre, and a fall guy may be as guilty as others who escape punishment. As the story unfolded, Young may have failed to understand that Haight was the principal culprit. He may have believed that Haight's sin lay in not controlling Lee. From the available evidence, we know that principal responsibility lays directly on Haight's shoulders—he planned the massacre, induced Dame to approve it, and ordered Lee and other militiamen to the killing field. Moreover, I find difficulty understanding Young's insensitivity in his comment to Lee, saying the emigrants deserved their fate, and in his comment at Mountain Meadows, that the Lord had taken a little vengeance. Clearly, the emigrants had done nothing to merit murder at the hands of the Mormon militia.

8

Sermons

In the forty-two and a half years of Brigham Young's ministry—between his call to the Quorum of the Twelve Apostles in February 1835 and his death in August 1877—he gave thousands of sermons. In virtually all of the talks, as historian Ronald Walker pointed out, Young spoke extemporaneously—or more precisely, impromptu—on a broad range of topics. Clerks transcribed the text of many that were published in the *Journal of Discourses,* and scholar Richard Van Wagoner assembled a five-volume work packed with every report of Young's sermons he could locate, including transcripts from shorthand notes, newspaper articles, personal notes, and diary entries.

I suggest that he spoke impromptu because as Young explained: "I opened my mouth . . . and the Lord filled it." By contrast, some observers considered his sermons examples of "acid-tongued oratory," and others thought the caustic language far too corrosive. Hiram S. Rumfield, assistant treasurer of the Overland Mail Company, judged a sermon he heard as "filthy" and "profane." In a February 1859 sermon, Young spoke with earthy obscenity to characterize federal judge Charles E. Sinclair, who tried—unsuccessfully, as it turned out—to force Utahns to plead in his court for Buchanan's pardon, which they had already accepted.

Like Rumfield, many travelers witnessed Young's sermons. British explorer Sir Richard Burton recorded his impressions of a sermon he heard in 1860. After removing his hat, expectorating in a spittoon near the pulpit, and taking a drink of water, Young began to speak. "The opening phrases," Burton wrote, "were hardly audible," but as the address continued, Young's voice "rose high and sonorous, . . . [with] a fluence so remarkable," it was "almost a work of art, . . . pleasing and animated . . . fluent, impromptu, and well turned, spoken rather than preached." Its content was, however, "rather rambling and unconnected." His "gestures were easy and rounded, not without a certain grace, though evidently untaught."

Young's sermons impressed a diversity of people, including California emigrant William H. Knight, territorial secretary Amos Reed, Missouri businessman J. C. Hoagland, and Episcopal bishop Daniel S. Tuttle. Ralph Waldo Emerson considered Young's oratory deficient, but he also said Young delivered a message imbued with a "certain homespun sense." Wilford H. Munro, associate principal of Salt Lake City's St. Marks School, found that Young understood his audience, although he "was ungrammatical . . . witty . . . slangy . . . profane . . . sometimes . . . obscene." Nevertheless, Munro observed, the people clearly related to him. French naturalist Jules Rémy wrote that Young possessed "a remarkable talent as a mimic [with an] . . . underlying practical truth . . . [like a] pontiff and . . . moralist." Heber J. Grant, a twentieth-century church president, opined that Young exhibited a "wonderful capacity to hold his audience and to inspire those who heard him preach." Young did prepare a sermon ahead of time once when he knew Speaker of the U.S. House of Representatives Schuyler Colfax would sit in the congregation. Alas, one observer said it was a complete flop, "the worst sermon he had ever preached."

In his own defense, Young said he spoke emphatically and used profanity because he believed that respectable language was like the "wind"—it reached the ear but was soon "forgotten." If you want the people to "feel what you say," he insisted, "you have got to use language that they will remember." To impress his words on their minds, "in many instances we use language we would rather not use." In one St. George Temple speech, he had a striking way to emphasize a point: he whacked the stand with his cane with such force that one observer believed the dent would last "for a generation."

His sermons leading up to and during the Mormon Reformation of 1856–57 struck the congregants with similar force. In March 1856, six months before Jedediah Grant began the movement, Young said, "with regard to preaching; you need, figuratively, to have it rain pitchforks, tines downwards from this pulpit, Sunday after Sunday. Instead of the smooth, beautiful, sweet, still silk-velvet-lipped preaching, you should have sermons like peals of thunder."

At various times, he preached on conflicting sides of controversial issues. During the Mormon Reformation, he preached blood atonement. In 1859, following the Utah War and the Mountain Meadows massacre, he emphasized the need for peace and deplored bloodshed and criminal acts against non-Mormons. In a sermon to an elders' conference on November 14, 1858, he condemned those who sinned with their "eyes wide open." Members should "forsake that you know to be wrong." "If the bosom of the Almighty was not filled with compassion and mercy this people would have been consumed before this." "I am ready to forgive a man or woman seventy seven times a day who sin ignorantly in the integrity of their hearts, but when men whose hearts are full of understanding give way to iniquity, run greedily after wickedness can I for give them? Yes if the Lord will, but he cannot forgive, such offenders." By contrast, on June 3, 1860, he said, "I speak of those who have been in the habit of doing wrong, and thereby have lost confidence—pursue a course that will convince your brethren that you have reformed." In a sermon in 1871, he preached of God's compassion and said that "if they [the Mormons] expect to enter the celestial kingdom [to live with God and Christ,] they must overcome this weakness [not to forgive others] and the wicked dispositions they have inherited through the fall."

In addition to speaking on forgiveness, Young preached on the Latter-day Saint conception of salvation. Instead of believing that God relegates the dead either to Heaven or Hell as some Christians believed, or that God sends some mortals to Purgatory to cleanse themselves of sin as Catholics believe, Young insisted, that salvation is virtually universal. All except a select few Sons of Perdition (Satan) will be saved in some Heavenly mansion or what Mormons call one of the three degrees of glory. On one occasion, he preached, "All the names of the human family are written there [in the Lamb's Book of Life], and the Lord will hold them there until they come to the knowledge of the truth, that they can rebel against him, and can sin against the Holy Ghost; then they will be thrust down to hell, and their names be blotted out." Only those who had a sure knowledge revealed to them by God that they would have the capacity to "deny and defy the power and character of the Son of God—[and] . . . sin against the Holy Ghost" could become Sons of Perdition.

Although he spoke differently on occasion, he also said that those who proved unfaithful—the Sons of Perdition—would "decrease and decompose" into native elements. The revelation to Joseph Smith canonized as Section 76 of the Doctrine and Covenants promised a degree of glory to all, even the most wicked, except those who received the light—a personal revelation of the Holy Ghost—and denied the "Holy Spirit after having received it." These must have the knowledge to deny "the Only Begotten Son of the Father, having crucified him unto themselves and put him to an open shame."

Earning such damnation was impossible for ordinary humans. Judas Iscariot is the only Son of Perdition of whom we are aware. He earned that punishment because he had an absolute knowledge of Christ's ministry and Godhood. Any others would have needed to acquire the same knowledge and turned against Christ and the Holy Ghost. Young preached that neither Mormons nor non-Mormons need concern themselves with becoming Sons or Daughters of Perdition because of the small number who had received the Spirit and knowledge to this extent. Virtually all mankind will achieve some degree of glory, he said. "How much," Young asked, "does it take to prepare a man, or woman, or any being, to become angels to the devil, to suffer with him to all eternity? Just as much as it does to prepare a man to go into the celestial kingdom, into the presence of the Father and the Son, and to be made an heir to His kingdom, and all His glory, and be crowned with crowns of glory, immortality, and eternal lives. Now who will be damned to all eternity? Will any of the rest of mankind? No; not one of them."

If Mormons faithfully kept Christ's commandments, obtained their temple endowments and sealings, and obeyed Christ's teachings to the end of their mortal lives, Young said they would be resurrected with bodies of spiritual matter like God's and Christ's. In those bodies, they would supersede the laws of the physical universe, and the refined matter of which their celestial bodies were made would cease its physical changes. Instead, he said, their celestial bodies will increase in intelligence throughout eternity. As exalted beings, they would give birth to spirit children, and use their power and priesthood like God and Christ to organize preexisting elements into planets. In fact, Young believed that this process began while people were in mortality. If they were faithful on the earth, they could begin the process of achieving godhood here.

Mormon commentators have taken various position about whether people who have died could move from a lower degree of glory—what non-Mormons might call salvation—to a higher one and eventually reach exaltation and become gods. Young believed that this was possible. In a sermon in October 1859, he preached that mankind's progression could continue after death for those prepared to progress. If "he [a deceased man or woman] is not prepared to enjoy the glories of the celestial kingdom with God our Father . . . he is not prepared at once to enjoy a fulness of the glory promised to the faithful in the Gospel; for he must be schooled, while in the spirit, in the other departments of the house of God, passing on from truth to truth, from intelligence to intelligence, until he is prepared to again receive his body and to enter into the presence of the Father and the Son." Thus, Young believed that humans who had not prepared themselves completely on earth for the highest degree of glory—exaltation in the Celestial

Kingdom—could progress after death in the spirit world until, in the resurrection, they were prepared to ascend to the highest kingdom and to live eternally with the Father and the Son.

In addition to preaching on passing to higher glory, Young insisted on the importance of understanding the atonement and salvation through Christ's grace. In a sermon on May 12, 1867, Young "said there never was any world created and peopled nor never would be but what would be redeemed by the shedding of the blood of the savior of that world. . . . Adam made this world and himself to take a body and subject himself to sin that Redemption and Exaltation might come to man. Without descending below all things we cannot ascend above all things." In a sermon on June 28, 1874, he reiterated that "The Latter-day Saints are believers in the atonement of the Savior. . . . The Savior has requested us and all of his disciples to remember him as oft as we meet together, and to break bread in remembrance of his body which was broken for us, and to drink from the cup in remembrance of the blood that was shed for us."

Just as he spoke on eternal salvation, he also spoke on the need for compassion during mortality. He gave sermons in which he said the Lord expected husbands to treat their wives and families with kindness and love. In December 1858 he said, "when a man married a wife, he took her for better or for worse, and had no right to ill use her."

If Young spoke about compassion, he also urged the gathering to Zion (by which he meant Utah) the remnants of the House of Israel wherever the Saints might find them. The Lord had given Jacob, the Hebrew patriarch Abraham's grandson, the name Israel (meaning: he that strives with God), and from him the twelve Israelite tribes descended. For Mormons, the most important were the two tribes Ephraim and Manasseh, Jacob's grandsons and sons of Joseph. Young reminded the Saints that Jacob (Israel) had given the greater blessing to Ephraim instead of his older brother, Manesseh.

Until the death of Solomon, the twelve Israelite tribes formed one nation. After his death, ten Israelite tribes broke with Judah and Benjamin and founded a kingdom in the northern part of what had been Israel. Often called Ephraim, after its dominant tribe, the northern kingdom had its capital at Samaria. In 722 B.C.E. the Assyrians sacked Samaria, deported the Israelites to Assyria, and settled the land with emigrants. After a time in Assyrian captivity, some Israelites assimilated with other peoples, and others escaped to the north. Historians do not know where they went, but the ancient prophet Jeremiah prophesied that sometime in the future, they would return: "they shall come and sing in the height of Zion, and shall flow together to the goodness of the Lord" (Jeremiah 31:12).

Young and other Mormons expected to serve as agents in fulfilling Jeremiah's prophecy by converting Israelites and gathering them to Zion—Joseph Smith had received a revelation that gave them the charge to do so. Joseph Smith and Oliver Cowdery testified that in a vision in the Kirtland Temple, Moses appeared to invest them with "the keys [authority] of the gathering of Israel from the four parts of the earth, and the leading of the ten tribes from the land of the north" (Doctrine and Covenants 110:11). With that authority, Mormon missionaries proselytized to fulfill the prophecy. Young explained a partial fulfillment of the gathering of Israel in a sermon on April 8, 1855: "Will we go to the Gentile nations to preach the Gospel?" he asked rhetorically. "Yes, and gather out the Israelites, wherever they are mixed among the nations of the earth."

More specifically, Young and the other missionaries sought to gather descendants of Ephraim, which Young said, "has become mixed with all the nations of the earth, and it is Ephraim that is gathering together. It is Ephraim that I have been searching for all the days of my preaching, and that is the blood which ran in my veins when I embraced the Gospel . . . and when we send to the nations we do not seek for the Gentiles. . . . We want the blood of Jacob, . . . which runs in the veins of the people" no matter where they may be in "China, Russia, England, California, North or South

America, or some other locality." Although he sent missionaries to many distant lands, more narrowly in a sermon on May 31, 1863, he preached that the Sons of Ephraim "are the Anglo-Saxon race, and they are upon the face of the whole earth, bearing the spirit of rule and dictation."

All faithful Mormons had a way to determine if they belonged to the tribe of Ephraim or one of the other Israelite tribes, or if they had been adopted into a tribe of Israel. While organizing the church, Joseph Smith called his father as the presiding patriarch, and he and Young called patriarchs for each stake. One of the patriarch's duties is to declare through inspiration the lineage of the members to whom they gave patriarchal blessings. Among other things in the blessing was to declare the lineage of the member, though this was not always done during the church's earliest years. Presently available evidence shows that patriarchs declare most of those from or descended from northern Europeans to be from the tribe of Ephraim. I spoke with one patriarch who had given 528 blessings. He said all except seven came from the tribe of Ephraim, and six of that seven were from Manesseh. The outlier belonged to the tribe of Gad.

As Young preached on the gathering of Israel, he also considered and preached about those eligible to hold the priesthood. Determining eligibility for the priesthood is extremely important for Latter-day Saints, since all worthy men may be ordained to an office in the priesthood. Significantly, with the exception of a few general authorities, lay priesthood holders functioned in virtually all positions of responsibility in the church, except organizations over which women preside. Most priesthood holders, then and now, supported themselves and their families in other occupations while functioning in priesthood callings.

As Young considered who might hold the priesthood, sometime between 1847 and 1852 he made a ruling that denied the priesthood to all African Americans. That ruling remained a policy in the church until 1978—126 years later. Young had preached a progressive view of race relations in 1847, but by 1852 he would rule that African American men could not hold the priesthood.

While Joseph Smith was generally more progressive than Young's eventual position, during the church's early history, he had preached contradictory teachings on race and slavery. The Book of Mormon (2 Nephi 26:32–33) said all people were equal. It did not matter whether they were young or old, bond or free, male or female. By contrast, Chapter 7:22 of the Book of Moses, an 1830 revelation to Joseph Smith, distinguished between the people of the city of the Old Testament patriarch Enoch and the descendants of Cain, "who were black, and had not place among them." In 1833 Smith published a revelation saying that no one should hold another in bondage. In 1836, however, he said that southerners had a right to hold slaves. In 1844, during his run for the United States presidency, Smith proposed compensated emancipation to free all the slaves by 1850 by paying owners from the sale of public lands and by reducing the salary of members of Congress.

Whatever his views at various times, we can document at least three—Elijah Abel, Joseph T. Ball, and Q. Walker Lewis—and possibly five African Americans whom church officials ordained to the priesthood during Joseph Smith's ministry. Others who may have received the priesthood included Enoch Lovejoy Lewis and Peter Kerr (nicknamed "Black Pete"). There may have been others whom we cannot at present document. Joseph Ball actually served as president of the Boston branch of the church.

Sometime between 1847 and 1852, Brigham Young decided that the church would not ordain African Americans to the priesthood. In 1847 he had said that race "had no bearing on an individual's standing in the church," and in a paraphrase of Acts 17:26, Young said that of "one blood God made all flesh." In 1849, however, Young linked African Americans to the curse of Cain as Joseph Smith had, although he said that God would eventually remove the curse.

Young may have adopted his view that Cain's curse was a black skin from Protestants, many of whom preached the association as early as the eighteenth century. Such a borrowing is possible because Young did not claim to have received a revelation on the topic. Consistent with the notion of the affliction of dark skin, in a speech to the Utah legislature in 1852, Young recommended a law permitting slavery in Utah. At the same time, in what seems a contradiction, he also said, "I am as much opposed to the principle of slavery as any man."

Young's speech preceded the passage of a law authorizing slavery in Utah. The territory's 1852 slavery act included provisions that were not usually in southern slave codes. It prohibited the exportation of slaves from Utah territory, and it required masters to prove their ownership of a slave to the county probate court, to treat their slaves humanely, to educate them, and not to have sexual intercourse with them. In 1859 Young told newspaperman Horace Greeley that slavery was a "Divine institution." However, he also believed slavery was a curse to the masters, the same position taken by Robert E. Lee. Significantly, Young told Greeley that if Utah were admitted into the Union, it would enter as a free state. He was probably serious about this because even though there were some slaves in Utah, slavery did not flourish there. Nevertheless, he was also telling Greeley, an avowed abolitionist, what Greeley wanted to hear.

Despite previous ordination of African Americans to the priesthood, Young's rulings—that male blacks could not hold the priesthood and that men and women with any African blood could not participate in temple worship—established church policy until 1978. Throughout the late nineteenth century, several black members, and particularly Jane Manning James, petitioned for permission to participate in temple rituals. Church leaders denied their pleas, though they did allow James to perform vicarious baptisms. In 1978, however, after a revelation to church president Spencer W. Kimball, the church abandoned its previous policy, and since then any worthy male regardless of race may receive the priesthood, and worthy men and women of any race may participate in temple ordinances and worship.

In addition to topics such as race, Brigham Young sermonized on cosmology: the origin, evolution, and fate of the earth. His beliefs on cosmology were much more progressive than those on race. Young knew that Joseph Smith had rejected the prevailing doctrine of the duality of matter and spirit and taught instead that spirit was simply refined matter. Contrary to much of Christendom, Smith believed that God did not create the universe from nothing *(ex nihilo)*, but from preexisting matter. In June 1856 Brigham elaborated on Smith's views, preaching that matter constitutes the essence of everything in the universe. Young said that all matter, regardless of its physical form, whether a star or a flower, constantly changes. As Chase Kirkham, an expert on the topic, wrote, matter "is either improving and growing or dissolving and decomposing."

Applying his conception of composing and decomposing, Young recommended that Mormons construct the Salt Lake Temple from adobe rather than stone because he believed that stone had reached its peak of development and would decompose, while the adobe would continue to compose. He feared that stone, in the process of decomposition, would not last through the millennium. Fortunately, the builders did not heed his counsel, and the quartz monzonite Salt Lake Temple still stands.

In elaborating his cosmology, Young argued that the universe existed eternally on several basic principles. These were truth, knowledge, wisdom, power, and progress. By truth, the basis of his philosophy, he meant any self-sustaining eternal fact. Regardless of where truth currently existed, he believed it originated with God. Young rejected, however, the idea that scripture and revelation were the only sources of truth. He believed instead that it might currently be located anywhere gods or humans might find it, including in other religions, science, experience, and opposites such as good and evil. He preached that if human beings expected to progress eternally, they had an obligation to search everywhere for truth.

In connection with cosmology, Young spoke on the creation of the earth and the fall of Adam and Eve. His beliefs were closer to those of philosopher Alfred North Whitehead and the process theologians than to such Christian fathers as Augustine and traditional Catholics and Protestants. As with the Book of Mormon, he rejected the concept espoused by Augustine—that the curse on Adam and Eve, for eating the fruit of the tree of the Knowledge of Good and Evil, passed to all human beings as original sin.

Young's teachings were also close to, but not precisely like, those of the earliest Christian fathers, Irenaeus (died 202 C.E.), Clement of Alexandria (ca. 150–215 C.E.), and Basil the Great (330–379 C.E.). Believing that Adam's fall was a progressive act—one that benefited the human race—and that it presupposed Christ's atonement, Ireneaus wrote that Jesus Christ "did, through His transcendent love, become what we are, that He might bring us to be what He is Himself." Clement of Alexandria said that "the Word of God became man, that thou mayest learn from man how man may become God." Basil the Great insisted that humans were not just "being made like to God," but "highest of the being made God." Since writing this paragraph, I have also found that Mormon scholars and authors Fiona and Terryl Givens arrived independently at a similar view of the earliest church fathers.

Young's beliefs were like two Biblical passages. The Psalmist wrote in 82:6, "I have said, Ye are gods; and all of you are children of the most High." Jesus cited the Psalmist's phrase in defense of himself as his opponents accused him of blasphemy. In John 10:34 it is written: "Jesus answered them, Is it not written in your law, I said, Ye are gods?"

Young preached that although eating the forbidden fruit by Adam and Eve might have been a minor lapse, because it was also a progressive act that benefitted the human race since it made possible the bearing of children and fulfilling of the greater commandment to create physical bodies for God's spirit children. If Adam and Eve had not eaten the forbidden fruit, they would have remained in innocence in the Garden of Eden, and they could have borne no children, so there would have been no other human beings on the earth. Unlike many other Christians, Mormons believe that each individual person is a unique personality who has existed as such eternally. At some point in their eternal existence, each becomes a spirit child of God, destined to come to earth as a mortal being born to mortal parents. Producing mortal children was impossible for Adam and Eve in their immortal state in the Garden of Eden.

To understand how immortals like Adam and Eve could become mortal and have mortal children, it is necessary to understand that the motivating force in Young's preaching originated in his reinterpretation of Joseph Smith's teachings. With the possible exception of blood atonement, which Young abandoned after the Utah War and which the church leadership repudiated, the Adam-God theory was arguably Young's most controversial teaching. As scholar Chase Kirkham has noted, the Adam-God theory was really the Adam-Eve-God story of a protean or changeable Adam and Eve. Joseph Smith, and after him Brigham Young, solved to the satisfaction of faithful Mormons a problem that plagued traditional Christianity: How could a loving and sovereign God who made everything also create the evil that had pervaded the world throughout history? The Book of Job offers one solution in the Hebrew Bible: Mankind simply did not know enough to understand God's purposes. Answering the question differently, Young said that God didn't create evil. Like Joseph Smith, Brigham Young believed that God was not the creator of the universe in the sense that traditional Christianity believed He was. He did not create the world *ex nihilo*—from nothing. Most important, He gave His creations agency, generally called "Free Agency" in nineteenth- and early-twentieth-century Mormonism. Everyone could act for themselves. Free agency allowed Satan—Lucifer, the Devil, the Adversary—and those spirits who followed him to rebel. It also allowed humans to choose between the good offered by Christ and the evil offered by Satan.

For the faithful, such a creation and free agency allowed men and women the possibility of achieving godhood like Adam and Eve. In a statement later attributed to Lorenzo Snow but first spoken by Brigham while the Twelve served their mission in England, he told Snow, "As God was, so are we now; as he now is so shall we be." "Our Father," he preached, "was once born of parents, having a father and mother the same as we have." Eliza R. Snow, Lorenzo's sister and a wife to both Smith and Young, echoed this teaching for women when she wrote a poem of a Mother in Heaven, "Invocation or The Eternal Father and Mother," later set to music as "Oh My Father."

Scholars often use the term "myth" to refer to such teachings. Scholars view the term "myth" as a description of something that people believe and that motivates them. For scholars, a myth is not fiction, but rather a story by which a community charts its life. A major problem with the term "myth" is that popular usage has freighted it with such negative connotations that when average folk hear the term, they immediately believe it is a synonym for falsehood or fiction. I would argue that a better term than "myth" is "story." Moreover, I prefer to use the word "story" in the sense of the German word *Geschichte,* which means both history and story.

Young told stories through which the Saints patterned their lives and beliefs. He told the story of Adam and Eve as historical characters. As Young told the story, God commissioned Adam under the name Michael to assist Christ, the Jehovah of the Hebrew Bible, to shape preexisting matter into the earth. An immortal being—a god—Young said, Adam brought his goddess wife, Eve, from another planet to become the father and mother of the race of humans who were to cover the earth. Acting in a protean capacity, by eating the food of the earth, Adam and Eve became mortal again. As mortals, Adam and Eve could produce mortal children. If Adam, Eve, and their descendants remained faithful they could again become gods. Young taught that Adam and Eve had already reached godhood, and Adam had become the god of this earth. Young said that Adam was the father of Jesus Christ, a doctrine that other Mormon leaders consider heretical.

In addition to the Earth and other presently existing planets, Young preached that millions of worlds remained to be created from unorganized matter. Those members who kept their temple covenants could become the creators and uhr-parents of those worlds. Moreover, this process had gone on forever. He said, "there never was a time when there were not Gods and worlds, and when men were not passing through the same ordeals that we are now passing through. That course has been from all eternity, and it is and will be to all eternity." The temple ceremonies gave Mormons the keys that provided knowledge about this future. In the temple, men and women participated in endowments and sealings that prepared them, if they remained faithful, to reach this eternal goal. Young preached that God would eventually say to the faithful, "You have passed so far in the progression of perfection that you can now become independent, and I will give you power to control and organize and govern and dictate the elements of eternities. There is a vast eternity stretched out before you; now organize as you will."

Young related the story of the reason for Mormon temples to the Masonic tradition of the construction of Solomon's temple. Young had been a Master Mason, so he understood the relationship between Mormon doctrine, temple rituals, and Masonry. In a sermon, he taught that "In the days of Solomon, in the Temple that he built in the land of Jerusalem, there was confusion and bickering and strife, even to murder, and the very man [Hiram Abiff] that they looked to to give them the keys of life and salvation, they killed because he refused to administer the ordinances to them when they requested it; and whether they got any of them or not, this history does not say anything about."

Not all of Young's contemporary Mormon apostles agreed with his views. For instance, Young's views of a God who progressively gained knowledge conflicted with Orson Pratt's views of an omniscient, omnipresent, omnipotent, and unchanging God. Young told Pratt in no uncertain terms that he did not preach sound doctrine. Pratt promised Young to not teach his views, but he still had a perfect right to believe them. Nevertheless, the two engaged in numerous disputes over doctrine until Young died in 1877. After hearing one of Pratt's discourses, Young said, Pratt "drowns himself in his own philosophy, . . . they make me think 'O dear, granny, what a long tail our puss has got!'" Some associates recommended that Young discipline Pratt, but he refused to do so, insisting that if Pratt were chopped into inch pieces, "each piece would cry out, Mormonism is true."

Such disputes notwithstanding, belief in Young's stories helped to motivate Latter-day Saints to migrate more than a thousand miles to Utah, and to establish 350 settlements during his lifetime in places such as Utah, Wyoming, Colorado, Nevada, Idaho, California, Hawaii, and Arizona. These settlers lived at first in wretched conditions, suffering together in wagon boxes and dugouts. They endured cricket infestations, attacks on their livestock by ravenous wolves, harsh winters, and flash floods. They preached to convert Indians to Mormonism. In some cases, their preaching succeeded; in others their settlements displaced the Indians and forced them eventually to move to reservations. In some cases, they fought with the Indians over the land both had occupied.

The stories Young told convinced the Saints that if they remained faithful, they could overcome their transgressions of God's laws and become gods and goddesses like Adam and Eve. The stories informed the life of everyday Mormons. In the settlements, they engaged with the elements, the land, and the Indians. As they worked to change the wilderness into Euro-American civilization, they believed that if they remained faithful, they could people earths organized by their own priesthood power. For the faithful, such rewards were worth any sacrifice.

Young's theology of a God who progresses in knowledge has much to recommend it, particularly against atheism. He offers a plausible alternative to such atheists as Richard Dawkins, who argues in favor of natural selection and against irreducible complexity. As far as I know, Young never lectured on natural selection. Nevertheless, instead of contradicting it, Young's conception of God who continues to learn makes completely plausible a being who uses natural selection as a means of creating species. Such a god might learn to use natural selection to progress from the rudimentary eye of a flatworm to the binocular eye of a human being or the complex eye of an insect.

Some atheists argue against the existence of God by pointing out that the creation and development of the earth has been extremely messy. Given the history of the earth, they cannot believe that an omniscient God could have created such a mess as natural history reveals. After all, scientists estimate that of more than five billion species, perhaps 99 percent that ever lived on the earth have become extinct. If, as Young believed, God gained knowledge progressively, His lack of previous knowledge offers a theological explanation for these extinctions, including such messiness as the mass extinction of the dinosaurs.

In May 1871 Young discoursed extensively on the earth and science. He questioned the accuracy of the creation story in Genesis. He said that Moses "obtained the history and traditions of the fathers, and from these picked out what he considered necessary." It does not "matter," he said, "whether it is correct or not, . . . or whether he made it in six days or in as many millions of years, [this] is and will remain a matter of speculation in the minds of men unless he give revelation on the subject." He said, "We differ very much with Christendom in regard to the science of religion. Our religion embraces all truth and every fact in existence, no matter whether in heaven, earth, or hell. A fact is a fact, all truth issues forth from the Fountain of truth, and the sciences are facts as far as men have proved them." "The Lord is one of the most scientific men that ever lived; you have no idea of the knowledge that he has with regard to the sciences."

As part of his cosmology, Young preached that death was a part of life, and it simply consisted of the separation of body matter from spirit matter. In his view, after the spirit leaves the body, the life processes in the body cause it to decay. The body decomposes into the elements of which it was made, but, as in his environmental theology, Young preached that like all elements, these still have life in them. To resolve the separation of spirit and body matter, through the atonement of Jesus Christ, the body's elements will rejoin each other, and the spirit will reunite with the body.

Young also preached that our earth was not unique. Each planet, he said, had its own Adam, Eve, and Savior. Millions upon millions of planets either existed or their Adam and Savior would build them from preexisting but unorganized matter.

In addition to preaching about creation and peopling the earth, central to Young's perspective of eternal progress was the need for suffering. He believed that suffering on the earth helped to prepare human beings for greater lives here and in the hereafter by giving them the knowledge and experience to live in an exalted state with the gods after living a faithful mortal life. The facts gained from suffering, Young preached, added "knowledge, understanding, power, and glory, and prepare him [a human being] to receive crowns, kingdoms, thrones, and principalities, and to be crowned in the glory with the Gods of eternity." With such knowledge and exaltation, resurrected beings would gain the power to, in Chase Kirkham's words, "control matter and create planets." Young insisted that God had previously gone through a similar experience, and this experience had prepared Him for godhood. Young thought such teaching consoled faithful Mormons with the promise that if they endured their stressful lives on earth, they would receive exaltation and godhood in the hereafter, with all its responsibilities and blessings. In these teachings, he understood and elaborated Joseph Smith's teachings about the future expectations of the exaltation of faithful Latter-day Saints.

In effect, Young had turned the suffering by the Mormon people on its head. Instead of a curse, to endure suffering prepared the Saints for exaltation and godhood. "Do I acknowledge the hand of the Lord in persecution?" Brigham asked rhetorically. "Yes, I do. It is one of the greatest blessings that could be conferred upon the people of God." Such suffering taught the essence of good and evil to those Saints who persevered. Suffering prepared them to become gods and goddesses who could create and rule over new worlds. Through suffering, Christ descended below everything, as we must. The difference between Christ's suffering and ours, Young taught, was that Christ's atoned for the sins of all human beings. Christ was already a God, and our suffering prepares us for godhood.

Drawing teachings from the Book of Mormon, Young said that men and women learned from opposites: good and evil, virtue and vice, faith and faithlessness. Young's belief in the value of suffering and his belief in radical free agency offered the Saints reasons to believe in a benevolent and loving God who could allow such widespread suffering through war, famine, and genocide. If suffering prepared men and women for godhood, they benefitted if they endured such trials.

Young understood and could preach on the blessings of trials and persecution, in large part, from his own experience. He had organized and participated in the winter exodus from Missouri while Joseph Smith remained imprisoned under wretched conditions in Liberty, Missouri. After the murders of Joseph and Hyrum Smith, Young had contended with violence authored by Illinois militias and led the relocation of the Saints from Nauvoo. He directed the movement of the Mormon people while he brought his own families across Iowa to Winter Quarters, sending wagons and supplies for the poor who had insufficient means to evacuate and move. He led the pioneer company to Utah, and he worked beside them and the Mormon people to erect a settlement in Salt Lake Valley. "Time and time again," he preached, "have I left handsome property to be inherited by our enemies." Acknowledging the hand of the Lord in persecution, he called it "a blessing."

Young and the Mormon people endured suffering beyond the understanding of their twenty-first-century descendants. As Chase Kirkham has pointed out, the Harvard scholar Noah Feldman wrote that the Mormons "suffered greater religious persecution in its history than any other religious group in American history," and historian Gordon Wood argued that the Mormons endured the "greatest religious persecution in [United States] history"; they survived as the most "persecuted religion . . . [in] American history."

James Buchanan and some other politicians insisted that sending an army against the people of Utah and appointing anti-Mormons among the territorial officials sent to govern them had nothing to do with religion. By contrast, Colonel Johnston's adjutant, Maj. Fitz John Porter, threatened to kill the Mormons, and Col. James Carleton proposed to "make literally children of the mist of them."

Clearly, these officers expressed the intentions of other Americans more accurately than Buchanan.

Although he preached on such subjects as cosmology, Young had received only eleven days of schooling himself, and he recognized this shortcoming throughout his life. In spite of such a rudimentary education, Young read widely— in addition to studying Joseph Smith's teachings—and he spoke with many other people, particularly such visitors to Salt Lake City as Sir Richard Burton and Jules Rémy, who were well educated. His reading and discussions fed his exceptionally fertile mind. Because he considered education to be extremely important, especially in the quest for truth, and because he recognized his own deficiency, he sought to promote the education of the Mormons so they could have an advantage he did not. He sent at least five of his children, one daughter and four sons, to eastern schools for additional education. Little wonder that he expected the settlements to establish common schools—we would call them elementary schools—and academies. Public funds, donations, and tuition supported the schools. Young signed the legislation founding the public University of Deseret (now the University of Utah) in 1850 and endowed a number of private institutions, including Brigham Young Academy (now Brigham Young University) in Provo. He also chartered Brigham Young College in Logan shortly before his death. He expected the college to operate on the model of Oberlin College in Ohio, where students studied academic subjects and also practiced trades such as carpentry or blacksmithing. The college did not begin functioning until after he died. He was also unable to complete before his death plans for Latter-day Saints University in Salt Lake City—both of these institutions succumbed in competition with the state universities in Logan and Salt Lake City.

All too often, critics of Brigham Young have assumed that he controlled the Latter-day Saints through fear, coercion, and violence. We should understand, however, that these methods can control a people only if they have no way of escaping the system.

In Utah, most of those who wanted to leave the territory generally either did so, or they remained and fashioned their lives according to their own persuasion. Clearly, a few who wanted to leave could not do so because of violence—the Parrish-Potter murders are witness to that.

Many of those who left Utah chose moderate Mormonism by joining with Emma Smith in the Reorganization under her oldest son with Joseph Smith. Or like Wilford Woodruff's friend Alexander Badlam, some moved to California to engage in business. Some businessmen like brothers Samuel, David, Joseph, and Matthew Walker, and the Godbeites (an LDS offshoot of businesspeople and intellectuals), remained in Utah to run businesses outside the Mormon fold. Violence did exist in Utah, as historians Scott Thomas and Polly Aird have shown. Michael Quinn has argued that Utah harbored a "culture of violence." Most of it, however, as Thomas's study has shown, was uncoordinated vigilante action or commonplace criminal activity. Available statistics show that Utah was less violent than other areas of the West. In fact, Young wanted apostates to leave the community, so he could build Saints. "You nasty apostates, clear out," he said, as Polly Aird has reminded us. She has given us case studies of seven individuals who wanted to leave—and succeeded without too much difficulty. All of them believed that violence existed in the community, but Aird cited only Swiss emigrant, Frederick Loba, who made specific charges that are clearly questionable.

In many cases, those who wanted to leave could not because they were too poor or they owed debts that they could not pay. At times, the creditors and debtors could not agree on the extent of or even the existence of the debt. Such disagreements led in some cases to property confiscation by bishops or, in several instances, a demand by Brigham Young that the debtor pay what Young believed he owed before leaving.

A more pertinent question is: why would the Mormon people persevere by traveling a thousand miles to Utah and then disperse throughout the Mountain West, where they chose to live in relative poverty on hardscrabble farms, house their families in wagon boxes and dugouts, and dig irrigation ditches? They might have abandoned Mormonism and remained in the Midwest on prosperous farms blessed by summer rain. It seems ludicrous to believe they did what they did because of coercion. Rather, they found in Mormonism and Brigham Young's teachings a philosophy and way of life that offered happiness in this life and the expectation of an exalted one after death and resurrection.

The stories Young told and the precepts he taught led those who believed to love a man they called Brother Brigham. In more than forty-two years of sermonizing, Young covered a large number of topics. Significantly, although Young continued to use salty language during his entire ministry, the topics of his sermons became less spicy later in his life. Although he had spoken of blood atonement before the Utah War, afterward he spoke of the need for peace and kindness. In an 1860 sermon, he said he doubted that those who sinned willfully could receive forgiveness. In 1860 and 1871, he urged sinners to repent and change their ways so they could achieve the highest degree of glory and live with God and Christ eternally. Like other Mormon leaders since his time, Young believed the sin of Adam and Eve was beneficial to the human race because it opened the pathway for human beings to populate the earth. Between 1847 and 1852, his views on who could hold the priesthood changed radically, so that by the end of the period, he had condemned African American Mormons for more than a century and a quarter after his death to living without the blessings of the priesthood or temple ordinances. He apparently never changed his views that Adam was the god of this world and the father of Jesus Christ, a doctrine that other church leaders refused to accept. By contrast, Mormon leaders have generally continued to emphasize the importance of education, just as Young did.

9

Family Life and Polygamy

Young's faith in God and his certainty that humans could become gods and goddesses who could create kingdoms of their own provided part of the doctrinal grounding for nineteenth-century Mormon polygamy. At base, Mormons believed plural or patriarchal marriage was part of the restoration of all things, particularly of God's promises to Abraham—the polygamous patriarch who was the father of the covenant people—that through him all nations of the earth would be blessed. Young continued and expanded the doctrine, which Joseph Smith had told to a select few so they might go forward and "do the works of Abraham," as commanded in the Doctrine and Covenants Section 132. More expansively for those, like Young, with faith in nineteenth-century Mormon theology, it sealed the capstone on eternity. They believed that a man and wives who could manage multiple families gained some of the knowledge necessary to create and govern new worlds.

After at first rejecting polygamy, Young accepted it wholeheartedly. He eventually married fifty-five women, the most of any Latter-day Saint man. In the Mormon lexicon, Young was "sealed" to them in eternal marriage, which lasts for eternity, not just "until death do us part." Sixteen of these wives bore him twenty-six sons and thirty-one daughters. Eight of Young's wives, including Mary Jane

Bigelow (1827–1868, married [hereinafter m.]—1847, divorced [hereinafter d.]—1851) and Ann Eliza Webb (1844–1917, m. 1868, d. 1875), divorced him. In addition to his wives, he was sealed for eternity to thirty-one other women, telling Horace Greeley that he regarded them "as mothers rather than wives." In practice, he managed his own welfare program by providing for them as well as his connubial wives and children.

Fathering and managing these families in an age of patriarchal dominance—and especially during the forced exodus from Nauvoo and settlement in Utah—presented extraordinary challenges. By 1846, as the Mormons agreed, under violent force, to leave Nauvoo, Young had married twenty-one women; and as he traveled across Iowa to Kanesville and Winter Quarters in present-day Nebraska, he was sealed to nineteen more. Fifty family members left Nauvoo with him on February 18, 1846. Mary Ann Angell, his legal wife, brought six children with her, and children from previous marriages accompanied other wives. Young arranged for some of his wives to travel with their family or friends. Eliza R. Snow (1804–1887, m. 1844), for instance, traveled with the Steven Markham family and rarely saw Young as they emigrated. Several of his wives—Harriet Cook (1824–1898, m. 1843), Mary Elizabeth Rollins Lightner (1818–1913, m. 1845), Julia Foster Hampton (1811–1891, m. 1846), Mary (1821–1847, m. 1845) and Margaret (1823–1907, m. 1845) Pierce, Elizabeth Fairchild (1828–1910, m. 1844), Augusta Adams Cobb (1802–1886, m. 1843), and Mary Ann Powers (1816–1881, m. 1845)—remained in Nauvoo, many of them under extreme danger from vigilante attacks, until they could arrange transportation. Young assigned Joseph B. Noble, Almon W. Babbitt, and others to provide conveyance for them.

Some of the wives remained temporarily in towns that the Mormons established across Iowa. For instance, Emily Dow Partridge (1824–1899, m. 1844) and Zina Diantha Huntington (1821–1901, m. 1846) stopped briefly at Mount Pisgah, Iowa. Emily was caring for her baby, Edward Partridge Young. They did not join Young at Winter Quarters until spring 1847.

As Young struggled to transport his families from Nauvoo and arrange for their transportation to Winter Quarters, he carried an additional burden: overseeing the general exodus of all the Saints who agreed to move west. Approximately twelve thousand people lived in Nauvoo in 1844. Many of these were closely connected with the church leadership because most of the adults—perhaps five thousand, many of whom had families—received their endowments in the newly constructed temple during the winter of 1845–46.

As the 1847 companies arrived in Salt Lake City, they selected lands—called inheritances—for their town homes, yards, gardens, and outbuildings. In inheritances, the Mormons believed that God bequeathed the property to each person through His representatives, the church leadership. The beneficiary paid a $1.50-per-acre surveying fee, but otherwise, the land cost him nothing. Young choose a site on City Creek east and north of the temple lot. Until he could build houses there, Young made temporary accommodations for his families. He moved a number of wives and children to the Old Fort in what is now Pioneer Park between current Third and Fourth West and Third and Fourth South in Salt Lake City. As the Mormons abandoned the Old Fort, Young moved some of his wives and their children into a group of log houses called Log Row or Harmony House on his inheritance near present-day First Avenue. Harmony House included a long living room and five family rooms. Some of his wives lived temporarily in wagon boxes set on a trellis near Log Row. Margaret Pierce lived in the upper room of a recently constructed building nearby. Two of his wives lived in an adobe house built west of the future site of the Lion House. Mary Ann and her five children lived in an adobe house that was plastered white, known as the White House south of Log Row.

Over time, permanent dwellings replaced the temporary housing as Young constructed a complex of buildings, including three nearby homes. One of these, the Beehive House, designed in the Greek Revival style by Truman O. Angell, Mary Ann's brother, was built in 1853–54. Made of adobe bonded with slats of native pine on a foundation of hewn stone, the Beehive House still occupies the northwest corner of State Street and South Temple. Trained as a carpenter and joiner, Angell learned the rudiments of architecture from William Weeks, the architect of the Nauvoo Temple. After Angell designed the Beehive House—where Lucy Ann Decker (1822–1890, m—1842), Young's first plural wife, and her seven children lived—Young sent him on a mission to Europe to study architecture. Truman Angell also designed Young's office, which was built in 1852 between the future sites of the Beehive House to the east and the Lion House to the west.

In 1856 Angell designed the Lion House, an eclectic structure. The three-story Lion House got its name from the stone lion sculpted by William Ward that crouches over the south entrance. The Lion House accommodated twelve living wives with children, a number of childless wives, and some women for whom Young provided. Its lowest floor contained a kitchen, a long dining room, and a schoolroom. It also served as recreational space for the family. Situated on the second floor were a parlor for family gatherings, as well as nine apartments where several wives and their young children lived. Those who lived on that floor included Emily Partridge (1824–1899, m. 1844) and her children, Clarissa Decker (1828–1889, m. 1844) and her children, Emmeline Free (1826–1875, m. 1845) and her children, and Augusta Adams Cobb and her daughter, until they moved to a house on State Street (then called First East) north of current First South. In addition, several older women whom Young cared for lived on the floor. Some wives with children, childless wives, and older children occupied the top floor, which was fashioned with twenty bedrooms with dormer windows. These included Margaret Pierce and her son, Eliza R. Snow, Harriett Cook and her son, Harriet Barney (1830–1911, m. 1856) and her son, Eliza Burgess (1827–1915, m. 1852) and her son, Zina D. Huntington and her daughter, Martha Bowker (1822–1890, m. 1846), Ellen Rockwood (1829–1866, m. 1846), and briefly, Susannah Snivley (1815–1892, m. 1844).

The total complex of houses in the south, plus the outbuildings, yards, and gardens to the north and east, provided virtually everything the family needed. Amenities ranged from a blacksmith shop to a swimming pool. Members of Brigham's family could have their shoes made at a cobbler shop, order horseshoes from a blacksmith, get their horses shod at the barn, and obtain chairs and tables at the carpenter shop. Family members could attend school, shop at the family store, pick grapes from vines and fruit from the trees, or harvest vegetables in the gardens.

Most of the family lived in this complex for fifteen years. As the family grew in size and age, however, Brigham acquired or built separate homes for some wives. Emmeline Free with her ten children moved to a house on Main Street south of the complex. Emily Partridge and her seven children resided first on State Street and later on current Fifth East. Zina Huntington and her daughter lived on current Third South. Clarissa Decker had a home on State Street near the Social Hall. Harriett Barney and her son were domiciled on South Temple. Mary Van Cott (1844–1884, m. 1868) set up housekeeping on South Temple at the current site of the City Creek Center.

With most of his family situated in and around the South Temple complex, Young's wives divided responsibilities among themselves for the large community. Zina Huntington and Harriet Cook taught the children, holding school for the Young children in the Lion House until Brigham constructed a white schoolhouse east of his family complex. Eliza Snow, Lucy Bigelow, and Zina Huntington served as spiritual leaders for the community until Lucy left Salt Lake City.

Some of the wives eventually moved to other towns. Eliza Burgess and her son lived in Provo, fifty miles south of Salt Lake City. Lucy Bigelow and her three daughters transplanted to St. George in 1870. At age sixty-nine in 1870, Young himself would begin a yearly winter trip to St. George because of the warm climate there.

Young's family experienced both advantages and challenges with these arrangements. In the nineteenth century, daughters of working- and middle-class families were expected to learn the arts of household work and management. Young's daughter with Lucy Bigelow, Susa Young Gates, who was born in 1856, noted that many of the daughters missed out on such training. Instead, some wives and hired servants carried out many of these responsibilities. As a consequence, Susa said, she and many of the daughters "wasted a good deal of the rest of our time in useless frolic." She believed, nevertheless, that the religious convictions of the family held it together with very little—if any—strife or conflict among the families.

For nineteenth-century boys, life in a polygamous family offered a grounding for a much more conventional life. Society anticipated that young men would leave home to engage in professions, business, work, or a trade. Brigham's sons generally realized these expectations. Joseph A. Young constructed and operated railroads until his untimely death in 1875 at age forty-one. Young called both Brigham Jr. and John W. as counselors in the church's First Presidency. Brigham Jr.— often called "Briggie"— was also called to the Quorum of the Twelve Apostles in 1868 and served as a counselor to his father until Brigham died in 1877, at which point Briggie returned to the Twelve. John W. Young was sustained as a counselor to Brigham Young in 1873 and as his first counselor in 1876. The Twelve Apostles released him after Brigham's death in 1877 and sustained him as their counselor. After the Apostles released him from the latter position in 1891, his fortunes slid, and he lived in New York in humble circumstances, reportedly working as an elevator operator, at his death in 1924. Willard Young graduated as an engineer from West Point. He served in the engineer corps and was a professor at West Point. He subsequently served as a university and college president, commander of the Kansas City Engineering District during World War I, and director of the LDS church's building department later in life. Alfales Young earned a law degree at the University of Michigan and practiced law in Salt Lake City briefly, although he spent most of his life as a newspaper editor. Joseph Don Carlos Young earned a civil engineering degree at Rensselaer Polytechnic Institute in Troy, New York. Returning to Utah in 1879, he succeeded Truman Angell as church architect in 1887. He designed a number of edifices, including the Brigham Young Academy building in Provo, and he served as Salt Lake Temple architect during completion of construction. Feramorz L. Young spent two years at the Naval Academy at Annapolis, Maryland, before transferring to the Rensselaer Polytechnic, where he graduated the same year as Joseph Don Carlos. Brigham Heber Young engaged in a number of businesses before becoming president of an insurance and real estate company. Brigham Morris Young worked principally in organizing the Young Men's Mutual Improvement Association in communities throughout the Intermountain West. The YMMIA sponsored adult education and recreation. Lorenzo Dow Young worked in a number of businesses in Salt Lake City. Alonzo Young managed the wholesale shoe department in Zion's Cooperative Mercantile Institution (ZCMI), established by Young in 1868 and said to be the nation's first department store. Phineas Howe Young and Royal B. Sagers Young were partners in a music company in Salt Lake City.

Young's wives also excelled in many ways. In addition to those who served as teachers, a number managed Young family properties. Susannah Snivley, who had no children, moved to Forest Dale in southern Salt Lake City to manage Young's Forest Farm. Eliza R. Snow and her brother, Lorenzo, organized the Polysophical Society, a literary, theater, and music organization. In 1868 she reorganized the church-wide Latter-day Saint Relief Society, which had operated previously on the local level in some wards, and served as its general president until her death in 1887. Margaret Pierce managed Young's gristmill in what later became Liberty Park. Lucy Bigelow served as matron in the St. George Temple, supervising and participating in the vicarious temple work for numerous famous women. Zina D. Young served on the all-female board of Salt Lake City's Deseret Hospital and later as general president of the Relief Society.

In an age when women generally achieved status by marriage to prominent or successful men, several of Young's daughters were college educated, and some achieved considerable success in their own right. Young sent Vilate and another daughter to

Massachusetts for finishing school. Zina Young Card helped to establish the Mormon settlements in Canada. Susa Young Gates, who studied at the University of Deseret (now University of Utah), worked as a successful writer and editor for a number of Mormon publications, including the *Relief Society Magazine,* and worked diligently in the battle for women's rights. Maria Young Dougall served as First Counselor in the Presidency of the Young Women's Mutual Improvement Association, an organization to provide continuing education and recreation for young women. She was also active in Utah and nationally in promoting women's suffrage. In 1870, Ella Young Empey, Emily Young Clawson, Zina Young Williams, Maria Young Dougall, Caroline Young, Eudora Lovina (Dora) Young, and Phebe Young served as officers in the retrenchment association that Young proposed and Eliza R. Snow organized to promote frugal and virtuous living among young women.

Others, though prominent and active themselves, owed some of their status to the success of their husbands. Two of Young's daughters, Alice and Emily, married Hiram B. Clawson, Brigham Young's business manager and a successful businessman in the firms of Clawson and Eldredge and ZCMI. Ella Empey was the wife of Nelson A. Empey, vice president and director of the Deseret Agricultural and Manufacturing Association and an officer in ZCMI. After a failed marriage, Susa Young Gates married Jacob F. Gates, a prominent church leader and missionary. After two failed marriages, including one to Wilford Woodruff, Susa's sister Eudora married Albert Hagen, an attorney and clerk of the territorial supreme court.

Later in life, Young expanded his downtown housing complex. In 1873 he commissioned the construction of the Gardo House on South Temple across the street from the Beehive and Lion houses. William Harrison Folsom, one of Brigham Young's fathers-in-law, and Joseph Ridges, a talented builder, designed the house in the elaborate French Second Empire style. Young planned it as a suitable venue for receptions and other formal occasions.

Young promised Folsom's daughter, Harriet Amelia (called Amelia) (1838–1910, m. 1863), and Mary Ann Angell a life estate in the house, but construction was not completed until 1883, six years after his death. To solidify their occupancy, the two women actually moved into the house before workers finished the building.

The two women never really liked the Gardo House. Mary Ann died in 1882, before construction was finished, and after Young's death in 1877, the court awarded the house to the church in the settlement of his estate. Amelia declined to continue living there and moved back to the Lion House. Young's successor as church president, John Taylor, occupied it as his official residence, but he did so infrequently because of his need to flee Salt Lake City to hide out from U.S. marshals during much of the 1880s. The church's fourth president, Wilford Woodruff, held some meetings there, but after the completion of Woodruff Villa on Fifth East near 1600 South in 1891, he generally lived there rather than the Gardo House.

How do we judge the equity of accommodations and provisions for Young's families? The houses and conditions in which the wives lived varied. Residence in the multi-roomed Beehive House for Lucy Ann Decker was clearly superior to the rooms in the Lion House where a number of wives lived. Mary Ann Angell had a home of her own, and she lived briefly in the unfinished Gardo House. Nevertheless, by drawing on the family store, the gardens, and other amenities, family members lived in relative comfort, and Brigham Young's account books show a relatively equal distribution of goods and services to each of the families.

On balance, Young tried to provide accommodations for each of his wives, as well as education and other opportunities for his children. Given the size of his family, it seems remarkable that he and his wives and children accomplished as much as they did. Young had at least eight divorces from among fifty-five wives, but divorce in Utah was very easy. In many nineteenth-century states, adultery was the only basis for divorce except when a couple agreed to a separation from bed and board. Utah, by contrast, had no divorce law; all a couple had to do to divorce was agree to separate, which many did formally in court. If the couple had a church sealing, Young ordinarily granted a church divorce to women who applied for it. He was reluctant, however, to grant divorces to men. He considered men responsible to live with their wives in love and harmony. It is clearly a tribute to Young's faith and attention to the wives and children, but more extraordinarily, it is a testimonial to the faith of the wives and children to remain in marriages in which they had to live under such diverse circumstances.

As Leonard Arrington has noted, members of the family who lived in and around the Beehive-Lion House complex followed a general routine each day. After the hard times of the 1850s when the family had to ration its food, family members generally ate breakfast together in the morning. The meal usually consisted of toast, eggs, milk, and stewed fruit. The children attended school from nine to four with two hour-long recesses and a one-hour break for dinner at mid-day. In our current society, many urban families eat breakfast in the morning, a light lunch at mid-day, and a large dinner in the evening. Like many nineteenth-century families and many rural and small-town families today, Young's family ate substantial meal for dinner at mid-day and a light supper in the evening. After food shortages abated, the family generally built their noonday dinner around a meat dish—beef, lamb, bear, elk, or goose—during the week, with chicken on Sunday. Supper generally consisted of bread and milk or cornmeal mush, cheese, fruit, and bread.

When he was in town, Young met each day with his families who lived in and around the Beehive-Lion House complex. Generally, about fifty family members gathered in the late afternoon and evening. The families ate supper together at five o'clock, after which they held a meeting with gospel instruction and family fun, finishing with prayers at six-thirty. Following the prayers, the family held an evening devotional. In the devotional, Young counseled family members about various matters, including recreational activities or his advice about the problems of the young people.

Young expected all of his family members to come to the family meeting, prayers, and devotional. He observed that occasionally one or another of his wives or some of his children would fail to attend. The absent ones often offered excuses such as that they had gone to visit a sister, neighbor, or other relative. Because their children were scattered about the town, some wives said they could not assemble them. One wife or daughter might say that she was changing a dress, or putting on shoes, or getting ready to go to the theater. Young refused to accept such excuses, and he told the family in no uncertain terms that when the others met for prayers, all wives must attend with their children. They must "be ready to bow before the Lord and to make their acknowledgments to Him for His kindness and mercy and long-suffering towards us. . . . Strict attendance to my wishes in this respect will give joy to the heart of your Husband and Father."

Young generally acted as an indulgent and affectionate father, but he could be strict. For instance, one young boy had the habit of hitting his mother's hand as she held the dish and spoon he was supposed to use for bread and milk at suppertime, knocking it on the floor. Young advised his wife to lean the boy against the chair, and go on about her work. She did as he suggested. The boy leaned against the chair for a while, then he reached down and picked up the dish and spoon and placed them on the table. She reported that she had no further trouble with that boy. Sometimes, however, Brigham Young resorted to corporal punishment. One evening, while the family knelt together while Young said a prayer, one little daughter ran around noisily squealing and laughing. Young stopped praying, spanked the girl, and set her sobbing in her mother's arms. Then he resumed his prayer.

In an 1872 sermon, Young criticized some boys for their dangerous activities in the streets. Some of them taunted teamsters, challenging the drivers to run over them, or they forced carriage drivers to rein in their horses to avoid running them over. Young counseled that "if one of my boys attempts to obstruct the highway, take your whip and give him a good sound horse-whipping." On the other hand, he said, "I think of a truth, that a boy of mine never did this, never."

During the 1860s, Young promoted frugality and the Word of Wisdom, a series of health rules advised in a revelation by Joseph

Smith. He asked his family to observe the Word of Wisdom for their own sakes and to set an example for others. He urged his wives to sew their own clothes as much as possible, not to follow worldly fashions, and to dress frugally. His wife Zina designed a "Deseret Costume" that used far less material and boning than contemporary fashions.

Young urged his families to make certain his children had an adequate education. He counseled this, in part, to prepare them to speak intelligently with others when they served missions. In addition, he believed that a good education "will save them from the influence of evil." If parents do not educate their children, "when we are weighed in the balance we shall be found wanting."

Young expected his children to remain active in the church. Eleven of his sons filled missions, with eight of them laboring in England. Others accepted assignments to various areas, including Hawaii, the eastern United States, Switzerland, the American South, and Mexico. Young believed that missionary work helped young men to adopt "the principles which are to guide him through his future career, [if he has not] been dilatory and careless."

He urged his sons to take advantage of opportunities for self-education while they served. As he wrote to two sons in England, "you are in the midst of the world's activities, the discoveries of science and the masterpieces of inventive genius are within your reach and you have many bright opportunities of increasing your range of knowledge and widening your views of man and nature." He spoke from experience, having visited sites of historic, cultural, and scientific importance while on a mission in England.

Despite Young's efforts to provide equitable treatment for his families, all was not sweetness and light in Young's household—contrary to Susa Young Gates's supposition. I have relied on the research of Laurel Thatcher Ulrich for much of the information in the following paragraphs. As Ulrich noted, Augusta Adams

Cobb functioned as one disruptive force. She had seven children by Henry Cobb, including a daughter, Charlotte, who was the only child to accompany Augusta to Utah. She tried to take her baby, George, whom she called Brigham, with her, but he died on the way west. Dissatisfied with her small family in Utah, Augusta frequently begged Young for sexual relations to bear additional children. Born in 1802, she was forty-one years old when she married Young in 1843. By 1850, when she settled in Utah, she was forty-eight, and Brigham insisted she was too old to bear additional children. She disagreed quite vigorously and continued to demand marital relations. When Young refused, she asked him to allow her to consort with someone else—she even suggested Ezra Taft Benson, one of the Twelve Apostles—but Young continued to refuse her entreaties.

Augusta also resented that she saw Young so infrequently, and that she did not achieve status as a queen in the Mormon community. She had believed that by marrying him, her position would equal Mary Ann's. She was continually disappointed at being counted as merely an additional wife—one of the girls. After attempting without success to see Young over a long period, Augusta concluded that correspondence was her only alternative, and she penned a letter to him, writing, "My pen is my only weapon that God has given me to fight my way through this unfriendly World."

After enduring hunger in 1850, Augusta stole a bushel of corn from the tithing house to pay for some meat. In defending herself and threatening to do the same again in order to secure some tea, she wrote that "her husband has been sending it [tea] around to others and forgetting her." This was an intense rebuke of Young, who taught that a husband must support his families through his labor. She deserved the food from the tithing house, she said, because it was for the poor—and she was poor.

In large part, Augusta's dissatisfaction seems to have resulted from her background. Unlike most of Young's wives who came from working-class families, as a Massachusetts Adams, Augusta had been reared among the first households of the Bay State, and her former husband, Henry Cobb, was a successful merchant. She resented having to subsist on short rations, slop pigs, cut firewood, wear "thin" fabric, and do the other things plural wives did to care for themselves and to work together in the interest of the large household. She refused to learn to spin thread and weave cloth, though she said that her daughter, Charlotte, might learn if she chose.

Augusta antagonized Young's other wives by refusing to cooperate with them, and she declined to recognize Mary Ann as her superior. Along with other Mormon women, she belonged to the Council of Health and the Female Council of Health, organizations established to promote Thomsonian medicine, and she managed to irritate others in both organizations. In the Council of Health, for instance, she supported Dr. Jeter Clinton, while most members opposed him when he claimed to know more than others did. In addition to working as a physician, Clinton served as Salt Lake City coroner and alderman. After Brigham Young gave a discourse in which he urged that women could easily be delivered of babies just as animals and Indians were, she rebelled at the comparison of pregnant women with beasts and native Americans, though she agreed that male doctors should not deliver babies.

By contrast, as Ulrich has shown, Zina Huntington Jacobs came from a working-class background and fit well into Young's family. Instead of suing Zina for adultery and making her marriage to Young a *cause célèbre* as Henry Cobb did with Augusta, Zina's previous husband, Henry Jacobs, approved of her sealing to Young; Jacobs moved to California and remarried. In addition, Zina's brothers, Dimick and Oliver, had joined the church, and they provided familial support for their sister.

Zina taught school for the Young children, and she cooperated and participated happily with Mary Ann and Young's other wives. While she lived in the Old Fort, Dimick arranged space for her to teach fifty students. She taught school after moving to the South Temple complex, starting with some of Brigham's boys and later teaching larger groups of his children. Zina also participated in religious services, sometimes by speaking and singing in tongues.

In 1863, at age sixty-two, when many men would have looked forward to retirement, Young married twenty-four-year-old Amelia, daughter of church architect William H. Folsom and second cousin of Frances Folsom, whom President Grover Cleveland married during his first term as president. Many considered Amelia to be Young's favorite wife, and his actions support the claim: he commissioned the Gardo House, often called Amelia's Palace, for her and Mary Ann. Young frequently escorted Amelia to concerts and plays, and she accompanied him on his tours to southern Utah.

At the time of their marriage, Amelia would have learned that her husband was not a typical polygamist. Unlike Young, most polygamous men had two wives. No others had fifty, as Young did at the time of their marriage. Many Americans did not know Young was unique in this way, as lurid tales of Mormon polygamy led a gullible and in some cases prurient audience to believe that all Mormon men presided over harems with multiple wives. Nevertheless, several other leaders broke with the general pattern. Heber C. Kimball had forty-three wives (with sixteen divorces); George Q. Cannon, a counselor in the First Presidency, had five; Daniel H. Wells had seven (with one divorce); and Wilford Woodruff had nine (with four divorces).

Not all Mormon men entered polygamy as enthusiastically as Young. In practice, leaders often believed it necessary to encourage monogamous Mormon men to enter into patriarchal marriage. If a church leader called a monogamist to a bishopric, stake presidency, stake high council, or stake patriarch, he frequently urged or pressured the man to take a second wife. George Q. Cannon said he "did not feel like holding up his hand to sustain anyone as a presiding officer . . . who had not entered into the Patriarchal order of Marriage." Daniel H. Wells said any man "who can and will not obey it [plural marriage] shall be damned." In an 1878 sermon, Joseph F. Smith, then an apostle and later church president, made a similar statement in an extended argument for plural marriage.

Nevertheless, like some lay members, some general authorities remained monogamous. These included Anthony W. Ivins, member of a stake high council in St. George, a stake president in Mexico, and an apostle, and Anthon H. Lund, a mission president and apostle. Both Ivins and Lund later served in the church's First Presidency.

From the late 1880s and into the twentieth century, as Mormons campaigned to accommodate themselves to traditional American society, they began to argue that monogamists like Ivins and Lund were the norm. The Utah Commission, a federal body assigned to enforce the 1882 Edmunds Act (which prohibited polygamists from voting or serving in elective office), estimated that registration agents had disfranchised twelve thousand polygamists. During the struggle for statehood and after Utah entered the union, in an attempt to minimize the extent of polygamy, a number of church leaders extrapolated from that figure and estimated that only about 3 or 4 percent of Mormon men practiced plural marriage. That figure is statistically flawed because it counted only men who married polygamously as a percentage of the entire Mormon population, by assuming that women and children in polygamous families were not polygamous. Historian Kathryn Daynes, geographer Lowell C. Bennion, and others have recognized that it was more accurate to calculate the number of people living in polygamous families. Using census data, Daynes calculated that the percentage of polygamous families in Manti at 25 in 1850, 43 in 1860, 36 in 1870, 25 in 1880, and 7 in 1900. She could not calculate the 1890 percentage because the Utah census had burned. Bennion's research on Brigham City showed results similar to Daynes's for 1870. From what we currently know, statistics like Daynes's seem generally accurate for the nineteenth-century Mormon population.

Although we can generalize with these statistics for the entire population, the percentage of polygamous families in Mormon towns varied widely. Bennion determined that the percentage of polygamous households in 1870 varied from a low of 7 percent in Coalville in eastern Utah to 68 percent to the small southern Utah town of Pintura. Available evidence suggests that the peak percentage of polygamous families occurred during the Mormon Reformation of 1856–57, when leaders pressured men to enter the Patriarchal Order of Marriage. The high percentage Daynes found in the 1860 census resulted from this. After 1860 the percent of polygamous families in the Mormon population declined. Although some new marriages occurred after the 1890 Woodruff Manifesto—in which Woodruff announced a revelation in which he said that he intended to obey the law prohibiting polygamy "and to use my influence with the members of the Church . . . to have them do likewise" (Doctrine and Covenants, Official Declaration 1)—the incidence of polygamy in the orthodox Mormon community abated, as Daynes's statistics confirm.

Because we can with some confidence determine the percentage of polygamous families, and because Mormon leaders encouraged—even pressured—church members to enter into polygamy, we wonder whether most husbands and wives opted to remain in unhappy marriages, as Augusta Adams Young did? By examining family group records prepared by descendants, sociologist Phillip Kunz calculated the divorces in Utah for Mormons married between 1844 and 1890. He determined that 9 percent of polygamous husbands and 3 percent of polygamous wives divorced, while only 0.9 percent of monogamous marriages ended in divorce. Daynes, who used court records as well as family group sheets, found that 17.8 percent of Manti polygamous marriages ended in divorce. Statistically, the incidence of divorce among polygamous families exceeded that of monogamous families.

Bennion asked why only 25 to 30 percent of the Mormons lived in polygamous families, when Mormons believed that plural marriage was part of the restoration of all things and members were obligated to embrace the principal. Demographer Val Lambson answered by calculating that, in a stable population in which the numbers of men and women are relatively equal, as they were in the Mormon community, only 15 to 20 percent of the men and 25 to 30 percent of the women could marry polygamously. Clearly, the community could not sustain the large percentage of marriages contracted during the mid- to late 1850s. The unusual increase in that period, as Wilford Woodruff noted, occurred because relatively older men married teenagers who had barely reached menarche. Even in normal circumstances, because some leaders like Young and Kimball married more than two women, some Mormon men had difficulty finding anyone to marry. Some parents exacerbated this difficulty because they urged their daughters to marry successful men, and some prominent men competed with younger and less wealthy men for the attention of eligible women. On the whole, 25 to 30 percent of the families living in plural marriage in 1870 would have been a normal situation rather than evidence of lack or loss of faith.

Most non-Mormons had little concern for the percentage of families in polygamy. Instead, they insisted on and actively sought the institution's eradication. The national Republican platform in 1860 did not contain a plank attacking the "Twin Relics of Barbarism," as the 1856 platform had. Rather, it focused on eliminating slavery in the territories. In 1862, though, as Congress outlawed slavery in the territories, it attacked polygamy and the church itself by passing the Morrill Anti-Bigamy Act. The act prohibited polygamy in the territories and forbid any church from owning more than $50,000 worth of property in any territory.

Despite a public clamor, the anti-polygamy provision of the Morrill Act was essentially a dead letter until 1874, and the government did not enforce the property limitation until after 1887. Because Mormons controlled the empaneling of juries until 1874, no grand jury indicted a polygamist in Utah until passage of the Poland Act that year. Under this law, the county probate judges, generally Mormons, chose half the jury panels, and the clerks of the district courts, generally non-Mormons, picked the other half.

Following passage of the Poland Act, the U.S. attorney for Utah, William Carey, and the First Presidency agreed to bring a test case to determine the constitutionality of the Morrill Act. Mormons considered it an unconstitutional infringement of the free exercise clause of the Constitution's First Amendment. George Reynolds, a clerk in Young's office, agreed to stand trial, and Carey agreed not to bring suits against other alleged polygamists until the courts finally ruled in the Reynolds case. When Carey broke the agreement by securing an indictment against George Q. Cannon of the First Presidency, the Mormons refused to continue cooperating, and Reynolds fought unsuccessfully against conviction. After he was convicted in the district court, Reynolds appealed to the Utah territorial supreme court, which overturned his first conviction on a technicality. When, in his 1875 second trial, the jury found him guilty, Reynolds lodged an unsuccessful appeal to the territorial supreme court, and afterward appealed to the United States Supreme Court.

Responding to Reynolds's appeal, the chief justice of the U.S. Supreme Court, Morrison Waite, rendered the decision in *Reynolds v. United States* (98 U.S. 145, [1878]) upholding Reynolds's conviction. The court's decision essentially eviscerated the First Amendment's free exercise clause by ruling that Americans might believe anything they wished, but they could not practice religious principles that the nation's laws prohibited. Brigham Young lived long enough to learn of the district court and the territorial supreme court rulings, but he died the year before this decision.

Reynolds's conviction proved a pyrrhic victory for anti-polygamists, however, because of a Supreme Court ruling in *Miles v. U.S.* (103 U.S. 304 [1880]). Writing for the court, Associate Justice William B. Woods ruled that the prosecution must prove a previous marriage had occurred in order to convict a defendant of plural marriage. During the trial, John Miles admitted he had married Caroline Owens, who was the chief witness against him, but the prosecution could not prove he had married Emily Spencer polygamously. Because Miles testified he had married Owens and denied his marriage to Spencer, Owens—as his wife—could not testify against him, and the court threw out her testimony. Utah had no civil registration until 1887, so no records were available to prove either marriage. After the decision overturning Miles's conviction, without incontrovertible evidence of a polygamous marriage, the prosecution could not enforce the Morrill Act.

Thus, even in view of Reynolds's conviction, because of the difficulty of proving a marriage had taken place, Mormons could still practice polygamy with relative impunity by the time of Young's death in 1877. Nevertheless, because of statistical limits, the percentage of polygamous families surpassed its peak during the extraordinary conditions of the late 1850s. New plural marriages declined during the 1880s, and especially during the 1890s, after the Woodruff Manifesto.

Because of Young's extraordinarily large number of marriages, Young's family situation differed from most polygamous families that had two wives rather than many more. Despite his unusual situation, Young generally provided a conventional life for his children. Poorly educated himself, Young insisted on elementary (then called common) schooling for his children and college and finishing school for some of them. A number of his sons succeeded in nineteenth-century society, although the fortunes of some, like John W. Young, declined into poverty. A number of his daughters married well, and many participated in the community in significant ways.

With some exceptions, Young's families generally accommodated themselves to patterns Young fashioned for the large number of wives and children. He tried with relative success to provide each family equally with available goods and services. His wives in general accommodated themselves to a hierarchy of position or they complained but remained, though, as in the case of at least eight of them, they left the flock in divorce. Young had some difficulty securing attendance of all of his families at the daily family gatherings, but monogamous families undoubtedly had similar difficulties, especially with socially active women and willful children, particularly teenagers with their inevitable desire for independence. Young's family situation was certainly not the horrible state of affairs portrayed in the popular press and Republican Party rallies. Rather, on the whole, Young's families seem to have worked well generally in the unusual situation in which they found themselves.

10

The End of One War and the Duration of Another

Young and other Latter-day Saints had moved their families from Salt Lake City to Provo as part of the Move South during the Utah War, so troops of the Utah Expedition marched through a nearly vacant city and on to their newly established base at Camp Floyd well southwest of the city. After the army settled there, the Mormon and non-Mormon communities began the extremely difficult task of reconciling themselves to the results of the Utah War.

Reconciling the two sides was difficult, however. Federal judges Delana Eckels, John Cradlebaugh, and Charles Sinclair; Col. Albert Sidney Johnston and other army officers; and U.S. Marshal Peter Dotson made the reconciliation virtually impossible by refusing to recognize that President Buchanan's pardon meant absolution. In their normal dealings with the Mormon people, they denied that—despite the pardon—the Saints deserved the same rights, privileges, and cooperation afforded other American citizens. Pretending judicial ignorance, Judge Sinclair announced that he would insist that individual Utahns appear in his court to plead acceptance of the pardon. U.S. Attorney Alexander Wilson refused to countenance Sinclair's ploy, however, and the judge had to abandon his ill-advised ruling. Nevertheless, Cradlebaugh, Eckels, and Dotson refused to cooperate with Utah's local citizens in enforcing the law in general and in investigating and prosecuting the Mountain Meadows massacre in particular. Even after the Buchanan administration placed the army under civilian control, the judges continued to shun help from Utahns.

As historians Donald Moorman and Gene Sessions have shown, Johnston inadvertently helped the Mormons in northern Utah by sending soldiers to the northern overland trail in response to Shoshone and Bannock attacks on emigrant trains and mail carriers. Because of the reduced power of the Indians, Mormons successfully established fifty-one settlements in northern Utah during the three years the soldiers occupied Camp Floyd. These included towns in Cache Valley, which the Saints had abandoned when they moved south during the Utah War but were able to restore.

On the other hand, Brigham's people paid a high price for settling in Shoshone-Bannock territory. The Shoshones attacked Kington Fort near Ogden; Willard, south of Brigham City; and other settlements in Box Elder County. After Peter Maughan and a party of Mormons returned to Cache Valley in 1859, the Shoshones tried to dislodge the Mormons. A battle took place at Smithfield, seven miles north of Logan, after Mormon officials imprisoned a Shoshone man who had stolen a horse, then killed him as he tried to escape. The Shoshone troops, who had come to free their colleague, killed Mormon settler John Reed and wounded Samuel Cozens in a battle that followed the Indian's death. Chiding the settlers on the arrest and death of the Shoshone, Brigham Young wrote to Cache Valley leader Maughan, "I hope that the brethren will learn that the loss of a horse or two is not so much value as the life of a person."

Conflicts broke out as soldiers with pockets full of cash and looking for a good time went on leave from Camp Floyd. In Fairfield, near the camp, which the soldiers called Frogtown, and in Salt Lake City, troops encountered camp followers eager to unburden them of their money. This combination transformed the territorial capital's Main Street into a sinkhole of gambling, inebriation, and prostitution. Saloons, gambling houses, and brothels sprang up like weeds in an untended garden, and violence and murder made Main Street, nicknamed Whiskey Street, a place no respectable citizen dared visit—a condition that seems strange considering Young's homes were just around the corner, and one of his wives lived on Main Street.

Complementing the emigrant criminals, organized violence sprang from Mormon miscreants as well. Battles for the spoils of crime pitted William A. "Bill" Hickman's gang against Lot Huntington's. Huntington, a well-known cattle and horse thief and general desperado, backed by half-dozen men, called Hickman out on Christmas Day 1859, and charged that Hickman had informed on him. In an ensuing gunfight, both men wounded each other, Hickman so seriously that his friends thought he might die. Needing little or no evidence to support their charges, anti-Mormons attracted considerable public notice by loudly blaming Brigham Young for the violence and murders. Those who were poorly informed chalked up the murders to defunct organizations such as the Danites or fictitious conspiracies they called Brigham's Avenging Angels. However, Leonard Arrington, after careful study, believed the Danites and Avenging Angels did not exist in Utah, though Young did have Minutemen prepared to respond to emergencies. The charges of a nefarious organization would gain considerable public support in 1872 when Hickman, by that time excommunicated from the church for his criminal activities and working for former general Patrick Edward Connor, published his fabricated confessions with the assistance of journalist J. H. Beadle. Instead of accepting blame for his crimes, Hickman insisted he was under orders from Brigham Young—yet no one has ever proven Young ordered the murders he committed

Dissatisfied with their failure to implicate Young in Hickman's crimes, a group associated with Col. George H. Crossman, Camp Floyd's quartermaster, laid plans to entrap him, conspiring with John M. Wallace, a gambler from California, and Myron Brewer, a boyish-looking Mormon convert. Crossman enlisted David McKenzie, a Mormon engraver who worked in offices rented from Brigham Young, and with whom Crossman believed that Young cooperated, to engrave U.S. Treasury drafts drawn on the New York and St. Louis federal sub-treasuries. After organizing the scheme, Wallace placed Brewer and McKenzie in jeopardy so he could help Crossman in his plan to implicate Brigham Young. After Brewer tried unsuccessfully to pass some of the notes McKenzie had engraved in a card game, Crossman gave Brewer a free pass in order to bring charges against McKenzie—whom he had asked to engrave the notes—expecting to entrap Young as well, since McKenzie did his work in rooms the prophet owned. McKenzie ended up spending two years in prison, but he testified truthfully, saying that Young had played no part in the crime.

Convinced that McKenzie had taken the fall to shield Young, U.S. Marshal Peter Dotson raided the Deseret Currency Association offices, expecting to find evidence incriminating Brigham in the notes, files, and engraved plates. Dotson found no such evidence, but he wrecked some of Young's property in the raid. Young sued Dotson for damages and secured a judgment against the marshal for twenty-three hundred dollars. Dotson had to sell his house to pay the assessment, and he resigned in disgust after the government refused to support him.

Additional violence punctuated the conflicts between the army and the Mormon community. Because Congress had refused to extend the preemption and other land-acquisition laws to Utah Territory despite repeated requests from Young, the territorial legislature, and other Utahns, the army could legally ignore Utah's temporary land-distribution system. General Johnston designated military reservations in the rangelands used by Utah herders in Rush, Cedar, Skull, Tintic, and Goshen valleys. Holding a local permit, Bishop Daniel Spencer had used parts of Rush Valley to graze his cattle and run a saloon. In 1859 Johnston ordered Spencer's cattle removed, and when Spencer's nephew, Howard Spencer, who worked as a herder for his uncle, refused to comply, a confrontation ensued between him and soldiers commanded by lieutenants Louis

Henry Marshall and Alexander Murry. Murry ordered 1st Sgt. Ralph Pike to remove the cattle, but Spencer blocked his efforts. The evidence about what happened afterward is contradictory, but the outcome is not: Sergeant Pike bashed Howard Spencer over the head with his rifle butt, injuring him severely. Spencer lay on the verge of death, but Dr. Charles Brewer from Camp Floyd cleaned the wound, reduced the pressure of his swollen brain on his skull, and saved his life.

Indicted for attempted murder, Pike appeared in court in Salt Lake City. Spencer had partly recovered, and between sessions of court, he confronted Pike on the street, shot and killed him, and then fled. Pike's death motivated soldiers at Camp Floyd to attack the nearby Mormon town of Cedar Fort, where they destroyed buildings and haystacks. Johnston refused to hold those responsible accountable for the damages. A grand jury indicted Spencer for murder, but he escaped capture until 1889, when a federal jury acquitted him.

Rumors of these and other conflicts reached Brigham Young's office, but he could do little about the civilian-army conflicts. Among them was an altercation between a party of army officers that included Dr. Edward Covey on the one side and a group of lawmen that included Marshal John Sharp and deputy William H. Hennefer on the other. In the ensuing melee, one of the lawmen wounded Covey.

Covey carried a grudge to retribution. By 1860 the War Department had begun to reduce the force at Camp Floyd, and orders transferred Covey and a number of troops to New Mexico. While marching through Echo Canyon, the soldiers encountered Hennefer with a party of Mormon herders. Covey confronted Hennefer at gunpoint and, with the assistance of the other soldiers, stripped him naked, tied him to a wagon wheel, and whipped him nearly to death. After beating Hennefer, Covey demanded that the deputy return to Salt Lake City, show the wounds to Brigham Young, and tell him that he would have done the same to the prophet if he had been there. The soldiers then destroyed all of Hennefer's property, reportedly worth several thousand dollars. After recovering from the whipping, Hennefer tried to secure reimbursement from the army for the damages, but he failed just as the settlers at Cedar Fort had.

It is almost impossible to balance the social and economic cost to the people of Utah with the economic advantages they obtained by hiring on to construct Camp Floyd and sell supplies to the army. Such Mormon entrepreneurs as the Walker Brothers, Charles Woodmansee, William Staines, J. C. Kimball, William S. Godbe, and Jesse C. Little accumulated more wealth by trading with the army. Mormon workmen hired on as laborers and craftsmen at elevated wages. Brigham Young believed that some Mormons benefitted too much at the expense of the community, and he complained when some of them sold their grain to non-Mormon merchants for speculation while poor families starved. Non-Mormon merchants doing business in Utah benefitted as well, including Livingston and Kinkead; Miller, Russell, and Company; Perry, Radford, and Cabot; Brannon and Hockaday; Russell, Majors, and Waddell; Ben Holladay; and Gilbert and Gerrish, all of whom managed to enrich themselves through the trade.

Mormons also enjoyed a windfall from the closing of the fort. On July 16, 1861, as the last troops prepared to leave the camp, now renamed Fort Crittenden after Unionist Kentucky senator John Crittenden, the army destroyed the remaining arms and munitions. The command then auctioned $4 million worth of materiel and livestock for $100,000. Young urged Mormon businessmen not to bid against one another during the auctions, but his agent, Hiram B. Clawson, purchased a large part of the goods for Young.

By late July 1861, the troops had left Camp Floyd. They first went to Arizona and New Mexico, but as the Civil War intensified, they transferred to the Midwest and East. John Floyd, the anti-Mormon secretary of war, joined the Confederate army, as did Gen. Albert Sidney Johnston, who resigned his commission to become one of its leading generals. Johnston died in battle at Shiloh in 1862, and

Floyd, who served ignominiously at the Battle of Fort Donelson the same year, died in 1863. Both had become traitors—a charge they had leveled against the Mormons.

The army had left Fort Crittenden, but following the Confederate attack on Fort Sumter on April 12–13, 1861, news of the escalating war reached Utah—generally by the Pony Express, which brought news to Salt Lake City in about five days from St. Joseph, Missouri—between April 3, 1860, and October 1861. On October 17, 1861, the Pony Express became a relic of a bygone era as the telegraph line reached Salt Lake City, and on the 24th, the Pacific Telegraph Company completed the entire transcontinental telegraph link. The day after the telegraph reached Salt Lake, Young sent a message to J. H. Wade, the company president, in which he affirmed, "Utah has not seceded, but is firm for the Constitution and laws of our once happy country." In his reply, Wade complimented Young on his and the Mormon peoples' "patriotism and Union-loving sentiments."

Nonetheless, Mormon loyalty came into serious question shortly after New Year's Day 1862, although from a dubious source. Eager for equality with other Americans, Utahns continued to petition for admission into the Union, and in December 1861 the territorial legislature passed a bill authorizing a constitutional convention. Vetoing the bill, Governor John Dawson complained that the legislature had left too little time between the drafting of the constitution and the ratifying election. Commenting on the constitution and admission, Young said in February that the Utahns had proved themselves capable "to sustain self-government." The following month he said, "It is our right to frame our own laws, and to elect our own officers to administer them. . . . We will cling to the Constitution of our country, and to the Government that revers that sacred charter of freemen's rights; and if necessary, pour out our best blood for the defence of every good and righteous principle."

On December 31, 1861, shortly after the close of the legislative session, Dawson fled from Utah, reportedly because he made the mistake of propositioning the late Thomas Williams's widow. Several toughs, including Wood Reynolds, Jason Luce, and probably

Lot Huntington, John P. Smith, and Moroni Clawson intercepted and severely beat Dawson at Ephraim Hanks's mail station in Emigration Canyon. The Salt Lake City police arrested Huntington, Smith, and Clawson and charged them with beating Dawson. The policemen then shot the three prisoners "as they tried to escape."

Upon reaching Fort Bridger, Dawson wrote a scathing report to President Lincoln. Blaming the beating on Danites and calling Mormon loyalty to the Union "mythical," he charged that Mormon leaders had initiated the attack because he had vetoed the statehood bill. While it is true that Young had made critical comments about the Union, he commented unfavorably about the Confederacy as well, and there is no evidence that the gangsters beat up Dawson because of the veto. The Mormons did not need Dawson's approval to draft a constitution; they held a constitutional convention without his or anyone else's permission.

Young's views about Lincoln ran hot and cold throughout the president's tenure. Utah delegate John Bernhisel penned a letter to Young in December 1861 telling him that Lincoln had friendly feelings toward the Mormons, writing that it appeared that his friendship would continue. Young had not received Bernhisel's letter when, on December 10, he wrote to Wilford Woodruff, perhaps reflecting on Governor Dawson's current actions, condemning "cursed scoundrels [such] as Abe Lincoln and his minions . . . [who] have sought our destruction from the beginning."

In July 1861 Secretary of War Simon Cameron had written to California governor John G. Downey, authorizing him to raise a regiment of infantry and five companies of cavalry to protect the overland mail route and to establish garrisons in Nevada and Utah to guard the overland telegraph line. Young may not have learned of Cameron's request until December 1861, when word of the recruitment of troops in California passed through Salt Lake City on the telegraph line. Congress had established Nevada Territory from part of western Utah on March 2, 1861, and although its population was much smaller than Utah's, the Silver State would be admitted into the union on October 31, 1864, to provide three more electoral votes for Lincoln. Young believed that stationing

California troops in Utah was not only unnecessary but also a vicious slap at the Mormons. He argued that the Mormon militia could protect Utah and the overland mail route without outside help.

While these events unfolded in California, Utah's acting territorial governor, Frank Fuller, realized by April 1862 that the overland mail route remained unguarded. Fuller asked Lt. Gen. Daniel H. Wells, commander of the Utah territorial militia, to recruit a unit to guard the route. Some of the other federal officials wanted the superintendent of Indian Affairs, James Duane Doty, to lead the troops, but Brigham Young wired Washington through Delegate Bernhisel, offering Mormons for the duty. Fuller accepted Young's offer, and on April 25, 1862, Wells ordered Col. Robert T. Burton to guard the mail, persons, and property on the northern overland route. As they left for duty, Young counseled Burton's troops to refrain from drinking and swearing. He also cautioned Burton to treat everyone with kindness, including the Indians. In his efforts to guard the trail, Burton discovered, among other things, a cache of mail sacks at Ice Spring Station in Wyoming, many of which had been ripped open and looted of money. He concluded that whites rather than Indians had committed the robbery. His unit would serve until returning to Salt Lake City on June 1, 1862.

Burton's troops performed under territorial rather than federal authority, but on April 28, 1862, Adj. Gen. Lorenzo Thomas, following orders from Secretary of War Edwin Stanton and President Lincoln, ordered Brigham Young to "raise, arm, and equip one company of cavalry for ninety days' service . . . to protect" the telegraph and mail in the area near Independence Rock. On orders from Young, on April 29 Wells organized a cavalry unit commanded by Capt. Lot Smith. It seems ironic that Burton and Smith had been among the leading commanders of Mormon troops during the Utah War. The two and their soldiers now took up arms to fight for the United States in the Civil War, Burton under Wells's command and Smith under the command of Brig. Gen. James Craig at Fort Laramie. Following Craig's orders, Smith's cavalry searched for several Shoshone parties that had stolen livestock on the overland trail. Smith remained on the overland route until August 14, when the army released his unit in Salt Lake City.

Although Smith's cavalry failed to capture any of the Shoshones they sought, they did succeed in making the overland route safer. Before Smith's unit reached the overland route, Ben Holladay's overland stage company had stopped operating because of raids by Shoshone warriors, but after Smith's unit began its service, the stages began running again. Holladay telegraphed Young, thanking him for his positive response to Lincoln's request for troops.

Eight months before Smith returned to Salt Lake City, Irish emigrant and Stockton, California, resident, Patrick Edward Connor responded to Governor Downey's request by recruiting and organizing the Third California Volunteer Infantry Regiment. In March 1862, a month before Smith's unit left for the overland trail, Gen. George Wright, commander of the Department of the Pacific at San Francisco, ordered Connor to prepare to move east, and on May 26 Connor transferred his infantry to Camp Halleck near Stockton. On August 3, a couple of weeks before Smith's unit mustered out, Connor's regiment of 850 men arrived at Fort Churchill on the Carson River in Nevada.

From Fort Churchill, Connor stopped in Ruby Valley in northeastern Nevada on his way to Utah. After he reached Utah, instead of halting at Camp Floyd, he located his headquarters on the bench east of Salt Lake City. He named his post Camp Douglas (later to become Fort Douglas) for Illinois senator Stephen A. Douglas, whom Lincoln had defeated in the 1860 election and who had died in June 1861. After establishing Camp Douglas, Connor brought troops on from Fort Ruby, arriving by October 26, 1862.

Connor wasted little time revealing his hatred of the Mormons. In a dispatch from Ruby Valley to General Wright on September 14, 1862, he wrote that he found the Mormons "a community of traitors, murderers, fanatics and whores." Future comments like this coursed through Conner's missives to San Francisco. Nevertheless, while he was engaged in recruiting and marching his infantry to Fort Churchill, two units of Mormon militia served to guard the overland mail route. In contrast to Colonel Connor's charges, Lot

Smith's commander, General Craig, complimented the Mormons on their excellent service.

Connor's belief that the Mormons were traitors undoubtedly resulted from his perception of Brigham Young's action after Lot Smith's cavalry was mustered out. On August 24, 1862, Secretary of War Edwin Stanton authorized General Craig to enlist a hundred more men and to reenlist Lot Smith's cavalry for an additional ninety days. Utah territorial governor Stephen S. Harding met with Young to ask him to reenlist Smith's cavalry, but Young told him that this was not the time to do so. Harding interpreted the reply as evidence of disloyalty.

Young's attitude, however, was much more complicated. He had experienced conflicts with volunteer and state militia in Missouri and Illinois and regular army units led by Steptoe and Johnston in Utah. All four cases had resulted in conflict with the Latter-day Saints. Young believed that Utah's territorial militia was fully capable of protecting the territory from rebels and guarding the overland mail route against Indians. He feared that stationing an infantry unit from California in Utah with anti-Mormons serving as governor and judges would lead to further trouble for the Mormon people. He also considered it an affront that those selling supplies to the army had to take a loyalty oath.

Young took some measures both to protect his people and to gain whatever advantage he could from the army. He admonished the teachers in each ward to discourage women from going to Camp Douglas. He also appointed a central committee to set standard prices for supplies sold to the army.

Still, Young understood that the Mormons faced serious disadvantages. Young provided a buffer as territorial governor while Steptoe's unit was in Utah, and Governor Cumming had treated the Mormons fairly by controlling Johnston's troops after they abused the citizens of Provo. In 1861 Cumming had left to join the Confederacy, Dawson had fled the territory, and Governor Stephen Harding, who disliked the Mormons, had replaced him. On October 30, 1862, Young said crudely that "If you were to fill a sack with cow sh–t, it would be the best thing you could do for an imitation" of Governor Harding. Having long feared armies, and with Harding at the helm, Young opposed the re-enlistment of Smith's unit for service on the overland trail. He thought that the Mormons could easily do what the California volunteers were supposed to do, and he thought that anti-Mormonism motivated the dispatch of troops to Utah.

Young's fear of armies had developed over a long time. He had managed to avoid participation in the war in northern Missouri but had suffered himself and seen considerable suffering among the Mormons as they fled to Illinois. Anti-Mormon militiamen had killed Joseph and Hyrum Smith, an independent militia had attacked the Mormons in Nauvoo, and the Mormons had experienced considerable difficulty with some of Lt. Col. Edward Steptoe's troops. He feared that Connor had really come to oppose and perhaps fight the Mormons. Under the circumstances, he refused to encourage Smith's troops to reenlist while what he perceived as a hostile army had established a post in Salt Lake City.

Connor's attitudes about fanaticism, women, and murder may have had roots in generally negative perceptions about the Mormons. As a devout Roman Catholic, his religious convictions may well have led him to think of the Mormons as fanatics, and the general opposition to polygamy undoubtedly led him to believe that having multiple wives was prostitution. He used the well-known Anglo-Saxon pejorative "whores" in his letter. Even though statistics have shown that the incidence of murder in Utah was well below that of surrounding territories except during the Utah War, nineteenth-century stories emphasized the number of murders in Utah, and like many at the time, Connor thought them centrally directed.

Young considered Connor's hatred of the Mormon people and his location of an army post in Salt Lake City to be insults to him and his people. Nevertheless, he could do nothing to prohibit Connor from planting his soldiers at Camp Douglas. In reflecting, Young concluded that the post's location on the bench overlooking the city was "the best place they can be"—much better than Forts Crittenden or Bridger. He believed that at the other sites "they would go unrestrained," but at Salt Lake "they cannot do much hurt." Still, he also thought it "foolishly improvident" to base the soldiers in Salt Lake City if they intended to guard the overland mail route.

Like Young, when General-in-Chief Henry W. Halleck learned of Connor's decision to locate his headquarters at Salt Lake City, he considered it a poor location to protect the overland mail and stage route from Shoshone raiders. Halleck ordered Connor to relocate the Third California Volunteers to Fort Bridger, but Connor argued with Halleck by falsely insisting that Brigham Young planned to "oppose the Government of the United States in the spring" if Utah were not admitted into the Union. He also charged that the Mormons had cooperated with the Indians in the overland mail depredations. Supporting Connor, New Mexico's acting territorial governor, William F. M. Arny, charged that the Mormons intended to join the Confederacy. In fact, throughout the Civil War, Utah remained in the Union, although the Mormon people and their leaders complained of their treatment and frequently expressed discontent with both the Union and the Confederacy.

Although neither Connor nor Arny had any evidence for these assertions, their falsehoods helped keep the California Volunteers in Salt Lake City. General Wright ignored Halleck's orders and told Connor he could choose his own base. Connor enjoyed the active support of Governor Harding and of judges Thomas J. Drake and Charles B. Waite. Although Harding seemed friendly to the Mormons when he first arrived in Utah, he quickly sided with Connor and other anti-Mormons, calling the Mormons traitorous. In an address to the legislature in December 1862, he questioned the Mormons' loyalty and attacked polygamy.

Perhaps only Connor's hatred for the Indians equaled his hatred for the Mormons, and he ordered troops in his command to attack them, often indiscriminately. As his infantry marched across Nevada, he dispatched Maj. Edward McGarry's cavalry on Indian raids. After arriving in Utah, he sent McGarry to Cache Valley in November and December 1862 to fight Bear Hunter's band of Northwestern Shoshones. In these engagements, McGarry's troops killed a number of Shoshones, some in cold blood.

Not to be outdone by McGarry, in January 1863 Connor himself led troops in what turned into a massacre of Bear Hunter's and Sagwitch's bands of Shoshones, then camped near the Bear River a short distance from Franklin, Idaho. In the early stages of the battle, sixteen infantrymen died in combat, and another seven died afterward from wounds sustained in the fighting. After defeating the Shoshones in a flanking movement, however, Connor's troops unleashed a horrible massacre, killing Shoshone warriors, women, and children, and raping women indiscriminately.

Estimates of the number of Shoshones killed in the Bear River Massacre varied. Connor reported the Shoshone death toll at 224. Franklin resident Hans Jesperson said he counted 493 dead Shoshones on the battlefield. Frank Warner, Sagwitch's son, who was also known as Beshup Timbimboo, said the army killed 156. Bear Hunter died in the battle that preceded the massacre, but Sagwitch and some family members escaped. An accurate estimate would probably place the dead at nearly 300. Ignoring the massacre, Connor's whitewashed report called the engagement a military victory. Believing his version of the massacre, the War Department promoted him for the victory—to the permanent rank of brigadier general and the brevet rank of major general.

Connor and Harding continued to bombard civil and military officials with letters charging the Mormons with disloyalty, urging the stationing of more troops in Utah, and either proposing the annexation of Utah territory to surrounding territories or disfranchising the Mormons by giving more authority to federal appointees. They continued to charge that the Mormons cooperated with the Indians in committing depredations on the overland trail, and army and civil officials refused to believe that the Mormon people followed Brigham Young voluntarily. Brigham Young interpreted their efforts rightly as a campaign to eliminate Mormon control of Utah's government and eradicate their participation in civil administration.

The Mormon people, Young, and Lincoln's friends responded in various ways. Utah's civilian population held a protest assembly, met with governor Harding, and sent a petition to Washington.

In early 1863 a group of Lincoln's associates sent Col. J. M. Rosse to investigate the charges against the Mormons and report to the president. Rosse met with Brigham Young who told him emphatically "the allegation [that he was disloyal] is *utterly and absolutely false.*" He cited the Mormon response to the enlisting of the Mormon Battalion and the recruitment of troops to guard the overland mail route as examples of their loyalty. Professing his and the Mormon people's love for the Constitution and government, Young denounced the charges that the Mormons had assisted or encouraged the Indians in their depredations. However, he told Rosse that he emphatically resented that the government had sent troops to Utah when the Utahns themselves could easily have guarded the overland mail route, and they definitely did not need troops to guard themselves.

Nevertheless, throughout the succeeding years, Connor bombarded General Wright and his successor, Gen. Irvin McDowell, at San Francisco with letters requesting more troops and denouncing Brigham Young and the Mormons as traitors. He insisted that numerous "American citizens" wished to leave the territory but could not go without his protection. Connor charged that he was "fully satisfied that they [the Mormons] only wait for a favorable opportunity to strike a blow against the Union." He continued to allege that the Mormons worked with the Indians to attack civilians and mail carriers on the overland trail. In June 1863 Connor wrote, "The world has never seen a despotism so complete, so limitless, so transcendent." He admitted, however, that the Mormons had no love for the Confederacy. He also charged that the Mormons assisted the Indians in their depredations, but he said even if that were not true, the Indians lived near their settlements and the Mormons fed them.

Brigham Young viewed conditions much differently. The church president feared that the army would either try to kill him or arrest him for practicing polygamy. Preparing for a possible attack, the Mormons armed themselves and organized Minutemen to protect Young and guard the territory against possible Indian attacks. Utah delegate John Bernhisel tried unsuccessfully to disabuse federal officials in Washington of the charges the Mormons were traitors, but both he and William Hooper failed in their efforts to change Lincoln's mind about Young's disloyalty. Instead, on July 8, 1862, Lincoln signed the Morrill Anti-Bigamy Act with the results outlined in the previous chapter.

In March 1863 Judge John F. Kinney ordered Marshal Isaac Gibbs to arrest Brigham Young on a charge of practicing polygamy. Contrary to the fantasies of Connor and Harding, the army did not have to battle the Mormon militia to bring Young to court. After Gibbs delivered the summons, Young appeared voluntarily before Judge Kinney. Kinney admitted him to $2,000 bail, and scheduled him to appear at the next court term. The case would never come to trial.

At about the same time, President Lincoln had decided he would not try to attack the Mormons. He faced, after all, a much more serious problem in battling the Confederacy. He spoke about his policy both to Bernhisel and to Mormon journalist T. B. H. Stenhouse. As he often did, Lincoln couched his decision in an anecdote. He told the two Mormons that to avoid a log on a plot of land he was trying to clear, if the log were too wet to burn and too big to move, he simply plowed around it. Likewise, he told the two men he would leave Young alone if Young would leave him alone.

Perhaps aware of Lincoln's policy, the tenor of Connor's correspondence took a turn in spring 1863. The general wrote that if he were not to receive reinforcements as he had frequently requested, Washington should withdraw his command from Utah and accept Brigham Young's offer to guard the overland mail route. Perhaps in panic, General Wright ordered Connor on May 6 to raise one or more companies in Utah if the volunteers would enlist for three years or the duration of the war.

Neither the nation nor Connor found out whether the Mormons would have joined the Union forces in 1863. By the time Wright's order reached Utah, Lincoln had lowered a barrier in his relationship with the Mormons by removing Harding as Utah governor and sending him to Colorado as a judge while appointing Superintendent of Indian Affairs James Duane Doty as governor. Doty generally got along well with both Connor and the Mormons, but he refused to issue a call to recruit troops in Utah. In 1862 Lincoln had also appointed Hosea Stout as U.S. attorney for Utah—the only Mormon appointed to a major federal office in Utah between 1858 and 1890.

To the Mormons' disappointment Lincoln also removed territorial secretary Frank Fuller and Judge John Fitch Kinney. Fuller had enjoyed an amicable relationship with the Mormon community. Kinney, whose letters had contributed to Buchanan's decision to send the Utah Expedition to Utah, had returned as chief justice of the territorial supreme court, and had proved himself an even-handed jurist. The Mormons rewarded Kinney for his fairness by electing him their delegate to Congress—the only non-Mormon to serve as delegate until 1893.

With Harding's removal and Lincoln's announced intention to leave the Mormons alone, Young thought relations in Utah would run more smoothly. Working with both sides, Doty and Connor negotiated treaties with Pocatello's and Sagwitch's Shoshones and Sanpitch's Utes. In October 1863 Connor bragged that they had secured "the settlement of terms of peace with all the Indians within this military district from the Snake River on the north to the lower settlements of Utah, and from the Rocky Mountains on the east to Reese River on the west." Future events would prove his boast considerably overstated.

Doty accompanied Connor and a number of his infantry and cavalry units to escort a large number of civilians to Soda Springs on the big bend of the Bear River in Idaho. The civilians were followers of Joseph Morris, a Mormon apostate who had received revelations calling him as prophet to replace Brigham Young. In early 1861 Morris had established a collective settlement in South Weber, a site near the Weber River and the Weber-Davis County line.

Local Saints resented Morris's community and religion, and rowdy Mormon toughs harassed the Morrisite people even as local law enforcement did nothing to protect the them. Morris predicted Christ's Second Coming and the beginning of His millennial reign on a number of occasions. After these prophecies failed, some Morrisites became disillusioned and, led by William Jones, tried to leave the cooperative and take with them the property they had dedicated to the community. Refusing to allow them to do so, Morris had them imprisoned at the compound. Learning of the detentions, Judge Kinney ordered their release and sent a posse under Deputy Marshal Judson Stoddard to free them. Yet Morris burned the court order in front of Stoddard.

With Stoddard's failure, acting governor Frank Fuller ordered Robert T. Burton to lead a Nauvoo Legion unit to free the prisoners. In a violent overreaction, Burton's unit approached the compound with rifles, pistols, and a cannon. Morris refused to release the detainees, and Burton attacked with overwhelming military power, killing Morris and a large number of his adherents. Several posse members died in the fight as well, and Burton arrested several of the surviving Morrisite leaders. They were tried in Kinney's court and convicted of second-degree murder, but Governor Harding, believing the convictions unjust, pardoned the prisoners. Connor and Doty then escorted them to Soda Springs.

Brigham Young remained a burr under Connor's saddle, however, so the general again sent requests for more troops in the belief that he could suppress the "galling church tyranny" through martial law. The federal government refused to allow this, so the general turned to the promotion of mining in a failed attempt to overwhelm the Mormon population with non-Mormon miners. Connor expected that if non-Mormons knew of the extensive ore deposits in Utah's Wasatch and Oquirrh mountains, they would respond to the lure of wealth and flock to Utah. These newcomers, he expected, would "disabuse the [Mormon people] . . . of the false, frivolous, yet dangerous and constant, teachings of the leaders." Like many anti-Mormons, Connor believed that the church leaders had somehow deluded the otherwise intelligent Mormon people, and that non-Mormons would convert them by revealing the error of their beliefs.

To spur the search for ores, Connor authorized a liberal leave policy among his troops and helped to organize the first mining district in Utah. He expected the soldiers to prospect and mine, and he tried as much possible to advertise Utah's mining potential, participating in the organization of the West Mountain Quartz Mining district in the Oquirrh Mountains. Ironically, Mormon miners also helped in the organization of the mining district that took place at Mormon bishop Archibald Gardner's gristmill in West Jordan in December 1863.

Brigham Young had spoken frequently in opposition to precious-metal mining, preferring instead an economy based on farming, manufacturing, trade, and industrial mining. He favored the recovery of what he thought of as useful minerals such as coal, lead, salt, and iron, but thought that extensive prospecting for gold and silver would undermine solid economic development. Nevertheless, various Mormons engaged in the activity.

Connor also opened another line of attack by establishing a newspaper, the *Union Vedette.* Newspapers were the world's principal pre-electronic broadcast medium. Soldiers at Fort Douglas staffed the *Vedette* under its first editor, Capt. Charles H. Hempstead. While providing news of Fort Douglas, the *Vedette* campaigned for mining in Utah and published numerous anti-Mormon articles. Not incidentally, the paper preached patriotism while disparaging Young and the Mormon hierarchy as deluded traitors. In response, the church paper, the *Deseret News,* emphasized Mormon patriotism and editorialized for Utah's admission to the Union. The paper also reminded its readers that miners would need food that farmers could supply. Fortuitously, the Mormons had a non-Mormon ally in Congress with Judge Kinney as territorial delegate.

Never at a loss to find ways to attack Young and the Mormons, Connor had concluded by July 1864 that the Saints had launched a campaign to depreciate fiat currency the federal government issued, generally called greenbacks. To finance the war, Salmon Chase's Treasury Department had printed and circulated paper currency backed by neither gold, silver, nor something like the Federal Reserve, which was not established until 1914—the greenbacks had only the presumed ability of the government to redeem them. Their value actually fluctuated in relation to gold with the Union's fortunes in its battles with the Confederacy. Ignorant of what really drove their worth, Connor concluded at first that the decline in their value had originated with Salt Lake City's merchants, who had begun to insist on the payment for goods in gold. Flour, he pointed out, had increased in price from fifteen dollars to twenty-three dollars per hundred pounds. Shortly thereafter, in prejudiced ignorance, he insisted that Young was the real culprit because he urged the people to demand gold rather than greenbacks.

To counter what he perceived as Young's traitorous attack on the currency, Connor stationed an entire company as a provost guard under Captain Hempstead in a store opposite the south gate of the temple block. Connor simply did not understand that deficit financing by Congress and the printing of unsupported greenbacks had created the inflation. By mid-1864 their value had inflated to $2.58 in greenbacks to $1.00 in gold. Salt Lake City's merchants, including the Mormons, had simply responded to the inflation as any responsible businesspeople would, by increasing the price of goods and services.

Almost immediately after posting the provost guard in downtown Salt Lake City, both Connor and Young anticipated a conflict between the citizenry and the army. Recognizing the potential for violence, and acting on orders from Maj. Gen. Irvin McDowell who had replaced Wright in San Francisco, Asst. Adj. Gen. Richard C. Drum ordered Connor to "Remove the guards and troops rather than their presence should cause a war." On McDowell's orders, Drum wrote again that the worst thing that could possibly happen would be a war with the Mormons. "The object of troops being at this time in Utah is to protect the overland route," Drum reminded Connor, not "to correct the evil conduct . . . of the inhabitants of the Territory." He continued in no uncertain terms that "the major-general commanding . . . does not at this day deem it expedient to interfere by military force to regulate the currency in the District of Utah." Connor continued to insist that the disloyalty of the Mormons necessitated a strong force to convince them that war would be futile. Perhaps as a sop to Connor, McDowell authorized a small contingent of military police to deal with problems caused by soldiers, not to address any perceived difficulty with the Mormons.

Connor also proposed to conduct an aggressive campaign against the Indians east of Utah and outside his district. In correspondence with General-in-Chief Halleck, McDowell emphasized that he believed that if Connor were allowed to pursue his intended policy, instead of avoiding conflict, he would become embroiled in wars with both the Mormons and the Indians. McDowell gave Connor permission to travel to Denver on personal leave, but refused permission to move his troops east outside his district. Connor, already embarked, halted his troops at Fort Bridger.

By early 1865 battles led by generals Ulysses S. Grant and William T. Sherman had worn down the Confederacy to such an extent that Union victory seemed certain. Young had also come to understand that statehood for Utah would not arrive soon, nor would the federal government extend the land laws over Utah and allow its citizens to obtain clear titles to their farms, businesses, and homes. He said as much in a letter to Kinney. Moreover, he encouraged the *Deseret News* to let the *Vedette* rant and rave but to not respond to its allegations of disloyalty.

In February 1865 Young proposed that the Salt Lake City officials sponsor a major festivity to celebrate both the Union capture of Charleston, South Carolina, and Lincoln's second inauguration. On March 4 the city council, officers at Fort Douglas, and federal officials held a joint festivity. Governor Doty, Chief Justice John Titus, and Mormon leaders all gave speeches, and soldiers marched. On April 11 both Mormons and non-Mormons cheered after learning of Robert E. Lee's surrender to Grant two days earlier.

Then the city sank into mourning shortly after Lincoln's assassination on April 14. His carriage draped in black crape, Young flew the flags at his residence at half-staff. On April 21 representatives of all factions met in the Old Salt Lake Tabernacle on Temple Square in a memorial service for the slain president.

The Salt Lake Tabernacle, which replaced the Old Tabernacle, was then under construction, but it was not dedicated until 1867. William Harrison Folsom designed the sandstone piers that supported a roof of timbers constructed in a Remington lattice truss work designed by Henry Grow. Folsom designed the interior ceiling as a three-dimensional ellipse with the pulpit at the west focus and a point in the congregation at the east focus. Young had prescribed the specifications, commenting that the design mimicked "the best sounding board in the world . . . the roof of my mouth." As a result, in the pre-electronic age, the congregation enjoyed extraordinary acoustics, but only after the construction of a balcony that surrounded the lower floor to eliminate echoes that previously created poor acoustics.

Connor, whose command had been reassigned in February 1865 from San Francisco to Gen. Grenville M. Dodge's Department of the Missouri, wrote that his policies had pacified the Indians. He predicted that his policy of promoting mining would end Utah's isolation by attracting an influx of non-Mormons and bring about the demise of Mormonism. He missed the mark with both prophecies. Nevertheless, in a needless move made to prevent the Mormons from persecuting their opponents, the federal government decided to leave troops at Fort Douglas for the foreseeable future. After a visit with Brigham Young in June 1865, journalist Samuel Bowles agreed with Connor that the influx of more non-Mormons to Utah would "soon solve the polygamous problem,—rightly and without bloodshed."

In an addendum to his book *Across the Continent: A Summer's Journey to the Rocky Mountains, the Mormons, and the Pacific States with Speaker Colfax,* Bowles insisted that sometime in August or September 1865 after he and Speaker of the House of Representatives Schuyler Colfax had left Utah, Young had given a sermon in which "he said that nine-tenths of the people of the Territory were southern sympathizers; that the North was wrong, and this people sympathized with the South." I have tried without success to find any sermon during August and September 1865 in which Young said anything like the words that Bowles attributed to him. There are two collections of Young's sermons. One is the *Journal of Discourses,* a twenty-six-volume incomplete collection of sermons by general authorities given from 1851 to 1886. Another is Richard S.

Van Wagoner's *Complete Discourses of Brigham Young* (5 vols.; Salt Lake City: The Smith-Petit Foundation, 2009). Van Wagoner consulted every source he could find for all the sermons that Young gave, and he published multiple versions of many of the sermons. He found none given in August or September 1865 that even came close to including anything like the words Bowles attributed to Young, although a number of the sermons were not reported. None of Young's reported talks addressed the recent Civil War or the Confederacy. It would have been odd for Young to say such things at so late a date. Lee had surrendered in April, and Young and other prominent Mormons joined with non-Mormons in celebrating the Union success. Moreover, Young was traveling during most of those two months, giving instruction to the members and leaders in settlements on their church duties, with his itinerary taking him from Logan in the north, Tooele in the west, and St. George in the south.

Because Bowles was not actually in Utah during the two months, he probably got spurious information from an anti-Mormon who set out to paint a negative picture of the Mormons in general and Young in particular. Bowles, however, published information that he heard directly that painted a much different picture. In his text, Bowles reported his interview with Young in June 1865 in which Brigham told him "now that peace is established let all [rebels] be pardoned." Bowles quoted Young as saying that early in or during the war, he (Brigham) "would have disposed of the rebel chiefs that fell into the hands of the government without mercy or hesitation." Quoting Young, Bowles continued: "Had he been President when [Confederate diplomats James Murray] Mason and [John] Slidell were captured, he would have speedily put them 'where they never would peep.'" In fact, Union officials had removed Mason and Slidell from the British ship *Trent,* causing an international incident.

How do we understand the events from 1858 through the end of the Civil War? During the war, Mormon leaders spoke frequently on what they perceived as the reasons for the war and its outcome. As author

John Gary Maxwell has pointed out, some Latter-day Saint leaders wanted Utah to join the Confederacy. Young did not. Nevertheless, on occasion, Young said he viewed the conflict as God's retribution upon the United States for allowing Missouri and Illinois to persecute the Saints. Clearly, however, stationing of the California Volunteers in Utah outraged Young. He believed, as even Connor eventually admitted, that the Mormons could easily have guarded the overland trail routes as they did with Burton's and Smith's volunteers. In addition, Young found it insulting that the Union should station an army in Salt Lake City to make certain the Mormons did not engage in treason. Moreover, in spite of Connor's, Harding's, and the *Vedette*'s harping, there is no evidence of any Mormon activity that could reasonably be interpreted as treasonous. Nevertheless, because Young found the sending of outside troops to Utah an affront, he refused to promote Mormon service in the Union army. As historian Kenneth L. Alford has shown, some Mormons did serve, but with the exception of Burton's and Smith's units, Young did not encourage them to do so. Moreover, Utahns were never given the opportunity to organize volunteer units because neither Governor Harding nor Governor Doty, the officials who would have had to issue orders for such units, issued such a call, though Harding tried unsuccessfully to secure Young's cooperation to enlist them.

As we will see in the coming chapters, the years after 1865 proved extremely difficult for Brigham Young and the Mormon people. They faced continued persecution as they tried to build the Kingdom and improve their own lives. Changes in government policy eventually allowed them to obtain titles to the property they had occupied, but not before Young and others endured abuse of federal officials and war with the Indians.

11

Cooperation, Expansion, and Black Hawk

Although the Civil War had ended, Brigham Young and the Mormon people faced additional challenges. Construction of the transcontinental railroad, which Young heartily endorsed, led to outside competition with Utah's businesses. Before 1869 the long distance and slow wagon travel had buffered the Mormons from the threat of competition from outside non-Mormon firms. As the railroad threatened to eliminate those barriers, Young proposed cooperative manufacturing and marketing to protect the community, and he encouraged the reduction of wages, which some vigorously opposed. Young also feared that precious-metal mining would entice too many Mormons from occupations such as farming, manufacturing, and other occupations in their search for the mother lode. Opposition to Young's economic policy and the attraction of spiritualist séances, popular in the mid-nineteenth century, led to the disaffection and excommunication of several prominent Latter-day Saints. Young's belief in the unity of the sacred and the secular led him and others to invest heavily not only in businesses, but also in adequate venues for religious, dramatic, and musical activities. Undoubtedly, however, the Black Hawk War posed the most serious challenge to the Mormons. Post–Civil War conflict with American Indian tribes led to the deaths of numerous settlers and Indians, a number of horrible massacres, the abandonment of Mormon settlements in central and southern Utah, and removal of the Utes to the Uinta Basin.

As these events unfolded, Young and the Mormons found it extremely difficult to explain their point of view to non-Mormon critics. Many outsiders considered the Mormons to be non-Christian deviants, and they thought Young was a dictator who wielded absolute power. Far from serving as a despot, Young had a complex relationship with other church and local secular leaders and with the general church membership. Young met regularly with his counselors, the Quorum of the Twelve Apostles, and civic leaders to obtain counsel on church and community matters.

In the selection of replacements for general and local authorities, for example, Young discussed the candidates with his counselors and the apostles. He considered the apostles' recommendations fully before making a nomination, which then required apostolic approval. This procedure led to the calling of many leaders, including apostle and First Presidency member George Q. Cannon, one of the most capable of late nineteenth-century leaders. In LDS usage, a call is an assignment given by inspiration from someone in authority to a man or woman under his supervision to either serve in some position or perform some task.

Recognizing that he needed advice from a broader group than his counselors and the apostles, however, Young organized the School of the Prophets in 1867, resurrecting the name from an organization Joseph Smith had established in Kirtland. The name implies a theological purpose, but in addition to church doctrine and practice, the members discussed subjects such as the allocation of resources, the response to economic change—especially that caused by the railroad—and how to protect the community from social corruption. This broad agenda seemed reasonable to Latter-day Saints because, like Young, they did not believe in the separation of the spiritual and secular. At its peak, the Salt Lake City school included nearly a thousand prominent men and women; following that city's model, leaders in nearly thirty other towns organized schools of the prophets as well.

As they formed these new organizations, Young and church leaders also organized prayer circles of their friends, in which those present dressed in ceremonial clothing and joined in prayer. They also discussed religious and temporal matters while they met.

Establishing and operating Mormon settlements was much more complex than conventional wisdom would lead us to believe. Contrary to the popular image, Young did not call all of the Mormon emigrants to settle in various towns. Although he called many of the faithful to various areas to achieve a distribution of talents and occupations, many Mormons settled where they pleased. Leaders announced many of the calls from the pulpit at general conference, but some members ignored the calls—without adverse consequences. Others abandoned the towns to which Young sent them and returned to the more prosperous Salt Lake Valley. In addition, without his approval, local leaders engaged in such horrors as the Parrish-Potter murders, the Mountain Meadows massacre, and massacres during the Black Hawk War.

Although church leaders discussed such topics as murders and massacres, another matter seriously affecting the church in the 1860s was differences of opinion over church doctrine. In the interest of collegiality, the First Presidency and the Quorum of the Twelve Apostles met together in council in 1860 to discuss whether each of the fifteen men could consider themselves free to publish their views on doctrines with which the others disagreed. As the discussion progressed, Young insisted that the Spirit influenced his pronouncements on doctrine, but in the interest of harmony, those present agreed that they would avoid the discussion of controversial subjects. Despite this agreement, Mormon leaders' public preaching sometimes contradicted one another, and the discord may not be illustrated anywhere better than in the different views on the nature of God held by Brigham Young and Orson Pratt.

Young visited each of the Mormon towns as part of his stewardship, and he sent members of the Quorum of the Twelve Apostles to serve as leaders in many of the outlying towns. Since the twentieth century, all of the First Presidency and Twelve live near Salt Lake City, although they are often called on temporary assignments for duties such as serving as president in outlying areas of the church. In the nineteenth century, however, Young called members of the Twelve to supervise settlements throughout Utah and southern Idaho, and he sent others to direct church affairs still farther afield such as in Europe and on the East and West Coasts.

A number of examples are instructive. In 1853 Young called Lorenzo Snow to lead fifty families to Box Elder County to settle in Brigham City, a relatively unsettled area at the time some sixty miles north of Salt Lake City. Similarly, in 1851 Charles C. Rich and Amasa Lyman led a large party to establish a colony at San Bernardino in southern California, after which Young recalled the Saints from California in 1857 as the Utah War approached. In 1863 he also sent Rich to establish settlements in the Bear Lake region in southeastern Idaho with Paris, Idaho, as the principal hub. Lyman went to Fillmore, 150 miles south of Salt Lake City, in 1863 to lead the colonists in Millard County. Young sent Orson Hyde in 1855 to lead the settlers to Carson Valley, which was then a part of Utah Territory and later would become a piece of western Nevada. Hyde returned to Salt Lake City in 1857 to settle in Spring City, Utah, one hundred miles south of Salt Lake, where he oversaw the Sanpete and Sevier Valley settlements. Young called Franklin D. Richards in 1869 to settle in Ogden north of Salt Lake to lead settlements in Weber County and to serve as probate judge, and in 1861 Young had called Erastus Snow and Orson Pratt to go to Washington County in southwestern Utah to preside over the Cotton Mission. With the Civil War raging, Young believed the climate in southern Utah offered an excellent location to raise cotton and other subtropical crops. Pratt stayed only a short time there before returning to Salt Lake City, but Snow remained there to preside over the settlements in southwestern Utah and southeastern Nevada. In 1854 Young sent Ezra Taft Benson to Tooele, west of Salt Lake, and then in 1860 to Cache County in northeastern Utah.

These leaders represented the church leadership in various areas even as rails of the transcontinental railroad approached

Utah. Contrary to the belief of some, Young did not oppose the railroad. Rather, Young and the Mormon leaders wanted the railroad to reach Utah long before it actually arrived. After completion of the first transcontinental railroad in 1869, Young expected to build railroad connections to the various Mormon towns. As the crews constructed the roadbed west from Omaha and east from Sacramento, members at the School of the Prophets discussed its potential impact on the Mormon community. Many had ridden on the railroad in the East and Midwest, and they understood that it would collapse distance and time, and entrepreneurs would be able to sell mass-produced goods such as shoes more cheaply than local shoemakers could cobble them. Young expected competition with factories in the Midwest to reduce the wages of Utah workers. Furthermore, entrepreneurs, who had previously declined to invest in Utah mining because of the prohibitive expense of shipping ore and minerals by wagon, could soon access markets by railroad. Young knew that mining development would attract outsiders, many of them non-Mormons and some of them anti-Mormons.

During the Civil War, railroad construction had moved at a snail's pace. Central Pacific crews began building eastward from Sacramento in 1863, using what for them was cheap and expendable Chinese labor. The CP crossed the Sierra Nevada with difficulty because a roadbed of less than 2 percent grade required extensive blasting and tunneling. The Civil War delayed construction of the Union Pacific until 1865. After the war, however, the UP had less difficulty traversing the 1,085 miles from Omaha to Promontory Summit, Utah, than the CP did in building over the 690 miles from Sacramento, in part because they could lay rails on relatively flat land on the plains and cross the Rockies at South Pass, Wyoming, while the CP had to build through the rugged Sierras.

The Mormons had anxiously anticipated the railroad's construction since the 1850s, and Young and other church and business leaders invested in both the CP and the UP. To mitigate the impact on the Saints of the saloons, prostitution, and gambling that came with the hell-on-wheels railroad towns, Young negotiated contracts for grading the roadbed in Utah so the work would be done by

Mormon men, though both railroads tried later to get out of the contracts and ultimately cheated Young out of full payment for grading done by Mormon crews. Despite repeated demands for the money they owed him, he reluctantly accepted rails, ties, and some rolling stock at pennies on the dollar.

In an attempt to capitalize on the railroad's construction and transshipment by wagon to Montana, non-Mormons founded the town of Corinne near the Bear River in Box Elder County, where they expected to establish the formal junction of the two railroads. Young managed to finesse their plans by purchasing land in Ogden, a Mormon settlement, which he donated to the Central (later Southern) Pacific for its terminal and marshaling yards. Although the rails joined at Promontory Summit, the two railroads agreed on Ogden as the division between the lines. Young then killed the hopes of Corinne's developers by constructing the Utah Northern through Weber, Box Elder, and Cache counties to Franklin, Idaho. He had expected to build the line north to Montana, but when he could not finance the project, he sold the railroad to the Union Pacific, and the UP laid the track to Garrison, Montana. Corinne became just another small agricultural town.

The decision of Union Pacific engineers to bypass Salt Lake City by entering Salt Lake Valley through Weber Canyon to Ogden disappointed Young, but Young and Mormon businesspeople made the best of the situation by constructing the Utah Central Railroad from Ogden to Salt Lake in 1870. Young also managed to construct the Utah Southern from Salt Lake into Utah County and eventually to Chicken Creek (now Levan, fifty-two miles south of Provo) in Juab County. He had hoped to build the railroad to Mormon communities such as Fillmore, Beaver, Cedar City, and St. George, but that plan failed for lack of funds, just as the northern project had. The Union Pacific bought the Utah Southern, but instead of laying rails to the Mormon towns, it headed southwest to Milford and Minersville to tap the mines in southwestern Utah. Of the Mormon communities in southern Utah, the railroad reached only Cedar City, but not until 1923.

As railroad construction proceeded, Brigham Young also recognized the important role that women could play in meeting its challenges. After the death of Joseph Smith, Young at first opposed the reorganization of the Relief Society that Smith had organized in 1842. Responding to various needs, however, Mormon women took the initiative in the 1850s to organize Relief Societies in various town wards. They patterned these after the original organization to which many of them belonged. The Relief Society women offered help to needy Mormons and to Indians, and they strove to encourage high moral standards in their towns.

Recognizing the need to revive a church-wide Relief Society, Young called Eliza R. Snow, one of his wives and a woman of extraordinary skill and intelligence, to preside in 1867 as general Relief Society president. She traveled from town to town organizing local groups. In the process, the local Relief Society building became a mainstay of Mormon towns. In addition to providing charitable assistance to the needy, the Relief Societies joined with the Schools of the Prophets in an effort to undermine extravagance and promote frugality.

Young also recognized that beyond the Relief Society, women could play important roles in building God's kingdom in other ways. He thought it ludicrous that big, able-bodied men should tend store counters as clerks. Women, he said, could do such work. He also recognized the intelligence of women, encouraging them to secure educations as doctors and lawyers, and as the telegraph spread north and south throughout Utah, he encouraged women to work as telegraphers. Such an attitude, sexist perhaps by twenty-first-century standards, was clearly progressive in the nineteenth century. In addition, although Young considered the man as head of the family, he insisted that the husband and father must earn the respect of his family. Women, he said, need not follow or obey an abusive or unrighteous husband. As a result, he allowed women to divorce quite freely. Young and other church leaders also supported the proposal for women suffrage. Mormon women worked diligently on this project, which bore fruit in Utah as the legislature approved a measure in 1870 and non-Mormon acting governor Samuel A. Mann signed the legislation.

As he encouraged women to secure education, jobs, and the right to vote, Young, who had received very little formal education himself, championed not only schooling but also public enlightenment. As early as December 1854, he had met with Wilford Woodruff and a number of friends in the Salt Lake Sixteenth Ward schoolhouse to establish a philosophical society. Young persuaded those present to name the organization the Universal Scientific Society because, he said, "its name might be applicable to the universal diffusion of knowledge and science." The organization met only until late 1855, but the Deseret Agricultural and Manufacturing Society replaced it in 1856. The D. A. and M. functioned throughout the territorial period and conducted a territorial fair in which prizes were awarded for improvements and inventions. Significantly, the D. A. and M. conducted agricultural experiments to determine which plants flourished in Utah's soils and climate.

In meetings of the Universal Scientific Society, members listened to and participated in lectures and discussions on a number of topics. Young joined William Paul, for example, in lecturing on architecture. John Hyde talked on natural philosophy. George A. Smith spoke on Saracen history, and William Phelps told of the ten tribes of Israel. John Lyon lectured on poetry and read examples to those present. Thomas Hawkins spoke on conserving natural resources, and David Candland discussed the Crimean War. Jonathan Grimshaw instructed on music theory. Drs. Darwin Richardson and William France unveiled what was then known about genetics. Autodidact Orson Pratt told about the planets. Attorney Almon W. Babbitt talked about the American government, and Wilford Woodruff, a man of considerable experience, spoke on horticulture.

In a commitment to education shared by Young, his friends Eliza R. (also his wife) and Lorenzo Snow, the latter an apostle and brother to Eliza, recognized the importance of high- and middle-brow culture in the Latter-day Saint community. In 1854 they organized the Polysophical Society. The society promoted public education with friends by sponsoring lectures, musical presentations, literature readings, and poetry writing. The society continued to flourish until 1856, when, during the Mormon Reformation, Young's counselors Jedediah M. Grant and Heber C. Kimball attacked it, Grant saying it possessed an "adulterous spirit." Young held a different view, holding that he had no objection to literary and musical presentations if "they could be done in righteousness."

In fact, far from objecting to literature and music, Young thought the city needed both. He broke with his counselors and his strict Methodist upbringing by favoring dancing and the theater. "If I were placed on a cannibal island," he said, "and given a task of civilizing its people, I should straightway build a theater for the purpose." Young participated in the organization of the Deseret Dramatic Association in 1850, only three years after the founding of the frontier community. He directed that the participants open all rehearsals and performances with prayer, and that the actors and patrons refrain from smoking and drinking. Before the opening of the Salt Lake Theater in 1862, the dramatists performed in the Social Hall, a building a half block southeast of Young's residence, but after that year drama in Salt Lake City flourished.

Recognizing the need for a formal venue for dramatic and musical performances, Young had promoted the construction of the Salt Lake Theater. Designed by William Harrison Folsom, the building stood on the northwest corner of First South and State Street from 1862 to 1928. Patterned after the Drury Lane Theater in London, with three balconies and a floor that workmen could convert for dancing, the theater could seat 7,500 patrons. Astoundingly, this meant that it could accommodate 62 percent of Salt Lake City's 1860 population of 12,000. Clearly, everyone could attend one of multiple performances of a play or musical. Young and other community leaders purchased boxes in the theater. Personally, Young favored pleasant drama, but during his lifetime, the theater presented a number of Shakespeare's tragedies, including *Hamlet* nineteen times, *Macbeth* eighteen, *Richard III* fourteen, and *Othello* ten times.

Young also encouraged Mormons to build playhouses in other towns. In some places, the local church meetinghouse, used for church services on Sunday, doubled as a theater during the week. In others, the community constructed playhouses.

Because Young and most Mormons recognized no division between the religious and the temporal, the theater was viewed as part of religious life. Thus, in the Salt Lake Theater's early years, instead of paying the actors and staff, Brigham Young called them to serve on theatrical missions. Annie Adams Kiskaden remembered that in a minor uprising that may have occurred sometime in the mid to late 1860s, a number of actors and musicians objected to working for free. After all, they had to take time from their regular professions to rehearse and perform. Their service also endured much longer than a normal mission, and those missionaries who settled in Mormon towns earned their living through their normal professions. Following a rousing discussion in which the performers and stagehands confronted Young, he agreed to adopt a schedule of salaries. Along with the salaries, however, he established a schedule of monetary penalties for such infractions as coming late to rehearsal and failing to learn the play's lines.

Young viewed all music, not just clearly religious hymns, as a facet of the sacred life just as he did drama. On one occasion, he said, "There is no music in hell, for all good music belongs to heaven. Sweet harmonious sounds give exquisite joy to human beings capable of appreciating music." As early as August 1847, one month after the pioneers entered the Salt Lake Valley, the Mormons organized a choir. After construction of the Salt Lake Theater, Young selected British-educated musician C. J. Thomas to conduct the orchestra there. He noted Thomas's success with a number of musical organizations, and called him to direct the Tabernacle choir. In addition, with Young's encouragement, David Calder directed musical organizations that performed music by classical composers, including Hayden, Mozart, and Mendelssohn.

Young sought continued improvement in the church's music. In 1864 George Careless, a graduate of the Royal Academy of Music in London, arrived in Salt Lake City. After encouraging him to "lay a foundation for good music" in the Mormon community, Young called him in 1869 to replace Thomas as Tabernacle choir director. Careless served as taskmaster for what had been a small, undisciplined group of singers with varying abilities. He increased the tabernacle choir to three hundred voices by adding smaller, local choral groups, and on July 4, 1873, the choir offered its first formal concert. In 1876 Careless conducted Handel's *Messiah* in a performance that journalist Edward Tullidge called the birth of "supreme" musical culture in Deseret.

Thomas and Careless found excellent accompaniment for the choir after Joseph Ridges built the Tabernacle organ in 1867. Ridges patterned the pipe organ after the instrument in the Boston Music Hall, fashioning the organ's seven hundred pipes from wood, zinc, and tin and lead alloys, many of which he found in Utah. After the organ's construction, the choir directors induced local boys to pump the bellows to serve the organ pipes. Finding a better way to provide air for the pipes, technicians diverted City Creek to power the bellows. Although experts have rebuilt and enlarged the organ a number of times since 1867, the original casework and some of Ridges's pipes have endured for more than 150 years.

Clearly, Young considered education, drama, and music important, but he also recognized that the people did not live by culture alone, and he sought to promote economic expansion. As the railroad's arrival in Utah loomed, Young sought to mitigate the impact of economic change on Mormon communities. He believed that a cooperative economy would hedge against the competition. After 1861, as the California Volunteers occupied Utah, Young became increasingly concerned with the encroachment of non-Mormon merchants on the local market. As their numbers increased and the railroad approached, in cooperation with the Salt Lake School of the Prophets, Young ordered a boycott of non-Mormon merchants in 1868.

Young proposed to complement the boycott with cooperatives. Mormon missionaries had seen the operation of cooperatives in England and Scandinavia, and Young believed that a similar organization in Utah could facilitate both protection and growth. In October 1868 Young and a group of merchants organized Zion's Cooperative Mercantile Institution (ZCMI), a manufacturing and commercial cooperative. The bylaws of the organization required shareholders and institutional members to be full tithe-payers. They purchased the store of Nicholas S. Ransohoff, a Jewish merchant from Germany's Rheinland, and converted it into ZCMI's principal retail outlet. Businesses that joined the cooperative displayed the all-seeing eye and the motto "Holiness to the Lord" with the ZCMI name.

After opening its first store in March 1869, ZCMI functioned profitably until 1873, after which a nationwide economic recession followed by a depression plunged ZCMI into $1 million in debt and brought it to the verge of bankruptcy. Young had invested $268,000 in tithing funds and $77,200 of his own money in ZCMI, and he played a central role in propping it up. Hiram B. Clawson, Brigham Young's son-in-law who served for the first four years as ZCMI's general manager, insisted that the major goal of the cooperative was to offer bargain prices to the Mormon public. Significantly, however, as the depression abated in the mid to late 1870s, the Walker Brothers, Salt Lake City merchants and former Mormons, emerged in better financial shape than ZCMI. They seem to have offered more attractive prices, and the public seems to have patronized their store more often than the co-op. By 1875 ZCMI stock that had sold at $100 per share in 1869 had declined in value so much that some stockholders sought with difficulty to unload their shares at $50.

To complement the ZCMI store in Salt Lake City, Young envisioned a system of co-ops in the various Mormon towns. Responding to the prophet's suggestion, 150 communities opened a network of Cooperative Mercantile Institutions (CMIs). At first, the stock in these local organizations sold widely to Mormons. Over time, however, local entrepreneurs tended to purchase the stock from farmers, mechanics, and laborers who had little understanding of investments and dividends. Many of these entrepreneurs enjoyed monopoly power by publicizing their stores as "church" enterprises, and urging members to patronize them as a religious duty.

The founding of ZCMI, Young's opposition to precious-metal mining, and some dissident Mormons' adoption of spiritualism and its séances drove a wedge between the prophet and several community leaders. Young's announcement of the proposed founding of ZCMI in 1868 hit British emigrant and drug store owner William S. Godbe squarely in his pocketbook. Godbe, who had joined the church in England in 1850, immigrated to Utah in 1851 and subsequently became a polygamist, had recently constructed a new building in Salt Lake City and was plunged deeply into debt. He would have been foolish to close his business to avoid competing with the co-op, and he grew increasingly critical of Young's economic policies. Godbe's merchant friend, Henry W. Lawrence, also a British emigrant, thought the organization of ZCMI unsound because he believed it would concentrate commerce in one organization and tend to drive others out of business. Nevertheless, Lawrence supported the co-op at first.

Although Lawrence did not join Godbe at first, the latter secured the support of his friend Elias L. T. Harrison, a British emigrant, architect, and intellectual who had joined with him in a publication venture. In 1868 Godbe and Harrison financed the publication of the weekly *Utah Magazine.* With Harrison as editor, the magazine published high-class literature, and the *Deseret News* praised the content and the editor. By late 1869, however, the *Utah Magazine* had begun to challenge Young's economic policy and subtly encouraged spiritualism. When Young urged reducing wages to compete with those paid in midwestern factories, Godbe and Harrison responded by opposing wage reduction and supporting mining as "The True Development of the Territory."

Charged with apostasy for challenging Young's economic policy, Godbe and Harrison stood trial for their church membership before the presidency and members of the Salt Lake Stake in late October 1869. Godbe insisted on his religious orthodoxy and love for the church and its leadership. Nevertheless, Harrison and Godbe asserted their rights to speak their views and differ with the church leadership on economic matters. After a number of church leaders testified against the two businessmen, Young spoke as the final prosecution witness. He said he was not infallible, but rather that truth necessitated obedience to "the Lord Jesus Christ in everything." The church leaders present admitted that neither Godbe nor Harrison had, to their knowledge, committed any sin. Young, however, argued that sin would eventually come to light. Stake president George Wallace announced a verdict of excommunication. In a practice used at times in the nineteenth century, he asked the congregation to sustain the verdict. This must have been difficult for Young, because his step-daughter, Charlotte, was one of Godbe's wives. All present except Eli Kelsey, Henry Lawrence, John and Edward Tullidge, Joseph Silver, and James Cobb sustained the verdict. On Young's motion, Kelsey was excommunicated as well.

The assembly took no action against Lawrence or the others. Lawrence had supported ZCMI and promoted church businesses. In succeeding weeks, Young met with Lawrence and pleaded for "hours" that he remain in the fold. Nevertheless, in a trial before the Salt Lake Eighth Ward, Lawrence insisted, "I do not believe in being forced, but the principles must bear evidence upon their face. . . . God gives men light and intelligence for themselves, and I must be my own Judge as to what is right." He testified to Young's inspiration "a great many times," but he did not believe Young to be infallible, and he insisted that Young was wrong in this case. He was excommunicated.

As editor of the *Utah Magazine,* Harrison differentiated the views of what he called the New Movement from Mormon orthodoxy, writing on the right of individual judgment guided by "light" from "the throne of God." Godbe and Edward W. Tullidge, like Harrison a British emigrant and writer, believed conditions in Utah had changed. They argued that the American nation would subsume Utah because the territory could no longer remain sheltered from outside competition. Godbe and Harrison issued a "Manifesto," which read like liberal Protestantism tempered with spiritualism, in which they said they had begun the New Movement, but they were only its caretakers, and they did not intend to assume its leadership.

Godbe and Harrison went on to organize the Church of Zion, and in 1870 they changed the name of the *Utah Magazine* to the *Mormon Tribune,* and in 1871 to the *Salt Lake Daily Tribune and Mining Gazette.* Having broken with Young on economic matters, Harrison, Godbe, and Tullidge nevertheless maintained a friendly attitude toward the church. In 1873, however, Kansans Frederic Lockley, George F. Prescott, and A. M. Hamilton purchased the paper and turned it into an anti-Mormon organ. A group of anti-Mormons and Godbeites organized the Liberal Party at Corinne in February 1870, but in time, non-Mormons cut Godbe and his followers adrift from the party because they practiced polygamy. This left the Godbeites with a home in neither the non-Mormon nor the Mormon community, and such anti-Mormons as U.S. Marshal George Maxwell attacked the Godbeites because of their polygamy.

Organization of the Liberal Party changed the political complexion of Utah. Prior to 1870, Utah had no political parties, and the citizens selected candidates without party labels. In response to the organization of the Liberal Party, however, the Mormons organized the People's Party. Because of the small non-Mormon population in Utah, the People's Party generally won elections until 1889. One exception was a few years, 1874 to 1879, when an exploding population of non-Mormon miners in Tooele County managed to elect Liberal Party officers there.

In the meantime, the Godbeites recruited a president for the Church of Zion—Amasa Lyman, a member of the Quorum of the Twelve Apostles since 1842. Lyman had served as a counselor to Joseph Smith, but upon Smith's assassination, he returned to the Twelve. He had fulfilled a number of assignments, but in 1867 the First Presidency and Twelve dropped him from the quorum because of their understanding of his views on the atonement of Christ. Contrary to what some writers have assumed, Lyman did not believe that the atonement had no validity. Rather, as historian Leo Lyman has shown, he "consistently stopped short of acknowledging the literal role of Jesus Christ as the sinless sacrificial offering whose grace bridges the gap between human individual efforts to attain salvation and the demands of God's justice." In Lyman's view, people had to bridge that gap themselves. Unwilling to accept such subtle differences between that position and a denial of the efficacy of Christ's grace and His atonement, the other general authorities interpreted Lyman's position inaccurately as denying the atonement.

Another factor in Lyman's alienation was his strained relationship with Young. On the surface, the two remained friendly. Lyman worked diligently with George A. Smith on assignment from Young to heal the breaches in the Mormon kingdom caused by the Mountain Meadows massacre. He presided over the European Mission and carried out a number of other assignments. Nevertheless, the two often disagreed.

Lyman's sacking by the Quorum of the Twelve Apostles led to his break with the church. He lived mainly in Fillmore but visited Salt Lake occasionally. He met with Young at times, but spent more time with Godbe, Harrison, and T. B. H. Stenhouse, who with his wife Fanny were longtime Mormons who had joined the Godbeites. After serious deliberation, Lyman had decided by May 1870 to break with Young and assume the presidency of the Church of Zion.

Lyman and the Godbeites were not the only influential people deciding to sever their affiliation with the Latter-day Saints. In 1851 a woman named Elizabeth Green wrote Young asking him to remove her name from church records because she had decided to become a spiritualist. With a touch of humor, Young replied, "I have this day examined the records of baptisms for the remission of sins in the Church of Jesus Christ of Latter Day Saints, and not being able to find the name of 'Elizabeth Green' recorded therein I was saved the necessity of erasing your name therefrom. You may therefor consider that your sins have not been remitted you and you may consequently enjoy the benefits therefrom."

Young found significantly less humor in events taking place between 1865 and 1872. During those eight years, in addition to the challenges of confronting the changes caused by the railroad, the Godbeite dissent, and the loss of Amasa Lyman, Young and the Mormons faced a more serious series of fierce engagements known as Utah's Black Hawk War. The war forced the evacuation of a number of settlements in southern and south-central Utah and the deaths of numerous Euro-Americans and Indians. For the text on the Black Hawk War, I have relied almost exclusively on John Alton Peterson's *Utah's Black Hawk War* (Salt Lake City, 1998).

The leader of the uprising was Black Hawk (in Ute: Antonga), a chief in the Northern Ute confederacy. He may have been a brother of Walkara, but if not, he was a close relative. Like Walkara and the other chiefs, Black Hawk may also have been a Latter-day Saint.

Food shortages initiated the conflict. Utes throughout central and northern Utah had starved beyond imagination during winter 1864–65. The Mormons near whom they lived provided some food, but not nearly enough. Black Hawk and Jake Arapeen, the son of Arapeen, bragging that they would feed their people by taking cattle from the Mormons, began rustling livestock in central Utah's Sanpete Valley. Recognizing the potential for war, Utah chiefs Sow-ok-soo-bet (Arrow Feather—called Joe by the Mormons), An-kar-twets (Red Boy), and Toquana (Black Mountain Lion) tried in early April 1865 to negotiate with the Mormons in Manti to avoid conflict with Black Hawk's band. They failed in part because the Utes were starving and because a hotheaded Indian interpreter, John Lowry, got into a fight with a hotheaded Jake Arapeen. Arapeen, on horseback, confronted Lowry with an arrow strung in his bow. Lowry grabbed Arapeen by the hair and pulled him from his horse. While Lowry ran home for his gun, Black Hawk and Arapeen rode away before he could return. Continuing on the run, the two Utes and a small band of raiders killed one settler and escaped with a small herd of cattle.

From that point the raids increased. Later in April, Black Hawk and Arapeen, with a much larger band, rustled an estimated 125 head of Sanpete cattle. During the raid, the Utes killed three settlers. In an attempt to retrieve the cattle and avenge the dead settlers, five militiamen and three Utes died when, in a tactical masterstroke, Black Hawk lured the Mormons into an ambush in Salina Canyon. The Utes succeeded in defeating the would-be avengers and keeping the cattle and a number of horses.

Before the war began, however, officials in Washington had decided as early as February 1865 that they must do something to separate the Utes from the expanding Mormon settlements, even though after the initial conflicts in Utah Valley and the Walker and Tintic wars of the 1850s, the Mormons and Utes lived together in relatively amiable conditions. On February 23, 1865, Congress authorized Utah's superintendent of Indian Affairs, Orsemus H. Irish to negotiate a treaty with the Northern Ute chiefs. At Irish's request and the request of a number of chiefs, including Sowiette (Nearly Starved), Kanosh (Man of White Hair), Sanpitch (Bull Rush), and Tabby (The Sun), Brigham Young attended the treaty negotiations. The Black Hawk raids had already begun before negotiators could meet in early June 1865 at the abandoned Indian farm at Benjamin, west of Spanish Fork. Governor Doty did not attend because of illness, and General Connor refused to come because Brigham Young, whom he called "the arch traitor," would be there. When Irish, Young, and others got there on June 6, 1865, five hundred Utes had already arrived.

The financial arrangements Irish offered seem generous. The government proposed to give the Utes who agreed to move to the Uintah Reservation in eastern Utah a total of $1.1 million in specified yearly payments over a sixty-year period. The treaty also promised $30,000 for initial improvements at the reservation, including buying cattle for them to herd. In addition, the Bureau of Indian Affairs agreed to provide a $10,000 schoolhouse, grist- and sawmills, and homes for the chiefs. The first year's payment would have amounted to $65,000, equivalent to $1,032,228 in 2017 dollars, in addition to the improvements, cattle, school, mills, and homes. The major drawback for the Utes, however, was that they would have to relinquish their land in central and southern Utah and move to the Uinta Basin if they approved the treaty.

The Ute chiefs present authorized Sowiette, Kanosh, Sanpitch, and Tabby, the ones who had invited Young to attend the negotiations, to speak for them. After acknowledging Sowiette as the head chief, Kanosh said, "Brigham is the great Captain of all, for he does not get mad when he hears of his brothers and friends being Killed, as the California Captains do." The Black Hawk raids had indeed already led to the death of several settlers. Kanosh said the land belonged to both the Utes and the Mormons, and he wished that the two peoples could continue to live together. Sanpitch agreed, citing the verbal treaties and purchases the Mormons had made over the previous years. He said also that he would rather reject the annuities than give up the land they had lived on for as long as anyone could remember.

Perhaps misunderstanding that agreeing to the treaty would mean the separation of the Indian and Mormon communities, Young urged the chiefs to sign the treaty. He said even if they did not, the government would take their land anyway. Further, he said it really did not matter whether the Utes sold the land or not. The Mormons "shall increase: and we shall occupy this valley and the next, and the next, and so on till we occupy the whole of them." Clearly, for Young, it did not matter if the government took the land: the Mormons would occupy it. Under those conditions, Young said, "we are willing you should live with us." Young may not have understood that under the treaty, the Indians could not continue to live with them because they would have to move to the reservation.

In predicting future developments, Young knew that the government had always taken the land occupied by settlers and moved Indians to a designated reservation. The Mormons had begun to settle throughout the territory; and as Young told those assembled, after they established a mother settlement, they founded nearby towns that occupied land the Indians owned. Since at least 1852, Young had asked the Mormon people to live in peace with the

Indians, to encourage the natives to live with them, and to provide food when the Indians needed it. Young's policy of coexistence had not always succeeded, as demonstrated by the Walker and Tintic wars, conflicts in Box Elder and Cache valleys, and the Black Hawk–Arapeen raids in Sanpete County. But as Kanosh and Sanpitch pointed out, Young's approach had been more satisfactory than Connor's policy of planned extermination.

Nevertheless, Young's policy had aroused objections from federal officials. Garland Hurt rightly said that it placed an enormous burden on the Mormon people who had to share their food with the Indians. Connor had charged that allowing the Indians to live near their towns proved that the Mormons assisted them in their raids.

After Young spoke, the chiefs went to their lodges to consider Irish's offer. The next morning, June 8, 1865, Sanpitch remained in his lodge and refused to sign. Sowiette, however, said he would sign, and fifteen of the chiefs signed. A week later, Sanpitch came to Salt Lake City and signed the treaty. Tabby said that at the time Sanpitch was ashamed because his father and some others from the Sanpete tribes had participated in the Black Hawk–Arapeen raids. That was clearly not all there was to it, because Sanpitch and some of the others whose ancestral homes had not included the Uinta Basin did not want to relinquish their lands in central Utah and move there. On reflection, Sanpitch probably concluded that Young was right: whether they signed or not the government would take their land, although he apparently thought his people could continue to live with the Mormons. Irish signed for the government, and Young signed as a witness.

The treaty did not bring peace, however, and matters grew worse than before. The U.S. Senate refused to ratify the treaty, but the Bureau of Indian Affairs, with the force of the army behind it, began to move the Utes to the Uintah Reservation anyway. As Young predicted, the government did take their land, and the Indians received no compensation until they won only a small percentage of what it was really worth in post–World War II court cases. Few if any Utes alive in 1865 ever saw that money, for the cases had to await passage of the Indian Claims Commission Act of 1946.

As an additional blow, Congress in effect denied the sovereignty of Indian nations in 1871 by passing a rider to an appropriations act that ended the practice of negotiating treaties with Indian tribes. Although the federal government began moving the Utes to the Uintah reservation, Congress did not appropriate enough money to meet their needs during the transition from hunting and gathering to stockraising and farming, and because the Indians still needed food, Black Hawk and his raiders continued to attack Mormon settlements, rustle cattle, and battle the Nauvoo Legion.

As the raids continued, Young might have taken the prudent course and turned to the U.S. Army to fight the war. But Young feared the army and the government behind it more than he did the Utes. Although the Civil War had ended, Connor continued to demand that more soldiers be sent to Utah to fight the Mormons. When Speaker of the House Schuyler Colfax and house territorial committee chair, James M. Ashley, visited Utah, Ashley, in a confrontation with Brigham Young, threatened to lay waste to Utah as Sherman had Georgia, burning homes and raping Mormon woman until the Mormons gave up polygamy. Ashley anticipated that Connor would carry out his threat.

The Mormons expended large amounts of money lobbying Congress and various administrations to undermine proposals of Colfax, Ashley, Connor, and others while battling the Utes themselves. Young responded to the Utes' challenge by traveling to Utah and Sanpete Valleys during July 1865 to encourage the settlers to prepare for possible battles. He urged the Saints to sell their excess cattle and purchase weapons to prepare for a war if Connor attacked or if Black Hawk's raiders tried to rustle cattle. Young urged the settlers to protect themselves even if it meant killing some Ute raiders. While Young met with the settlers, Black Hawk's soldiers moved against Sevier Valley. Despite recently receiving a certificate from Salina's bishop calling them "friendly Indians," they killed two settlers near Salina and rustled three hundred cattle near Glenwood.

In a tragic response to the raid, Brig. Gen. Warren Snow mustered the Sanpete militia, but instead of pursuing the Utes, the

Sanpete troops attacked a Paiute camp near Burrville and killed men and women indiscriminately. The Sanpete soldiers justified the raid by saying they found there some belongings of the two dead settlers. Even though Snow rebuked his troops for killing women and children, he became a symbol for the Utes of untamed violence. Not wanting to attract the attention of the U.S. Army, Young suppressed stories of the battle and massacre, and he soon reversed course in his policy. After the militia failed on numerous occasions to capture Black Hawk's raiders in eastern Utah, Young ordered the Nauvoo Legion to stop fighting the Indians. On Young's instructions, Dimick Huntington met with Sanpitch to tell him that the Legion had stopped fighting and to ask that he let Black Hawk know. Most of the Saints, including Warren Snow, greeted Young's proposal favorably. Although Snow became a symbol of violence to the Utes, he, too, wanted to end hostilities.

Black Hawk rejected Young's initiative, however, declaring he would fight to the death. Trying to make good on his threat, Black Hawk with Jake Arapeen and a party of Indians attacked the city of Ephraim. Unprepared for such raids, Ephraim's peaceful Scandinavian settlers failed to respond effectively. After killing seven settlers and mutilating others, Black Hawk's raiders escaped with a herd of a hundred cattle that they drove to a redoubt in eastern Utah. Later, a Ute raid on Circleville in southern Utah led to the deaths of four settlers. All told, Indians had killed twenty-five settlers and wounded eight during 1865, and they had rustled approximately two thousand cattle and horses.

Young knew that despite his proposed cease-fire, the settlers would have to arm themselves and remain vigilant. Hearing of the attack on Ephraim, he responded with anger at the "stupidity of our settlements and their recklessness of life." He had, he said, counseled the settlers for "many years" to build forts, buy guns, and prepare to defend themselves against possible attack. Nevertheless, he understood that "the architects of Zion [must] . . . work with such material as the Lord has provided, stupidity, wooden shoes, and cork brains thrown into the bargain."

The raids in Sanpete, Sevier Valley, and Circleville were only a prelude to a region-wide campaign. Sending recruiters throughout the Mountain West, Black Hawk gathered soldiery from virtually all the Ute bands in Utah, Arizona, New Mexico, Colorado, Nevada, and Wyoming. Increasing his power, he created an intertribal army by recruiting Navajos, Paiutes, Goshutes, and even some Apaches and Hopis. Astoundingly, by 1866 Navajos, generally Ute enemies, made up half of Black Hawk's raiders. These were Navajos who had not surrendered to Brig. Gen. James H. Carleton and Kit Carson and gone to Bosque Redondo in 1864—those Navajos did not return to their homeland until mid-summer 1868. By contrast, largely because of his fear that they might lose the goods, services, and annuities promised in the 1863 Fort Bridger Treaty, Washakie succeeded in keeping most Shoshones from enlisting in Black Hawk's army. Still, as the size and scope of Black Hawk's troops increased, his goals expanded from rustling cattle to driving whites from the region.

Responding to the raids, Young and other Mormon leaders continued to urge settlers to prepare for conflict. During the winter of 1865–66, Brigham Young in Salt Lake City and Orson Hyde in Spring City advised the settlers to send cattle to Salt Lake to trade for weapons. To their distinct disadvantage, most Mormons had disobeyed Young's previous instructions to buy weapons; Hyde went so far as to issue the hollow threat to excommunicate those who refused to trade cattle for weapons.

In contrast to Mormon reluctance to arm themselves, the Indians traded livestock from their raids for high-quality rifles. Black Hawk got help from American and Mexican arms dealers of the sort who manage to benefit themselves in almost all wars. The dealers traded guns and ammunition with Black Hawk for cattle, horses, and the women and children his raiders kidnaped from other tribes. In fact, by negotiating such trades, Black Hawk's troops accumulated better arms than the Mormon militia. A number of the Indian raiders had Henry or Spencer .44 caliber or .52 caliber breach-loading repeating rifles that could hold sixteen (Henry) or seven (Spencer) rimfire shells. They were much superior to the muzzle-loading rifles and the breach-loading single-shot rifles such as the Ballards or Sharps and especially the less accurate muskets owned by many of those Mormon militiamen who had weapons—and many had none. Both Indians and Mormons shared two disadvantages since they had difficulty securing rimfire ammunition, and black powder (the only kind available then) damaged the chambers and barrels of the weapons when fired in large quantities.

Properly armed or not, both the Indians and Mormons believed they were acting on the side of a higher cause. Black Hawk and his raiders considered themselves Indian patriots. Brigham Young called them a "predatory band of outlaws" who attracted others to their "murder and robbery . . . [to gratify] their murderous and thievish propensities." Young insisted they were not a tribe, but a "band of renegade Indians . . . [who united] together for purposes of plunder." The Mormons believed they served a higher cause because they were building God's Kingdom in the American West. Moreover, they wanted the Indians to join and live with them.

On January 8, 1866, Black Hawk pulled together a band of Ute, Navajo, and Apache raiders to attack the Whitmore ranch at Pipe Springs on the Arizona strip north of the Grand Canyon. Together, they killed James Whitmore and Robert McIntyre while taking three hundred cattle, a large sheep herd, and some horses. A unit of the Nauvoo Legion from St. George under Capt. James Andrus killed a large number of otherwise peaceful Paiutes they found with clothing and cattle belonging to the Whitmores. The dead Paiutes had not joined in the raids, but because they had some of Whitmore's and McIntyre's clothing and livestock in their possession, even Young considered them accessories. We might justifiably consider the killings a massacre.

As the Black Hawk War unfolded with increasing fury in 1866, Brigham Young and the Mormons grappled with a second front as an enemy in Washington, D.C., fashioned tactics to reconstruct Utah while they reconstructed the Southern states. Congressman James Ashley proposed an initiative to dismantle Utah Territory. He failed, but in testimony before Congress, Utah chief justice John

Titus urged the government to send five thousand troops to Utah to enforce anti-polygamy laws. When Titus failed also, General Connor journeyed to Washington to give corroborating testimony. Young said that asking Connor to testify about the Mormons was like inviting "Nero to give testimony against the Christians" or Herod to provide a reference "about the character of John the Baptist and whether Jesus is the Christ."

With these threats from Washington in mind, Young believed the Utahns needed to bring the Black Hawk War to a close as soon as possible. By early 1866 Utes in Sanpete Valley under the leadership of Sanpitch, who was generally friendly to the Mormons, had begun announcing threats against the settlers. This surprised many Mormons because the Sanpitch Utes had not joined Black Hawk in numbers as large as many of the other tribes and bands.

Thinking that a hostage policy might succeed where force of arms had failed, Young responded to Sanpitch with a tactic that proved disastrous. Through militia commander Daniel H. Wells, Young sent orders to capture Sanpitch and three other Indians and imprison them until Black Hawk came to terms. Young expected that holding these Indians as hostages would convince leaders who had not joined in raiding like Sowiette, Kanosh, Tabby, Toquana, Antero, and Sanpitch to induce Black Hawk to end the war.

Acting on Young's orders sent through Wells, Brig. Gen. Warren Snow rounded up eight of the Sanpete Utes, including Sanpitch and Ankawakits, Tabby's brother-in-law. They all had signed the Spanish Fork Treaty, and none of them had participated in the raids. By March 16, 1866, Snow had jailed them in irons in the second story of Manti's Sanpete County Courthouse. Sanpitch admitted that he had given Black Hawk supplies and that several of his band had joined Black Hawk, but he had not joined the raiders.

After taking the hostages, Snow sent a unit to attack a camp containing Indians who had joined Black Hawk. In the attack, his troops killed a Ute, and they captured three whom John Kanosh identified as raiders. After a drumhead court martial, Snow summarily executed the Utes. Frightened by Snow's action, the Ute hostages, including Sanpitch, tried to escape from jail, but Mormon militiamen overtook and killed them, and Moroni City settlers killed a woman and her child who had helped them. In a tragic ending to the hostage policy, militiamen killed Sanpitch in the San Pitch Mountains as he tried to flee.

The imprisonment of hostages and the subsequent killings poisoned the relations with bands of friendly Indians led by Sowiette and Kanosh. Young and Snow had both ordered the Mormons not to kill women and children, but settlers had murdered them anyway. Both men knew that the hostage tactic had failed and led to strained relations with nearly all the Utes in central Utah. Frightened by the murders, nearly all of those who had remained in Utah and Juab valleys fled from the region and eventually moved to the Uintah Reservation.

In retrospect, Young expressed sorrow that the hostage policy had failed to end the war on peaceful terms. "We do not want to kill the Indians; it is painful and repugnant to our feelings . . . but it will not do for us to sit down and see our brethren and Sisters killed by them, and not take measures to prevent such occurrences." Young particularly grieved over the death of Sanpitch and the strained relations with Kanosh and Sowiette because they had valiantly opposed Black Hawk's war against the Mormons.

Close on the heels of the killing of Sanpitch and the Utes at and near Manti, in April 1866 settlers in Circleville in southern Piute County arrested twenty Paiutes. They killed six who tried to escape and then massacred the rest, including women and children, except four children. Paiute tradition says that two of the captives escaped. When Brigham Young learned of the Circleville massacre, he condemned both the horrible deed and the settlers for excusing this cruel act as a "necessity of war." He said that God's curse rested on Circle Valley because "a band of our Lamenite brethern and their families, were here cruely slain." In contrast with Young, Apostle Orson Hyde justified the murders.

Following the failure of the hostage policy and the Circleville massacre, Young returned to a peace and vigilance policy. He sent Dimick Huntington to the Uintah Reservation to try to pacify Tabby and Toquana. Huntington failed, and he managed to escape with his life only because Sowiette saved him. Angered by the violence of the Manti militia and the Circleville settlers, the Utes chose Tabby as head chief in place of Sowiette. Utes under Tabby's leadership, aroused by the murders and by the failure of the federal government to provide food and housing at the reservation, forced an army unit and the federal officials to flee from the reservation. As the war continued and relationships with previously friendly Utes deteriorated, Utah superintendent of Indian Affairs Franklin H. Head asked Maj. Gen. John Pope to send federal troops. Pope and his superior, Maj. Gen. William T. Sherman, refused. They did send some troops to New Mexico, but the army took severe cuts to reduce its size during the late 1860s, and Pope said they did not have enough troops to send any to Utah. The refusal pleased Young, and the Nauvoo Legion carried on the fight without federal assistance.

Anxious for peace, in 1866 Young ordered settlers to abandon small towns and move to larger towns if they could not muster a force of 150 armed men. He again instructed the towns to build substantial forts and assign significant numbers of armed herdsmen to guard livestock. At the same time, he admonished church members that the Indians were "human beings and the descendants of Abraham," to be treated "with proper kindness and consideration." At Young's insistence, Wells mustered 100 men from the Wasatch Front and sent them to Sanpete and Sevier Valleys.

Young also prepared to send $5,000 worth of supplies to the Uintah Reservation to help feed the Utes under Tabby's leadership. Young's offer came too late to pacify Tabby, however. Outraged by Sanpitch's death, Tabby dispatched warriors to raid near Spanish Fork and Heber City, and he sent Utes to raid Kanosh's Pahvant herds because of their friendship with the Mormons.

Undeterred by the attacks, Young sent twenty-five cattle and a load of flour to the reservation in May 1866. Superintendent Head and a militia unit accompanied Young's supplies, and Head brought some presents as well. After a tense confrontation with the still-angry Tabby, the Indians accepted the gifts, though some Utes returned them. Tabby nevertheless said that he could not control some of the younger Utes, and he demanded Warren Snow's death to avenge the killing of Sanpitch and the other hostages. Tabby had no control over Black Hawk, who, with three hundred Utes and Navajos, moved on Manti bent on attacking Snow's hometown and killing him. In response, Wells sent 125 more militiamen to Sanpete and Sevier.

Clearly beyond Tabby's control, Black Hawk continued his raids. In June 1866 Black Hawk and Tamaritz, who had become his chief lieutenant and who later changed his name to Shenavega (Saved by Almighty Power), captured three hundred cattle from Scipio in northern Millard County. The settlers in this small town ignored Young's order to abandon the town or fort up. After the attack there, Brig. Gen. William B. Pace from Gunnison led troops to battle Black Hawk in the Sevier River Canyon at Gravelly Ford. The engagement ended in a draw, but Pace's troops managed to wound both Black Hawk and Tamaritz severely before retreating. Black Hawk's wounds remained unhealed, and they contributed to his surrender two years afterward and to his death two years after that.

Brig. Gen. Warren Snow in Manti also mustered troops to pursue Black Hawk but, perhaps influenced by Young's increasingly pacifistic attitude, he withdrew before engaging in battle. Young valued human life too much to remain an aggressive militarist. Increasingly, the Mormon leader favored a policy of forting up and guarding livestock rather than sending troops to recover stock and punish aggressive Utes. Wells observed Young's new policy by sending 350 troops from the Wasatch Front to Sanpete and Sevier valleys and pressing the settlements to construct forts.

Young made clear his opposition to killing in a letter to Bishop Thomas Callister of Fillmore following James Ivie's cold-blooded murder of Panikary, an inoffensive Pahvant Ute. Young deplored the murder by "a man *professing* to be a Latter-day Saint," and recommended a murder trial. Packed with Ivie's friends, the jury acquitted him. Disappointed at the outcome of the trial, Callister excommunicated Ivie.

Despite Young's policy of forting up and guarding livestock, some battles took place. Nauvoo Legionaries achieved victories over renegade Utes in battles at Thistle, a town at the junction of Sanpete Valley and Spanish Fork Canyon and at Diamond Fork, a tributary of the Spanish Fork River. The troops from Utah and Sanpete Valleys inflicted considerable damage on the Ute warriors, and they recaptured small herds of livestock the Indians had rustled. Nevertheless, Black Hawk's raiders made another successful raid in July 1866, but Black Hawk's fortunes had clearly taken a turn for the worse. The defeats at Thistle and Diamond Fork and Young's current policy of vigilance and forting up seem to have led Tabby and Sowiette to believe they needed to come to terms with Young. Tabby and Sowiette sent a delegation from the reservation to Salt Lake City to meet with Young and sue for peace. Young agreed, even though Tabby's brother, Jim, had been part of the Thistle raiding party.

In spite of all the raids, Young understood that the Utes on the reservation suffered from insufficient food, so he sent his associate, William Wall, with twenty sacks of flour for Tabby. Wall found Tabby, Sowiette, Toquana, Joe, Jim, and several others north of the reservation and across the Uinta Mountains at Fort Bridger trading with white men and with Washakie and his Shoshones. After giving Tabby Young's message of peace, Wall reported that the Ute chief promised again to try to dissuade reservation Indians from rejoining Black Hawk's raiders.

Following on the victories and the efforts to secure peace, Wells launched three well-supplied Nauvoo Legion expeditions into the Canyon Country of eastern Utah to try to locate Black Hawk's redoubts. Brig. Gen. William Pace, Col. Heber P. Kimball, and Capt. James Andrus led these expeditions. They found a large number of corrals but few of the livestock and fewer Indians, but they did learn more about the geography of the region.

In the meantime, Young continued to preach peace and vigilance and to condemn the murder of peaceful Indians. He again invited the Utes to live with the Mormons, and "in the name of the Lord Jesus Christ, . . . [he] forbid any elder or member in this church slaying an innocent Lamanite!" He condemned also such whites as non-Mormons Richard James and Isaac Potter who supplied weapons and ammunition to the Indians and who participated in some of the raids. In August 1866, as a token of his peaceful intentions, Tabby and a number of Utes traveled to Heber City where they and the settlers held a barbecue and party. Tabby told those in attendance there had been enough killing of whites and that he, too, wanted peace.

Yet the war had not ended. Black Hawk attacked Glenwood to try to kill Warren Snow, who had come there. Perhaps angered at their failure to kill Snow, the Utes murdered and dismembered Jens Peter and Caroline Petersen and Mary Smith. This slaughter led Brigham Young to order the abandonment of all Sevier Valley settlements. Settlers from Sanpete helped the Sevier residents to move themselves and their possessions to Sanpete Valley.

The evacuation of Sevier settlements was only the beginning of the removal of towns of Mormon people from central and southern Utah. Between 1866 and 1871, in an attempt to avoid human death and loss of livestock, Brigham Young ordered the evacuation of a large number of other settlements. John Wesley Powell, famed explorer of the Colorado River and Grand Canyon, estimated that Black Hawk had driven "eight or ten thousand white people . . . from their homes." Powell may have overestimated the numbers, but it is difficult to overrate the extent of the damage the Black Hawk War did to Mormon settlements. Many settlers returned to their homes after the war only to find them occupied by others or in a state of unrecognizable disrepair. Whites, Mormon and non-Mormon alike, were not the only people to suffer. The Utes experienced even more permanent injury from being dispossessed of their ancestral lands.

Whether Black Hawk became discouraged because of Young's policy of abandoning settlements, his increasing lack of success, or his declining health, he had, by August 1867, wearied of war. Wounded at Gravelly Ford, stricken with tuberculosis, and suffering from venereal disease, Black Hawk had reached the end of his raiding career. On August 10, 1867, three weeks after a raid failed at Paragonah in Southern Utah, Black Hawk rode to the Uintah Reservation and announced he and two other chiefs wanted peace.

He and a hundred of his followers met with Orson Hyde late in June 1868 at Mount Pleasant, where he signed a peace treaty. In August 1868 he led Tamaritz and two other chiefs to Strawberry Valley to meet with Superintendent Head and interpreter Dimick Huntington.

On a number of occasions, Brigham Young had insisted that if the Utes did not stop killing and robbing they would decrease until they became "extinct." Black Hawk reportedly came to believe that his illness and the illness of other Utes had resulted from Young's prophecy. Bad blood between some Mormons and some Utes continued long after the war had ended, and a currently unknown Mormon killed Jake Arapeen, some of James Ivie's relatives threatened to kill Black Hawk, and Tabiona wanted to kill James Ivie. More than a few outraged Utes still wanted to kill Warren Snow, and unprovoked murders of Utes continued for years.

In an attempt to heal the breach with the Mormons, Black Hawk visited with Brigham Young in Salt Lake City in May 1869. Young urged Black Hawk to make peace with the people. From July to December 1869, a sick and increasingly debilitated Black Hawk in the company of Ute chiefs Mountain (Black Hawk's brother) and Tamaritz visited all of the major towns between Spanish Fork and St. George. Greeted by musicians in each community, Black Hawk spoke to assembled congregations, expressing "sorrow" because of the raids and killings. As Brigham Young urged, the congregations unanimously voted to forgive him, although some of the settlers continued to bear grudges.

Throughout the Black Hawk War, various officials questioned the legality of the Nauvoo Legion's administration. Technically, Young could give advice to Lt. Gen. Daniel H. Wells as a citizen, but he held no official authority—Wells held his position by appointment of the territorial legislature. Although the Utah Territorial Organic Act designated the territorial governor as the Nauvoo Legion's commander-in-chief, Wells commanded the militia, and he conducted the war as Brigham Young advised. Governor Charles Durkee, who served from 1865 to 1869, during the bulk of the Black Hawk War, deplored the situation, as did Brig. Gen. James F. Rusling, whose report in 1866 condemned the Mormons and their militia. Nevertheless, neither Durkee nor the army officers sought to change the arrangement. In 1870, as the Black Hawk War wound down, however, Governor J. Wilson Shaffer removed Wells, appointed Patrick Edward Connor as commander, and prohibited any drills without his express order.

Despite Black Hawk's surrender, some raids continued until 1872, when the federal government established Fort Cameron at Beaver in southern Utah. Although the Senate failed to ratify the Spanish Fork Treaty, the federal government used the army to force the Utes who had not already done so to move to the Uintah Reservation. In 1881 the government established Fort Thornburgh in the Uinta Basin in part to keep the Utes on the reservation. The government also provided some assistance to the Utes, but it was far less than they should have received under the unratified treaty.

The Black Hawk War and the Indians' forced removal to the reservation fundamentally changed the relationship between the Mormons and Utes. Previously, after the first conflicts in Utah Valley, the Utes had lived in close proximity to the Mormon settlements. At the Spanish Fork negotiations, both Young and a number of the chiefs had said they hoped they could still live together. Young's hostage policy, the murders of Sanpitch and his associates, and the massacre of a nearby Indian settlement—whether Warren Snow ordered it or not—made cooperative settlement impossible. Black Hawk recognized as much when he changed his military policy and set as his goal the eradication of Mormon settlements. His attack on Scipio was the opening chapter in that policy. By 1868, however, he recognized that such a policy would never succeed because Young had concentrated the Mormons in larger settlements and sent additional troops to aid settlers in Sanpete and Sevier Valleys. As his health declined, Black Hawk came to realize that his raids were increasingly futile.

The war had confirmed that Young and the Mormons could make serious mistakes as well. Young's hostage policy led to the murders of at least nine Indians, all of whom—but particularly Sanpitch—had remained friendly despite Black Hawk's efforts to recruit among them. The tragic the death of Sanpitch eliminated one of Utes' most thoughtful and friendly leaders. Saddened by his death, Young deplored the loss of a church member as well and denounced the massacre of innocent Paiutes in three settlements, which had taken place in spite of Young's policy of avoiding conflict with non-combatants. Ill-informed, fearful, or malevolent settlers had killed these people. A tragedy of the first order, the Black Hawk War had resulted from the expansion of Mormon settlements and the hunger of Utes living near them.

The Black Hawk War ended in a whimper between 1868 and 1872, but it was not the only challenge with which Young had to contend between 1865 and 1872. Although the completion of the transcontinental railroad facilitated the immigration of the faithful to Utah, Young and his people faced serious difficulty in addressing the economic challenges brought with the railway's completion. Young worked to protect the Mormons by organizing the cooperative movement, ZCMI, the School of the Prophets, the Relief Society, and a retrenchment organization for young women. After Young's death, the cooperative stores generally morphed into locally owned businesses. As for ZCMI, it encountered serious difficulty during the depression that overwhelmed the United States in 1873, but it continued to sell goods well beyond World War II. The Relief Society and the Young Women's Mutual Improvement Association, which grew out of retrenchment, flourished in the Mormon community. In addition, the Mormons improved their cultural and religious lives by completing construction of the Salt Lake Tabernacle and the Salt Lake Theater. As we will see in the next chapter, during the last years of his life, as Young struggled with increasingly poor health, he worked to promote equality in the Mormon community through the United Order. He also took great strides in promoting spirituality through the construction of the first temple in Utah.

12

The Final Years

The arrival of the railroad, the expansion of mining, the end of the Black Hawk War, the defiance of the Godbeites, and the prosecution of polygamy ushered in the final years of Brigham Young's life. Numerous developments made the years between 1870 and his death in 1877 exciting, productive, and challenging. Young inaugurated several initiatives to build God's Kingdom. These included organizing cooperative United Order communities and businesses; realigning the membership of the Quorum of the Twelve Apostles by time of ordination rather than by age; revitalizing priesthood quorums and stake and ward organizations so all males over age twelve would belong to a quorum and each church unit would be properly led; extending additional rights to women; and expanding ritual worship through the construction of the St. George Temple. Young also demonstrated significant appreciation for the services to the Mormon community of Thomas and Elizabeth Kane by hosting them on a visit to Utah. Meanwhile, in concerted attacks on Young and the Mormon people, federal officials tried in various ways to thwart the expansion of the Mormon commonwealth. Some sought unsuccessfully to undermine Mormon power by reducing the size of Utah and sending an army to eradicate the Saints. Federal officials arrested Young and other

Mormon leaders, alleging that they had committed murder. A judge allowed a polygamous wife to try to secure alimony in a divorce suit against Young. With Young's approval, one of his clerks sought a judicial ruling on the question of whether the Constitution's First Amendment provision guaranteeing the free exercise of religion protected plural marriage.

Young's boldest initiative may have been his proposal to remake Mormon economic life by reintroducing the Law of Consecration and Stewardship, which had failed under Joseph Smith's leadership. Young named it the United Order of Enoch, but most Mormons just called it the United Order. Between 1854 and 1856, Young had tried unsuccessfully to secure the consecration of each member's property for the benefit of the poor. A number of Latter-day Saints, including Young and such Indian leaders as Ute chief Arapeen, signed deeds of consecration. The church did not take the property most likely because the members pushed back.

Some United Orders organized from 1864 through the 1870s actually functioned for substantial lengths of time; most, however, failed within a few years. The first organized and longest enduring United Order was the Brigham City cooperative. In 1854 Brigham Young sent Elder Lorenzo Snow, of the Quorum of the Twelve Apostles, to preside over Brigham City. To accompany Snow to Brigham City, Young dispatched a party of members with skills ranging from blacksmithing to shoemaking.

In 1864 two developments led to the founding of a store as the first link in a chain of Brigham City's cooperative businesses. First, a large group of Scandinavian immigrants poured into the town, bolstering the community by introducing a diverse collection of backgrounds and skills. Second, Young and Snow discussed in detail the economic future of Brigham City. Young had already begun to anticipate the cooperative movement, an economic plan originating in Europe that was designed to reduce the cost of goods, and he urged the apostle to organize cooperative commercial and manufacturing departments to benefit the members.

In 1864 Snow established the cooperative general store in Brigham City as a joint stock corporation. By 1869 the co-op store had two hundred shareholders and capital stock of twenty thousand dollars. Instead of paying dividends, salaries, or wages in cash, the store and the other cooperative enterprises paid in scrip that patrons could use to purchase locally made goods at the store. The cooperative also issued an alternative scrip to buy imported goods. Both types of scrip apparently circulated at a discount outside the co-op.

The cooperative store was the first of a growing number of enterprises financed both by issuing new shares and by profits from existing businesses. Through the use of local labor paid mostly in stock, the co-op built a tannery. After incorporating as the Brigham City Mercantile and Manufacturing Company in 1870, the co-op added a number of other businesses during the next decade, including a woolen mill, sheep herds, a dairy, a hat and cap factory, a silk operation, sawmills, a lime kiln, a blacksmith shop, and a furniture factory. There was also a tin workshop, a rope works, a greenhouse, a broom factory, a cooperage, and a brush manufacturing plant. An education department provided schooling for the children. Significantly, the Brigham City cooperative weathered the depression following the crash of 1873 while other cities felt the impact of national economic collapse more fully. This success impressed a number of national observers, including Edward Bellamy, author of the national best-selling utopian novel, *Looking Backward.*

Snow established a number of these enterprises at considerable distance from Brigham City. For instance, the cooperative opened a cotton farm near Washington City some 360 miles south of Brigham City. In 1874, as Young organized United Orders in other communities, the Brigham City cooperative adopted the title "United Order," although it remained a collection of cooperative enterprises. Brigham City's citizens owned stock in the co-op and worked in its various businesses, but none of them consecrated their personal or real property to the collective. Nevertheless, in April 1878 Lorenzo Snow remembered that Brigham Young's praise for the cooperative: "Brother Snow has led the people along, and got them into the United Order without their knowing it." By that time, many of the other United Orders had failed or were on the verge of failure.

Despite Brigham Young's optimism, the Brigham City cooperative eventually failed as well. In 1877, the year of Young's death, the subsequent failure seemed unlikely because it had reached its peak of prosperity. By the mid-1880s, however, the cooperative, deeply in debt, had to sell a number of its businesses to private investors, and by 1888 the factories had closed down, leaving only the co-op store in operation. In 1895 the bankrupt cooperative passed into receivership.

In 1872, as the Brigham City cooperative expanded, Young and a number of other church leaders began preaching the need for a church-wide United Order of Enoch. Young frequently traveled to Mormon settlements outside of Salt Lake City to preach to the Saints and to determine their attitudes and faithfulness, and by 1870 he was regularly spending the winter in the warmer climate of St. George. In 1871 Miles Romney designed an adobe home for him, and the people of St. George constructed it at their expense.

On February 9, 1874, on one of his winter sojourns in St. George, Young gathered three hundred members and organized the St. George United Order. Those present approved and signed an agreement that specified the roles of officers, set wages, and established a mechanism for appraising property pledged to the United Order. Unlike the Brigham City Cooperative, those who joined the St. George United Order pooled both capital and labor, not just capital alone. Dividends were to be calculated at the end of five years based on the value of property dedicated to the order, and members could withdraw after five years by reclaiming half of the property they had dedicated. Despite an enthusiastic start, the St. George members voted to disband the cooperative in 1877, and by 1880 they had dissolved the order, largely because wealthy members were reluctant to leave their property in the collective. Some prosperous members considered the United Order impractical from an economic perspective, while Young viewed it idealistically from a religious perspective.

In 1874 the church leaders did not anticipate dissolution, and Young and George A. Smith prepared an outline of the religious principles embodied in the United Order. Concurrently, church leaders began to preach and organize United Orders in southern Utah. Young and Smith envisioned an order like those mentioned in Acts 2:44, in which the early Saints "had all things common"; and 4th Nephi: 3, where "they had all things common among them; therefore there were not rich and poor, bond and free, but they were all made free and partakers of the heavenly gift." The Saints expected to found a place like the community organized by the Old Testament patriarch Enoch, whose name Young used as a title of the movement. Moses 7:18 mentions the community: "And the Lord called his people Zion, because they were of one heart, and one mind, and dwelt in righteousness; and there was no poor among them."

On April 6, 1874, the day the general conference usually started, Young, Smith, and Erastus Snow left St. George, even as Orson Pratt told the Tabernacle congregation that the leaders had postponed general conference for a month so they could organize United Orders in all Mormon communities. As he proceeded north from St. George, Young established United Orders in Rockville, Virgin, Shunesburg, and Toquerville in Washington County. He moved on to towns in Iron County, where he founded them in Kanarraville and Paragonah. Continuing toward Salt Lake, he launched a United Order in Beaver.

In instituting the one in Beaver, Young emphasized that he did not view the institution as a means of enriching himself or the local leaders. Rather, Young said he intended the order "to elevate the poor, and make them comfortable and happy as the rich." Young made it clear that he "wanted no poor in our midst." Young and other church leaders set up United Orders in Mormon towns in Idaho, Wyoming, Nevada, Arizona, and northern Mexico, as well as virtually every Latter-day Saint town in Utah. The leadership patterned most of these United Orders on the St. George model.

The intent of the United Orders was perhaps too idealistic even for committed Latter-day Saints, and most of them dissolved within a few years. Some of the reasons seem quite evident. The wealthy became increasingly anxious about the management of the property they had dedicated to the order, and some workers also seemed unable to labor efficiently enough to satisfy the managers or the wealthy who had previously owned the property.

Young recognized that in a large community like Salt Lake City, he could not set up a single United Order to encompass the entire city. Instead, he and other leaders founded them in each of the city's twenty wards. These were not, however, simply smaller ones patterned on the St. George model. Rather, the General Authorities encouraged each of the wards to engage in some cooperative business. The Nineteenth Ward, for instance, converted a private business that made "soaps, concentrated lyes, sal soda and axle grease" into a United Order enterprise. In addition, a number of tradespeople, such as the tailors, organized United Orders that functioned like guilds. Young himself belonged to United Order Number 1 in Salt Lake City, for businessmen. Ironically, Young engendered some resentment because, unsure about the ability of others to manage his property, he did not pledge all of his holdings to the United Order as he had in 1855. Nevertheless, using the Salt Lake City model, the leaders founded multiple United Orders in other larger cities as well, including four in Logan and Ogden and three in Provo.

Some Mormons have looked back nostalgically on the United Order of Orderville, a town in Long Valley on what is now U.S. Highway 89, about twenty-five miles north of Kanab, a town on the Arizona border. The Orderville settlers had previously starved as they scratched out a hardscrabble existence on the Muddy River in southeastern Nevada. Brigham Young visited those settlements in 1870, and their living conditions appalled him. When he released them from the Muddy Mission and freed them to move elsewhere, many of the settlers moved to Mount Carmel, a town about nineteen miles north of Kanab. Because of conflicts over land use, many pulled up stakes again and moved a few miles north to establish a settlement they called Orderville. As they incorporated the United Order of Orderville in July 1875, the residents deeded all their real and personal property to the order, and the members lived as a single family. All men and women of the same age and gender received the same wages regardless of their occupation. One caustic observer, who obviously failed to understand Orderville's religious foundation, said that the town "bore more resemblance to a Christian military camp than to an individualistic society of free men and women."

Brigham Young understood that he intended to create a religious community of dedicated Saints. When Young spoke of his vision for the United Order of Enoch, he anticipated a community like Orderville: all should live together, sharing everything. In Orderville, families lived in dwellings owned collectively, a pattern he also envisioned. Young even spoke of a miniature railroad that would run through the mess hall to deliver food to the diners. Orderville did not construct such a railroad, but in most respects, their United Order conformed to Young's plan. The whole community ate meals together in shifts, until 1880 when a flood destroyed the ovens. After that disaster, Orderville began to fall apart. Instead of rebuilding the ovens, they began dining as individual families, and in 1883 Orderville's leadership stopped treating everyone equally. Instead of paying the same wage to all workers of the same gender and age, the leaders began to set wages on their calculation of the relative value of the work each person did. Also in 1883, the leaders authorized each family to purchase a town lot and a cow for itself. The supervisors also began to arrange lease agreements with unit managers, which allowed them to earn profits in addition to wages.

These internal changes placed the order on the road to a capitalistic system, and the federal government struck a fatal blow by enforcing the Edmunds Act of 1882. In 1884 U.S. deputy marshals began to hunt down polygamous husbands, which included most Orderville men. Unlawful cohabitation was the legal term, but the federal officials interpreted the law to apply only to men living with more than one woman in the marriage relationship. Those who fornicated with prostitutes or mistresses could do so with safety, at least from the marshals, though perhaps not from diseases or from community disapproval. Still, the marshals' raids accelerated the path toward capitalism, and the order dissolved in 1885.

———

The federal government had already begun pressing its efforts to destroy the church in the 1870s by attacking Brigham Young and other Mormons. President Ulysses S. Grant appointed New York judge James B. McKean, formerly a Civil War colonel, as chief justice of the Utah territorial supreme court in 1870, and in 1872 McKean told Grant's brother-in-law—Julia Dent Grant's brother, Judge Louis Dent—that "God" had called him to a "mission." His mission in Utah, he said, "is as much above the duties of other courts and judges as the heavens are above the earth, and whenever or wherever I may find the Local or Federal laws obstructing or interfering therewith by God's blessing, I shall trample them under my feet."

One of the laws on which he trampled was the 1852 Utah territorial law on empaneling juries. Territorial statute required the county probate judges to pull the names of candidates for a jury from a box containing the names of men who were taxpayers living in the court's jurisdiction. At the time, women could not serve on juries. Shortly after McKean assumed the bench, he ruled that the Utah territorial courts were United States district courts in which the U.S. marshal could simply pick jury members off the street, and the judge could empanel juries from those the marshal selected. The marshal found both non-Mormons and Mormons on the street, but McKean excluded from the juries Mormon men who refused to say that polygamy was adultery.

A grand jury McKean empaneled that was packed with anti-Mormons returned indictments against Mormon officers Brigham Young, George Q. Cannon, and Daniel H. Wells, as well as Godbeite convert Henry W. Lawrence. Significantly, instead of indicting the men for polygamy under the Morrill Act of 1862, the jury charged them with lewd and lascivious cohabitation and adultery under a territorial statute, coinciding with McKean's insistence that polygamy was adultery. Certainly, the territorial legislature had not intended the statute to apply to polygamous marriages, since many of the legislators were themselves polygamists. When Young appeared in McKean's court to answer the accusation, the judge admitted him to $5,000 bail but, in a flourish of judicial drama, he announced "that while the case at bar is called '*The People versus Brigham Young,*' its other and real title is, 'Federal Authority versus Polygamic Theocracy.'" "A system," he charged, "is on trial in the person of Brigham Young."

In 1872 McKean launched a second attack on Brigham Young and Daniel H. Wells, together with Hosea Stout. In 1868 William A. "Bill" Hickman had been excommunicated from the church for his murderous activities. He claimed that this resulted from his refusal to commit a murder for Young, but there is no evidence for that assertion other than Hickman's purported confessions, which were edited and published by anti-Mormon author J. H. Beadle. Bearing a grudge against Young and other church leaders for his excommunication, Hickman began working for Young's archenemy Patrick Connor and he met with attorney Robert N. Baskin to confess his evil deeds. He told Baskin the stories of multiple murders he had committed as the leader of squad of assassins, and he insisted he had killed people on Brigham Young's orders. Hickman said that during the Utah War, he and Hosea Stout had murdered munitions dealer Richard Yates, swearing that Brigham's son, Joseph A. Young, had relayed his father's orders for the killing. In a public statement, however, Joseph Young repudiated Hickman's assertion, denying that he had conveyed such orders. Hickman repeated his confession to McKean's anti-Mormon grand jury, and on January 2, 1872, U.S. Marshal Matthewson T. Patrick arrested Young and Stout. Young's attorneys Thomas Fitch and Julius C. Bates, both non-Mormons, tried to get Young released on $500,000 bail, but McKean sentenced Young to house arrest and sent Stout to the city jail.

It was the U.S. Supreme Court, however, that thwarted James McKean's plans to try the church in the person of Brigham Young for adultery or murder. McKean's Achilles heel bared itself in an unlikely dispute over a liquor license. Salt Lake City, like a number of places in Utah, had levied relatively high fees for operating saloons, and one owner, Paul Englebrecht, refused to pay. Jeter Clinton, a Salt Lake alderman and justice of the peace, levied a fine of more than fifty-nine thousand dollars on Englebrecht for declining to pay the fee. When he appealed the judgment to McKean's court, one of the judge's packed juries ruled against Clinton, and McKean threw out the fine. Clinton in turn appealed to the U.S. Supreme Court, and in April 1872 the high court ruled that McKean must follow territorial law in empaneling juries. The decision in *Clinton v. Englebrecht* (80 U.S. 434; 1872) negated not only the indictments against Young but also some 130 indictments issued by McKean's illegal juries.

Undeterred by the judgment in the Clinton case, McKean found another way to trample on Young. In July 1873, in one of the most bizarre divorce cases in American history, Ann Eliza Webb Dee Young, one of Young's plural wives, applied to McKean's court for a divorce. Alleging mental cruelty, she demanded $1,000 a month in alimony, $20,000 in legal fees, and $20,000 from his estate. Through his attorney, Thomas Fitch, Young replied that he believed Ann Eliza was still married to James Dee. Even if Ann Eliza were not, Fitch said, Young was married to Mary Ann Angell Young, and could not have legally married Ann Eliza. The two of them had joined together, he said, in a religious "plural or celestial marriage," rather than a marriage recognized by the territory.

In a February 1874 ruling, McKean refused to accept Young's explanation. He ordered Young to pay Ann Eliza five hundred dollars per month in alimony pending the outcome of the litigation. Utah had no laws governing marriage, the judge said, and any union was legal providing that the two parties were competent to marry. Young appealed McKean's ruling to the territorial supreme court, but McKean refused to stay the case pending Young's appeal.

Instead he fined Young twenty-five dollars for contempt of court and ordered him to spend a night in the penitentiary. A number of local non-Mormons, including Young's vocal opponent, Patrick Connor, thought McKean's order was absurd, but Young slept in the pen that night. President Grant removed McKean from the bench in March 1875, when he declined to recuse himself in a mining case in which he was alleged to have a personal interest. Several years later, the U.S. attorney general ordered a subsequent chief justice, Michael Schaeffer, to dismiss the case. After all, if the courts recognized Ann Eliza's divorce suit as legal, they would have to recognize plural marriage as legal, which federal officials considered ludicrous.

After Ann Eliza separated from Young, she also apostatized from Mormonism. For the next several years, she earned a comfortable living and a national reputation by revealing what she insisted were the horrible secrets of Mormonism in lectures given principally in the East and Midwest. She also published an exposé about what she insisted were personal experiences in a book titled *Wife No. 19, or, The Story of a Life in Bondage.* Had she been better informed, she would have known she was actually wife number fifty-five or thereabout.

If Young gave much thought to the exposé, he didn't dwell on it. His mind and heart carried more concern for the spiritual welfare of the Saints. As such, he accomplished a great deal during the last years of his life. In addition to trying to promote the United Orders and endowing a number of educational institutions, Young fostered construction of a temple in St. George.

The Mormons in the Cotton Mission at St. George had struggled with Mother Nature since they answered Young's mission call in 1861. Available farmland was scarce, and the fickle Virgin and Santa Clara rivers presented constant hazards. Settlers in the region lived in a desert that received less than six inches of precipitation each year, and on inopportune occasions, cloudbursts would smash down 20 percent or more of the annual rainfall within an hour or so. These deluges swelled the rivers into torrents of water, rocks, and mud that changed their courses and washed out dams the settlers had constructed to irrigate their crops.

As Mormons in the Cotton Mission suffered from flash floods, Young also concerned himself with their spiritual welfare and that of other faithful members. Most particularly he longed for the erection of a temple, a proper place for members to participate in the most sacred Latter-day Saint rituals, which included baptisms for the dead, endowments for the living and dead, and sealing for time and eternity. Work on the Salt Lake Temple had begun in 1853, but construction on this massive edifice moved at a snail's pace. In the meantime, the Saints had begun performing rituals in the Council House on Salt Lake City's Main Street after its completion in 1852. Since 1855 they had participated in temple ordinances in the Endowment House on the northwest corner of Temple Square, performing vicarious baptisms for the dead, but they did no vicarious endowments for deceased relatives there.

The hiatus in performing endowment and sealing rituals for the dead apparently occurred because Young, following Joseph Smith's example, had ruled that the Mormons must perform such rituals only in a temple. As Young considered this matter, he thought perhaps the members could construct a smaller temple in St. George more rapidly than the larger Salt Lake Temple. After he came to St. George for the winter in December 1870, he asked those present during a council meeting in Erastus Snow's "Big House" on January 31, 1871, "what they thought of building a temple in St. George." Elder Snow, leader of the Washington County community, "greeted the suggestion with: Glory! Hallelujah!!" Those present then "unanimously voted in favor of the measure."

On November 9, 1871, Young led the groundbreaking ceremony for the temple. He marked the spot for the southeast cornerstone to hold sacred records, and said that a capstone would be placed above it near the top of the temple where temple records would be stored. Then he turned a few shovelfuls of dirt and gave the shovel over to other leaders to follow his example. After they, too, had broken ground, he led those present in the Hosanna Shout, which consisted in shouting three times, "Hosanna, Hosanna, Hosanna to God and the Lamb," and clapping hands three times after each shout. Those present followed the hosannas by saying, "Amen, Amen, and Amen," and accompanying these words with clapping as well. In April 1874 he placed records in a box in the cornerstone and dedicated them to rest there, as he said, "until the Savior comes."

Young called for volunteers from southern Utah and from Mormon towns throughout the territory to help build the temple. Workers dedicated their time without pay, although the church credited the equivalent of their labor to the tithing account. The building of the St. George Temple was a monument to the dedication of church members—laborers came from far and wide. Men harvested lumber on Mount Trumbull, Arizona, in stands seventy to eighty miles south of St. George. Stonemasons built the foundation from a quarry in a volcanic mesa west of St. George, and workers erected the walls from sandstone obtained from a quarry north of the city. Young himself donated the temple's baptismal font and the statues of twelve oxen—representing the twelve tribes of Israel—on which the font rested. Workers covered the outside walls with white plaster that shone in the desert sun, and in 1875 those who joined the United Order were re-baptized in the font in the partially constructed temple. Construction may have cost as much as eight hundred thousand dollars, equivalent to more than sixteen million dollars in 2017.

After the Saints finished the building in early 1877, Young called Wilford Woodruff, Brigham Young Jr., Alexander F. McDonald, and L. John Nuttall to write down the endowment ceremony. The Mormons had apparently never written the complete ceremony since practicing it in Nauvoo, and the four men wrote from memory. Young read and approved what they wrote and dictated as well a lecture for presentation in the temple that incorporated his Adam-God theory, including his belief that Adam was the father of Jesus Christ. After Young's death, the church leadership repudiated the doctrine and removed the lecture from the temple ceremony. We do not know exactly when the General Authorities removed the lecture or whether it was used in all temples. Members also swore an oath of vengeance in which they promised to pray for God's retribution against the murderers of Joseph and Hyrum Smith. This was removed from the temple ceremony during the early 1920s.

Although Young had promoted the temple's construction enthusiastically, he did not dedicate the St. George Temple himself. He suffered from a severe case of gout and rheumatism, which incapacitated him to such a degree that he had to walk with a cane. During the temple dedication service, men carried him in a chair from place to place. Nevertheless, other church leaders gave three dedicatory prayers. Young assigned Wilford Woodruff to prepare the dedicatory prayer and read it in the baptismal room on January 1, 1877. Erastus Snow offered a second dedicatory prayer in the main floor assembly room, and Brigham Young Jr. offered a prayer in the sealing rooms in the upper level. After the prayers, the congregation returned to the assembly room, and Brigham Young spoke to those present. At one point when talking about the Devil, he struck the pulpit with his cane so hard that it carried a mark for future generations. Young called Woodruff as the first temple president, and he called one of his wives, Lucy Bigelow Young, as temple matron. Woodruff also married one of Young's daughters by Lucy, Eudora Lavina, as a plural wife, and she bore him one child who died shortly after birth. Eudora Lavina later divorced Wilford and reportedly eloped with attorney Albert Hagan, clerk of the territorial supreme court.

As construction of the temple testifies, although some authors have considered Young an extremely pragmatic leader, he was also deeply religious. Before joining Mormonism, Young had belonged to the most radical offshoot of Methodism. Among other differences, Reformed Methodism organized by congregations instead of bishops and circuit riders and practiced faith healing and personal revelation. After learning of Mormonism, speaking in tongues attracted Young, and he engaged in it in America and in England at a time the practice was relatively widespread. Young spoke in tongues infrequently after arriving in Utah, though he reportedly did to a group of Indian leaders in the early 1850s.

In addition to speaking in tongues, Young obtained knowledge and direction from dreams and visions. In Nauvoo, before ever seeing Utah, he dreamed he saw "in the west many beautiful hills & barren & valley skirted with timber." George A. Smith reported that Young's description of his dream of the Salt Lake Valley was so vivid that Smith recognized Ensign Peak when he first saw it. In commenting on Young's visions, historian D. Michael Quinn wrote: "At conference on 6 April 1862 he said: 'I have had visions and revelations instructing me how to organize this people so that they can live like the family of heaven.'" Quinn also noted the influence that other visions had on Young. Before the expulsion of church members from Missouri in 1838, Young had a vision of the scattering of Mormons, and the future establishment the New Jerusalem. On February 17, 1847, Wilford Woodruff reported that Young experienced "an exceedingly sick day." As Quinn noted, however, that night, as he later told Willard Richards, he "went into Eternity, & came back again." He met with Joseph Smith and saw the premortal spiritual life of future human beings. Quinn wrote that after Young reached the Salt Lake Valley, he saw a vision of the Salt Lake Temple with the six spires that would actually be built, although no architectural plans existed at the time. Young later had a vision of the organization of the Kingdom of God into families.

Young also found comfort, inspiration, and insight in a wide variety of dreams. As author Clair Barrus on the website *Mormon Chronicles* noted, some dreams—"such as a dream of his family while he was overseas"—were of those closest to him whom he missed. In a dream while he was away, he dreamed of "repeatedly kissing his wife." Barrus wrote also that in many of Young's dreams he met with and received counsel from Joseph Smith. In those dreams, Smith spoke to him from the spirit world. Barrus found that on one occasion, Young had such a traumatic experience while four teeth were being extracted that he fainted, and while unconscious he dreamed of devils.

While Young believed in revelations and dreams, he also pursued temporal activities such as a frequent exchange of letters with Thomas L. Kane, who had assisted the Mormons during their past trials. In his correspondence, Young had frequently urged Kane and his wife Elizabeth to visit Utah. After delaying for some time, the couple, their two sons, and an African-American servant came west in 1872–73. After visiting with Young in Salt Lake City, the Kane party accompanied Young and his entourage to St. George. The Kanes spent the winter in southern Utah, where Elizabeth noted that Thomas, who suffered frequently from serious ailments, seemed to recover in the southern Utah climate. Elizabeth wrote two books about her experiences and travels in Utah, and Young frequently commented on the exceptionally valuable service Kane had given the Mormons.

Young appreciated the support of friendly non-Mormons like Kane, but he also believed that women could assist in the church's work, and in addition, they had an important role to play in the economic and political life of Utah Territory and the church. With Young's encouragement, and the active lobbying by Latter-day Saint women, women in Utah achieved a degree of political power shared only by women in Wyoming at the time. At the ratification of the U.S. Constitution, women who owned property in Massachusetts, New York, New Jersey, and Rhode Island could vote, but the state legislatures soon took that right from them. In 1870 Utah's gender composition was quite different from Wyoming's. In Utah women made up 48 percent of the population, whereas in Wyoming they made up only 20 percent. Several eastern and midwestern congressmen led by George W. Julian of Indiana had argued that if women could vote in Utah, they would overthrow Utah's polygamous leadership. Young knew they were wrong, and he urged the legislature to grant suffrage to Utah's women. His counselor, George Q. Cannon, published editorials in the *Deseret News* championing the cause of women as a progressive measure. "With women to aid in the great cause of reform," Cannon wrote, "what wonderful changes can be effected!" Utah women—led by Charlotte Ives Godbe, Young's stepdaughter, and Mormon women Emmeline B. Wells and Sarah

Kimball—lobbied aggressively for the reform by holding rallies and urging acting governor Samuel A. Mann to sign the bill that granted women the vote after the legislature passed it. He did so on February 12, 1870, and among the first women to vote was Seraph A. Young, an attorney and Brigham Young's grandniece. The U.S. Congress would abolish women's suffrage in Utah seventeen years later with the Edmunds-Tucker Act of 1887, but, responding to the will of the people, the Utah Constitutional Convention restored woman suffrage at statehood in 1896.

Young supported the extension of woman suffrage while suffering from ill health, a condition he had endured since the 1850s. Between 1875 and 1877, his condition grew increasingly fragile. During those years, despite poor health, he made a number of changes in the church organization that established precedents for the future. In 1835, when Oliver Cowdery, David Whitmer, and Martin Harris ordained the original members of the Quorum of the Twelve Apostles, Joseph Smith ranked their seniority by age, from oldest to youngest. In that ordering, Thomas B. Marsh had served as president of the Quorum until his excommunication in March 1839. Young became second in seniority when David W. Patten, who was older than Brigham, died in the Battle of Crooked River in October 1838. Because of Marsh's excommunication, Young succeeded as president of the Quorum. With Young's ordination as church president in December 1847, Orson Hyde then became president of the Quorum because he was second oldest among the original Twelve.

In 1861, however, Young changed the precedent by ruling that succession in the church leadership should follow from date of ordination rather than by age. During the Mormon war in Missouri, Hyde had become disaffected, and the apostles dropped him from the Quorum between May 4 and June 27, 1839. After Orson Hyde's return to fellowship, Joseph Smith had placed him in the Quorum in his original position. In April 1875, however, Young decreed that he should hold the position in the Twelve he would have held at his re-ordination in June 1839. Orson Pratt had been a member of the original Twelve, but he had been excommunicated from August 1842 until January 1843, and Young ruled that his position should obtain from his re-ordination in January 1843.

Brigham Young's rule placed John Taylor and Wilford Woodruff ahead of both Hyde and Pratt. Joseph Smith had called John Taylor and Wilford Woodruff to the Twelve at the same time, but Taylor, who was a year and a half younger than Woodruff, had been ordained in December 1838, four months before Woodruff's April 1839 ordination. Under Young's rule, although Woodruff was older than Taylor, Taylor moved ahead of Woodruff in succession. The church membership had never sustained Taylor as president of the Twelve, but in fall 1875, Young declared that Taylor was president of the Quorum. The General Authorities did not actually resolve the question of succession to the church's presidency until September 1877, a month after Young's death, when on Woodruff's motion, the Twelve sustained Taylor as quorum president. As the senior apostle, Taylor succeeded Young as church president.

In addition to reorganizing the Twelve, Brigham Young initiated a number of other changes in church organization. John Taylor summarized the reason for Young's action in June 1877 when he said, "Many things have been left apparently at loose ends." Some stake presidents lacked counselors, some had no high councils, and some had called Seventies— members who serve as missionaries as members of the stake high council. In addition, the church leadership had not set apart or ordained all leaders for their positions. Some church members considered the Salt Lake Stake as the church's central stake with authority over the thirteen stakes that had been organized at the time. In a situation Mormons would consider highly unusual today, apostles presided concurrently as stake presidents over six of the thirteen: Charles C. Rich (Bear Lake), Brigham Young Jr. (Cache), Erastus Snow (St. George), Orson Hyde (Sanpete), Lorenzo Snow (Box Elder), and Franklin D. Richards (Weber). One presiding bishop, Edward Hunter, was supposed to handle all of the church's financial affairs, but the General Authorities had actually assigned fifteen presiding bishops to collect and distribute tithing and exercise some ecclesiastical leadership over various regions. In some cases, irregularities existed in ward bishoprics and quorums of priests and teachers who were supposed to serve as the major intermediaries between the ward bishopric and the individual families and members.

Brigham Young had probably allowed such organizational lapses to occur because he had concerned himself principally with other matters of church governance. He had spent considerable time establishing colonies from 1847 until the 1870s, directing Utah War operations during the mid-1850s, establishing cooperatives during the 1860s, supervising campaigns in the Black Hawk War from 1865 to 1872, and founding United Orders for several years beginning in 1874. In his last major effort at colonization, Young dispatched settlers to the Little Colorado region in eastern Arizona in 1876.

On top of all of these efforts, construction of the St. George Temple in the early 1870s and its dedication in January 1877 had placed additional pressure on Young. This was the first temple the Saints had constructed since the abandonment of Nauvoo in 1846. Unlike ward meetinghouses and stake tabernacles, it was the House of the Lord—for Latter-day Saints, it created a connection between the temporal and the eternal, a link between Heaven and earth. Construction of the Salt Lake Temple had already been moving ahead very slowly, but it was meant to serve the Saints in the Wasatch and Oquirrh regions. Including the one in Salt Lake, Young had divided the Mormon towns into four temple districts, although the realization of that division had to await the construction of three more temples. Young expected that the four temples would serve the spiritual needs of Latter-day Saints in the areas in which most of them lived. The St. George Temple served settlements in southern Utah, Arizona, and southern Nevada. Temples to be constructed at dedicated sites in Manti and Logan were to serve the Mormons in, respectively, south-central Utah and in northern Utah and southeastern Idaho.

As noted, the temples offered a link between Heaven and earth, but Young understood that in addition, the Latter-day Saints needed an orderly temporal and spiritual connection "to consolidate the interests, feelings, and lives of the members of the Church" in properly organized wards and stakes. He expected to organize, as he said, "the holy Priesthood after the pattern given us of our Father in Heaven." Under Young's direction, at stake conferences held between April 4 and August 26, 1877, he and members of the First Presidency and the Twelve organized seven new stakes and reorganized the previously existing thirteen. Local men or outsiders called to move to the stakes replaced the apostles as stake presidents, and for those in such counties as Tooele where no stake had previously existed, the visiting authorities organized stakes and called and set apart new stake leaders. The visiting authorities also organized or reorganized ward bishoprics and priesthood quorums.

Significantly, the reorganization touched individual members in ways most had not experienced. Perhaps the most important changes took place in the revitalization of bishoprics by calling or regularizing the calling of more than 180 bishops and more than 240 bishop's counselors. In reorganizing stake presidencies and ward bishoprics, the visiting authorities instructed local leaders to improve the functioning of Sunday Schools and Young Men's and Young Women's Mutual Improvement Associations. They admonished the local leaders to reactivate the priesthood quorums by extending calls to all worthy mature men and teenage young men as priesthood holders and members of quorums.

Young and his counselors also issued a circular letter to local leaders outlining the priesthood reorganization they and the apostles had undertaken. Among salient points were the instructions that a bishopric must consist of three high priests, the church would have only one presiding bishop, and each member must be properly enrolled in a ward. When members moved from one ward to another, the previous ward must send a recommendation to the ward into which the member had moved. The circular also reiterated the instructions on auxiliaries. The reorganization that Brigham Young had initiated continued in the local wards and stakes during his last illness and after his passing in August 1877.

Because of declining health, Young called additional counselors to serve in the First Presidency. Those called included Joseph

F. Smith in 1866; George Q. Cannon, Brigham Young Jr., and Albert Carrington in 1873; and John W. Young in 1874. Young subsequently called John W. Young as first counselor following George A. Smith's death on September 1, 1875. The death of Smith, first cousin of Joseph Smith and First Counselor in the church's First Presidency since 1868, unnerved Young, who had suffered severely following the deaths of his second counselor, Jedediah Grant, on December 1, 1856, and his first counselor and closest friend, Heber C. Kimball, on June 22, 1868. Smith, just 5 feet, 10 inches tall but a man of more than 250 pounds, was only 58 when he died. Young, who, himself, suffered from extremely poor health at the time, wept bitterly at Smith's funeral, and reportedly had an extremely difficult time recovering from the pain caused by the death of his confidant and close friend.

Young had suffered from bouts of ill health at least since the mid-1850s. Already ill during the 1860s, Young's health deteriorated almost steadily during the 1870s, and after 1873 he was frequently incapacitated. Among other ailments, he suffered from the rheumatism and gout that required he be carried from room to room during dedication of the St. George Temple in January 1877. Well-educated medical doctors, including his nephew and personal physician, Seymour B. Young, could do little to cure the diseases that plagued him, which was not surprising, considering how rudimentary medical knowledge remained in the 1870s. For someone born in 1801, as Young was, life expectancy was thirty-six years. Many children died before age ten, but those who lived beyond that age, on average, lived only forty years. Young, obviously, beat the odds by quite a few years.

Seymour B. Young graduated in 1873 from the University Medical College of New York, and a year later, Brigham Young began consulting him. As early as 1858, Young experienced persistent urinary blockages, and in December 1858 he had ordered "first quality" silver and rubber catheters from St. Louis. We do not know when Young began to catheterize himself, but reports indicated that Seymour Young gave him additional instruction during the 1870s after he became Young's physician.

Young's illness ran headlong into the prosecution of John D. Lee, whose first trial for the Mountain Meadows massacre, held in Beaver, Utah, lasted two and a half weeks, from Tuesday, July 20, to Saturday, August 7, 1875. On July 30, 1875, during the first trial, both Brigham Young and George A. Smith submitted affidavits testifying that as a consequence of their ill health, they could not attend the trial and instead submitted depositions. Some authors have accused Young and Smith of faking illness to avoid having to testify, but Smith, who was clearly ill, died only a few weeks after giving the deposition, and Young, who had suffered for years from urinary blockage, might have placed his life in jeopardy under the strain of testifying during the trial. The pressure of a grueling cross-examination by Robert Baskin, who used the first trial to try unsuccessfully to prove that Young had ordered the massacre, might well have exacerbated his already fragile health. Indeed, in October 1875, three months after Young's deposition, the trauma of self-catheterization led to a spasm and hemorrhage.

Still, Young insisted on traveling to St. George for the temple dedication in January 1877, and he followed up with extensive travel the following summer to supervise the massive priesthood reorganization. After lecturing to the church's bishops at the Council Hall in Salt Lake City on the night of August 23, 1877, he began vomiting and experienced diarrhea and cramps. Doctors Seymour Young, Washington F. Anderson, and Joseph M. and Francis D. Benedict attended Young and called his ailment cholera morbus, a nineteenth-century diagnosis for abdominal pain accompanied by "vomiting and purging of bilious matter" with "a good deal of nausea" and "spasmodic pain in the stomach, which is sometimes excruciating." Young's condition continued to deteriorate until he died six days later on August 29.

At that point in time, the diagnosis of cholera morbus covered a multitude of unknown conditions—including appendicitis. Later in the century, after physicians understood the symptoms, Seymour Young reflected on Young's condition and concluded that Brigham Young had died of appendicitis. In fact, Young probably died of the disease now known as peritonitis from a ruptured appendix.

Friends moved Brigham's body to the tabernacle, where he lay in state from September 1, 1877, through noon on September 2. More than twenty-five thousand people passed by his casket. In 1873 he had prescribed the program for his funeral, at which George Careless directed music by the Tabernacle choir. George Q. Cannon, his friend, counselor, and an executor of his estate, conducted the funeral. Cannon spoke, as did his counselor Daniel H. Wells and apostles Wilford Woodruff, Erastus Snow, and John Taylor. An entourage of four thousand—who, at Brigham's request, wore colors other than black—accompanied the casket to a small cemetery Young had designated on what is now First Avenue. His remains lie there today in a wooden casket he designed surrounded by a stone vault.

Even though Young suffered from rapidly worsening health during the 1870s, he refused to slow down, investing his energies as much as his health allowed to serve the church he loved. The evening of his final illness, he was instructing the church's bishops at the Council House. In his heart of hearts, Young envisioned a fellowship with no poor, so he organized the United Orders to try—unsuccessfully, as it proved—to build a community of equals. Although debilitated from increasingly painful diseases, he endured personal attacks from Bill Hickman, Ann Eliza Young, Robert Baskin, and James McKean, and suffered at a distance during the trial of John D. Lee, who, with the Iron County Militia, had murdered 120 innocent people and, in their horrid attacks, caused irreparable harm to the church he loved. In spite of these setbacks, Young reorganized the Quorum of the Twelve Apostles and the local wards and stakes. He responded positively to dreams and visions, and he believed strongly that the church must construct temples to tie Heaven and earth together. Living through such events with all his shortcomings and faults, Young persisted as an extraordinary leader who had escorted the Saints from violence in the Midwest to erect a Godly kingdom in the Intermountain West.

13

Some Final Thoughts

Religion had guided Brigham Young's life since he was old enough to make choices for himself. He had joined the Reformed Methodists, a relatively radical church at the time that practiced faith healing and personal revelation. He left that church after reading the Book of Mormon and learning of the Pentecostal features of early Mormonism. After his baptism and ordination to the Mormon priesthood, he began proselytizing for his new church. Upon first meeting Joseph Smith, he spoke in a tongue that Joseph said was the pure Adamic language. Similar Pentecostal experience continued through the dedication of the Kirtland Temple and into Young's mission in the United Kingdom. After the trek to Utah, Young continued to believe in revelation and dream-conveyed messages. He reduced his practice of glossolalia, but other church members continued it well into the 1920s.

While Young believed in revelation and the atonement through Christ's death and resurrection—that he was engaged in God's work—others disagreed, punctuating their disagreement with attacks on the church and its members. Violent opposition would follow the Mormons wherever they settled. At least one perceptive observer recognized part of the reason. In 1831, the year after Joseph Smith published the Book of Mormon and founded what was then called the Church of Christ, French aristocrat Alexis de Tocqueville visited the United States to study prisons. Tocqueville wrote about his observations of American society in the book *Democracy in America,* an insightful examination of Jacksonian America.

Tocqueville does not mention Mormonism by name, but the Latter-day Saint experience fits easily into his analysis of the abuse of an unpopular minority in a democratic nation. Tocqueville argued that such populations had virtually no protection in America from the "omnipotence of the majority." He observed that in America majorities could encourage "legal despotism in the legislator but at the same time . . . [induce] arbitrariness in the magistrate. . . . Backed by the opinion of the many and strengthened by their support, officials will then dare to do things that astonish even a European accustomed to the sight of arbitrary rule. Within the bosom of liberty habits are thus formed that may one day do it great harm."

Mormons did not need to read Tocqueville to understand how and why majorities oppressed them. By the early 1840s they considered leaving the United States. After the organization of the Council of Fifty in 1844, the Latter-day Saints began to look for a place to settle where they could avoid persecution. They considered Texas, at the time an independent republic. They also studied California, a territory on the northern fringe of the Mexican empire, and Oregon, then under joint occupation by the United States and Great Britain. After examining all of the evidence available, including reports of John Charles Frémont's explorations in the West, they agreed upon the Great Salt Lake region. Young's comments in sessions of the Council of Fifty provide an insight into his choice of the Great Salt Lake as a new home for the Mormons. Contrary to some Mormon folklore, Young did not receive a revelation to settle on the Wasatch Front as he overlooked the Salt Lake Valley from Emigration Canyon; he knew where the Saints would settle when they left Nauvoo.

Through the lens of Tocqueville's book and the Mormons' own observations, we can examine Young's changing attitudes and reactions to violence and understand why he feared armies. Throughout his life, Young witnessed a great deal of majority-supported "legal despotism." Historian Ronald Walker has argued that Young was a pacifist. In view of his reaction in various ways to differing conditions, it seems more accurate to conclude that Young preferred to avoid violence but he would act pragmatically. While he lived in Kirtland, Young first heard of the tyranny of the majority in Missouri, as state officials turned a blind eye while vigilantes drove the Mormons from Jackson County. He joined Zion's Camp, in which the Mormons tried unsuccessfully but without violence to help those expelled regain their property. Under attack because of his support for Joseph Smith, Young fled Kirtland, Ohio, in the winter of 1838 to settle with his family near Far West in northwestern Missouri. Militiamen in that state fought and killed his friends and raped Mormon women, but Young refused to participate in the war. Instead, he helped refugees leave the state when Governor Lilburn W. Boggs issued his infamous extermination order and their bloody feet marked the path to Illinois. After the Mormons built Nauvoo into a thriving city, members of a non-Mormon militia unit murdered Joseph and Hyrum Smith and wounded John Taylor while they were imprisoned but under the ineffective protection of Governor Thomas Ford. Reflecting on Smith's murder, Ford wrote Joseph's clerk, William W. Phelps, that he deplored the assassination but welcomed the prophet's death. Yet instead of fighting the independent militias that killed Mormons and drove them from Nauvoo, Young led the Mormon exodus to Utah.

In Utah, Young experienced additional upsetting experiences with armies. One of the first came with Bvt. Lt. Col. Edward Steptoe's assignment to Utah in 1854. Even though the government paid well for supplying Steptoe's forces, furnishing food for his troops, camp followers, and animals emptied Mormon larders. Conflicts with Steptoe's soldiers included a Christmastime riot and Lt. Sylvester Mowry's inducing of Mormon women to abscond with the army to California.

Because Congress organized Utah as a territory in 1850 rather than admitting it as a state as it did California, Young and the

Utahns had to contend with anti-Mormon federal appointees. Letters from these officials denouncing the Mormons flooded Washington, D.C. Many charged correctly that the Mormons tried to live in peace with the Indians. Others claimed that the Latter-day Saints colluded with the region's tribes to attack the overland mail and emigrants. Some like Judge John Fitch Kinney were essentially well meaning but misunderstanding as he complained about the jury's verdict in the trial of Pahvants for the murder of Lt. John Gunnison and seven others in Gunnison's surveying party. Federal appointee David H. Burr and his deputies conducted and approved fraudulent land surveys, yet Buchanan accepted Burr's complaints about Mormon control of land and resources. The president declined to investigate the criminal surveyors until after the Utah War of 1857–58, though significantly, he did not reappoint Burr. Buchanan probably sent an army to Utah in part because of Judge William W. Drummond's flagrant lies, for Buchanan's summary of the justification for dispatching the army to Utah seems to parallel Drummond's charges.

Buchanan's decision to dispatch troops against the Mormons further confirmed Young's fear of armies. The president charged the Mormons with rebellion, and when the Mormons attacked the army's supply trains to obstruct the Utah Expedition, he charged treason. Whether treasonous, rebellious, or not, Young's response was understandable. He harbored a reasonable and deeply ingrained fear of armies that experiences in Missouri, Illinois, and Utah had infused in his soul. Young's fear played a major role in his efforts to hinder the troops who marched on Utah in 1857, especially when accurate rumors reached him that many of the soldiers, including Johnston's adjutant, Fitz John Porter, said they intended to murder Mormons.

Of Young's own views on Mormon-authored violence, it seems accurate to conclude they were inconsistent largely because, in most cases, they were pragmatic responses to difficult conditions. As his experiences in Missouri and Illinois demonstrated, Young opposed violence. Nevertheless, he sent the Mormons to settle on Indian lands, and, as with most Euro-Americans, conflict arose as a result. Young told the Mormon settlers to treat the Indians kindly, but his two orders conflicted with each other. As Indian agent Garland Hurt noted, the Mormon settlements undermined the Indians' economic base. On the other hand, Hurt also observed that Young's policy of feeding the Indians, adopted in 1852, burdened the Mormon settlers.

In both the short and long runs, settlements that Young established contributed to the Walker, Tintic, and Black Hawk wars. In response to the Indian opposition, Brigham Young pursued inconsistent policies. He ordered the extermination of Utah Valley Utes in 1850 because of incomplete information, but by 1852 he had adopted a policy of defense and conciliation. In each of these wars, Young eventually returned to defense and conciliation, which helped to restore peace.

Events in the Black Hawk War show Young's inconsistency. Young rebuked Circleville citizens for murdering the innocent Paiutes they captured. On the other hand, he made a tragic and costly mistake by ordering Warren Snow to take several Indians hostage in the hope that it would end the war. Young's and Snow's mistake led to the deaths of at least nine Utes, including Sanpitch, one of the friendliest of Utah Indians. These deaths also frightened the Utes into abandoning central Utah and caused the failure of Young's policy of encouraging the Utes and Mormons to live peaceably together.

The hostage policy proved disastrous as a wartime measure, and like Young's preaching of blood atonement, it led to violence. Young preached the doctrine at various times between 1852 and 1856, but more frequently during the Mormon Reformation of 1856–57. After 1857 he stopped promoting blood atonement, though in his thorough collection of Young's sermons, historian Richard Van Wagoner cites what he believes are other examples. These, however, are about a person shedding his or her blood as a testimony rather than about shedding blood to atone for sins. Explanations of Young's preaching have ranged all the way from scholar Leonard Arrington's argument that the sermons were rhetoric to historian Will Bagley's belief that he meant literally what he said. Adopting a middle ground, Young biographer John Turner argues that "Young primarily considered the doctrine a prod to repentance," citing Young's instructions to Isaac Haight. Nevertheless, as Turner points out, "several brutal acts of violence indicated the dangerous nature of [Young's] rhetoric."

On balance, Arrington and Turner seem correct to understand Young's teaching as rhetoric, but Turner is also correct to say that some Mormons interpreted Young's sermons as a license for violence. The most flagrant example occurred in Springville, where Bishop Aaron Johnson misrepresented a letter from Young about the flight of John Ambrose and Thomas Betts to justify the murder of William Parrish and his son, Beason. A grand jury later indicted Johnson, but he succeeded in avoiding capture.

Young, himself, could at times ignore his opposition to violence and authorize its use. The Ambrose-Betts case is an example. In the Utah war, though Young ordered non-lethal attacks on wagon trains, he authorized armed resistance if the army advanced past Fort Bridger. Fortunately, Thomas L. Kane's intervention made violent resistance to the army unnecessary.

Although the contending armies spilled no blood in the Utah War, the war was not a bloodless confrontation as some have claimed. Deaths resulted from a Bannock-Shoshone attack on Fort Limhi that some federal contractors may have encouraged. Other deaths occurred in Utah among arms dealers. Mormons under the leadership of Porter Rockwell murdered five members of the John and William Aiken party near Nephi, but Young may not have ordered those deaths, as some authors have argued. Young's role in the murder of arms dealer Richard Yates is also debated—William Hickman insisted that Young ordered it through Joseph A. Young, but Joseph Young and Daniel Jones denied that he did.

In addition to these murders, the worst atrocity occurred at Mountain Meadows in southern Utah in September 1857. Controversy over Brigham Young's role in the Mountain Meadows massacre persists to this day. Four scholarly biographies of Young, published between 1971 and 2012—two of them by non-Mormons, Stanley P. Hirshson and John G. Turner, one by a Mormon, Leonard

J. Arrington, and one by a cultural Mormon, Newell Bringhurst—all argue that he did not order the massacre. In addition to the biographies, histories of the massacre written by various authors divide into two groups. William Wise, Sally Denton, and Will Bagley insist that Young decreed the killings. Juanita Brooks, Ronald W. Walker, Richard E. Turley Jr., and Glen M. Leonard deny it.

Some authors have cited John D. Lee's alleged confessions as evidence that Young ordered the massacre. Historian Chad Orton has assembled what seems convincing evidence to demonstrate that W. W. Bishop and others associated with him heavily edited and doctored the alleged confession in which John D. Lee or Bishop may have written that he "always believed" Young had ordered the murders through George A. Smith. Throughout his lifetime, Lee vigorously denied Young's culpability, and he refused to save his life in his first trial by implicating Young and other Mormon leaders. The confession he gave to U.S. Attorney Sumner Howard said he had "considered" that Young had ordered the massacre rather than he "believed" that Young had done so, as is written in his alleged confession. After examining the evidence, William MacKinnon, the principal authority on the Utah War, argues that Young deserved a Scotch verdict of "not proved." After examining the evidence collected in the LDS Church History Library in over a year and a half while working as an editor for the book by Walker, Turley, and Leonard, I am convinced that Young did not order the massacre. Moreover, we have positive evidence that Young sent directions to Isaac Haight through James Haslam to allow the Arkansas party to proceed unmolested.

Still, the massacre did occur. Why? Young's decision to dispatch George A. Smith to warn the Saints of the approaching army and the possible attacks of troops from the south may have contributed to the anti-emigrant sentiment in Cedar City. A published sermon by Isaac Haight, however, shows that he needed no encouragement from Smith to order the massacre.

More to the point, the lengths to which stake president and militia commander Isaac Haight went to order the massacre places the blame squarely on his shoulders. Haight sent John D. Lee to initiate the attack. He lied to his high council, but agreed to send James Haslam to secure advice from Brigham Young. Then, he ignored Haslam's mission and sent out troops on his own initiative. He convinced his militia superior, Parowan Stake president William Dame, to approve the massacre despite a vote against it by Dame's high council. After the massacre, Haight sent Lee to lie to Young by misdating the massacre and reporting the horrible tragedy as an Indian massacre, as Wilford Woodruff's diary clearly demonstrates.

After Young learned of the massacre and Kane brokered a resolution of the Utah War, Young demonstrated his basic inclination to promote peace and justice. He sent George A. Smith and Amasa M. Lyman south to preach peace, and he proposed to go south himself, to bring the Mountain Meadows perpetrators to court. Unfortunately, Judge Delana Eckels and U.S. Marshal Peter Dotson—who could have cooperated—refused to do so, and Governor Alfred Cumming, U.S. Attorney Alexander Wilson, and Wilson's assistant could not convince the other officials to hold trials at the time in towns in southern Utah where they could bring witnesses to testify. Thus, the two trials that did take place had to wait until 1875 and 1876 when, despite nine indictments, including that of Isaac Haight, John D. Lee was the only person convicted and executed for a crime for which the stake president and militia leader bore the principal responsibility.

The peaceful end of the Utah War did not end the threat of army-authored anti-Mormon violence. During the Civil War, Brigham Young and the Mormons contended with anti-Mormon and anti-Indian Patrick Edward Connor and the California volunteers. Connor frequently requested more troops to fight the Mormons, insisting that Brigham Young and the Latter-day Saints were traitors who waited only for the propitious moment to rise up against the Union. Young announced emphatically that the Mormons were loyal to the Union, but he also believed that God had brought Civil War to the United States as punishment for the nation's mistreatment of the Mormons. He also emphasized that the Mormons did not need Connor to guard the overland mail route, which they had done themselves during the early months of the war. Guarding the mail route was the ostensible reason for sending Connor's troops to Utah, but Connor assumed the added task of preparing to fight the Mormons and exterminating Indians.

In the October 2013 Latter-day Saint General Conference, Elder Dieter F. Uchtdorf, now in the Quorum of the Twelve Apostles but at the time Second Counselor in the church's First Presidency, emphasized that the church leaders did not think themselves or past leaders perfect. "There have been times when members or leaders in the Church have simply made mistakes," he said, adding: "imperfect people make mistakes."

Brigham Young clearly made mistakes. His public statements could, at times, be crude. Nevertheless, we would seriously underestimate Young if we judge him solely on the violence that accompanied his leadership at times and on the crude comments he sometimes made. We should not forget the strength of his religious beliefs and activities and his role in settling the Intermountain West. Young's religious philosophy anticipated an optimistic and progressive present and future for all mortals except the few Sons of Perdition, and, unfortunately, African Americans. Young believed in a God who increased in knowledge through experience. He believed that faithful human beings could become gods, and by accumulating knowledge, as God had, they could organize and govern new worlds. He believed that Adam and Eve were protean beings who came to earth as a god and goddess, and through eating mortal foods became mortal and the father and mother of the human race. As god of the earth, Young believed Adam was the father of Jesus Christ.

Some of Young's teachings have worn well, but others have not. The church leadership has repudiated Young's Adam-God theory including the concept that Adam fathered Jesus Christ. In 1889 the First Presidency and Quorum of the Twelve Apostles denied the church believed in or preached blood atonement. In 1978, through a revelation to President Spencer W. Kimball, the First Presidency, Quorum of the Twelve Apostles, and church membership disavowed Young's views on African Americans.

Some teachings, however, have become significant facets of Latter-day Saint beliefs and practices. Among those is the belief that human beings are perfectible, and that they can become like God. Young's teachings about the importance of the temple also remain central to Mormon doctrine.

Young and the Mormon people hurried to complete the Nauvoo Temple so that five thousand worthy members could receive their sealings and endowments before they had to flee from Nauvoo. Under his direction, endowment and sealing rituals continued in the Council House and Endowment House in Utah. Young dedicated the sites for the Salt Lake and Manti Temples, the latter only four months before his death. Young dedicated the site for the St. George Temple in 1872, and, though suffering from gout and rheumatism, officiated at its dedication in January 1877, eight months before his death. Orson Pratt dedicated the site for the Logan Temple, and Brigham's son and First Counselor, John W. Young, officiated at the groundbreaking, both three months before Young's death. Young oversaw the rewriting of the temple ceremony by a committee headed by Wilford Woodruff; and one of Young's wives, Lucy Bigelow Young, served as St. George Temple matron.

That Young considered the construction and operation of temples the central feature of Mormon religious life is completely understandable. The temples are the "House of the Lord," and through the ceremonies and rituals performed in them, Latter-day Saints tied Heaven and earth together and prepared faithful men and women to return to God. Marriage in the temple, called "sealing" by the Latter-day Saints, united husband and wife not just until "death do you part" but "for time and eternity."

Young expected not only Mormons married in the temple but all Latter-day Saint husbands and fathers to govern their families in love and kindness. Following that philosophy himself, Young supplied accommodations for each of his families, including the sixteen wives who bore him children and those others who did not. The conditions under which they lived were diverse, but as Leonard Arrington pointed out, the goods and services each received were relatively equal. He met regularly with his families to instruct them in how to live loving and worthy lives.

In general Young got along well with most of his wives. Nevertheless, at least eight of his wives divorced him, and some of the wives who remained with him were not completely content. Laurel Thatcher Ulrich cited the example of August Adams Cobb, who was clearly dissatisfied with her situation. Some wives, such as Mary Ann Angell, Eliza R. Snow, and Zina Diantha Huntington, were quite happy. Both Eliza and Zina achieved considerable status in the community, including their service as general Relief Society presidents. Young's divorce from Ann Eliza Webb Dee, however, was extremely messy. After Young's death, because of the difficulty of deciding which of the properties, bonds, and equities in Young's possession belonged to him and which to the church, a few family members led by Emeline (or Emmeline) A. Young, believed that too much of the estate had gone to the church, and they entered a suit against the executors. The executors succeeded in negotiating an out-of-court settlement.

Beyond incorporating loving care of wives and families in his preaching and action, Young spent considerable time facilitating various aspects of economic development for the improvement of the community. By taking contracts for grading the roadbed, he helped with the coming of the railroad to Utah, which he had long anticipated. Disappointed that it did not come through Salt Lake City, he nevertheless built lines north and south to connect some Mormon settlements together and to the transcontinental line. Unfortunately for Utah, the railroads cheated Young and the Mormons out of much of the revenue for their work.

In addition to facilitating the arrival of the railroad, Young promoted the development of local railroads, urban rail lines in Salt Lake City, various other businesses, the cooperative movement, and United Orders. Behind these efforts stood Young's salutary religious philosophy that God's people should live in harmony and equality. Co-op ZCMI did not succeed as fully as some authors have insisted, and we owe a debt to businessman and author Larry

King for ferreting out the story of ZCMI and the depression of the 1870s. The loss of the Godbeite leaders and Amasa Lyman hurt the Mormon community. The United Order movement largely failed, even though some like the Brigham City cooperative lasted from the 1850s until the 1890s. The United Orders like the one in St. George generally failed within a few years of their organization. The Orderville United Order lasted for longer, but leaders soon began to introduce capitalistic principles, which changed it fundamentally.

The lack of success of the United Orders disturbed Young, but perhaps the low point in his life occurred in his relationship with federal officials, especially Judge James B. McKean. McKean charged into Utah on a crusade to crush the Mormons in general and Brigham Young in particular. He proceeded illegally, and though he caused Young to spend money, time, anguish, and a night in prison, he eventually lost because the U.S. Supreme Court checkmated him.

In spite of the efforts of federal officials to thwart Young's leadership, he served as host to numerous prominent travelers who passed through Salt Lake City. Sojourners included Sir Richard Burton, Jules Rémy, Solomon Nunes Carvalho, Mark Twain, Ulysses S. Grant, William T. Sherman, Ralph Waldo Emerson, Horace Greeley, and Tom Thumb. *Goodwin's Weekly* on April 4, 1914, reported that during his conversation with Tom Thumb, the little man remarked, "I cannot understand polygamy." We see Young's ready wit in his reply, "Neither could I when I was your size."

Although Young was always ready with a witty comment, he was deadly serious about the organization over which he presided. The priesthood reorganization that Young initiated late in his life proved extremely important to the church's continued health and growth. Regularizing the organization of stake presidencies, high councils, and bishoprics, in addition to returning members of the Quorum of the Twelve Apostles to general church duties, influenced the future development of the church. Inaugurating the means of enrolling all members in wards and men in priesthood quorums began a process of strengthening the church that continued into the twentieth century. Regrouping the Twelve by seniority rather than age set a precedent that has influenced the composition of the Quorum and of the First Presidency. Encouraging the stakes and wards to promote auxiliaries for young men and women and the Sunday School for general religious instruction has provided additional opportunities for members to participate in service, recreation, and religious education.

Young's attitudes and actions about women proved important in promoting their activity in the church and the larger community. Although his ideas seem antiquated today, in the nineteenth century, they were progressive. Giving women the responsibility for their own Relief Society, supporting women's political activity, and encouraging women to study medicine, law, telegraphy, sales, and other professions was extremely important for their progress and for the health of the community.

In addition to promoting opportunities for women, Young, though poorly educated himself, believed in the importance of education. He promoted the expansion of public, private, and informal education for his own family and for the community at large, though he opposed tax-supported public education. Some of Young's educational enterprises like Brigham Young College in Logan failed, and only LDS Business College remains from LDS University. Nevertheless, the community owes a debt to Young for supporting the establishment of the public University of Utah and endowing the private Brigham Young University. Young's love of music and the theater and the institutions he established as vehicles of improvement have also influenced Mormon and secular communities to the present. Unfortunately, the Salt Lake Theater failed during the 1920s.

While we recognize Young's promotion of education, we can also understand his enthusiasm for sugar production, the Iron Mission, the Lead Mission, and the Cotton Mission, although they failed. Young was a mercantilist; he wanted the Mormon commonwealth to become self-sufficient. He hoped to facilitate a favorable balance of trade with the country outside the Mormon settlements, but he was far ahead of his time. In 1891 the church initiated what became the Utah-Idaho Sugar Company. Iron production began in Provo in 1922, and during World War II, the federal government constructed the Geneva Steel Plant at Vinyard in central Utah. Iron from Iron Mountain west of Cedar City, from which settlers had little success in mining and smelting into various implements, later supplied factories in Utah and California.

Young tried to promote iron, lead, and salt mining, but he opposed gold and silver mining. His justification seemed reasonable at the time: He wanted to build communities rather than encourage the Saints to scurry through the hills in search of El Dorado. Opposition to such mining died with him. John Taylor, George Q. Cannon, and such Mormon entrepreneurs as John Beck and Jesse Knight invested in and developed mines during the 1880s and afterward. These mines made some Mormons and non-Mormons very wealthy.

Opposition to precious-metal mining went hand in hand with Young's successful efforts to expand and build Mormon settlements. Young's greatest economic achievement lay in establishing 350 settlements during his lifetime. These settlements were generally successful—as Lynn Rosenvall, professor of geography at the University of Calgary, has calculated, only sixty-three, or 18 percent, failed by 1900.

A number of scholars have recognized Young's success in organizing companies of Mormons and sending them to establish towns. Howard Lamar, Sterling Professor Emeritus of history and former president of Yale University, has said that Brigham Young was the greatest colonizer in the history of the American West. Jonathan Hughes, professor of economic history at Northwestern University, selected William Penn and Brigham Young as examples of *The Vital Few* who promoted economic progress as protagonists of idealism and economic development through planned settlement. Milton R. Hunter's revised and published Ph.D. dissertation written at the University of California, Berkeley, labeled Young "The Colonizer." Leonard Arrington called Young the American Moses.

Perhaps equal to the importance of establishing settlements, Young rose to assume leadership, and he may have led in the salvation of a church that many in the United States and Europe expected to expire with Smith's death. His leadership skills, religious teachings, and enthusiasm inspired thousands to join and remain in the church as it endured under consistent attack from anti-Mormons and the federal government. His successors as church presidents—John Taylor, Wilford Woodruff, Lorenzo Snow, and Joseph F. Smith—all served under his guidance, and they persisted in building on the foundation that Young had established. Some churches that were organized or flourished during the Second Great Awakening have survived just as the LDS church did, while others have died out or have left only vestiges of themselves. Significantly, none of these churches experienced the persistent persecution the Mormons endured during the nineteenth century. Absent the strong, gifted, and indeed, inspired leadership that Brigham Young gave the Saints, the Church of Jesus Christ of Latter-day Saints might well have died out as well. Faithful members loved Brigham Young, and they willingly followed him into the Indians' land, the Mormons' considered wilderness, to build towns. Most remained faithful despite continued persecution because they believed in his message and his leadership.

Bibliography

Published Primary Sources

Alford, Kenneth L. *Utah and the American Civil War: The Written Record.* Norman, Okla.: Arthur H. Clark, 2017.

Anderson, Devery S., ed. *Salt Lake School of the Prophets, 1867–1883.* Salt Lake City: Signature Books, 2018.

Anderson, Devery S., and Gary James Bergera, eds. *The Nauvoo Endowment Companies, 1845–1846.* Foreword by Richard S. Van Wagoner. Salt Lake City: Signature Books, 2005.

Buchanan, James. "First Annual Message to Congress on the State of the Union, December 8, 1857." Available online at Gerhard Peters and John T. Woolley, *The American Presidency Project.* Accessed July 19, 2018. http://www.presidency.ucsb.edu/ws/?pid=29498.

Bullock, Thomas. *Journals of Thomas Bullock.* Edited by Will Bagley. Kingdom in the West: The Mormons and the American Frontier, vol. 1. Spokane, Wash.: Arthur H. Clark, 1997.

Bowles, Samuel. *Across the Continent: A Summer's Journey to the Rocky Mountains, the Mormons, and the Pacific States with Speaker Colfax.* Springfield, Mass.: Samuel Bowles & Company, 1865.

Carvalho, Solomon Nunes. *Incidents of Travel and Adventure in the Far West.* Edited by Bertram Wallace Korn. Philadelphia: The Jewish Publication Society of America, 1954.

Chamberlain, Solomon. "Autobiography of Solomon Chamberlain." Accessed January 30, 2014. http://www.boap.org/LDS/Early-Saints/SChamberlain.html.

Clark, James R. *Messages of the First Presidency of the Church of Jesus Christ of Latter-day Saints, 1833–1964.* 6 vols. Salt Lake City: Bookcraft, 1965–75.

Clayton, William. *An Intimate Chronicle: The Journals of William Clayton.* Edited by George D. Smith. Salt Lake City: Signature Books, 1995.

Davidson, Karen Lynn, David J. Whittaker, Mark Ashurst-McGee, and Richard L. Jensen, eds. *The Joseph Smith Papers, Histories, Volume 1: Joseph Smith Histories, 1832–1844.* Salt Lake City: The Church Historian's Press, 2012.

Derr, Jill Mulvay, Carol Cornwall Madsen, Katt Holbrook, and Matthew J. Grow. *The First Fifty Years of Relief Society: Key Documents in Latter-day Saint Women's History.* Salt Lake City: The Church Historian's Press, 2016.

Grow, Matthew J., and Ronald W. Walker. *The Prophet and the Reformer: The Letters of Brigham Young and Thomas L. Kane.* New York: Oxford University Press, 2015.

Hafen, LeRoy R., and Ann W. Hafen. *Mormon Resistance: A Documentary Account of the Utah Expedition, 1857–1858.* Lincoln: University of Nebraska Press, 1958.

Jesse, Dean C., Mark Ashurst-McGee, and Richard L. Jensen. *The Joseph Smith Papers: Journals, Volume 1: 1832–1839.* Salt Lake City: The Church Historian's Press, 2008.

Lee, John Doyle. *A Mormon Chronicle: The Diaries of John D. Lee, 1848–1876.* Edited by Robert Glass Cleland and Juanita Brooks. 2 vols. San Marino, Calif.: Henry E. Huntington Library and Art Gallery, 1955; reprint edition, Salt Lake City: University of Utah Press, 1984.

———. *Mormonism Unveiled, Including the Remarkable Life and Confessions of the Late Mormon Bishop, John D. Lee, and Complete Life of Brigham Young.* Edited by W. W. Bishop et al. Albuquerque, N.Mex.: Fierra Blanca Publications, 2001. Reprint of St. Louis, Mo.: D. M. Vandawalker, 1891.

MacKinnon, William P., ed. *At Sword's Point, Part 1: A Documentary History of the Utah War to 1858.* Kingdom in the West: The Mormons and the American Frontier, vol. 10, edited by Will Bagley. Norman, Okla.: Arthur H. Clark, 2008.

———, ed. *At Sword's Point, Part 2: A Documentary History of the Utah War, 1858–1859.* Kingdom in the West: The Mormons and the American Frontier, vol. 11, edited by Will Bagley. Norman, Okla.: Arthur H. Clark, 2016.

Mace, Wandle. "Autobiography (1809–1846)." Journal of Wandle Mace. Typescript. Harold B. Lee Library, Brigham Young University, Provo, Utah. Accessed July 19, 2018. http://www.boap.org/LDS/Early-Saints/WMace.html.

Roberts, B. H., ed. *History of the Church of Jesus Christ of Latter-day Saints: Period I: History of Joseph Smith, the Prophet by Himself.* 6 vols. 2nd ed., rev., Salt Lake City: Deseret Book, 1969.

———, ed. *History of the Church of Jesus Christ of Latter-day Saints: Period II from the Manuscript History of Brigham Young and Other Original Documents.* Salt Lake City: Deseret News, 1966.

Rogers, Jedediah S., ed. *The Council of Fifty: A Documentary History.* Salt Lake City: Signature Books, 2014.

Smith, Joseph, *Journals, Volume 3: May 1843–June 1844. The Joseph Smith Papers.* Edited by Andrew H. Hedges, Alex D. Smith, Brent M. Rogers. Salt Lake City: The Church Historian's Press, 2015.

——— et al. *The Joseph Smith Papers, Administrative Records, Council of Fifty, Minutes, March 1844–January 1846.* Edited by Matthew J. Grow, Ronald K. Esplin, Mark Ashurst-McGee, Gerrit J. Dirkmaat, and Jeffrey D. Mahas. Salt Lake City: Church Historian's Press, 2016.

Stout, Hosea. *On the Mormon Frontier: The Diary of Hosea Stout.* Edited by Juanita Brooks. 2 vols. Salt Lake City: University of Utah Press and Utah State Historical Society, 1964.

Tuttle, Daniel Sylvester. *Missionary to the Mountain West: Reminiscences of Episcopal Bishop Daniel S. Tuttle, 1866–1886.* Foreword by Brigham D. Madsen. Salt Lake City: University of Utah Press, 1987.

U.S. Census Bureau. "1870 Census: Volume 1. The Statistics of the Population of the United States." Accessed July 19, 2018. https://www.census.gov/library/publications/1872/dec/1870a.html.

Woodruff, Wilford. *Wilford Woodruff's Journal.* Edited by Scott G. Kenney. 9 vols. Midvale, Utah: Signature Books, 1983–85.

Young, Brigham. *The Complete Discourses of Brigham Young.* Edited by Richard S. Van Wagoner. 5 vols. Salt Lake City: Smith-Pettit Foundation, 2009.

———. CR12341: Brigham Young Office Files, 1832–1878. https://eadview.lds.org/findingaid/0002803451/. Accessed November 21, 2018.

———. *Diary of Brigham Young, 1857.* Edited by Everett L. Cooley. Salt Lake City: University of Utah Library Tanner Trust Fund, 1980.

———. *Letters of Brigham Young to His Sons.* Edited by Dean C. Jessee. Salt Lake City: Deseret Books, 1974.

———. *The Office Journal of President Brigham Young, 1858–1863, Book D.* Edited by Fred C. Collier. Hanna, Utah: Collier Publishing Company, 2006.

Young, Brigham, et al. *Journal of Discourses by Brigham Young, President of the Church of Jesus Christ of Latter-day Saints, His Two Counselors, the Twelve Apostles, and Others.* G. D. Watt, reporter. 26 vols. Liverpool [place of publication varies]: F. D. Richards [editor varies]; London: Latter-day Saints Book Depot, 1855–86.

Young, Mary Ann Angell, and Eliza R. Snow. "Heroines of the Church: Biography of Mary Ann Angell Young." *The Juvenile Instructor* 26 (January 1, 1891): 18–20, (January 15, 1891): 56–58, (February 1, 1891): 94–96.

Books

Alexander, Thomas G. *Brigham Young, the Quorum of the Twelve, and the Latter-day Saint Investigation of the Mountain Meadows Massacre.* Leonard J. Arrington Mormon History Lecture Series, no. 12. Logan: Utah State University Press, 2007.

———. *Things in Heaven and Earth: The Life and Times of Wilford Woodruff, a Mormon Prophet.* Salt Lake City: Signature Books, 1991.

Alford, Kenneth L. *Civil War Saints.* Provo, Utah: Brigham Young University Religious Studies Center, 2012.

Anderson, C. LeRoy. *Joseph Morris and the Saga of the Morrisites.* Logan: Utah State University Press, 1988.

Arrington, Leonard J. *Brigham Young: American Moses.* New York: Alfred Knopf, 1985.

———. *Great Basin Kingdom: An Economic History of the Latter-day Saints, 1830–1900.* Cambridge, Mass.: Harvard University Press, 1958.

Arrington, Leonard J., Feramorz Y. Fox, and Dean L. May. *Building the City of God: Community and Cooperation among the Mormons.* 2nd ed. Urbana: University of Illinois Press, 1992.

Backman, Milton V., Jr. *The Heavens Resound: A History of the Latter-day Saints in Ohio, 1830–1838.* Salt Lake City: Deseret Book, 1983.

Bagley, Will. *Blood of the Prophets: Brigham Young and the Mountain Meadows Massacre.* Norman: University of Oklahoma Press, 2002.

Baugh, Alexander L. *A Call to Arms: The 1838 Mormon Defense of Northern Missouri.* Provo, Utah: Joseph Fielding Smith Institute for Latter-day Saint History, 2000.

Bigler, David L. *Fort Limhi: The Mormon Adventure in Oregon Territory, 1855–1858.* Kingdom in the West: The Mormons and the American Frontier, vol. 6, edited by Will Bagley. Spokane, Wash.: Arthur H. Clark, 2003.

Bigler, David L., and Will Bagley. *The Mormon Rebellion: America's First Civil War, 1857–1858.* Norman: University of Oklahoma Press, 2011.

Bringhurst, Newell G. *Brigham Young and the Expanding American Frontier.* Library of American Biography. Boston: Little, Brown, 1986.

———. *Saints, Slaves, and Blacks: The Changing Place of Black People within Mormonism.* Westport, Conn.: Greenwood, 1981.

Bringhurst, Newell G., and Darron T. Smith, eds. *Black and Mormon.* Urbana: University of Illinois Press, 2004.

Brooks, Juanita. *The Mountain Meadows Massacre.* [2nd edition.] Norman: University of Oklahoma Press, 1962.

Bush, Lester E., Jr. *Health and Medicine among the Latter-day Saints.* New York: Crossroad, 1993.

Bushman, Richard Lyman. *Joseph Smith, Rough Stone Rolling.* New York: Alfred Knopf, 2005.

Christensen, Scott R. *Sagwitch: Shoshone Chieftain, Mormon Elder, 1822–1887.* Logan: Utah State University Press, 1999.

Cobb, John B., Jr. and David Ray Griffin. *Process Theology and Introductory Exposition.* Philadelphia: Westminster Press, 1976.

Denton, Sally. *American Massacre: The Tragedy at Mountain Meadows, September 1857.* New York: Alfred Knopf, 2003.

Firmage, Edwin Brown, and Richard Collin Mangrum. *Zion and the Courts: A Legal History of the Church of Jesus Christ of Latter-day Saints, 1830–1900.* Urbana: University of Illinois Press, 1988.

Fluhman, J. Spencer. *"A Peculiar People": Anti-Mormonism and the Making of Religion in Nineteenth-Century America.* Chapel Hill: University of North Carolina Press, 2012.

Furniss, Norman F. *The Mormon Conflict, 1850–1859.* New Haven: Yale University Press, 1960.

Givens, Fiona, and Terryl Givens. *The Christ Who Heals: How God Restored the Truth that Saves Us.* Salt Lake City: Deseret Book, 2017.

Grow, Matthew J. *"Liberty to the Downtrodden": Thomas L. Kane, Romantic Reformer.* New Haven, Conn.: Yale University Press, 2009.

Hardy, B. Carmon. *Doing the Works of Abraham: Mormon Polygamy—Its Origin, Practice, and Demise.* Kingdom in the West: The Mormons and the American Frontier, vol. 9, edited by Will Bagley. Norman, Okla.: Arthur H. Clark, 2007.

Harris, Matthew L., and Newell G. Bringhurst, eds. *The Mormon Church and Blacks: A Documentary History.* Urbana: University of Illinois Press, 2015.

Hickman, Bill, and J. H. Beadle. *Brigham's Destroying Angel: Being the Life, Confession and Startling Disclosures of the Notorious Bill Hickman, Danite Chief of Utah.* Salt Lake City: n.p., 1870.

Hicks, Michael. *Mormonism and Music: A History.* Urbana: University of Illinois Press, 1989.

Hirshson, Stanley P. *The Lion of the Lord: A Biography of the Mormon Leader, Brigham Young.* 2nd ed. London: J. M. Dent & Sons, 1971.

Homer, Michael W. *Joseph's Temples: The Dynamic Relationship Between Freemasonry and Mormonism.* Salt Lake City: University of Utah Press, 2014.

Hughes, Jonathan. *The Vital Few: American Economic Progress and Its Protagonists.* London: Oxford University Press, 1973.

Hunter, Milton R. *Brigham Young: The Colonizer.* Independence, Mo.: Zion's Printing and Publishing Company, 1945.

Jackson, Richard H., ed. *The Mormon Role in the Settlement of the West.* Charles Redd Monographs in Western History, no. 9, edited by Thomas

G. Alexander and Howard A. Christy. Provo, Utah: Brigham Young University Press, 1978.

Jenson, Andrew. *Church Chronology*. 2nd ed. Salt Lake City: Deseret News, 1914.

———. *Latter-day Saints Biographical Encyclopedia*. 4 vols. Salt Lake City, 2012.

Kane, Elizabeth Wood. *A Gentile Account of Life in Utah's Dixie, 1872–73*. Edited by Norman R. Bowen and Mary Karen Bowen Solomon. Salt Lake City: Tanner Trust Fund, University of Utah Library, 1995.

———. *Twelve Mormon Homes Visited in Succession on a Journey through Utah to Arizona*. Edited by Everett L. Cooley. Salt Lake City: Tanner Trust Fund, University of Utah Library, 1874.

Kerstetter, Todd M. *God's Country, Uncle Sam's Land: Faith and Conflict in the American West*. Urbana: University of Illinois Press, 2006.

Larson, Gustive O. *The Americanization of Utah for Statehood*. San Marino, Calif.: Huntington Library, 1977.

Leonard, Glen M. *Nauvoo: A Place of Peace, a People of Promise*. Salt Lake City: Deseret Books; Provo, Utah: Brigham Young University Press, 2002.

LeSueur, Stephen C. *The 1838 Mormon War in Missouri*. Columbia: University of Missouri Press, 1987.

Locke, John. *Second Treatise on Civil Government*. The Project Gutenberg EBook of Second Treatise of Government: E-book 7370, 2010.

Long, E. B. *The Saints and the Union: Utah Territory during the Civil War*. Urbana: University of Illinois Press, 1981.

Lovelock, James. *Gaia: A New Look at Life on Earth*. 3rd ed. Oxford: Oxford University Press, 2000.

Lyman, Edward Leo. *Amasa Mason Lyman: Mormon Apostle and Apostate—A Study in Dedication*. Salt Lake City: University of Utah Press, 2009.

Madsen, Brigham D. *Glory Hunter: A Biography of Patrick Edward Connor*. Salt Lake City: University of Utah Press, 1990.

———. *The Shoshoni Frontier and the Bear River Massacre*. Salt Lake City: University of Utah Press, 1985.

Maxwell, John Gary. *The Civil War Years in Utah: The Kingdom of God and the Territory That Did Not Fight*. Norman: University of Oklahoma Press, 2016.

Moorman, Donald R., and Gene A. Sessions. *Camp Floyd and the Mormons: The Utah War*. Salt Lake City: University of Utah Press, 1992.

Newell, Linda King, and Valeen Avery. *Mormon Enigma: Prophet's Wife, "Elect Lady," and Polygamy's Foe*. New York: Doubleday, 1984.

Palmer, Richard F., and Karl D. Butler. *Brigham Young: The New York Years*. Charles Redd Monographs in Western History, no. 14. Provo, Utah: Charles Redd Center for Western Studies, 1992.

Peterson, John Alton. *Utah's Black Hawk War.* Salt Lake City: University of Utah Press, 1998.

Putnam, Robert D., and David E. Campbell. *American Grace: How Religion Divides and Unites Us.* New York: Simon and Schuster, 2010.

Quinn, D. Michael. *The Mormon Hierarchy: The Origins of Power.* Salt Lake City: Signature Books, 1994.

———. *The Mormon Hierarchy: Extensions of Power.* Salt Lake City: Signature Books, 1997.

———. *The Mormon Hierarchy: Wealth and Corporate Power.* Salt Lake City: Signature Books, 2017.

Reeve, W. Paul. *Making Space on the Western Frontier: Mormons, Miners, and Southern Paiutes.* Urbana: University of Illinois Press, 2006.

———. *Religion of a Different Color: Race and the Mormon Struggle for Whiteness.* Oxford: Oxford University Press, 2015.

Roberts, B. H. *Comprehensive History of the Church of Jesus Christ of Latter-day Saints, Century One.* 6 vols. Salt Lake City: Deseret News Press, 1930.

Rogers, Brent M. *Unpopular Sovereignty: Mormons and the Federal Management of Early Utah Territory.* Lincoln: University of Nebraska Press, 2017.

Sessions, Gene Allred. *Mormon Thunder: A Documentary History of Jedediah Morgan Grant.* Urbana: University of Illinois Press, 1982.

Shipps, Jan. *Mormonism: The Story of a New Religious Tradition.* Urbana: University of Illinois Press, 1985.

———. *Sojourner in the Promised Land: Forty Years among the Mormons.* Urbana: University of Illinois Press, 2000.

Smith, George D. *Nauvoo Polygamy: "But we called it celestial marriage."* 2nd ed. Salt Lake City: Signature Books, 2011.

Spencer, Clarissa Young, and Mabel Harmer. *Brigham Young at Home.* Salt Lake City: Deseret Book, 1961.

Staker, Mark Lyman, *Hearken O Ye People: The Historical Setting of Joseph Smith's Ohio Revelations.* Salt Lake City: Greg Kofford Books, 2009.

Talmage, James E. *The House of the Lord: A Study of Holy Sanctuaries Ancient and Modern.* Salt Lake City: Deseret News, 1912.

Tocqueville, Alexis de. *Democracy in America.* Translated by Arthur Goldhammer. The Library of America. New York: Literary Classics of the United States, 2004.

Turley, Richard E., Jr., and Barbara Jones Brown. *After the Massacre.* New York: Oxford University Press, forthcoming.

Turner, John G. *Brigham Young: Pioneer Prophet.* Cambridge, Mass.: Belknap Press of Harvard University Press, 2012.

Ulrich, Laurel Thatcher. *A House Full of Females: Plural Marriage and Women's Rights in Early Mormonism, 1835–1870.* New York: Alfred A. Knopf, 2017.

Van Wagoner, Richard S. *Sidney Rigdon: A Portait of Religious Excess.* Salt Lake City: Signature Books, 1994.
Walker, Kyle R. *William B. Smith: In the Shadow of the Prophet.* Salt Lake City: Greg Kofford Books, 2015.
Walker, Ronald W. *Heroes, Hero Worship, and Brigham Young.* 2016 Leonard J. Arrington Lecture, Utah State University, November 15, 2016.
———, Richard E. Turley Jr., and Glen M. Leonard. *Massacre at Mountain Meadows.* New York: Oxford University Press, 2008.
———. *Wayward Saints: The Godbeites and Brigham Young.* Urbana: University of Illinois Press, 1998.
Whitney, Orson F. *History of Utah.* 4 vols. Salt Lake City: George Q. Cannon and Sons, 1892–1904.
Wise, William. *Massacre at Mountain Meadows.* New York: Thomas Y. Crowell, 1976.
Yorgason, Blaine M., Richard A. Schmutz, and Douglas D. Alder. *All That Was Promised: The St. George Temple and the Unfolding of the Restoration.* Salt Lake City: Deseret Book, 2013.

Dissertations and Theses

Gentry, Leland H. "The History of the Latter-day Saints in Northern Missouri, 1836–1839." Ph.D. diss., Brigham Young University, 1965.
Kirkham, James Chase. "Worlds Without End: The Cosmological Theodicy of Brigham Young." M.A. thesis, Utah State University, 2012.
Thomas, Scott K. "Violence across the Land: Vigilantism and Extralegal Justice in the Utah Territory." M.A. thesis, Brigham Young University, 2010.

Articles, Book Chapters, and Unpublished Manuscripts

Aird, Polly. "'You Nasty Apostates, Clear Out': Reasons for Disaffection in the Late 1850s." *Journal of Mormon History* 30 (Fall 2004): 129–207.
Alexander, Thomas G. "An Experiment in Progressive Legislation: The Granting of Woman Suffrage in 1870." *Utah Historical Quarterly* 39 (January 1970): 20–30.
———. "Carpetbaggers, Reprobates, and Liars: Federal Judges and the Utah War (1857–58)." *The Historian* 70 (Summer 2008): 209–38.
———. "Conflict and Fraud: Utah Public Land Surveys, 1855–57, and The Subsequent Investigation." *Utah Historical Quarterly* 80 (Spring 2012): 108–31.
———. "Thomas L. Kane and the Mormon Problem in National Politics." In *Col. Thomas L. Kane and the Mormons,* edited by David J. Whittaker. Provo, Utah: BYU Studies; Salt Lake City: University of Utah Press, 2010, 57–88. Reprinted in *BYU Studies* 48 (2009): 57–88.

Bibliography

Alford, Kenneth L. "Indian Relations in Utah During the Civil War." In *Civil War Saints*, edited by Kenneth L. Aford, 202–25. Provo, Utah: Brigham Young University Religious Studies Center, 2012.

Anderson, Gary Clayton. "The Native Peoples of the American West: Genocide or Ethnic Cleansing?" *Western Historical Quarterly* 47 (Winter 2016): 407–33.

Arrington, Leonard J. "Blessed Damozels: Women in Mormon History." *Dialogue: A Journal of Mormon Thought* 6 (Summer 1971): 22–31.

———. "The Deseret Telegraph: A Church-Owned Public Utility." *Journal of Economic History* 11 (Spring 1951): 117–39.

———. "The Mormon Cotton Mission in Southern Utah." *Pacific Historical Review* 25 (August 1956): 221–38.

———. "The Mormon Tithing House: A Frontier Business Institution." *Business History Review* 28 (March 1954): 24–58.

———. "The Transcontinental Railroad and Mormon Economic Policy." *Pacific Historical Review* 20 (May 1951): 143–57.

Barris, Clair. "Excerpts of *The Dreams of Brigham Young*." *Mormon Chronicles*. Posted November 9, 2011. http://mormon-chronicles.blogspot.com/2011/11/dreams-of-brigham-young.html.

Beeton, Beverly. "Woman Suffrage in Territorial Utah." *Utah Historical Quarterly* 46 (Spring 1978): 100–120.

Bennett, Richard E. "'We Know No North, No South, No East, No West': Mormon Interpretations of the Civil War, 1861–65." In *Civil War Saints*, edited by Kenneth L. Alford, 93–105. Provo, Utah: Brigham Young University Religious Studies Center, 2012.

Bergera, Gary James. "The Orson Pratt–Brigham Young Controversies: Conflict within the Quorums, 1853 to 1868." *Dialogue: A Journal of Mormon Thought* 13 (Summer 1980): 7–58.

Bigler, David L. "Garland Hurt the American Friend of the Utahs." *Utah Historical Quarterly* 62 (Spring 1994): 149–70.

Bitton, Davis, and Val Lambson, "Demographic Limits of Nineteenth-Century Mormon Polygyny." *BYU Studies* 51, no. 4 (2012): 7–26.

Briggs, Robert H. "The Tragedy at Mountain Meadows Massacre: Toward a Consensus Account and Time Line." Juanita Brooks Lecture Series, St. George, Utah, March 13, 2002.

Buerger, David John. "'The Fullness of the Priesthood': The Second Anointing in Latter-day Saint Theology and Practice." *Dialogue: A Journal of Mormon Thought* 16 (Spring 1983): 10–44.

Bush, Lester E., Jr. "Brigham Young in Life and Death: A Medical Overview." *Journal of Mormon History* 5 (1978): 79–103.

Christy, Howard A. "Open Hand and Mailed Fist: Mormon Indian Relations in Utah, 1847–52." *Utah Historical Quarterly* 46 (Summer 1978): 216–35.

———. "The Walker War: Defense and Conciliation as Strategy." *Utah Historical Quarterly* 47 (Fall 1979): 395–420.

Crawley, Peter. "The Constitution of the State of Deseret: A Keepsake Issued by the Friends of the Harold B. Lee Library in Commemoration of the Library's Two-Millionth Volume." Vol. 19. Provo, Utah: Friends of the Harold B. Lee Library, 1982.

Crockett, Robert D. "A Trial Lawyer Reviews Will Bagley's Blood of the Prophets." *FARMS Review* 15, no. 2 (2003): 199–254.

Cronon, William. "The Trouble with Wilderness; or, Getting Back to the Wrong Nature." In *Uncommon Ground: Rethinking the Human Place in Nature,* edited by William Cronon, 69–90. New York: W. W. Norton, 1983, 1996.

Dickson, Ephraim D., III. "Protecting the Home Front: The Utah Territorial Militia during the Civil War." In *Civil War Saints,* edited by Kenneth L. Alford, 142–59. Provo, Utah: Brigham Young University Religious Studies Center, 2012.

Gee, Elizabeth D. "Justice for All or for the 'Elect'? The Utah County Probate Court, 1855–72." *Utah Historical Quarterly* 48 (Spring 1980): 129–47.

Hartley, William G. "The Nauvoo Exodus and Crossing the Ice Myths." *Journal of Mormon History* 43 (January 2017): 30–58.

———."The Priesthood Reorganization of 1877: Brigham Young's Last Achievement." *Brigham Young University Studies* 20 (Fall 1979): 3–36.

Heath, Steven H. "Notes on Apostolic Succession." *Dialogue: A Journal of Mormon Thought* 20 (Summer 1987): 44–57.

Johnson, Jeffrey O. "Was Being a Probate Judge in Pioneer Utah a Church Calling." Paper presented at the annual conference of the Mormon History Association, Casper, Wyo., May 2006.

King, Larry. "Analyzing the Success of ZCMI in Pioneer Utah." Paper Presented at the Annual Convention of the Mormon History Association, Snowbird, Utah, June 11, 2016.

Kirkham, J. Chase. "'Tempered for Glory': Brigham Young's Cosmological Theodicy." *Journal of Mormon History* 42 (January 2016): 128–65.

Lambert, Neal E., and Richard H. Cracroft. "Literary form and Historical Understanding: Joseph Smith's First Vision." *Journal of Mormon History* 7 (1980): 33–37.

MacKinnon, William P. "'Lonely Bones': Leadership and Utah War Violence." *Journal of Mormon History* 33 (Spring 2007): 121–78.

McKiernan, F. Mark. "The Conversion of Sidney Rigdon to Mormonism." *Dialogue: A Journal of Mormon Thought* 5 (Summer 1970): 71–78.

Madley, Benjamin. "Reexamining the Genocide Debate: Meaning, Historiography, and New Methods." *American Historical Review* 120 (February 2015): 98–139.

Morgan, Dale L. "The Administration of Indian Affairs in Utah, 1851–1858." *Pacific Historical Review* 17 (1948): 383–409.

O'Neil, Floyd A., and Stanford J. Layton. "Of Pride and Politics: Brigham Young as Indian Superintendent." *Utah Historical Quarterly* 46 (Summer 1978): 236–50.

Orton, Chad. "John D. Lee, W. W. Bishop, and *Mormon Unveiled.*" Paper presented to the Utah Valley Historical Society, February 9, 2016.

Parshall, Ardis E. "'Pursue, Retake & Punish': The 1857 Santa Clara Ambush." *Utah Historical Quarterly* 73 (Winter 2005): 64–86.

Pearson, Lisa Madsen, and Carol Cornwall Madsen. "Innovation and Accommodation: The Legal Status of Women in Territorial Utah, 1850–1896." Edited by Patricia Lynn Scott and Linda Thatcher, 36–81. *Women in Utah History: Paradigm or Paradox.* Logan: Utah State University Press, 2005.

Powell, Jay. "Fairness in the Salt Lake County Probate Court." *Utah Historical Quarterly* 38 (Spring 1970): 256–72.

"Question: Was the 'Adam-God' theory ever taught as part of the temple endowment ceremony as something called 'the lecture at the veil'?" *FairMormon.* Accessed September 26, 2016. http://en.fairmormon.org/Mormonism_and_temples/Endowment/Adam-God_and_the_%22Lecture_at_the_Veil%22.

Quinn, D. Michael. "Brigham Young: Man of the Spirit." *Ensign* (August 1977). Accessed August 13, 2018. https://lds.org/ensign/1977/08/brigham-young-man-of-the-spirit?lang=eng.

Radke-Moss, Andrea. "Beyond Petticoats and Poultices: Finding a Women's History of the Mormon-Missouri War of 1838." Paper presented at Beyond Biography: Sources in Context for Mormon Women's History, Brigham Young University, Provo, Utah, March 3, 2016.

Rooker, C. Keith, Marvin S. Hill, and Larry T. Wimmer. "The Kirtland Economy Revisited: A Critique of Sectarian Economics." *BYU Studies* 17, no. 4 (1977): 389–475.

Schindler, Harold, and Ephraim D. Dickson III. "The Bear River Massacre: New Historical Evidence." In *Civil War Saints,* edited by Kenneth L. Alford, 226–35. Provo, Utah: Brigham Young University Religious Studies Center, 2012.

"Seixas, Joshua." The Joseph Smith Papers. Accessed January 23, 2014. http://josephsmithpapers.org/person/joshua-seixas.

Staker, Mark. "Black Pete and Early Mormonism." *Rational Faiths.* Posted February 16, 2014. Accessed May 23, 2016. http://rationalfaiths.com/black-pete-early-mormonism.

Stuart, Joseph R., and Kenneth L. Alford. "The Lot Smith Cavalry Company: Utah Goes to War." In *Civil War Saints,* edited by Kenneth L.

Alford, 126–41. Provo, Utah: Brigham Young University Religious Studies Center, 2012.

Talmage, James E. "The Eternity of Sex." *Young Woman's Journal* 25 (October 1914): 600–604.

Walker, Kyle R. "William B. Smith and the Josephites." *Journal of Mormon History* 40 (Fall 2014): 73–129.

Walker, Ronald W. "The Tintic War of 1856: A Study of Several Conflicts." *Journal of Mormon History* 42, no.3 (July 2016): 35–67.

———. "'Proud as a Peacock and Ignorant as a Jackass': William W. Drummond's Unusual Career with the Mormons." *Journal of Mormon History* 42, no. 3 (July 2016): 1–34.

———. "Toward a Reconstruction of Mormon and Indian Relations, 1847–1877." *BYU Studies* 29 (Fall 1989): 23–42.

White, Richard. "'Are You an Environmentalist, or Do You Work for a Living?' Work and Nature." In *Uncommon Ground: Rethinking the Human Place in Nature*, edited by William Cronon, 171–85. New York: W. W. Norton, 1983, 1996.

Index

References to illustrations appear in italic type.